Lecture Notes
in Business Information Processing

483

LNBIP reports state-of-the-art results in areas related to business information systems and industrial application software development – timely, at a high level, and in both printed and electronic form.

The type of material published includes

- Proceedings (published in time for the respective event)
- Postproceedings (consisting of thoroughly revised and/or extended final papers)
- Other edited monographs (such as, for example, project reports or invited volumes)
- Tutorials (coherently integrated collections of lectures given at advanced courses, seminars, schools, etc.)
- Award-winning or exceptional theses

LNBIP is abstracted/indexed in DBLP, EI and Scopus. LNBIP volumes are also submitted for the inclusion in ISI Proceedings.

Boris Shishkov

Editor

Business Modeling and Software Design

13th International Symposium, BMSD 2023
Utrecht, The Netherlands, July 3–5, 2023
Proceedings

 Springer

Editor
Boris Shishkov
Bulgarian Academy of Sciences
Institute of Mathematics and Informatics
Sofia, Bulgaria

Faculty of Information Sciences
University of Library Studies and Information
Technologies
Sofia, Bulgaria

Interdisciplinary Institute for Collaboration
and Research on Enterprise Systems and Technology
Sofia, Bulgaria

ISSN 1865-1348   ISSN 1865-1356 (electronic)
Lecture Notes in Business Information Processing
ISBN 978-3-031-36756-4   ISBN 978-3-031-36757-1 (eBook)
https://doi.org/10.1007/978-3-031-36757-1

This Springer imprint is published by the registered company Springer Nature Switzerland AG
The registered company address is: Gewerbestrasse 11, 6330 Cham, Switzerland

Preface

Everybody is talking about **Artificial Intelligence, Cyber Technology, ChatGPT,** and so on, but what's the point? It was around 30 years ago today when I saw a book written by *Simon Haykin* and explicitly addressing NEURAL NETWORKS. Around 5 years earlier we were all curious to see inspiring and visionary statements of *Isaac Asimov,* touching upon *Artificial Intelligence, robots,* and so on. And also in the early 1990s, the inspiring scientist and visioner *Mark Weiser* stated (in his '91 essay entitled *"The Computer for the 21st Century"*) that *"**specialized elements of hardware and software, connected by wires, radio waves and infrared, will be so ubiquitous that no one will notice their presence"**.* Why is the Public so "impressed" today and not then? Well, *ChatGPT* would be able to answer with a high degree of precision many questions concerning a poem of *Shakespeare* (for example) but would *ChatGPT* be able to answer even an easy question concerning a *Bulgarian* poem that is not popular worldwide? Indeed, the answer would be in good *Bulgarian* but the answer itself would be inadequate, in our view. Hence, it is for sure neither that *Artificial Intelligence* is ARTIFICIAL (not at all driven by *Humans*) nor that it is real INTELLIGENCE by itself. Why? Because *Artificial Intelligence, Cyber Technology,* and *ChatGPT* are all essentially fueled by MACHINE LEARNING and TRAINING DATA. They are in turn *conceptualized, prepared* and *provided,* driven by HUMAN intelligence and we have doubts that any artificial thing would just go and learn on its own. Looking at the 1990s, we seriously doubt that the progress (beyond implementations that were not possible then) is so impressive, after *Haykin, Asimov,* and *Weiser,* except for the huge abundance of *sensor data* and *Internet data* showering us "for free" every second. This makes it easy to supply **training data** and use **machine learning algorithms.** Even though the above example is simple and *Artificial Intelligence* (*AI*) can "do" much more, we argue that any *AI*-driven (technological) solution is "nothing" without its underlying **DESIGN, RULES,** and **REGULATIONS.** *Designs* are <u>HUMAN-driven</u> because they reflect *requirements* of the service USER (most IT services are about fulfilling the desires of *Humans* and even if a *machine* would be the service user, this would reflect a part of a process whose ultimate goal is to serve a *Human*). *Rules* and *regulations* are <u>HUMAN-driven</u> as well because they essentially reflect *societal norms, human behavior standards, public values, legislation,* and so on, which cannot be MACHINE-driven in any way. Indeed, *AI*-driven systems may be pro-active, they may initiate collaboration among each other but: (i) Whatever they initiate should conform to the *underlying designs* and if something would go "out of control", this would have been mainly the fault of those who have DESIGNED those systems; (ii) Whatever comes out as a result of the behavior of an *AI*-driven system should be considered in a broader perspective; if the system would do things that are not societally adequate, then *institutional mechanisms* should be activated, as in the case of unproper behavior of a person. For this reason, we argue that *the bombastic claims concerning the power of AI, the danger of AI, the new era marked by AI, and so on, are greatly exaggerated.* Further, we argue that most *AI*-driven solutions essentially depend on a software "rocket-carrier"; said otherwise, *AI* needs *software* in order for *AI*-driven services to be delivered. Finally, *AI*-driven solutions are to be integrated in existing business processes in order to "solve" anything. Therefore the **ENTERPRISE modeling**, the **design of SOFTWARE**, and their **ALIGNMENT** remain key challenges and failures here would only be more damaging when powerful *AI*-related capabilities are engaged. At the same time, *AI* and *Big Data* lead to *increased requirements* when servicing a *Human* because a person can be in different situations with different access to data, having different related needs and so on. Hence, we need a high degree of precision when *determining the situation of the user* and his or her corresponding *needs*. Nevertheless, *AI* and *Big Data* are also enabling in this regard because the abundance of *sensor data* and *predictions-driven data*, make it possible to determine the user situation. That is why **CONTEXT AWARENESS** remains a key desired feature of most current *information systems*. Considering these challenges brings us together in the **BMSD Community – Business Modeling and Software Design.**

This book contains the *proceedings* of **BMSD 2023** (the 13th International Symposium on *Business Modeling and Software Design*), held in *Utrecht, The Netherlands*, on *3–5 July 2023* (https://www.is-bmsd.org). *BMSD* is an annual event that brings together researchers and practitioners interested in enterprise modeling and its relation to software specification.

Since 2011, we have enjoyed **twelve successful BMSD editions**. The first BMSD edition (**2011**) took place in **Sofia, Bulgaria**, and the theme of BMSD 2011 was: "**Business Models and Advanced Software Systems**." The second BMSD edition (**2012**) took place in **Geneva, Switzerland**, with the theme: "From Business Modeling to Service-Oriented Solutions." The third BMSD edition (**2013**) took place in **Noordwijkerhout, The Netherlands**, and the theme was: "Enterprise Engineering and Software Generation." The fourth BMSD edition (**2014**) took place in **Luxembourg, Grand Duchy of Luxembourg**, and the theme was: "Generic Business Modeling Patterns and Software Re-Use." The fifth BMSD edition (**2015**) took place in **Milan, Italy**, with the theme: "Toward Adaptable Information Systems." The sixth BMSD edition (**2016**) took place in **Rhodes, Greece**, and had as theme: "Integrating Data Analytics in Enterprise Modeling and Software Development." The seventh BMSD edition (**2017**) took place in **Barcelona, Spain**, and the theme was: "Modeling Viewpoints and Overall Consistency." The eighth BMSD edition (**2018**) took place in **Vienna, Austria**, with the theme: "Enterprise Engineering and Software Engineering - Processes and Systems for the Future." The ninth BMSD edition (**2019**) took place in **Lisbon, Portugal**, and the theme of BMSD 2019 was: "Reflecting Human Authority and Responsibility in Enterprise Models and Software Specifications". The tenth BMSD edition (**2020**) took place in **Berlin, Germany**, and the theme of BMSD 2020 was: "Towards Knowledge-Driven Enterprise Information Systems". The eleventh BMSD edition (**2021**) took place in **Sofia, Bulgaria** (*We got back to where we once started!*), and the theme of BMSD 2021 was: "Towards Enterprises and Software that are Resilient Against Disruptive Events." The twelfth BMSD edition (**2022**) took place in **Fribourg, Switzerland**, with the theme: "Information Systems Engineering and Trust." The current edition brings BMSD back to

The Netherlands (ten years after BMSD-Noordwijkerhout-2013) – to Utrecht. BMSD-Utrecht-2023 marks the **13ᵗʰ EVENT**, with the theme: *"INCORPORATING CONTEXT AWARENESS IN THE DESIGN OF INFORMATION SYSTEMS."*

We are proud to have attracted distinguished guests as keynote lecturers, who are renowned experts in their fields: **Hans-Georg Fill**, *University of Fribourg*, Switzerland (2022), **Manfred Reichert**, *Ulm University*, Germany (2020), **Mathias Weske**, *HPI - University of Potsdam*, Germany (2020), **Jose Tribolet**, *IST - University of Lisbon*, Portugal (2019), **Jan Mendling**, *WU Vienna*, Austria (2018), **Roy Oberhauser**, *Aalen University*, Germany (2018), **Norbert Gronau**, *University of Potsdam*, Germany (2017 **and 2021**), **Oscar Pastor**, *Polytechnic University of Valencia*, Spain (2017), **Alexander Verbraeck**, *Delft University of Technology*, The Netherlands (2017 **and 2021**), **Paris Avgeriou**, *University of Groningen*, The Netherlands (2016), **Jan Juerjens**, *University of Koblenz-Landau*, Germany (2016), **Mathias Kirchmer**, *BPM-D*, USA (2016), **Marijn Janssen**, *Delft University of Technology*, The Netherlands (2015), **Barbara Pernici**, *Politecnico di Milano*, Italy (2015), **Henderik Proper**, *Public Research Centre Henri Tudor*, Grand Duchy of Luxembourg (2014), **Roel Wieringa**, *University of Twente*, The Netherlands (2014), **Kecheng Liu**, *University of Reading*, UK (2013), **Marco Aiello**, *University of Groningen*, The Netherlands (2013), **Leszek Maciaszek**, *Wroclaw University of Economics*, Poland (2013), **Jan L. G. Dietz**, *Delft University of Technology*, The Netherlands (2012), **Ivan Ivanov**, *SUNY Empire State College*, USA (2012), **Dimitri Konstantas**, *University of Geneva*, Switzerland (2012), **Marten van Sinderen**, *University of Twente*, The Netherlands (2012), **Mehmet Aksit**, *University of Twente*, The Netherlands (2011), **Dimitar Christozov**, *American University in Bulgaria – Blagoevgrad*, Bulgaria (2011), **Bart Nieuwenhuis**, *University of Twente*, The Netherlands (2011), and **Hermann Maurer**, *Graz University of Technology*, Austria (2011).

The high quality of the BMSD 2023 technical program is enhanced by two keynote lectures delivered by outstanding Dutch scientists: **Willem-Jan van den Heuvel**, *Tilburg University* (the title of his lecture is: "Data Meshes Fueling MLOps: Toward Frictionless Collaboration Between the Operational and Analytical Panes") and **Roel Wieringa**, *University of Twente* (the title of his lecture is: "Value-Driven Requirements Engineering") who was also a keynote lecturer at BMSD-Luxembourg-2014 (see above). Next to that, the presence (physically or distantly) of former BMSD keynote lecturers is much appreciated: *Norbert Gronau* (2017, 2021), *Alexander Verbraeck* (2017, 2021), *Roy Oberhauser* (2018), and *Mathias Kirchmer* (2016). The technical program is further enriched by a panel discussion (featured by the participation of some of the abovementioned outstanding scientists) and also by other discussions stimulating *community building* and facilitating possible *R&D project acquisition initiatives*. Those special activities are definitely contributing to maintaining the event's high quality and inspiring our steady and motivated Community.

The BMSD'23 Technical Program Committee consists of a Chair and 111 Members from 37 countries (*Australia, Austria, Brazil, Bulgaria, Canada, China, Colombia, Denmark, Egypt, Estonia, Finland, France, Germany, Greece, India, Indonesia, Italy, Latvia, Lithuania, Grand Duchy of Luxembourg, Malaysia, Mexico, New Zealand, Palestine, Poland, Portugal, Russia, Singapore, Slovak Republic, Slovenia, Spain, Sweden,*

Switzerland, Taiwan, The Netherlands, UK, and *USA,* listed alphabetically) – all of them competent and enthusiastic representatives of prestigious organizations.

In organizing BMSD 2023, we have observed **highest ethical standards**: We guarantee *at least two reviews per submitted paper* (this assuming reviews of adequate quality), under the condition that the paper fulfills the BMSD'23 requirements. In assigning a paper for reviewing, it is our responsibility to *provide reviewers that have relevant expertise.* Sticking to a **double-blind review process**, we guarantee that a reviewer would not know who the authors of the reviewed paper are (we send anonymized versions of the papers to the reviewers) and an author would not know who has reviewed his/her paper. We require that a reviewer *respects the reviewed paper* and would not disclose (parts of) its content to third parties before the symposium (and also after the symposium in case the manuscript gets rejected). We *guarantee against conflict of interest* by not assigning papers for reviewing by reviewers who are immediate colleagues of any of the co-authors. In our decisions to accept / reject papers, we **guarantee against any discrimination based on age, gender, race, or religion**. As it concerns the EU data protection standards, **we stick to the GDPR requirements**.

We have demonstrated for a 13th consecutive year a high quality of papers. We are proud to have succeeded in establishing and maintaining (for many years already) a high scientific quality (as it concerns the symposium itself) and a stimulating collaborative atmosphere; also, our Community is inspired to share ideas and experiences.

As mentioned already, BMSD is essentially leaning toward **ENTERPRISE INFORMATION SYSTEMS (EIS)**, by considering the **MODELING OF ENTERPRISES AND BUSINESS PROCESSES** as a basis for **SPECIFYING SOFTWARE**. Further, in the broader EIS context, BMSD 2023 addresses a large number of research areas and topics, as follows:

› **BUSINESS PROCESSES AND ENTERPRISE ENGINEERING** - *enterprise systems; enterprise system environments and context; construction and function; actor roles; signs and affordances; transactions; business processes; business process coordination; business process optimization; business process management and strategy execution; production acts and coordination acts; regulations and business rules; enterprise (re-) engineering; enterprise interoperability; inter-enterprise coordination; enterprise engineering and architectural governance; enterprise engineering and software generation; enterprise innovation.*

› **BUSINESS MODELS AND REQUIREMENTS** - *essential business models; reusable business models; business value models; business process models; business goal models; integrating data analytics in business modeling; semantics and business data modeling; pragmatics and business behavior modeling; business modeling viewpoints and overall consistency; business modeling landscapes; augmented- and virtual- reality-based enterprise modeling; requirements elicitation; domain-imposed and user-defined requirements; requirements specification and modeling; requirements analysis and verification; requirements evolution; requirements traceability; usability and requirements elicitation.*

› **BUSINESS MODELS AND SERVICES** - *enterprise engineering and service science; service-oriented enterprises; from business modeling to service-oriented solutions; business modeling for software-based services; service engineering; business-goals-driven service discovery and modeling; technology-independent and platform-specific service modeling; re-usable service models; business-rules-driven service composition; web services; autonomic service behavior; context-aware service behavior; service interoperability; change impact analysis and service management; service monitoring and quality of service; services for IoT applications; service innovation.*

› **BUSINESS MODELS AND SOFTWARE** - *enterprise engineering and software development; model-driven engineering; co-design of business and IT systems; business-IT alignment and traceability; alignment between IT architecture and business strategy; business strategy and technical debt; business-modeling-driven software generation; normalized systems and combinatorial effects; software generation and dependency analysis; component-based business-software alignment; objects, components, and modeling patterns; generic business modeling patterns and software re-use; business rules and software specification; business goals and software integration; business innovation and software evolution; software technology maturity models; domain-specific models; croscutting concerns - security, privacy, distribution, recoverability, logging, performance monitoring.*

› **INFORMATION SYSTEMS ARCHITECTURES AND PARADIGMS** - *enterprise architectures; service-oriented computing; software architectures; cloud computing; autonomic computing (and intelligent software behavior); context-aware computing (and adaptable software systems); affective computing (and user-aware software systems); aspect-oriented computing (and non-functional requirements); architectural styles; architectural viewpoints.*

› **DATA ASPECTS IN BUSINESS MODELING AND SOFTWARE DEVELOPMENT** - *data modeling in business processes; data flows and business modeling; databases, OLTP, and business processes; data warehouses, OLAP, and business analytics; data analysis, data semantics, redundancy, and quality-of-data; data mining, knowledge discovery, and knowledge management; information security and business process modeling; categorization, classification, regression, and clustering; cluster analysis and predictive analysis; ontologies and decision trees; decision tree induction and information gain; business processes and entropy; machine learning and deep learning - an enterprise perspective; uncertainty and context states; statistical data analysis and probabilistic business models.*

› **BLOCKCHAIN-BASED BUSINESS MODELS AND INFORMATION SYSTEMS** - *smart contracts; blockchains for business process management; blockchain schemes for decentralization; the blockchain architecture - implications for systems and business processes; blockchains and the future of enterprise information systems; blockchains and security / privacy / trust issues.*

› **IoT AND IMPLICATIONS FOR ENTERPRISE INFORMATION SYSTEMS** - *the IoT paradigm; IoT data collection and aggregation; business models and IoT; IoT-based software solutions; IoT and context awareness; IoT and public values; IoT applications: smart cities, e-Health, smart manufacturing.*

BMSD 2023 received 65 paper submissions from which 29 papers were selected for publication in the symposium proceedings. Of these papers, 11 were selected for a 30-minute oral presentation (full papers), leading to a **full-paper acceptance ratio of 17%** (compared to 22% in 2022, 23% in 2021 and 2020, 22% in 2019 and 19% in 2018) - an indication for our intention to preserve a high-quality forum for the next editions of the symposium. The BMSD 2023 authors come from: Belgium, Brazil, Bulgaria, Finland, Germany, Jordan, Grand Duchy of Luxembourg, Portugal, Sweden, Switzerland, The Netherlands, and USA (listed alphabetically); that makes a total of 12 countries (compared to 9 in 2022, 16 in 2021 and 2020, 10 in 2019, 15 in 2018, 20 in 2017, 16 in 2016, 21 in 2015, 21 in 2014, 14 in 2013, 11 in 2012, and 10 in 2011) to justify a strong international presence. Three countries have been represented at all thirteen BMSD editions so far – **Bulgaria**, **Germany**, and **The Netherlands** – indicating a strong European influence.

Clustering BMSD papers is always inspiring because this gives different perspectives with regard to the challenge of **adequately specifying software based on enterprise modeling**. (a) As it concerns the BMSD'23 Full Papers: some of them are directed towards BUSINESS PROCESS MANAGEMENT AND DIGITAL TRANSFORMATION, while others are touching upon CHANGE MODELING IN BUSINESS PROCESSES, the relation between BUSINESS MODELING AND TACIT KNOWLEDGE, ENTERPRISE MODELING WITH CONVENTIONS, and SEMIOTICS; some papers address CONTEXT AWARENESS, and in particular: the INCORPORATION OF TRUST INTO CONTEXT-AWARE SERVICES and the VR-DRIVEN VISUALIZATION OF ENTERPRISE CONTEXT DYNAMICS, while others are taking a broader perspective on VR, considering its combination with CONCEPTUAL MODELING; some papers address issues concerning ORGANIZATIONAL CAPABILITIES and SERVICE PLATFORMS, while the eleventh full paper is touching upon OBJECT-ORIENTED SPECIFICATIONS. (b) As it concerns the BMSD'23 Short Papers: some of them are directed towards SEMIOTICS, BPMN, DOMAIN-SPECIFIC MODELING, and ENTERPRISE ARCHITECTURES, while others are touching upon EXPERT MODELS, TRUST, and PUBLIC VALUES; some papers consider AR in support of BUSINESS MODELING, while others address the relation between AI and CHANGE CAPABILITY driven by the goal of achieving OPERATIONAL AGILITY; a paper addresses the comparison between SENSOR-BASED COMPUTING and PREDICTIVE DATA ANALYTICS for usage in CONTEXT-AWARE APPLICATIONS, while other papers consider SOFTWARE ENGINEERING PROCESS IMPROVEMENTS and the MONITORING OF TECHNICAL DEGRADATIONS; a paper touches upon RULE-BASED BUSINESS INFORMATION SYSTEMS, while other papers consider OBJECT-ORIENTED SPECIFICATIONS and DATABASE TRIGGERS; finally, in the perspective of INTERNET-OF-THINGS and SMART (HOME) ENVIRONMENTS, some papers address, VULNERABILITIES, CYBERSECURITY, and the SENSOR-DRIVEN TRAFFIC MANAGEMENT.

BMSD 2023 was organized and sponsored by the *Interdisciplinary Institute for Collaboration and Research on Enterprise Systems and Technology* (*IICREST*), co-organized by the *Open University of the Netherlands*, and technically co-sponsored by *BPM-D*, *Cesuur B.V.*, and the *Dutch Research School for Information and Knowledge*

Systems (SIKS). Cooperating organizations were *Aristotle University of Thessaloniki (AUTH)*, *Delft University of Technology (TU Delft)*, *Institute of Mathematics and Informatics* - Bulgarian Academy of Sciences, the UTwente *Digital Society Institute (DSI)*, and *AMAKOTA Ltd.*

Organizing this interesting and successful symposium required the dedicated efforts of many people. First, we thank the *authors*, whose research and development achievements are recorded here. Next, the *Program Committee members* each deserve credit for the diligent and rigorous peer reviewing. Further, appreciating the hospitality of the *Open University (OU) of the Netherlands*, we would like to mention the excellent organization provided by the *IICREST team* (supported by its *logistics partner, AMAKOTA Ltd.*) – the team (words of gratitude to *Aglika Bogomilova*!) did all the necessary work for delivering a stimulating and productive event, supported by the *OU team* (words of gratitude to *Lloyd Rutledge*!). We are grateful to *Coen Suurmond* and *Alexander Verbraeck* for their inspiring support with regard to the organization of BMSD 2023. We are also grateful to *Springer* for their willingness to publish the current proceedings and we would like to especially mention *Ralf Gerstner* and *Christine Reiss*, appreciating their professionalism and patience (regarding the preparation of the symposium proceedings). We are certainly grateful to our *keynote lecturers, Prof. Willem-Jan van den Heuvel* and *Prof. Roel Wieringa*, for their inspiring contribution and for their taking the time to synthesize and deliver their talks.

We wish you inspiring reading! We look forward to meeting you next year in *Luxembourg, Grand Duchy of Luxembourg*, for the *14ᵗʰ International Symposium on Business Modeling and Software Design (BMSD 2024)*, details of which will be made available on: https://www.is-bmsd.org.

June 2023   Boris Shishkov

Organization

Chair

Boris Shishkov   Institute of Mathematics and Informatics - BAS (Bulgaria), University of Library Studies and Information Technologies (Bulgaria), IICREST (Bulgaria)

Program Committee

Marco Aiello	University of Stuttgart, Germany
Mehmet Aksit	University of Twente, The Netherlands
Amr Ali-Eldin	Mansoura University, Egypt
Apostolos Ampatzoglou	University of Macedonia, Greece
Paulo Anita	Delft University of Technology, The Netherlands
Juan Carlos Augusto	Middlesex University, UK
Paris Avgeriou	University of Groningen, The Netherlands
Saimir Bala	Humboldt University of Berlin, Germany
Boyan Bontchev	Sofia University St. Kliment Ohridski, Bulgaria
Jose Borbinha	University of Lisbon, Portugal
Frances Brazier	Delft University of Technology, The Netherlands
Bert de Brock	University of Groningen, The Netherlands
Barrett Bryant	University of North Texas, USA
Cinzia Cappiello	Politecnico di Milano, Italy
Kuo-Ming Chao	Coventry University, UK
Michel Chaudron	Chalmers University of Technology, Sweden
Samuel Chong	Fullerton Systems, Singapore
Dimitar Christozov	American University in Bulgaria - Blagoevgrad, Bulgaria
Jose Cordeiro	Polytechnic Institute of Setubal, Portugal
Maya Daneva	University of Twente, The Netherlands
Robertas Damasevicius	Kaunas University of Technology, Lithuania
Ralph Deters	University of Saskatchewan, Canada
Claudio Di Ciccio	Sapienza University, Italy
Jan L. G. Dietz	Delft University of Technology, The Netherlands
Aleksandar Dimov	Sofia University St. Kliment Ohridski, Bulgaria
Teduh Dirgahayu	Universitas Islam Indonesia, Indonesia

Dirk Draheim	Tallinn University of Technology, Estonia
John Edwards	Aston University, UK
Hans-Georg Fill	University of Fribourg, Switzerland
Chiara Francalanci	Politecnico di Milano, Italy
Veska Georgieva	Technical University – Sofia, Bulgaria
J. Paul Gibson	T&MSP - Telecom & Management SudParis, France
Rafael Gonzalez	Javeriana University, Colombia
Paul Grefen	Eindhoven University of Technology, The Netherlands
Norbert Gronau	University of Potsdam, Germany
Clever Ricardo Guareis de Farias	University of Sao Paulo, Brazil
Jens Gulden	Utrecht University, The Netherlands
Ilian Ilkov	Kyndryl, The Netherlands
Ivan Ivanov	SUNY Empire State College, USA
Krassimira Ivanova	Institute of Mathematics and Informatics – BAS, Bulgaria
Marijn Janssen	Delft University of Technology, The Netherlands
Gabriel Juhas	Slovak University of Technology, Slovak Republic
Dmitry Kan	Silo AI, Finland
Marite Kirikova	Riga Technical University, Latvia
Stefan Koch	Johannes Kepler University Linz, Austria
Vinay Kulkarni	Tata Consultancy Services, India
John Bruntse Larsen	Technical University of Denmark, Denmark
Peng Liang	Wuhan University, China
Kecheng Liu	University of Reading, UK
Claudia Loebbecke	University of Cologne, Germany
Leszek Maciaszek	University of Economics, Poland
Somayeh Malakuti	ABB Corporate Research Center, Germany
Jelena Marincic	ASML, The Netherlands
Raimundas Matulevicius	University of Tartu, Estonia
Hermann Maurer	Graz University of Technology, Austria
Heinrich Mayr	Alpen-Adria-University Klagenfurt, Austria
Nikolay Mehandjiev	University of Manchester, UK
Jan Mendling	Humboldt University of Berlin, Germany
Michele Missikoff	Institute for Systems Analysis and Computer Science, Italy
Dimitris Mitrakos	Aristotle University of Thessaloniki, Greece
Ricardo Neisse	European Commission Joint Research Center, Italy
Bart Nieuwenhuis	University of Twente, The Netherlands
Roy Oberhauser	Aalen University, Germany

Olga Ormandjieva	Concordia University, Canada
Paul Oude Luttighuis	Le Blanc Advies, The Netherlands
Mike Papazoglou	Tilburg University, The Netherlands
Marcin Paprzycki	Polish Academy of Sciences, Poland
Jeffrey Parsons	Memorial University of Newfoundland, Canada
Oscar Pastor	Universidad Politecnica de Valencia, Spain
Krassie Petrova	Auckland University of Technology, New Zealand
Prantosh K. Paul	Raiganj University, India
Barbara Pernici	Politecnico di Milano, Italy
Doncho Petkov	Eastern Connecticut State University, USA
Gregor Polancic	University of Maribor, Slovenia
Hende*rik* Proper	Vienna University of Technology, Austria
Mirja Pulkkinen	University of Jyvaskyla, Finland
Ricardo Queiros	Polytechnic of Porto, Portugal
Jolita Ralyte	University of Geneva, Switzerland
Julia Rauscher	University of Augsburg, Germany
Stefanie Rinderle-Ma	University of Vienna, Austria
Werner Retschitzegger	Johannes Kepler University Linz, Austria
Jose-Angel Rodriguez	Tecnologico de Monterrey, Mexico
Wenge Rong	Beihang University, China
Ella Roubtsova	Open University, The Netherlands
Irina Rychkova	University Paris 1 Pantheon Sorbonne, France
Shazia Sadiq	University of Queensland, Australia
Ronny Seiger	University of St. Gallen, Switzerland
Denis Silva da Silveira	Federal University of Pernambuco, Brazil
Andreas Sinnhofer	Graz University of Technology, Austria
Valery Sokolov	Yaroslavl State University, Russia
Richard Starmans	Utrecht University, The Netherlands
Hans-Peter Steinbacher	FH Kufstein Tirol University of Applied Sciences, Austria
Janis Stirna	Stockholm University, Sweden
Coen Suurmond	Cesuur B.V., The Netherlands
Adel Taweel	Birzeit University, Palestine
Bedir Tekinerdogan	Wageningen University, The Netherlands
Ramayah Thurasamy	Universiti Sains Malaysia, Malaysia
Jose Tribolet	IST - University of Lisbon, Portugal
Roumiana Tsankova	Technical University - Sofia, Bulgaria
Martin van den Berg	Utrecht University of Applied Sciences, The Netherlands
Willem-Jan van den Heuvel	Tilburg University, The Netherlands
Han van der Aa	University of Mannheim, Germany
Marten van Sinderen	University of Twente, The Netherlands

Damjan Vavpotic	University of Ljubljana, Slovenia
Alexander Verbraeck	Delft University of Technology, The Netherlands
Hans Weigand	Tilburg University, The Netherlands
Roel Wieringa	University of Twente, The Netherlands
Dietmar Winkler	Vienna University of Technology, Austria
Shin-Jer Yang	Soochow University, Taiwan
Benjamin Yen	University of Hong Kong, China
Fani Zlatarova	Elizabethtown College, USA

Invited Speakers

Willem-Jan van den Heuvel	Tilburg University, The Netherlands
Roel Wieringa	University of Twente, The Netherlands

Abstracts of Keynote Lectures

Data Meshes Fueling MLOps: Toward Frictionless Collaboration Between the Operational and Analytical Panes

Willem-Jan van den Heuvel

Tilburg University, The Netherlands
w.j.a.m.vdnheuvel@tilburguniversity.nl

Abstract. Today, data is no longer viewed as merely a tacit derivative of enterprise applications, but rather a shareable, discoverable and composable product in itself. In the wake of this trend, the notion of a data mesh has emerged referring to a largely distributed data computing paradigm to share, discover, package and ingest analytical data as data products. In this keynote, we will argue how data meshes might fuel MLOps (and vice versa), facilitate frictionless collaboration between autonomous teams of data-product developers and consumers, promoting continuous delivery and integration. In this way, data mesh would achieve higher levels of alignment of the operational and analytical data panes, whilst breaking down the silos between data engineers and analysts. Several examples of data meshes and products will be discussed, cases presented, and open issues revealed.

Value-Driven Requirements Engineering

Roel Wieringa

University of Twente, The Netherlands
r.j.wieringa@utwente.nl

Abstract. In the digital economy, software systems are used not just to save cost but to create value for companies. They are used to create a value proposition for customers, to coordinate with partners and to collect revenue from services delivered online. This requires a value-driven and network-oriented approach to requirements engineering. In this talk I present an approach based on over 20 years of research in networked business modeling, and on real-world experience using this approach in business. I structure the requirements problem in four levels: What value proposition must be supported by ICT? Who participates in the value network that collaborates to offer this proposition? What are the revenue models to be supported? What are the requirements on ICT, data, and coordination that follow from this? The talk is illustrated with numerous practice cases. This talk is based on the upcoming book, Digital Ecosystems: How to Create, Capture and deliver Value in Business networks. TVE Press 2023, which Roel Wieringa wrote together with Jaap Gordijn.

Contents

Short Papers

Full Papers

Modeling Change in Business Processes

Christof Thim[1] , Norbert Gronau[1] , Jennifer Haase[1] , Marcus Grum[1(✉)] ,
Arnulf Schüffler[2] , Wiebke Roling[2] , and Annette Kluge[2]

[1] Universität Potsdam, August-Bebel-Str. 89, 14482 Potsdam, Germany
mgrum@lswi.de
[2] Ruhr-University Bochum, Universitätsstraße 150, 44801 Bochum, Germany

Abstract. Business processes are regularly modified either to capture
requirements from the organization's environment or due to internal optimization and restructuring. Implementing the changes into the individual work routines is aided by change management tools. These tools
aim at the acceptance of the process by and empowerment of the process executor. They cover a wide range of general factors and seldom
accurately address the changes in task execution and sequence. Furthermore, change is only framed as a learning activity, while most obstacles
to change arise from the inability to unlearn or forget behavioural patterns one is acquainted with. Therefore, this paper aims to develop and
demonstrate a notation to capture changes in business processes and
identify elements that are likely to present obstacles during change. It
connects existing research from changes in work routines and psychological insights from unlearning and intentional forgetting to the BPM
domain. The results contribute to more transparency in business process models regarding knowledge changes. They provide better means to
understand the dynamics and barriers of change processes.

Keywords: Intentional Forgetting · Routines · Business Processes ·
Unlearning

1 Introduction

Changes are regularly planned in business processes either through redesign or
incremental improvement. Discussions about organizational change have been
centred around the strategy and methods of redesign and adaption of business
process models. Analysis, implementation and automation are of primary concern. Even though process models are also means of management and communication within the organization, they do not play an important role in planning and executing change management initiatives. Change methods are seldom targeted towards specific tasks or employees. The extent and awareness of
prior knowledge are also not addressed. Change on the organizational level is
often hindered by the inertia of existing routines. Change management is centred around establishing the new process and seldom considers the impeding

B. Shishkov (Ed.): BMSD 2023, LNBIP 483, pp. 3–17, 2023.
https://doi.org/10.1007/978-3-031-36757-1_1

effects of existing, incorporated routines on the uptake of new processes. It has been shown that individuals tend to stick to their current beliefs and methods as long as they can successfully apply them [45]. Research on unlearning [22, 25] and intentional forgetting [9, 24] has investigated effects regarding the interaction between older knowledge and newly learned information, identifying factors leading to relapse, locating them in business processes and routines and finding ways to manipulate them can ease the change.

Business process modelling has neither been concerned with describing model changes over time nor with capturing factors influencing process learning, unlearning or forgetting. Therefore, this paper aims to extend business process models insofar as they can be used to identify changing activities and sequences and locate factors influencing relapse. While identifying changes in a process is generally applicable, we concentrate on the individual ability to inhibit the execution of activities when identifying and managing the change behaviour. Our research question is, therefore:

How can cues provoking relapse in business processes be mapped to business process models to plan, analyze and control change activities?

Three existing approaches inform the development: Process variability modelling, to capture differences between similar process models on a schema level; changes in work routines, which describe the behavioural aspect of change and the psychological foundations of unlearning and in the long term forgetting, which explain cognitive aspects of change (Sect. 2). A notation of process variability modelling is extended concerning temporal aspects and annotations for influencing factors (Sect. 4). The result is demonstrated using examples from an experiment researching process changes (Sect. 5). The proposed notation contributes to existing business process modelling research by capturing temporal variability in process models. It furthermore provides a link between schema-related changes in the business process models and organizational routines as enacted sequences of action. Moreover, it identifies manageable factors in the work environment and links those to the process model variants.

2   Related Literature

The development of the modelling notation is based on three theoretical realms, each representing a different level of modelling: business process model variants, organizational routines and cognitive operations of unlearning and forgetting. The changes in the scope of this paper stem from conscious design decision on the organizational level which ought to be performed and routinized by the actors within the business process. Emergent changes from individual or group behaviour which is generalised for the organisation is not considered here.

Business processes formally define the sequences of tasks to achieve an organizational goal. Different aspects of similar processes are captured in process variability modelling. Changes can thus be seen as temporal variants of one process. While business processes are normative, organizational routines are enacted activities stemming from their participants' joint sense-making.

They carry both behavioural and socially normative aspects. In the best case, routines and business processes are aligned. Especially during change projects, routines are expected to drift, temporarily diverge and realign with the business processes [3]. The direction of the shift in routines is connected to the agency of their participants [16]. Individual variance in routine execution is based on intention, motivation, and knowledge about the routine. Thus, the individual level, especially the cognitive operations of learning, unlearning and forgetting, must be regarded to manage change in business processes. While there is extensive literature on change and learning, this paper focuses on the factors of knowledge substitution, suppression and elimination.

2.1 Business Processes Model Variability

A business process structures all activities, their sequence and constraints, and the associated resources necessary to achieve an organizational goal [13]. While business process modelling primarily focuses on standardization, research has recently shifted towards different variants of process execution, their efficient adaptation and the reuse of process elements [49] mostly centred around information system support at run time [11,39].

Variability modelling at design time on the schema level, on the other hand, tries to capture different processes with the same goal, similar tasks and sequences but different domain-specific implementations before they are executed. Instead of maintaining each specific model variant separately (multi-model approach) [21], different implementations can be consolidated into one complex model which is easier to manage and eases variability identification. The consolidated version of the model (customizable process model) [29] contains variation points that highlight diverging implementations in the control flow (task insertion, deletion or substitution as well as changes in decision paths) and in the different use of resources (roles, systems, tools) for the specified tasks. Thus, variability modelling must consider flexibility in the association between tasks and resources. Besides structural changes to the process model, the content of the task or activity can differ. As work instructions change within a task, the actor has to adapt without executing a different task.

Process variants are often considered only between different domains. However, customizable process models capture differences in general. Thus, we reframe their usage towards variability over time (temporal variability). By that rationale, changed processes are variants occurring at different points in time [31]. (R1) Requirement 1 is therefore formulated as follows: The modelling notation needs to consider temporally different process models with changing actors and artefacts.

Switching from the initial business process to the modified version is not seamless [8]. The executed instances of the process model will therefore contain a mix of older and newer elements. By analyzing the instances concerning their closeness to pure process variants, activities and situations prone to relapse can be identified. This performative perspective is described in organizational routines.

2.2   Change in Organizational Routines

Changes in the business process model need to be enacted by the process participants. Organizational routines tie the organisational expectation (target process) to the individual interpretation and execution. Routines are defined by repetitiveness, a recognizable pattern, interdependent action, and multiple actors [16]. They are structurally constrained [46,52], yet possess endogenous dynamics [37]. The behaviour shown in routines might diverge from the organizationally designed process [7] as it tends to drift [16,38], undergo conscious modification [18] and produces varying sequences of action triggered by exception, error and improvisation [36]. It thus has to be distinguished between aspired changes (in the business process model) and implemented change (in the performative routines). Analyzing routines and generalizing the observed activities can thus inform the design of business processes changes [44].

In order to manage change though interventions, the causes of variation need to be detailed further. One central concept of explaining routine dynamics is the actor's agency [14]. Routine variability is therefore shaped both by the actors' orientation, and intention as well as its situational and organizational embeddedness [25]. Actors possess certain degrees of freedom to translate normative aspects into performance. The organizational setting and knowledge about the existing routine define this freedom. Lazaric & Denis [30] differentiate between declarative and procedural knowledge. Declarative knowledge provides facts and events. Procedural knowledge, on the other hand, describes how different actions should be executed. Cohen & Bacdayan [12] claim that routines store procedural knowledge. A successful shift in routines thus needs to incorporate the modification of existing procedural knowledge. Concepts of unlearning and intentional forgetting describe which factors drive the change of the underlying knowledge.

(R2) To generalise performative aspects of the change, requirement 2 states that the individual differences in process execution need to be connected to elements at the schema level.

2.3   Unlearning and Forgetting

Behavioral adaption is preceded by knowing the expected or successful patterns and the ability to inhibit unwanted patterns. Feldman [15] argues that routine dynamics are primarily concerned with learning, whereas Hedberg [22] includes unlearning and forgetting. While new information generates new options in routine performance, prior knowledge and experience can restrain variability therein [25] and interfere with adapting to the new routine as employees tend to relapse into the old routine. Older routines can also interfere with new knowledge as cognitive capacity is allocated for routine performance and the consolidation of new information. Intentionally inhibiting the recall of undesired tasks and objectives can free cognitive capacity [2,40] and ease the transition. This paper, therefore, concentrates on modelling these operations instead of learning. Two concepts can be used to explain the elimination or suppression of older knowledge: unlearning and forgetting [27].

On the routine level, unlearning is either substituting, overwriting, disregarding, or stopping to show an unwanted behaviour [48]. Enforcement and enactment are sufficient to overwrite it, if executed long enough [23, 34]. Fiol and O'Connor [17] identify three steps of unlearning: destabilizing and discarding an old routine as well as the subsequent establishment of a new one.

The unlearning concept has been criticized from the psychological perspective [26, 42]. The term forgetting is preferred as it also connects to broader explanations of the underlying cognitive aspects. Forgetting is generally defined as inhibiting the recall of previously learned information [43] and addresses both accidental and intentional aspects. The intentional aspect of forgetting includes active suppression and sorting out knowledge without a functional equivalent [9, 40, 50, 51]. The individual is therein aware about unwanted, habituated routines and actively aims at inhibition.

Research on forgetting has identified different mechanisms and modes of inhibition. Disuse of knowledge and interference of new and old knowledge elements [4, 10]. The interference perspective explains why old knowledge elements resurface instead of newly learned and why variability in executing the new actions is generated. Retrieval cues play an important role in this process. They can trigger and impact recall [19, 40]. The strength of a retrieval cue depends on its availability in the environment, and its exclusiveness for a specific memory item (cue overload) [33]. Since older, consolidated cues possess a higher retrieval strength, learning the new routine is delayed. The presence of cues for undesired memory items leads to complete or partial relapse.

Kluge & Gronau [28] classify cues into sensory, routine-related, time and space, and situational strength cues. Sensory cues are based on smell, taste, tactile and visual stimuli. Routine-related cues are connected to a routine's actors, objects, information and task sequences. Time and space-related cues define the location and time of routine execution, e.g. powering down the machinery at a production workplace when the shift ends. Situational strength cues are provided by external entities and mark the desirability of a behaviour [32]. These cues are related to supervisory activity and the associated incentive system [1].

By eliminating or presenting retrieval cues, relapse can be influenced. In the organizational context, this is achieved by managed forgetting [24], which encompasses "processes that deliberately impede the recall of certain organizational memory items, and do not provide these memory items and information elements in the case of a certain query to support an organization's changed strategic goal achievement" [28].

The work setting can be structured through cue manipulation, and inhibition of old activities is easier as older memory items are less likely to be retrieved. Relapse would occur less often. It is, therefore, beneficial to highlight changes in business processes concerning these cues [47]. Not all cues are equally accessible for manipulation in a controlled change process. While there might be some experimentation with sensory cues, their impact on inhibition in a work setting is uncertain. Thus, this paper concentrates on routine, time and space, and situational strength cues.

Beyond that, separate activities can also serve as a cue and lead to cascading effects and trigger further interlocking activities. The execution of an older activity automatically leads to the retrieval of old procedural knowledge and the execution of the old activity sequence. When planning and managing changes, these activities should be identified and addressed.

(R3) Thus the third requirement states that the modelling notation needs to highlight potential cues in the work environment. The availability and removal of cues in tasks must be annotated on the model level.

3   Methods

The development of the notation to model changes in business processes is guided by the design-science approach [35]. The previous section has presented the motivation, the theoretical foundations and the requirements of the notation. An appropriate base notation for capturing variability is selected based on the review of LaRosa et al. [29] and according to the requirements. This notation is extended with elements that capture the expected variance in performed routines and the impact of associated artefacts (cues) on forgetting.

The resulting notation is demonstrated using the processes and data from an experiment concerned with changing work routines. A medical product's existing production process was modified so that changes could be introduced in a controlled fashion. Experimentation was conducted in a hybrid lab simulation consisting of material (robot, transport system, workpieces) and simulated components (machinery, control system, product). In one lab session, participants were intensively trained in the original process, assuring routinization. The process was changed in a second session with a short introduction and practice of the changes. The participants' activities after the change, their performance, relapse and search activities were observed and logged. The experiment is described in detail at [20].

Data was collected by direct observation, logging of machine interactions, analysis of process-related paperwork and through head-mounted eye-tracking. Activity sequences were generated by combining and coding the data sources. The demonstration section (5) will present the original and changed processes from this experiment as variants. It will highlight potential relapse occasions and allocate the identified cues to these activities. The transition between the process variants will be demonstrated by presenting selected process instances from the data collected during the process execution in the experiment. The following section describes the elements and application of the notation to model changes.

4   A Notation to Model Change in Business Processes

Following the design science approach, the artefact (notation to model change in business processes) is designed according to the requirements derived from the theoretical considerations in Sect. 2:

1. The modelling notation needs to consider temporally different process models with changing actors and artefacts.
2. The notation should be able to generalise different instances and their relevant artefacts at the schema level.
3. The modelling notation must highlight potential work environment cues. The availability and removal of cues in tasks must be annotated on the model level.

The requirements guide the selection of an appropriate base language and the design of the extension of this language.

4.1   Selection of a Variability Modelling Approach

Regarding R1, the base notation should support modelling control flow variability, the annotation of different resources, and other relevant artefacts. There are different ways in which variability can be considered during design time. Based on the review of LaRosa et al. [29] on different variability modelling notations, most approaches support control flow variability, yet only Configurable Integrated Event-driven Process Chains (C-iEPCs) [41] and Configurative Process Modeling (CPM) [5] support resource and object modification. Both are extensions of the EPC language and provide a conceptual model. C-iEPCs capture variability by switching nodes on or off, activating or eliminating possible actions, and control flows. Customization of process models is achieved by marking different model elements (functions and connectors) as configurable and annotating these with requirements and guidelines. Process variants are derived from the customizable model by evaluating the requirements and setting the node switches. Conversely, CPM annotates specific aspects of the process model, e.g. functions, resources, and objects with domain-specific attributes. The customizable model contains all domain aspects. By switching and combining domain attributes, process variants are generated.

Both modelling approaches fulfil the requirement to model change, and CPM is more flexible concerning the usage of annotations. Furthermore, it has been used for (technical) change management purposes before [6]. It is therefore selected as the base for the change and forgetting extension. Instead of using the full specification with event-function-event sequences, a simplified version is applied that omits dispensable events without semantic value to eliminate noise.

4.2   Extension to Model Change in Business Processes

Annotations in CPM are flexible about different domains. Depicting temporal changes needs to apply constraints and extend the notation with further attributes. Tasks and activities are denoted as functions to be consistent with the EPC language. As CPM does not possess a meta-model or extension definition, the annotations were designed in line with the existing CPM-additions to EPC as purely graphical representations.

Process Schema. Abstracting from the domain-specific annotation, change on the process schema level can be modelled by annotating the variance points with their presence in the as-is and the aspired model. The annotation thus considers function persistence (no annotation), removal (annotated with as-is), insertion (annotated as target), as well as changes in the execution of the function (annotated with content). Besides changes in the functions and control flow, the work environment can be changed too, e.g. by modifying information systems or machinery. The presence of objects and resources is factual in a changed work environment. There is no relapse in the object, just in its usage. It, therefore, does not make sense to annotate the object itself but rather the edges associated with the task. Thus, a dashed, undirected line depicts a supposed discontinued use of this object in the target process. The same can be applied to persons, roles, organizational units, and information (R1).

Process Instances. Modeling on the schema level captures both work environments in a single diagram. During the transition from the as-is to the target process, different instances or routines can emerge from the customizable model, containing a mixed set of as-is and target elements resulting from the exploratory process of learning and inhibition. The model is thus not used to derive domain-specific models but to serve as a container for possible instances in the transition. Concrete instances can be compared to two ideal instances containing all as-is elements or all target elements to monitor and manage the change process (R2).

Cues. As cues may govern inhibition and in the long term forgetting of procedural knowledge and thus change in routines, their influence has to be accounted for in the modelling notation (R3). The general approach is to annotate model elements to be suspected to act as a retrieval cue with a circle in the top right corner of the element containing a (C) (for an unspecified cue).

Routine-related cues (objects, information, actors) are active if they are present during the execution of the process. They can be introduced into the process model by annotating the respective model element or by adding a cue element when it only provides context for the process and has not been modelled yet, e.g. provided handbooks or documentation. Routine-related cues are specified with an (R) in the annotation.

While routine-related cues can be presented or removed, time- and space-related cues are contextual and should be differentiated from routine-related cues. They can also be associated with specific process model functions, indicating that it is executed at a specific time or space. Time-related cues are highlighted using a (T), and space-related cues using an (S).

The third type of cue is situational strength cues (instructions, incentives, supervisory activities). They can also be associated directly with the function as well. Using the (I) as an indicator for this type of cue, it is possible to identify specific managerial interventions in the learning process and pinpoint potential misalignment of incentives.

However, situational strength cues are often not specified for one function but for a process outcome or the execution of the complete process. In CPM, groups of elements, e.g. branches after a split, can be annotated. An overarching impact can be highlighted by using this grouping and annotating the group with the specific cue. Annotating groups of functions can also indicate cascading effects if a task triggers a relapse into an old task sequence. The task itself serves as a cue for retrieving the subsequent task. Figure 1 summarizes the annotation elements.

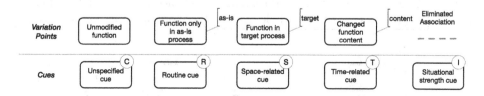

Fig. 1. Elements of the notation

The following section will present the application of the notation using the processes and data from the described lab experiment.

5   Demonstration: Findings from a Change Experiment

In the demonstration, the abstract variant model of the business process is designed as the starting point, and cues are added in the subsequent step. The instances and indications about the influence of cues are depicted in a third step (see Fig. 2). As only an outtake of the experiment is presented, the focus lies on only one sub-process executed by one worker, which provides sufficient variance points and cues.

5.1   Process Variants and Influencing Cues

The original process in the experiment described the steps needed to produce an artificial knee joint, from selecting and checking the blank to setting up and checking the machinery and performing quality assurance as a last step (see 3). The target process was changed in several aspects. Actions were removed, e.g. documenting the extraction of the blank from the warehouse and refilling the lubricant for grinding. Other actions were inserted, such as scanning the blank's QR code in the warehouse and securing, cleaning and calibrating the machine. The third type of change was related to how the specific task had to be executed, e.g. participants had to measure the dimensions of the workpiece in centimetres (original process), which was changed to inches in the target process.

Potential cues were intentionally selected during experiment planning. All environmental cues were present during the initial training and after the change.

Thus, the participants had the chance to relapse. While many possible cues exist, this demonstration is limited to a selected set to exemplify the notation. Thus, for extracting the blank from the warehouse, the documentation form is thought to act as a cue, which might trigger the action of filling out the form. Furthermore, the machine interface was marked as a cue for the operation of the machinery. Regarding actor-related cues, the quality check activity was used to discuss potential faults with the subsequent worker, which is thought to act as a cue. Different situational strength cues were used, e.g. different instructions were presented on notice cards attached to the machine. Furthermore, participants were instructed about the expected production time per piece. Both situational cues impact the process change as a whole and are therefore annotated accordingly.

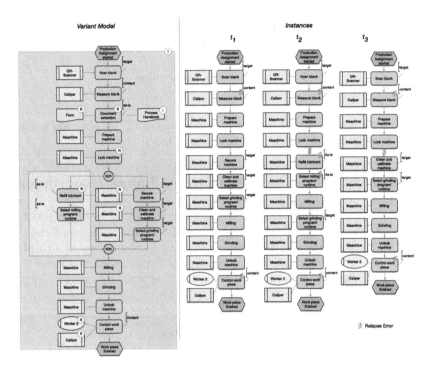

Fig. 2. Process variant model

5.2   Captured Instances

During the experiment, participants were observed in their process execution. The variant model allows capturing these instances and comparing them to the original and target processes. By assessing the closeness of an instance to each process, the progress of change can be monitored, and difficulties in adaptation and patterns of relapse can be identified.

Instances were selected from one participant, ordered by their execution time. Tasks annotated with as-is highlight relapse, while target-annotated tasks are executed correctly. It also needs to be noted that the sequence of tasks must also be considered. Target tasks do not only need to be executed but the correct order must be maintained. The associated cues indicate that the work environment might provide distractions from the target process and lead to relapse.

Analyzing the instances can be used to develop managerial interventions. The triggering cue could be removed from the environment by identifying relapse-associated task-cue associations. If this is not possible, additional cues can be added to overpower the influence of an existing cue. Especially situational cues, such as incentives, instructions and supervisory feedback, can be feasible to suppress the cue's influence by setting the employees' intention to forget the old task.

The demonstration presented the application of the suggested notation to model change and inhibition. Individual relapse behaviour is indicated. The participant reproduced most parts of the process after the initial instruction. During the experiment, relapse occurred more often and on different occasions (see Fig. 2).

6 Conclusions

Re-designing business processes initiate changes in the execution of activities for the process participants. Change management activities should ease the transition from the original to the target process. This intersection between process modelling and change management has been under-researched. This paper contributes to ongoing research by presenting an approach to link the fields.

A process variant model notation, which incorporates the original process alongside the changed process, has been developed on a general level of process change. This notation provides means to track progress and relapse in change by comparing the process model to performed routines captured in instances. It thereby connects the design aspects of process modelling to the behavioural aspects of organizational routines. It has been shown that process executors have problems with adaptation in specific tasks or process segments. The presented approach provides means to identify and control these segments.

Relapse behaviour was also connected to the cognitive effects of retrieval cues present in the work environment. On a more specific level, relevant classes of cues were presented and highlighted in the process model. By identifying and manipulating the cues, individuals can be directed towards suppressing and forgetting the execution of an older routine. This paper, therefore, contributed to the research on process change by presenting intentional forgetting through cue manipulation as an additional concept in change management, which can be aided by the use of process models.

Besides the contributions of this paper, the limitations of the presented approaches and future research areas need to be discussed as well. One limitation concerns the type of change addressed here. Variability modelling is applicable if the range of domains and changes is low. Only one episodic change was demonstrated. Variability models and their analysis might expand if a continuous change needs to be captured with multiple, overlapping time-frames. This is should be addressed in further research, e.g. by investigating how models are trimmed in cross-domain settings for which variability modelling was originally developed.

Furthermore, instance analysis, e.g., process mining, is only easily applicable if all work is performed within information systems that log the activities. As in production environments or warehousing, manual activities are hard to capture exactly. New approaches to tracking, e.g. through wearables and correlations of time and place, need to be developed along with optical recognition methods to gather data for these analyses. The data collection is also limited by objections of work councils and data protection concerns. In addition, the customisable model needs to be formally interpretable. The proposed notation is only a graphical representation which needs to be integrated into existing meta-models in future works.

Having addressed the obstacles of data collection and comparision to the variability model, it needs to be said that this demonstration did not consider the necessary effort to model and analyse changes. It can be argued, that with a sufficient automation in data collection, the insights on the individual level can outweight the substantial effort for the annotated models.

Regarding identifying relevant cues, generalization about the influence of specific cues has to be underpinned with additional research and observations, as current findings see cues as highly individual. However, the knowledge about the existence of cues can guide the observation of changing routines and the development of change management interventions. Thereby, change activities are more accurate and better fit the specific change situation.

References

1. Aguirre, C., Gómez-Ariza, C.J., Andrés, P., Mazzoni, G., Bajo, M.T.: Exploring mechanisms of selective directed forgetting. Front. Psychol. **8**(316) (2017). https://doi.org/10.3389/fpsyg.2017.00316
2. Altmann, E.M., Gray, W.D.: Forgetting to remember: the functional relationship of decay and interference. Psychol. Sci. **13**(1), 27–33 (2002). https://doi.org/10.1111/1467-9280.00405
3. Azad, B., Daouk-Oyry, L., Otaki, F.A.: How routines drift-in-check while being inhabited by agents? Acad. Manage. Proc. **2016**(1), 10898 (2016). https://doi.org/10.5465/ambpp.2016.10898abstract
4. Baddeley, A.D., Logie, R.H.: Working memory: the multiple-component model., book section models of working memory, pp. 28–61. Cambridge University Press, Cambridge, UK (1999)
5. Becker, J., Delfmann, P., Dreiling, A., Knackstedt, R., Kuropka, D.: Configurative process modeling- outlining an approach to increased business process model usability. In: Khosrow-Pour, M. (ed.) 4th Information Resources Management Association International Conference (2004). https://doi.org/10.4018/978-1-59140-261-9.ch157

6. Becker, J., Janiesch, C., Knackstedt, R., Rieke, T.: Facilitating change management with configurative reference modelling. Int. J. Inf. Syst. Chang. Manage. **2**(1), 81–99 (2007). https://doi.org/10.1504/ijiscm.2007.013883

7. Becker, M.C., Lazaric, N., Nelson, R.R., Winter, S.G.: Applying organizational routines in understanding organizational change. Ind. Corporate Change **14**(5), 775–791 (2005). https://doi.org/10.1093/icc/dth071

8. Betsch, T., Haberstroh, S., Molter, B., Glöckner, A.: Oops, i did it again–relapse errors in routinized decision making. Organ. Behav. Hum. Decision Processes **93**(1), 62–74 (2004). https://doi.org/10.1016/j.obhdp.2003.09.002

9. Bjork, R.: Intentional Forgetting in Perspective: Comments, Conjectures, and Some Directed Remembering, pp. 453–481. Lawrence Erlbaum, Mahwah, NJ (1998)

10. Chandler, C.C.: Specific retroactive interference in modified recognition tests: evidence for an unknown cause of interference. J. Exper. Psychol.: Learn. Memory Cogn. **15**, 256–265 (1989)

11. Cognini, R., Corradini, F., Gnesi, S., Polini, A., Re, B.: Business process flexibility - a systematic literature review with a software systems perspective. Inf. Syst. Front. **20**(2), 343–371 (2016). https://doi.org/10.1007/s10796-016-9678-2

12. Cohen, M.D., Bacdayan, P.: Organizational routines are stored as procedural memory: evidence from a laboratory study. Organ. Sci. **5**(4), 554–568 (1994)

13. Dumas, M., La Rosa, M., Mendling, J., Reijers, H.A.: Fundamentals of business process management. Springer, Berlin Heidelberg (2013). https://doi.org/10.1007/978-3-642-33143-5

14. Emirbayer, M., Mische, A.: What is agency? Am. J. Sociol. **103**(4), 962–1023 (1998). https://doi.org/10.1086/231294

15. Feldman, M.S.: Organizational routines as a source of continuous change. Organ. Sci. **11**(6), 611–629 (2000). https://doi.org/10.1287/orsc.11.6.611.12529

16. Feldman, M.S., Pentland, B.T.: Reconceptualizing organizational routines as a source of flexibility and change. Adm. Sci. Q. **48**(1), 94–118 (2003). https://doi.org/10.2307/3556620

17. Fiol, C.M., O'Connor, E.: Unlearning established organizational routines-part i. Learn. Organ. **24**(1), 13–29 (2017)

18. Garud, R., Kumaraswamy, A., Karnøe, P.: Path dependence or path creation? J. Manage. Stud. **47**(4), 760–774 (2010). https://doi.org/10.1111/j.1467-6486.2009.00914.x

19. Gronlund, S., Kimball, D.: Remembering and forgetting: from the laboratory looking out, pp. 14–52. Routledge, New York NY (2013)

20. Haase, J., Schüffler, A.: Studying cue-dependend and intentional forgetting in organizations: a methodological approach. In: Proceedings of the 52nd Hawaii International Conference on System Sciences (2019). https://doi.org/10.24251/HICSS.2019.658

21. Hallerbach, A., Bauer, T., Reichert, M.: Capturing variability in business process models: the provop approach. J. Softw. Main. Evol.: Res. Pract. **22**(6–7), 519–546 (2010). https://doi.org/10.1002/smr.491

22. Hedberg, B.: How Organizations Learn and Unlearn, vol. 1, pp. 3–27. Oxford University Press (1981)

23. Hislop, D., Bosley, S., Coombs, C.R., Holland, J.: The process of individual unlearning: a neglected topic in an under-researched field. Manage. Learn. **45**(5), 540–560 (2014)

24. de Holan, P.M.: Managing organizational forgetting. MIT Sloan Manage. Rev. **45–51**(2), 45 (2004)

25. Howard-Grenville, J.A.: The persistence of flexible organizational routines: the role of agency and organizational context. Organ. Sci. **16**(6), 618–636 (2005). https://doi.org/10.1287/orsc.1050.0150

26. Howells, J., Scholderer, J.: Forget unlearning? how an empirically unwarranted concept from psychology was imported to flourish in management and organisation studies. Manage. Learn. **47**(4), 443–463 (2016). https://doi.org/10.1177/1350507615624079

27. Klammer, A., Gueldenberg, S.: Unlearning and forgetting in organizations: a systematic review of literature. J. Knowl. Manage. **23**(5), 860–888 (2019). https://doi.org/10.1108/JKM-05-2018-0277

28. Kluge, A., Gronau, N.: Intentional forgetting in organizations: the importance of eliminating retrieval cues for implementing new routines. Front. Psychol. **9**, 51 (2018). https://doi.org/10.3389/fpsyg.2018.00051

29. La Rosa, M., Van Der Aalst, W.M.P., Dumas, M., Milani, F.P.: Business process variability modeling: a survey. ACM Comput. Surv. **50**(1), Article 2 (2017). https://doi.org/10.1145/3041957

30. Lazaric, N., Denis, B.: Routinization and memorization of tasks in a workshop: the case of the introduction of ISO norms. Ind. Corporate Change **14**(5), 873–896 (2005)

31. Lu, R., Sadiq, S., Governatori, G.: On managing business processes variants. Data Knowl. Eng. **68**(7), 642–664 (2009). https://doi.org/10.1016/j.datak.2009.02.009

32. Meyer, R.D., Dalal, R.S., Hermida, R.: A review and synthesis of situational strength in the organizational sciences. J. Manage. **36**(1), 121–140 (2010)

33. Nairne, J., Pandeirada, J.: Forgetting. Learning and memory: a comprehensive reference **2**, 179–194 (2008)

34. Nguyen, N.: The journey of organizational unlearning: a conversation with William H. starbuck. Learn. Organ. **24**(1), 58–66 (2017)

35. Peffers, K., Tuunanen, T., Rothenberger, M.A., Chatterjee, S.: A design science research methodology for information systems research. J. Manage. Inf. Syst. **24**(3), 45–77 (2007)

36. Pentland, B.T.: Conceptualizing and measuring variety in the execution of organizational work processes. Manage. Sci. **49**(7), 857–870 (2003). https://doi.org/10.1287/mnsc.49.7.857.16382

37. Pentland, B.T., Hærem, T.: Organizational routines as patterns of action: implications for organizational behavior. Ann. Rev. Organ. Psychol. Organ. Behav. **2**(1), 465–487 (2015). https://doi.org/10.1146/annurev-orgpsych-032414-111412

38. Pentland, B.T., Liu, P., Kremser, W., Hærem, T.: The dynamics of drift in digitized processes. MIS Q. **44**(1), 19–47 (2020). https://doi.org/10.25300/MISQ/2020/14458

39. Rinderle-Ma, S., Reichert, M., Weber, B.: On the formal semantics of change patterns in process-aware information systems. In: Li, Q., Spaccapietra, S., Yu, E., Olivé, A. (eds.) ER 2008. LNCS, vol. 5231, pp. 279–293. Springer, Heidelberg (2008). https://doi.org/10.1007/978-3-540-87877-3_21

40. Roediger, H.L., Weinstein, Y., Agarwal, P.K.: Forgetting: preliminary considerations, pp. 1–22. Psychology Press, New York, NY, US (2010)

41. Rosemann, M., van der Aalst, W.M.P.: A configurable reference modelling language. Inf. Syst. **32**(1), 1–23 (2007). https://doi.org/10.1016/j.is.2005.05.003

42. Salvato, C., Rerup, C.: Beyond collective entities: multilevel research on organizational routines and capabilities. J. Manage. **37**(2), 468–490 (2010). https://doi.org/10.1177/0149206310371691

43. Schooler, L.J., Hertwig, R.: How forgetting aids heuristic inference. Psychol. Rev. **112**(3), 610 (2005)
44. Seidel, S., Watson, R.T.: Integrating explanatory/predictive and prescriptive science in information systems research. Commun. Assoc. Inf. Syst. 47 (2020). https://doi.org/10.17705/1CAIS.04714
45. Starbuck, W.H.: Unlearning ineffective or obsolete technologies. Int. J. Technol. Manage. **11**(7–8), 725–737 (1996). https://doi.org/10.1504/ijtm.1996.025463
46. Sydow, J., Schreyögg, G., Koch, J.: On the theory of organizational path dependence: clarifications, replies to objections, and extensions. Acad. Manage. Rev. **45**(4), 717–734 (2020). https://doi.org/10.5465/amr.2020.0163
47. Thim, C., Gronau, N., Kluge, A.: Managing change through a work environment which promotes forgetting. In: Proceedings of 52nd HICSS 2019. University of Hawai'i at Manoa (2019). https://doi.org/10.24251/HICSS.2019.660
48. Tsang, E.W., Zahra, S.A.: Organizational unlearning. Hum. Relat. **61**(10), 1435–1462 (2008). https://doi.org/10.1177/0018726708095710
49. Valenca, G., Alves, C., Alves, V., Niu, N.: A systematic mapping study on business process variability. Int. J. Comput. Sci. Inf. Technol. **5**(1) (2013). https://doi.org/10.5121/ijcsit.2013.5101
50. Wixted, J.T.: The psychology and neuroscience of forgetting. Ann. Rev. Psychol. **55**, 235–269 (2004)
51. Wixted, J.T.: A theory about why we forget what we once knew. Curr. Direct. Psychol. Sci. **14**(1), 6–9 (2005)
52. Yi, S., Knudsen, T., Becker, M.C.: Inertia in routines: a hidden source of organizational variation. Organ. Sci. **27**(3), 782–800 (2016). https://doi.org/10.1287/orsc.2016.1059

Realizing Appropriate Process Standardization – Basis for Effective Digital Transformation

Mathias Kirchmer[(✉)]

Scheer Americas, Inc., Affiliated Faculty, University of Pennsylvania, Philadelphia, PA, USA
mtki2006@msn.com

Abstract. Process standardization has a significant impact on the performance of companies. It has become especially important as a foundation to deliver the best value from digital transformation initiatives. The importance of process standardization requires the development of a systematic approach as presented in this paper. This approach addresses required context-driven variants and considers all components of a business process, hence, organization, data, functions, deliverables and control flow. Levels of detail and abstraction of the standardization are defined based on the specific goals. The realization of process standards leverages process reference models as a core enabler as well as appropriately defined process governance to sustain the standardized processes.

Keywords: Business Process Management · Digital Transformation · Process Design · Process Governance · Reference Models · Standardization

1 The Value of Process Standardization for Digitalization

Business process standardization significantly impacts process performance and is a key driver in establishing successful business processes across an organization [1, 2]. This section defines process standardization and shows why it is especially important in the context of a digital transformation. Standardization helps realize the full value of digitalization initiatives. A discussion why standardization still requires variants of business processes is used to explain the need for a systematic approach to achieving appropriate standardization, leveraging process management methods and tools.

1.1 The Relation Between Process Standardization and Digital Transformation

Standardization, in general, is the process of implementing and developing inputs, work processes or outputs. This requires the acceptance of different parties that include companies, users, interest groups, standards organizations and governments. It can help maximize compatibility, interoperability, safety, repeatability, or quality [3–5]. Business process standardization refers to the design and realization of organization-wide uniform business processes. Examples are establishing a procure-to-pay process the same

B. Shishkov (Ed.): BMSD 2023, LNBIP 483, pp. 18–31, 2023.
https://doi.org/10.1007/978-3-031-36757-1_2

way in different product units of a company or customer service processes in various regional units of an organization. Standardization helps to make processes more efficient, effective and simplifies their automation [2]. This leads to its special importance for digitalization initiatives.

Digital transformation (used synonymously to digitalization) refers to integrating products and services with people, leveraging digital technologies, which are usually based on the internet. The value from these digital technologies is delivered through appropriately designed and implemented new or significantly improved business processes [6].

Process standardization enables successful digitalization. Process standardization allows an efficient digitalization approach that delivers the best value since good practices for a specific business process can be easily rolled out across the organization [2]. The standard processes are realized through the consistent use of digital technologies, such as automated workflows, in various organizational units of a company.

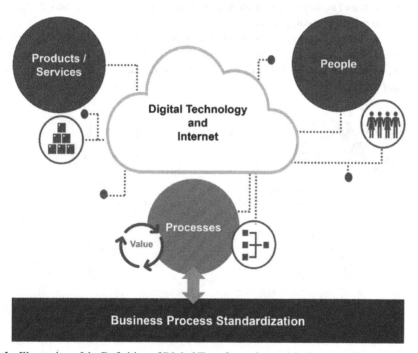

Fig. 1. Illustration of the Definition of Digital Transformation and the Impact of Business Process Standardization

The definition of digital transformation with the impact of process standardization is visualized in Fig. 1 [7]. The value business process standardization brings to digital transformations is now examined further.

1.2   The Value of Process Standardization for Digital Transformation

A direct effect of process standardization is the efficient role out of automation solutions and digital technologies in general [2]. Solution components can be aligned with the standard processes and applied in all relevant business units. This simplifies, not only the digital transformation, but also the following maintenance of the digital solutions. The result is a reduction of the total cost of ownership.

The standardization of processes enables a consistent customer experience, for example, across different regions and countries. Organizations with international clients, such as in the aerospace industry, gain significant competitive advantage through this consistency. This standardization effect is significant in digital transformation initiatives since they often focus on customer-facing front-office processes [6].

Standardized processes can be adjusted faster across an organization to reflect changing customer, supplier, or other market requirements. The adjustment only has to be identified once and can then be rolled out in all business units the same way. The result is a higher degree of agility for a company. The flexibility of digital solutions is leveraged effectively to provide ongoing value.

The management of processes toward compliance with legal or other requirements is simplified through process standardization. This is especially true for operational compliance since controls and checks only have to be defined once and then applied in all relevant business units.

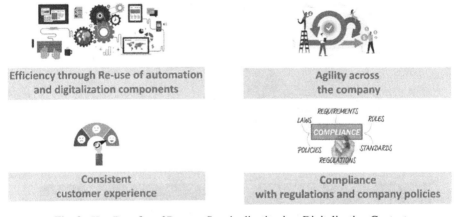

Fig. 2. Key Benefits of Process Standardization in a Digitalization Context

These key benefits of process standardization, especially in a digitalization context, is summarized in Fig. 2.

1.3   Process Standardization Still Requires Variants

The standardization of processes across business units of an organization can only be done to a certain degree due to the business context of a process. This business context, such as geography with specific legal requirements, a variety of products and channels or different target markets, may require variations of processes that cannot be avoided.

International organizations with operations in different countries must follow country-specific laws. These region-specific requirements lead to corresponding business processes and, with that, to country-specific variants, for example, in the finance area. Supporting digital solutions need to be extended accordingly.

A wide variety of products and services also leads to unavoidable process variants. A company, for example, that uses wood as a raw material to produce building products and a variety of paper products ends up with variants in its supply chain and production processes. Insurance firms with different products, such as property, casualty, life, and car insurance, will require variations of a series of processes, e.g., in their underwriting processes. A company that supports different sales or procurement channels has to accommodate those through appropriate process variants. A simple example is the acceptance of customer orders through a web page and mail orders, depending on the business unit. The result is a variation of the order-to-cash processes.

An organization that serves significantly different client groups, such as end-clients and retail clients, has to adjust to those client groups. This results in process variants depending on the client group targeted in a specific business unit to accommodate, e.g., the needs of professional clients with specific delivery and payment approaches and private customers.

Considering required standardization limitations by identifying necessary variants is the basis for of a successful standardization approach. There are several other reasons for organizations to accept process variants. However, practical experience has shown that other reasons, like different qualification levels or cost impacts can be overcome. Figure 3 shows the valid reason for process variants and examples for other explanations.

Examples for valid reasons for process variants

Fig. 3. Reasons for Business Process Variants - Examples

The requirement for process variants, hence, the limitations of process standardization does not only impact the transformation and implementation of business processes. It also leads to the needs to continuously managing these process variants from a business and technology point of view. Hence, process management capabilities, such as process governance, have to be adjusted accordingly.

2   Dimensions of Process Standardization

To manage process standardization effectively, it is important to understand what exactly is standardized and to what degree. This means the different dimensions of process standardization must be defined. Therefore, the components of a process that are addressed for standardization are identified. Then it is distinguished between the degree of detail and abstraction of the standardization.

Determining the degree of standardization of the different process components and the level of detail and abstraction is the first step of planning for appropriate process standardization. It leads to a realistic context-aware standardization approach delivering on the desired benefits.

Systematically considering the dimensions and degree of standardization allows to combine advantages of standard processes with the benefits of consciously allowed variations, e.g., to meet needs of specific customer groups. At the end this optimizes the overall value for the organization.

2.1   Process Components to Be Standardized

A business process consists of different components that can be examined to determine what areas process standardization addresses. According to the widely used ARIS framework developed by Scheer [8] the following views on a process can be distinguished [9]:

- Organization: Who is involved in the process, e.g., which companies, departments or roles?
- Data: Which Information is used or produced in the process?
- Function: What is done in the process, which activities are carried out?
- Deliverable: What does the process produce, why do we need it?
- Control: How do all those views fit together? Who is doing what, in which flow logic, by means of which data to produce which deliverables?

Each component of the business process can be described on the business level and the information technology level, addressing the digital realization of the process components. In practice, the underlying digital solutions, such as software products, are commonly described as part of the function view [9].

Effective process standardization addresses all the components of a business process. Standardizing roles simplifies the exchange of people and increases the agility of an organization. Master and transaction data are standardized to enable the same software solutions across the processes. It also allows using the same analytics to manage the process towards the expected goals, such as enhanced customer experience or compliance goals. The standardization of functions and deliverables enables all standardization benefits discussed before: it allows the use of the same digital solutions, leads to consistent customer experience, and enhances agility and compliance. Part of the standardization of the deliverables is the definition of standard metrics and performance indicators to manage the outcomes toward the business goals. Good practices in this area can be leveraged across the company if processes are standardized. Standard control flows lead to a consistent process logic, which is important, for example, to realize compliance requirements. Addressing all those process components allows the standardization of the underlying digital technologies.

The components of business processes and their relevance for process standardization are illustrated in Fig. 4. These process components are addressed in the design, implementation, execution, and control of the standard processes around the entire process lifecycle.

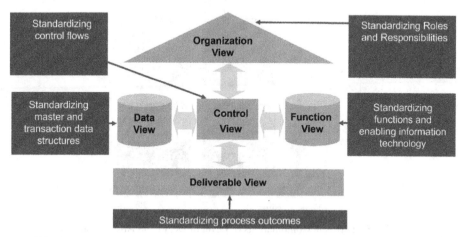

Fig. 4. Components of Process Standardization based on the ARIS Architecture [8]

2.2 Level of Detail and Abstraction of Standardization

The components of a business process are standardized on different levels of detail and abstraction. That means we define what is done in a standard process (level of detail) and how this is executed (level of abstraction).

A low level of abstraction enforces the use of the same digital solutions across the standard processes with the advantages discussed previously. The definition of a standard process on a high level of abstraction leaves room for different ways of executing a process, hence the use of different digital technologies. This can be important, for example, if using the same enabling digital technologies across the different business units is not desired, e.g., because of differences in the size of the business units or local availability of specific software systems.

A high level of detail of the definition of a process standard leaves little to no room for deviations in the different business units executing standard processes. Things are done a certain way, no exception. This is important, e.g., to ensure compliance, for example in finance related processes. A low level of detail of process standardization leads to a higher degree of freedom for the people executing the process. This could be desirable in subprocesses that require a lot of creativity, such as in research and development processes, or a high flexibility, e.g., when dealing with clients in business development situations or to resolve issues.

The appropriate level of detail and abstraction allows for adjusting the standardization of the process to the specific context of a business process. It helps to focus on the key goals of the standardization initiatives.

Figure 5 shows examples of the combination of different levels of detail and abstraction of functions of a business process.

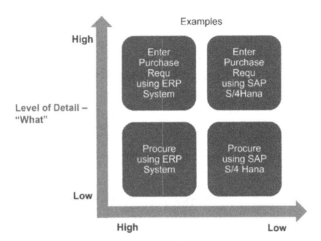

Fig. 5. Different Combinations of Level of Detail and Abstraction

3   Realizing Process Standardization

The realization of process standardization leverages various business process management capabilities. In this chapter, some key tools and approaches are discussed, enabling the design and implementation of standard processes and the following maintenance of the process standard. This includes the use of company-specific process reference models to define the standard, leveraging stakeholder journey planning to come to a consistent stakeholder experience, the use of process simulation to validate the effects of process standardization as well as the role of the process management and governance organization to sustain the process standardization.

3.1   Designing Standard Processes

The basis for implementing process standards is the structured definition of those standards in appropriate process models. The use of BPMN diagrams [10], for example, allows the specification of all ARIS views of the processes and definition of the desired level of detail and abstraction of the standardization. Figure 6 shows a sample BPMN diagram with a high level of detail and low abstraction.

The different process views, as well as the level of abstraction and detail, are determined by the goals of the standardization, and reflected in the design of the process. If a key goal of the standardization is, for example, to use a specific software system to optimize software maintenance cost, a low abstraction level is required since the specific application is included in the design. This is often combined with a high level of detail to ensure users follow the logic of the software. The definition of standard organization units, such as roles, may be less relevant.

Consistent customer or supplier experience is achieved through an appropriate process logic that can be defined on a relatively high level of abstraction since the technical realization is not relevant for the customer. Supporting the process with different applications is fine as long as they deliver consistent outcomes.

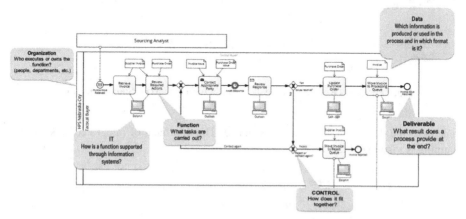

Fig. 6. BPMN Diagram with ARIS Views in a high level of detail and low abstraction

The design of the process standard is used as a company-wide reference model [9, 11]. It is the starting point for implementing the standard processes in different business units. To reflect the required process variations, the reference models identify the core of the standard process that should be the same across all business units and the areas with acceptable variants, possibility even defines the valid variants.

As starting point for the definition of company-specific reference models, industry or software reference models can be used as accelerators [11]. In digital transformation initiatives, the software reference models show the business impact of the software. These models are then adjusted to the company-specific needs by adding or removing content while considering the impact on software maintenance.

The use of process reference models as a basis to implement standard business processes is illustrated in Fig. 7.

In cases of stakeholder experience is a key goal of the standardization, such as customer, supplier or employee experience, it is important to take an outside-in look at the processes. This helps to understand the point of view of the specific stakeholder group. Stakeholder journey planning is a process management tool to address this aspect [12].

To operationalize the realization of the future experience, integrated customer journey planning is required. Every touch point of the stakeholder with the company is linked to the underlying processes. This allows the focused improvement of those processes

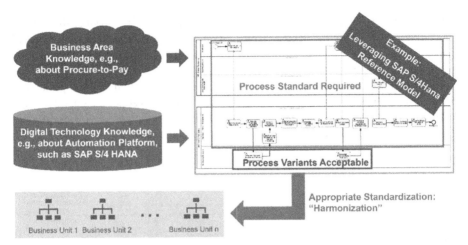

Fig. 7. Process Reference models as Basis for appropriate Standardization

to achieve the desired stakeholder experience. The approach of integrated stakeholder planning is visualized in Fig. 8.

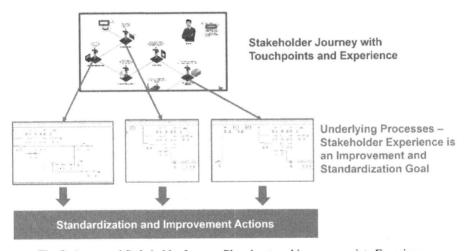

Fig. 8. Integrated Stakeholder Journey Planning to achieve appropriate Experience.

3.2 Validating and Implementing Standard Processes

Before implementing the defined standard processes, a validation of the effects of the process standard minimizes the risk of unplanned business issues and enables the realization of expected benefits. Process simulation achieves this by providing cost, cycle time or scalability information. While this is important to prepare any implementation of a new or significantly changed process, the simulation is especially significant for process standardization since the roll-out of the standard multiplies the effects of the process change.

Process simulation also helps determine for which business units the standardization is not beneficial. A major insurance company, for example, developed a reference model to roll out highly automated process standards for their placement and policy servicing processes. The simulation of the standard process showed a saving potential of over 50% in larger country organizations. However, it also provided the information that the investment is not justified in several smaller country businesses, with lower transaction volumes and a smaller number of products.

The standard processes described in BPMN-based reference models are simulated using a process modeling and repository tool [9]. Figure 9 illustrates the use of process simulation. It compares as-is processes with the new standard process. The same simulation approach can be sued to compare different standard scenarios to identify the best solution.

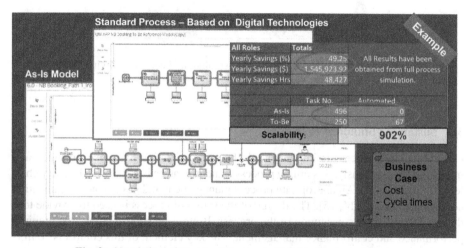

Fig. 9. Simulation of Standard Process to Validate Business Effects

The variable components of the standard process reference model are adjusted for every business unit. The result is the specific process model that drives the implementation of the standard in one specific business unit. This process model is the basis for configuring or developing the digital components supporting the process, for example, an automation platform. The same model also guides the people change management to align people and technology with the process standard [13].

The people change management often also requires documentation of the as-is processes to understand the overall impact of the new standard process. This is especially important when process standardization is used to roll-out of a process innovation [7]. The approach is visualized in Fig. 10.

Leveraging digital technologies that provide business content, such as enterprise resource planning systems, help to implement and enforce a process standard. The related software-based reference models visualize the Business impact of the software and guide its company-specific configuration.

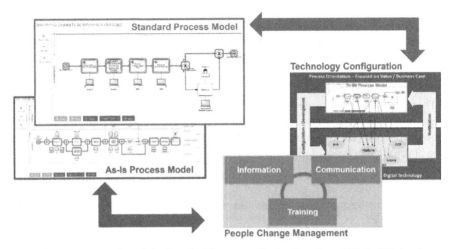

Fig. 10. Implementation of the Standard Process, aligning People and Digital Technology

3.3 Sustaining Standard Processes

Once a standard process is implemented, the standardization has to be managed and maintained continuously. Sustaining process standardization has shown to be a key challenge in practice [4]. An appropriate process management and governance organization addresses this issue [14, 15]. The design of the standard process is used to provide top-down guidance for the execution of the process. Bottom-up control allows the required performance and conformance management. The key element of this control is conformance management, hence, continuous check and management of the actual process instances and their variations compared to the standard. This allows the definition of actions to reduce the number of un-wanted variants systematically. The conformance control is complemented by appropriate performance metrics, verifying the achievement of specific benefits.

Sustaining process standardization effectively and with reasonable effort requires appropriate process management tools. The process reference models, and business units' specific variants are managed in a digital process modeling and repository tool. The conformance and performance management are supported through process mining and other analytics tools. Maintaining process governance economically is realized through a digitalized governance approach [16].

A well-established process management discipline is the foundation of realizing the value of process standardization and maintaining and adjusting it as required [15, 17]. The process management organization helps to adjust standards as required. Required initiatives are triggered through the process governance organization.

Figure 11 shows an example of a process management and governance organization. It highlights typical roles, like process owner, steward, and sponsor, as well as examples of typically used process management tools.

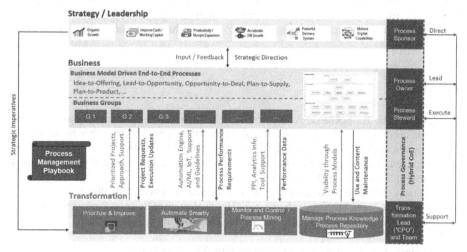

Fig. 11. Example for a Process Management Organization to sustain Standardization

The process management discipline establishes the capabilities to build and sustain process standardization. It is the key enabler of effective business process standardization.

4   Process Standardization – Now a Mainstream Topic

The standardization of business process across and organization has become a key topic for organizations, especially in the context of digital transformation initiatives. An increasing number of companies sees this topic even more important than the traditional process optimization. It lays the foundation for efficient digitalization and ongoing improvement of processes. However, while there is a significant amount of research and practice information available about process improvement and optimization, process standardization is less researched. This paper contributes to fill this gap by showing how process management methods and tools can be used to systematically realize an appropriate context-aware process standardization.

To continue to advance the approach of process standardization more research is required, for example in the following areas:

- Management of process reference models with information about standardization and allowed variations.
- Detailed approach to process standardization and its integration into the process management capabilities of an organization.

- Governance organization and related governance processes to sustain process standardization.

Process standardization has become a foundation for successful digital transformation. It's importance continues to grow accordingly. Process standardization is an important component of a value-driven process management discipline. It contributes to strengthen the role of process management to realize the full value from digitalization [18].

References

1. Münstermann, B., Eckhardt, A., Weitzel, T.: The performance impact of business process standardization: an empirical evaluation of the recruitment process. Bus. Process Manage. J. **16**(1), 29–56 (2010). https://doi.org/10.1108/14637151011017930
2. Westerman, G., Bonnet, D., McAffee, A.: Leading Digital – Turning Technology into Business Transformation. Boston (2014)
3. Wikipedia (ed.): Standardization (2023). en.wikipedia.org/wiki/Standardization
4. Franz, P., Kirchmer, M.: Standardization and Harmonization of Business Processes – Enabling Agile Customer Service in a Digital World. BPM-D Publications, London, Philadelphia (2016)
5. Mintzberg, H.: The Structuring of Organizations. New York (1979)
6. Scheer, A.-W.: Enterprise 4.0 – From disruptive business model to the automation of business processes. Saarbrucken (2019)
7. Kirchmer, M.: Agile innovation through business process management: realizing the potential of digital transformation. In: Shishkov, B. (ed.) Business Modeling and Software Design. BMSD 2022. Lecture Notes in Business Information Processing, vol. 453 (ISBN: 978-3-031-11509-7). Springer (2022). https://doi.org/10.1007/978-3-031-11510-3_2
8. Scheer, A.-W.: ARIS – Business Process Frameworks, 2nd edn. New York, e.a, Berlin (1998)
9. Kirchmer, M.: High Performance through Business Process Management – Strategy Execution in a Digital World, 3rd edn. New York, e.a, Berlin (2017)
10. Fisher, L: BPMN 2.0 Handbook – Methods, Concepts, Case Studies and Standards in Business Process Modelling Notation (BPMN), 2nd edn. Lighthouse Point (2012)
11. Kirchmer, M., Franz, P.: Process reference models: accelerator for digital transformation. In: Shishkov, B. (ed.) BMSD 2020. LNBIP, vol. 391, pp. 20–37. Springer, Cham (2020). https://doi.org/10.1007/978-3-030-52306-0_2
12. Kalbach, J.: Mapping Experiences: a Complete Guide to Customer Alignment through Journeys, Blueprints and Diagrams, 2nd edn. Beijing, Boston, e.a. (2021)
13. Kirchmer, M.: Process-led Digital Transformation: Value-driven, Data-based and Tool-enabled. https://digital-transformation.cioreview.com/vp/bpmd/process-led_digital_transformation:_value-driven,_data-based_and_tool-enabled/, 10/2022
14. Franz, P., Kirchmer, M.: Value-driven Business Process Management – The Value-Switch for Lasting Competitive Advantage. New York (2012)
15. Kirchmer, M.: The process of process management – mastering the new normal in a digital world. In: Proceedings of the 5th International Symposium on Business Modelling and Software Design, Milan, July 6–8, 2015
16. Kirchmer, M.: Digital transformation of business process governance. In: Shishkov, B. (ed.) BMSD 2021. LNBIP, vol. 422, pp. 243–261. Springer, Cham (2021). https://doi.org/10.1007/978-3-030-79976-2_14

17. Cantara, M.: Start up your business process competency center. In: Documentation of the Gartner Business Process Management Summit. National Harbor (2015)
18. Antonucci, Y., Fortune, A., Kirchmer, M.: An examination of associations between business process management capabilities and the benefits of digitalization: all capabilities are not equal. Bus. Process Manage. J. **27**, 124–144 (2021). https://doi.org/10.1108/BPMJ-02-2020-0079

Serious Game-Based Haptic Modeling - An Application-Oriented Approach for Sequentially Developing New Business Models from Tacit Knowledge

Norbert Gronau[1,2] , Malte Teichmann[1,2(✉)] , and Edzard Weber[1]

[1] University of Potsdam, August Bebel Street 89, 14482 Potsdam, Germany
{norbert.gronau,malte.teichmann,edzard.weber}@wi.uni-potsdam.de
[2] Weizenbaum Institute for the Networked Society, Hardenbergstraße 32, 10623 Berlin, Germany

Abstract. The authors propose that while tacit knowledge is a valuable resource for developing new business models, its externalization presents several challenges. One major challenge is that individuals often don't recognize their tacit knowledge resources, while another is the reluctance to share one's knowledge with others. Addressing these challenges, the authors present an application-oriented serious game-based haptic modeling approach for externalize tacit knowledge, which can be used to develop the first versions of business models based on tacit knowledge. Both conceptual and practical design fundamentals are presented based on elaborated theoretical approaches, which were developed with the help of a design science approach. The development of the research process is presented step by step, whereby we focused on the high accessibility of the presented research. Practitioners are presented with guidelines for implementing their serious game projects. Scientists benefit from starting points for their research topics of externalization, internalization, and socialization of tacit knowledge, development of business models, and serious games or gamification. The paper concludes with open research desiderata and questions from the presented research process.

Keywords: Serious game · Tacit knowledge · Business model · SECI-model · Conversion sequences · Design science

1 Introduction

Advancing digitalization increases customer demands for sustainable products, and tougher international competition makes new business models necessary. In addition to *explicit knowledge* (e.g., patents, process descriptions, etc.), companies have *tacit knowledge*. This knowledge is based, among other things, on employees' experience and is anchored in the respective employees' competencies, convictions, and individual mental schemata. *Tacit knowledge* represents most of the knowledge resources in a company, which is also associated with the potential for new business models. The problem

B. Shishkov (Ed.): BMSD 2023, LNBIP 483, pp. 32–55, 2023.
https://doi.org/10.1007/978-3-031-36757-1_3

is that, on the one hand, people often do not know that they have this knowledge. On the other hand, this knowledge is also difficult to articulate. As a result, companies often have the tacit potential for new business models, but these still need to be discovered in practice. This is associated with these challenges:

1. The success of business models depends on the synergies of different inter- and intra-organizational actors (e.g., suppliers, raw material providers, etc.)
2. These actors have different *tacit knowledge*, which decisively determine a persons competencies and thus their potential to develop new business models.
3. *Tacit knowledge* is difficult to make explicit, making it hard to use for new business models.

These points lead to the following research question:

RQ: How can gamification and serious games be used to generate explicit business models from tacit knowledge?

To develop new business models from existing *tacit knowledge*, innovative methods are consequently necessary. Following [1], we understand the conversion of *tacit knowledge* as a purposeful way to develop business models. This paper presents an *application-oriented serious game-based approach for the haptic modeling of new business* models based on players' *tacit knowledge*. To create the approach, we realized a design science research-oriented method (DSRM). Figure 1 introduces the method of [2] and its application in the paper:

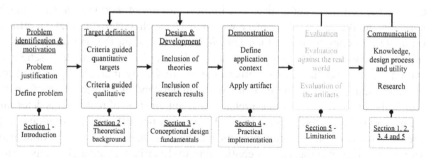

Fig. 1. The research method used in the paper following [2].

Following the outlined research approach, the paper is structured as follows. The *Problem identification* was realized in the introduction. Next, we present the characteristics of *tacit knowledge* (Sect. 2.1), gamification and flow states (Sect. 2.2), and serious games (Sect. 2.3) in the second step as part of the *final target definition* (Sect. 2.5). A presentation of the game mechanics follows, including its conceptional design fundamentals (*Design & Development*; Sect. 3) and their exemplary practical implementation in the context of *bioeconomy-sensitive circular economy* (*Practical implementation*; Sect. 4), usable as a starting point for other serious games. Finally, the paper concludes with a conclusion, and further research needs in section five.

2 Theoretical Background – Target Definition

This section overviews the theoretical foundations on which we developed the approach. Section 2.1 introduces basics of *tacit knowledge* and the *SECI-model* based on [3] and [4]. Next, we briefly introduce gamification and its associated flow state (Sect. 2.2) and serious games (Sect. 2.3). Following the DSRM, the research project's design goals and principles are derived by merging the theories in Sect. 2.5.

2.1 Tacit Knowledge

The work of [3] and [4] are considered landmarked contributions for the notion of *tacit knowledge*. The authors distinguish between *explicit* and *tacit knowledge*. Their approach aims to make *tacit knowledge* available throughout the organization by converting it into *explicit knowledge*. *Explicit knowledge* is rational and objective knowledge that describes the past or the present context-free. This knowledge can exist context-free in theories (understood as abstract attempts to explain reality) or data. The systematic representation occurs in numbers, words, drawings etc. [4], with which intersubjective comprehensibility is reached. In the form of data or numbers, *explicit knowledge* can be processed by a computer and stored in databases [3, p. 60]. In contrast, *tacit knowledge* is defined as embodied knowledge arising from concrete actions or experiences. Due to its application orientation, it is primarily understood as situation-specific knowledge. *Tacit knowledge* is embodied in experiences, actions, emotions, and values of individuals, context-specific and subjective. The implementation of *tacit knowledge* is tied to the situation and the action taking place within it. These characteristics make it difficult to formalize and communicate. *Tacit knowledge* includes, on the one hand, a cognitive dimension, which, following the work of [5], includes mental models, schemata, attributions, and expectations. Cognitive models are fed by individually created and manipulated analogies of the individual's world understanding. These models form the basis of individual processes of interpretation and anticipation of reality, thus determining the individual's perception of the world. Verbalization is difficult, but simultaneously it represents a kind of mobilization process. On the other hand, the technical dimension marks the presence of informal and challenging to describe technical elements, which include concrete know-how, crafts, and skills [3, p. 60]. These skills are acquired in years of practical experience, and the agent's explication of explanatory models, principles of action, or logical sequences is rarely possible (see also [4]). The *SECI-model* aims to make *tacit knowledge* available throughout the enterprise by converting it into *explicit knowledge*. Their interaction is conceptualized as *knowledge conversion*, the characteristics of which are described as follows:

Socialization: Describes the creation of *tacit knowledge* from *tacit knowledge*, primarily through sharing everyday experiences between two or more subjects. The acquisition is possible through a verbal and nonverbal exchange, provided that the knowledge-acquiring individual experiences the effect context and the associated emotions and intentions of the knowledge-sharing individual [3, p. 63]. However, the effect on the actual body of knowledge of the organization is limited since socialized *tacit knowledge* has yet to be fully available to the organization [3, p. 70].

Externalization: Describes the emergence of *explicit knowledge* from *tacit knowledge*. Externalization is conceptualizing *tacit knowledge* with the help of sequential metaphors and analogies. Although the resulting knowledge concepts are often incomplete, at the same time, an interpersonal exchange (e.g., in a group discussion) about recognized conceptual maluses is stimulated. Following this, modeling is possible to codify the (previously tacit) concepts. Nonaka and Takeuchi see externalization as the essential element in the growth of organizational knowledge [3, p. 63].

Combination: Describes the emergence of *explicit knowledge* from *explicit knowledge*. This occurs primarily through the addition, systematization, or categorization of documents, database entries (e.g., data on telephone connections) or other information. Likewise, the integration (or triggering) of medium-term into (or out of) long-term concepts (e.g., product strategy from strategic corporate planning) describes a form of combination. However, such knowledge still needs to expand the organizational knowledge corpus. In practice, this can be described, for example, by applying a best practice method (e.g., in a written management summary), to a defined problem.

Internalization: Describes the emergence of *tacit knowledge* from *explicit knowledge*. This can arise, for example, through engagement with models or concepts that have been externalized from the *tacit knowledge* of others.

This figure (Fig. 2) represents the *SECI-model*:

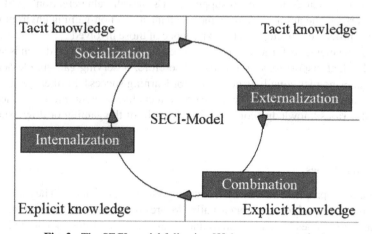

Fig. 2. The SECI-model following [3] (own representation).

2.2 Gamification and Flow State

The usage of gamification in commerce, sharing, consumption, innovation, and ideation [6] or eLearning in schools and universities [7, 8] has been extensively researched.

Researchers identified that using game-typical elements in education and training could help maintain learning motivation constantly high through its problem-solving and competitive character [8]. In the work context, gamification is often used as an intervention. The research investigates either the effect of gamification on internal communication and interaction [9, 10] or its effect on usually tedious work processes [11]. Building on the concept of gamification, serious games are an innovative means of continuing education, which offers companies the opportunity to prepare early for future developments, such as a change in the knowledge structure or necessary qualifications for a company. Depending on the game design, the gamification of knowledge content can also be helpful in particular educational contexts [6]. The context of learning, knowledge acquisition, and sharing with games and an intrinsic motivation experience can be described using the flow theory researched [12]. Accordingly, joy and pleasure arise in an intrinsically motivated activity when challenge and ability are balanced. The person succeeds with seemingly no effort in the tasks s/he faces and enjoys the process. In the beginning, the abilities can be relatively low, but they increase during the activity. However, when an imbalance between requirements and abilities arises, stress, anxiety, boredom, or disinterest may arise [12].

The concept of gamification includes two relevant aspects: On the one hand, it refers to the "use of game mechanics in non-gaming contexts" [13]. Examples of these mechanics are clear sequences, certain limits, and clearly defined rules [14]. On the other hand, gamification is not simply reducible to the sum of the single game elements. In other words, good storytelling is necessary [15]. Furthermore, defining gamification from an experienced-oriented perspective is "a process of enhancing a service with affordances for gameful experiences in order to support user's overall value creation" [16]. Gamification refers to "the application of game mechanisms in non-gaming environments to enhance the processes enacted and the experience of those involved" [17]. The effectiveness of gaming elements for learning, e.g., in serious games, however, depends strongly on the individual dispositions of a learner. Therefore, observing gaming elements and pedagogical principles equally is necessary for learning success. Furthermore, overemphasizing gaming elements may have adverse effects like addiction to the gameplay or the lack of serious knowledge content for the benefit of the gaming or flow experience [18].

2.3   Serious Games

Games are an appropriate means for conveying knowledge content. They are "Games [which] may be played seriously or casually. We are concerned with serious games in the sense that these games have an explicit and carefully thought-out educational purpose and are not intended to be played primarily for amusement. This does not mean that serious games are not, or should not be, entertaining." [19]. Following this, the concept of serious games subsumes all sorts of games "in which education (in its various forms) is the primary goal, rather than entertainment" [20]. They are characterized by the fact that an increased positive feeling can accompany learning and that learners are emotionally addressed. Especially today´s generation grew up adapting the increased flow of information through digital media and, thus, prefers games to conventional or serious work [21]. Eventually, for those new learners, parallel processing and connected, interlinked learning processes are natural ways of gaining knowledge [8]. Even older employees can profit from game-based learning formats for re-contextualizing knowledge [22].

In addition, players should actively deal with the learning content of the gaming environment to progress in the game and, within this, in their learning or knowledge exchange. Players are constantly motivated to continue playing by challenging game situations. The more a person dives into the gaming environment, the higher the probability that the flow state remains [18]. Clearly formulated goals, direct feedback, and balanced tasks are the prerequisites for flow. A flow state is recognizable by the concentration, the sense of control, and the loss of self-doubt of the test persons [12]. Playing serious games results in the flow state in which people gain, share, or understand knowledge without noticing.

In consideration of [18] and [15], the following table (Table 1) highlights the necessary design categories for personal flow experiences in serious games.

Table 1. Relevant game design categories for personal flow experiences

Design cat	Feature	Description
Game design	Unified storytelling	An overarching story that links individual game elements together
	Specified goals and objectives	Specified goals and objectives that a person must fulfill within the story being told by the game
	Clearly defined tasks	Clearly defined quantifiable tasks that a person must fulfill to reach goals and objectives
	Clearly defined rules	Rules that contribute to a comprehensible game experience and an undisturbed flow of play
Gaming environment	Constant and direct feedback	Successes (and failures) continuously affect the gaming environment
	Changing environment	The environment adapts to the knowledge progress and additional learning content
	Comprehensible/Traceable progress	The environment shows the progress comprehensibly for the players
	Various game elements	The environment should incorporate various game elements, designed to support both play and learning

2.4 Bioeconomy-Sensitive Circular Economy

Corona conditions challenge global supply chains. Climate change and associated extreme temperature fluctuations pose enormous challenges to seasonal businesses [23].

Regional and cross-regional players can gain crucial competitive advantages through high adaptability in supply chains, production, and value creation processes [24]. An increased focus on a bioeconomy-sensitive circular economy enables companies to be ecologically and economically agile. A bioeconomy approach encompasses the generation, development, and use of biological resources, processes, and systems to provide products, processes, and services in all economic sectors as part of a sustainable economic system [25]. Precisely, this results in using biogenic raw materials, for example. The overarching goal is a sustainable and circular economy. Regional and supra-regional players can use collective bioeconomic knowledge to develop business-enhancing innovations, climate-neutral developments [25], and new business fields. The associated bioeconomic transformation is to be understood as moving away from fossil raw materials toward a sustainable, regionally oriented circular economy focusing on renewable resources and innovative technologies. The ideal situation is a closed raw material cycle supported by regional actors and a few supra-regional actors.

Bioeconomic circular economies are organized in regional networks. These networks include key regional stakeholders: Local industrial and craft enterprises, municipalities, associations, schools, public institutions, and farms [26]. For bioeconomic concepts to work in a region, stakeholders must jointly develop business models. Likewise, regional topography (e.g., the proportion of farmland and forest area), infrastructure status (e.g., roads´ quality for transportation), and economic (e.g., the high proportion of agricultural products) and socio-cultural (e.g., regional age structure) factors must be considered, too. Individuals, organizations, or institutions are often well-connected and have regional business relations and knowledge [25, 27]. However, regional actors need to work together to address the potential challenges of a bioeconomic approach in a targeted way. Unfortunately, there is often a lack of opportunities to develop joint bioeconomic business models.

2.5 Theoretical Fundamentals – Final Target Definition

From a theoretical perspective following the outlined baseline of *tacit knowledge* and [1], we understand the intersubjective-oriented creation of a business model as the *knowledge conversion* of *tacit knowledge* (e.g., individual experiences, individual insides in processes etc.) into *explicit knowledge* (e.g., a draft of a business model). The different *knowledge conversations* between the two knowledge dimensions happens in individuals and on a group level. On the group level, different persons (e.g., introvert or extrovert) with different market backgrounds (e.g., producer, retailer etc.) and different motivations (e.g., strengthening owns market positions) work together. Considering the highlighted theoretical background of gamification and serious games, we understand both approaches as fruitful instruments for addressing the challenges of converting *tacit knowledge* in *explicit knowledge*. Following the DSRM approach, we formulated ten basic assumptions which describe the theoretical fundamentals of our *application-oriented serious game-based approach for the haptic modeling of new business*. In the next step, we derived one game goal from every assumption, that we want to address in our game design.

The intended holistic goals of the serious game also serve as quantitative targets in the research process (Table 2).

Table 2. Holistic serious game goals

Nr	Assumption	Knowledge conversion	Game goals
1	Business models are artifacts of *explicit knowledge* based on the *tacit knowledge* of different persons	All	Developing of a business models based on players *tacit knowledge* as the game goal, realized in the *game design* and *gaming environment*
2	The transformation of *tacit knowledge* into *explicit knowledge* is possible through knowledge conversation	All	Supporting the externalization of *tacit knowledge* through the game design
3	The complete *tacit knowledge* of individuals or groups is not externalizable in a single step, thus requiring a sequential approach, resulting in the principle of *conversion sequences*	All	Supporting the sequential externalization of *tacit knowledge* by the principle of *conversion sequences* through the usage of different game features in the *game design*
4	*Conversion sequences* must be done in small steps and build on each other to reduce possible acceptance barriers	All	Showing the progressive externalization of *tacit knowledge* in the *gaming environment*
5	Results of conversion sequences must be recorded as *explicit knowledge* to secure essential *tacit knowledge* for further *conversion sequences*	Externalization	Saving *explicit knowledge* by using various game elements in the *gaming environment*, depending on the *game design*
6	The exchange of *tacit knowledge* in a group through socialization results in the extended *tacit knowledge* of the group	Socialization	Triggering the knowledge exchange between the players trough an interaction-oriented *game design*
7	The exchange of *tacit knowledge* in a group through socialization helps individuals uncover their *tacit knowledge*	Socialization	Supporting an individual to reflect others knowledge trough the usage of various game features in the *gaming environment*
8	The internalization of (partially) explicit artifacts helps to generate further *tacit knowledge* in the group	Internalization	Incorporating knowledge internalization with the usage of different game features in the *game design*

(continued)

Table 2. (*continued*)

Nr	Assumption	Knowledge conversion	Game goals
9	Internalization of (partially) explicit artifacts helps individuals discover and later externalize their *tacit knowledge* through new perspectives	Internalization	Incorporating knowledge internalization with the usage of different game features in the *game design*
10	The complete explicit artifact - a business model - represents the combination of all explicit partial artifacts generated in the individual conversion sequences	Combination	The *game design* should result in an *explicit knowledge* artefact which consists of all explicit artifacts from every conversion sequence

3 Conceptional Design Fundamentals - Design and Development

According to the DSRM, this third section outlines the design process, which is defined as a process between theory-based requirements on a (starting point) and a practical artifact design (ending point). The artifacts goal is to fulfill the holistic goals derived from theory (Table 2) with the help of the artifact design. Consequently, theory-oriented goals had to be transferred into an application-oriented approach. A successful design process reduces the abstraction level and transforms theory into a usable artifact. Therefore, we decrease the abstraction level in each successful design step of the artifact development. The design process outlined here starts at a high abstraction level and is gradually transformed into a concrete artifact – an *application-oriented serious game-based approach for the haptic modeling of new business.*

At a medium level of abstraction, the identified goals (Sect. 2.5) should be realized with the help of the design category *game design* underlying the serious game. The *game design* thus forms the second design level of the presented serious game. Furthermore, the design category *game design* must have certain features to guarantee the theoretical basis for a flow experience (Sect. 2.2). Accordingly, the goals of the serious game were matched with the features of the *game design*.

Table 3 presents the results in a consolidated way.

Table 3. Matched *game design* features and game goals

Feature	Goal	Practical implementation
Unified Storytelling	1, 10	The game-based development of the business model is to be placed in an overarching plot, representing a self-contained storyline with a concrete starting and ending point. The narrated content should adapt to the business area for which the business model is to create
Specified goals and objectives	2, 3, 4	The storyline consists of separate to-play but plot-related rounds. Each round concludes with a goal that the players must achieve. A round's goal is divided into individual content-specific and objectively measurable objectives
Clearly defined tasks	3, 4, 5, 6, 7, 8, 9	Individual objectives consist of different tasks which the players must solve. Tasks are related to the storyline and have a measurable degree of success. The cumulative degree of success of all tasks results in the degree to which an objective has been successfully solved
Clearly defined rules	1, 2, 3, 4, 5, 6, 7, 8, 9	The rules of the game drive the narrative of the storyline by logically connecting the plot of the separative rounds. Within a round, the rules map the principle of *Conversion sequences* by linking the objectives within a round to knowledge conversions of *Internalization, Socialization, Externalization* and *Combination*

The design category *gaming environment* practically realizes the *game design* and thus represents the third design level of the serious game. Exemplary are game objectives with certain tasks (*game design*) whose completion actively affects the *gaming environment* (e.g., a completed house in a construction simulation). Likewise, *gaming environments* have special flow-promoting features that must be oriented to the overall game goals. Table 4 lists which goals have been conceptually linked to the features.

Table 4. Matched *gaming environment* features and Game goals

Feature	Goal	Practical implementation
Constant and direct feedback	All	The *gaming environment* must constantly inform about the progress of the game. Progress must be visible immediately so as not to jeopardize the flow experience. A constant flow experience has a positive effect on *sequential knowledge conversion*
Action active environment	3, 4, 5, 6, 7, 8, 9	Players´ haptic game experience must change directly with the game progress. Players need to see that their playful actions have a direct and feelable impact on the *gaming environment*. Likewise, the *environment* must promote engagement with one's own *tacit knowledge* through haptic changes
Comprehensible/ Tracable progress	3, 4, 5, 6, 7, 8, 9	The players must be able to comprehend their actions and externalization steps in order to be able to carry out different conversion sequences. The *gaming environment* must contribute accordingly to making progress constantly visible through different game elements
Various game elements	All	The *gaming environment* must contain various game elements that can both represent existing *tacit knowledge* and motivate people to engage with the game element itself. In addition, game elements must also contribute to concrete externalization activities

4   Practical Implementation

In the following section, we present the exemplary practical implementation of the conceptional design fundamentals in the context of *bioeconomy-sensitive circular economy*. For this purpose, the paper shows how the individual features of the design category *game design* and *gaming environment* were transferred to a practical level. To illustrate this, we choose the overarching plot *Development of business models in the bioeconomic circular economy*. We developed the game for regional actors who want to develop new bioeconomy-sensitive businesses with other actors. The unique thing about regional actors is that they have much *tacit knowledge* besides concrete knowledge networks (e.g., business relationships). *Tacit knowledge* applies - especially in rural areas - to topographical peculiarities and knowledge about other people's competencies, unique selling points of companies, or institutions that are not immediately apparent and tend to build on bilateral experience. We briefly explain the scientific background of the plot – the challenge of business model creation in a *Bioeconomy-sensitive circular economy* – in Sect. 2.4. Based on this, we derived objectives in Sect. 4.1 and matching tasks in Sect. 4.2 and Sect. 4.3. We also describe the developed game elements used by the players. Finally, in the last Sect 4.4, we outlined the rules for the serious game.

4.1 Specified Goals and Objectives

The players must develop a regionally significant bioeconomic business model in the serious game. The model should highlight the individual strengths of regional stakeholders, link them with each other and identify potential starting points for regional circular economies. In addition to the business effectiveness, regional specifics (see previous section) of the bioeconomic circular economy shall be discussed among the players involved the game. The resulting model represents the first version of a business model, which the players can further develop after the serious game. For this purpose, the players take on the role of different regional actors relevant in their region (e.g., a metal processer, a farmer, a carpenter, director of a vocational school) which are relevant for the emerging bioeconomy-sensitive business model. The round and rounds' objectives were defined according to the plot, considering the focus on bioeconomic circular economies. The following Table 5 provides an overview of the rounds, rounds´ goals and objectives.

Table 5. Rounds, rounds´ goals and objectives

Nr	Round	Goal	Objective 1	Objective 2	Objective 3
1	Topography	Mapping the topography	Farm land	Green area	Rivers and lakes
2	Infrastructure	Building the infrastructure	Transportation	Digital	Social
3	Business sectors	Locating the businesses	Primary	Secondary	Tertiary
4	Business actors	Understanding the actors	Competences	Qualifications	Products/services
5	Business processes	Defining the processes	As-It-Is	Target-oriented	Free
6	Model building	Extracting the model	Debate	Develop	Formalize

4.2 Play the Plot – Outlining "Clearly Defined Tasks" for Rounds 1, 2 and 3

The first three rounds are primarily about defining the *gaming environment*. Knowledge necessary for this is often freely available (e.g., in [google] maps) and has few tacit aspects. Therefore, the players should be playfully motivated to haptically transfer their knowledge associated with the region into the *gaming environment*. The haptic approach forms the basis for the later flow feeling since the players "create" the playing field by hand and thus become an active part of the storyline. Possible acceptance barriers to giving away own knowledge are thereby reduced. The approach also promotes the exchange of players and results in a familiar atmosphere. The following tables show which objectives have been assigned to which tasks for the first, second and third rounds. We also describe the game elements the players should use to solve the task. The used game elements are designed so that their haptic usage leads to an active change in the *gaming environment*. The (traceable) progress of each round (respectively each goal) in the *gaming environment* is also displayed. Table 6 shows tasks and game elements for round 1, Table 7 for round 2 and Table 8 for round 3.

Table 6. Tasks and game elements of round 1

Objectives	Task	Description	Game elements
Farm land	Place farm land	The players should model the regional farm-land	Sheets of *grain-yellow paper*
Greenland	Place forest area	The players should place regional forests	Sheets of *deep-green paper*
	Place grassland	The players should place regional grassland	Sheets of *light-green paper*
Lakes and rivers	Set lakes	The players should place lakes	Sheets of *blue paper*
	Set rivers	The players should set rivers	Blue *masking tape*

Table 7. Tasks and Game elements of round 2

Objectives	Task	Description	Game elements
Transportation	Place solid routes	The players should place solid routes, save for transportation	*Grey Masking tape* (e.g., concrete streets)
	Place non-solid routes	The players should place non-solid routes, not save for transportation	*Brown masking tape* (e.g., filed roads)
	Place bridges and underpasses	The players should place bridges and underpasses as a bottle-neck for transportation	*Wood-colored wooden bridges* *Black-colored wooden bridges* for underpasses

(continued)

Table 7. (*continued*)

Objectives	Task	Description	Game elements
Digital	Show dead zones	The players should show areas with no net coverage	*3D-printed small transmission masts*
	Show critical zones	The players should show areas with unstable net coverage	*3D-printed medium transmission masts*
	Show save zones	The players should show areas with stable net coverage	*3D-printed large transmission masts*
Social	Place houses	The players should place houses to mark residential areas	*3D-printed houses*
	Place education	The players should place educational institutions	*3D-printed school buildings, kindergartens* etc
	Place so-cial places	The players should place social organizations in their region	*3D-printed fishing rod, hunter stand, barbells*
	Show regional specifics, only YOU know	The players should reveal regional specifics only they know, rooted in their experience and all-day business	E.g., *figures of wild boars* (for model increased accident rates) or *model-railroad tracks* (for model upcoming infrastructure)

Table 8. Tasks and game elements of round 3

Objectives	Task	Description	Game elements
Primary	Place farms	The players should place all farms in the area	*3D-printed barns, biogas plans* etc
	Place fishing	The player should place fishing industry	*3D-printed fishing vessel, fishing boat*
	Place mining	The players should place mining industry	*3D-printed iron bar*

(*continued*)

Table 8. (*continued*)

Objectives	Task	Description	Game elements
Secondly	Place industries	The players should place all kinds of industries	*3D-printed factory buildings*
	Place crafts	The players should show all craftsman's and handicrafts	*3D-printed workbenches, windmills, baker oven* etc
	Place constructions	The players should place all construction firms	*3D-printed mason trowel, saw* etc
Tertiary	Place energy	The players should place regional energy suppliers	*3D-printed waterdrop, power plant* etc
	Place freight forwarders	The players should place opportunities for transportation and shipping, e.g. forwarding agents	*3D-printed trucks, transporters* and *bicycles*
	Place service firms	The players should place all kinds of service firms	*3D-printed car workshop, asclepius staff* etc

4.3 Go with the Flow – Outlining "Clearly Defined Tasks" for Round 4, 5 and 6

The *gaming environment*, haptically defined in the first three rounds, is used in the fourth, fifth, and sixth round to engage with players' *tacit knowledge*. Although *knowledge conversion* is targeted in all (including the first three) rounds, the fourth round primarily pursues the externalization of player-specific *tacit knowledge*: Different players often have different knowledge about regional actors that is neither publicly available (e.g., missing information on an enterprise website about a traditional craft technique) nor known to other players (e.g., through a different business focus). We primarily designed the tasks accordingly to externalize this *tacit knowledge* into *explicit knowledge* via pre-defined and self-definable game elements - the so called *gamecards*. Since players also watch other players play (or externalize it into *tacit knowledge*), there is a simultaneous internalization of others' *tacit knowledge*. Likewise, conversations between the players about the tasks are likely, to socialize *tacit knowledge*. Table 9 shows the tasks and their associated game elements.

The fifth round begins with another *externalization* and *socialization* task. The players have to model *As-It-Is* business processes. These existing processes can represent all kinds of knowledge and resource flows as well as transport routes and other connections (e.g., sports club sponsorships of a local car dealer). The further course of the game in the fifth round depends on the previous course of the game and the developed group dynamics. If the first ideas for a business model have already emerged in the conversations or socialization between the players, they can continue with *free process modeling*. Here, the players should briefly outline their ideas and the role of regional actors, which the game leader notes down. Afterward, the necessary processes are modeled on the

Table 9. Tasks and game elements of round 4.

Objectives	Task	Description	Game elements
Competencies	Attribute pre-defined competencies	Players should assign predefined competencies from a pool of possible competencies to the business actors	Pre-defined *light-red colored competence (game-)cards* that name and describe a specific competence (e.g., Innovativeness, strong network etc.)
	Attribute undefined competencies	Players should assign self-defined competencies to the business actors	Writable *light-red colored competence (game-)cards*, on which players can name and describe a self-defined competence
Qualifications	Reveal pre-defined qualifications	Players should assign predefined qualifications from a pool of possible qualifications to the business actors	Pre-defined *light-blue colored qualification (game-)cards* that name and describe a specific qualification (e.g., ISO9000)
	Reveal undefined qualifications	Players should assign self-defined qualifications to the business actors	Writable *light-blue colored competence (game-)cards*, on which players can name and describe a self-defined qualification
Products/Services	Describe pre-defined products	Players should assign predefined products and services to the business actors, common for regional actors	Predefined *light-green colored product (game-) cards* that name and describe a common product or service (e.g., locksmith)
	Describe undefined products	Players should assign self-defined products and services to the business actors	Writable *light-green colored product (game-) cards*, on which players can name and describe a self-defined product or service

gaming environment. If concrete ideas have yet to emerge, the game leader intervenes by distributing task cards. These cards contain predefined business models for which the players must develop and model processes in the *gaming environment*. Further *free modeling* can be conducted if momentum develops in the group due to *target-oriented modeling*. Regardless of the nature of the modeled processes, the game leader should note as much information as possible to capture *tacit knowledge* in all facets. As in the fourth round, the players (except in *target-oriented modeling*) use writable *gamecards* to describe their modeling processes by externalizing their *tacit knowledge*. Finally, the cards are applied to the modeled processes in *gaming environment*. Table 10 shows the tasks and game elements for round 5.

Table 10. Tasks and game elements of round 5.

Obj	Task	Description	Game elements
As-It-Is	Knowledge flows	The players should model and describe *existing* knowledge flows between business actors	*Scarlet-red wool strings* and writable *white-colored knowledge (game-)cards*
	Resource flows	The players should model and describe *existing* resource flows between business actors	*Navy-blue wool strings* and Writable *white-colored resource (game-)cards*
	Transport routes	The players should model and describe *existing* transport routes between business actors	Emerald-green wool strings and writable *white-colored transport (game-)cards*
	Other connections	The players should model and describe other *existing* connections, relevant for the region	Purple wool strings and writable *white-colored other connections (game-) cards*
Target-oriented	Knowledge flows	The players should model and describe knowledge flows between business actors for a *pre-defined* business model	Salmon-red wool strings pre-defined *white-colored knowledge (game-)cards*
	Resource flows	The players should model and describe resource flows between business actors for a *pre-defined* business model	Baby-blue wool strings and pre-defined *white-colored resource (game-)cards*
	Transport routes	The players should model and describe transport routes between business actors for a *pre-defined* business model	Light-green wool strings pre-defined *white-colored transport (game-)cards*

(continued)

Table 10. (*continued*)

Obj	Task	Description	Game elements
	Other connections	The players should model and describe other connections, potentially relevant for *pre-defined* business model	Grey wool strings and writable *white-colored other connections (game-) cards*
Free	Knowledge flows	The players should model and describe knowledge flows between business actors for a *self-defined* business model	Chimney-red wool strings and writable *white-colored knowledge (game-)cards*
	Resource flows	The players should model and describe resource flows between business actors for a *self-defined* business model	Ultramarine-blue wool strings and writable *white-col. Resource (game-)cards*
	Transport routes	The players should model and describe transport routes between business actors for a *self-defined* business model	Olive-green wool strings and writable *white-colored transport (game-)cards*
	Other connections	The players should model and describe other connections, potentially relevant for *self-defined* business model	Gold-yellow wool strings and Writable *white-colored other connections (game-) cards*

The sixth and last round marks the end of the serious game. The *gaming environment*, haptically modelled over the first fifth rounds, is a first haptic version of a bioeconomy-sensitive business model. The model includes, therefore, necessary competences, qualifications, and products/services of regional actors as part of an over-arching value creation process, including detailed descriptions as well as regional potentials (e.g., local handicraft, which can shorten supply chains immensely by providing a partial product) and challenges (e.g., a bridge with too little load capacity, which requires long transport routes by switching to another bridge). As a result, in the gaming environment, all players' *tacit knowledge* is captured in the haptic model itself and in the *explicit knowledge* artifacts of the respective rounds (e.g., the *knowledge (game-)cards*). The sixth round aims to debate and develop the *gaming environment* for a circular improvement of the underlying bioeconomy-sensitive business model. Finally, after the last circle, the model will be formalized for further use. Table 11 shows the tasks and their associated game elements for round 6.

Table 11. Tasks and game elements of round 6

Objecive	Task	Description	Game elements
Debate	Debate the *gaming environment*	The players should debate the modeled gaming environment. The goal is to talk about, e.g., possible process modifications as well as necessary infrastructure modifications and, finally, identify best practice solutions	The *gaming environment* itself
Develop	Develop the *gaming environment*	The players should model changes necessary to realize business models directly in the *gaming environment*	Every used game element in the gaming environment (e.g., *3D-printed buildings, ultramarine-blue wool strings* etc.) and additional game elements (e.g., another writable *light-green colored product (game-)cards*)
Formalize	Formalize the model	The players and the game masters should jointly formalize the model based on an established modeling language (e.g., KMDL, BPMN, PMDL etc.)	-

4.4 Clearly Defined Rules - Preserving the Flow (of the Game)

In this section, we outline the rules that define the gameplay initially, drive the flow of the game and give orientation to the players of a serious game. Following their outlined characteristic in Table 3, we distinguish between general rules (*general rules*) (Table 12), rules concerning a specific round (*inter-round rules*) (Table 13), and rules that determine how rounds interact with each other (*intra-round rules*) (Table 14).

Table 12 shows the *general rules* of the serious game.

Table 13 shows the *inter-round rules* of the serious game.

Table 14 shows the *intra-round rules* of the serious game.

Table 12. *General rules* of the serious game

Name	Description
Specified roles	The serious game is prepared and managed by one or more game masters. Game masters must have methodological competence, communication skills, and design ability. Persons with relevant *tacit knowledge* are playing the game as players. Players can come from individual companies or other organizations
An overarching plot defined in advance of the game	The plot defines the content focus of a serious game and, vice versa, the final developed business model. Therefore, the plot's content should be oriented toward the needs of the players and represent a self-contained story. The gamemasters define the plot before the game, including practical related content and scientific knowledge. They also prepare the *gaming environment*
Support haptic modeling trough room conditions	Successful gaming or modeling is achieved through haptic modeling. Players change the *gaming environment* through their haptic actions, making game progress visible on the playing field. The gamemasters prepare the room accordingly: enough space for modeling, enough game elements for all players, sufficient lighting, ergonomic modeling conditions (e.g., sufficiently high tables)
Customized game elements	The Game Masters adapt the haptic game elements used to the plot before the game, especially to 3D-printed models and topographic elements. Each new game element is assigned a specific use and associated properties

Table 13. *Inter-round rules* of the serious game

Name	Description
Defined start and end point	Each round represents a self-contained section of the overall story. Accordingly, the individual objectives are to be aligned with it

(continued)

Table 13. (*continued*)

Name	Description
Focus on knowledge conversion(s)	Each round should primarily focus on one or two knowledge conversions (where other conversions should not be excluded). Gamemaster should align the associated objectives and tasks to the chosen knowledge conversions
Changing the gaming environment	Solved tasks and related sequential conversions must lead to a change in the *gaming environment*, understandable and comprehensible for the players. Any changes per round are to be conceptually defined by the gamemasters
Providing options for socialization	Regardless of the primary targeted knowledge conversion, every single round must give time and space for the socialization of *tacit knowledge*. This can be done through both specific tasks and scheduled breaks from play

Table 14. *Intra-round rules* of the serious game

Name	Description
Progressive development - Plot	The narrative of different rounds must build on each other. With the completion of one round, the narrative basis for the next round must be created. At the end of the game, the successive expiring rounds must form a narrated plot
Progressive development - Environment	Depending on the successively told plot, the completion of a round must lead to further development of the *gaming environment*. Haptic changes through haptic modeling of knowledge (as artefacts of *explicit knowledge*) mark the end of a round
Maintaining the overall game goal	The serious game's goal is to haptically model business models based on the players' *tacit knowledge*. If the game character or the flow experience is too intense after a round, the gamemasters have to intervene in a regulating way

5 Conclusion and Further Research Potentials

We presented an innovative approach to transforming *tacit knowledge* into *explicit knowledge* using serious game-based haptic modeling. Players can transform *tacit knowledge* into the first version of a business model through the presented approach and its practical implementation. The underlying research project was implemented using a design science approach. Table 15 highlights the papers main contributions.

Table 15. Contribution of the research

Name	Description	Section
Holistic game goals	The paper presents a first theoretical approach to how serious games can help to explicate *tacit knowledge* into *explicit knowledge*	2.5
Holistic game goals	The paper presents holistic goals for serious games, according to which practitioners and researchers can design their games to explicate *tacit knowledge*	2.5
Usage of game environment	The paper shows how concrete *knowledge conversions* of the popular *SECI-model* can be combined with gaming environments	3
Usage of game design	The paper shows how concrete *knowledge conversions* of the popular *SECI-model* can be combined with game design elements	3
General rules	The paper presents generalized game rules for preserving the flow in serious games that can give a basis for other game concepts	4.4

The paper presents promising ideas for designing serious game concepts, however, its evaluation is limited in scope. While the rules and basics of the game have been introduced in Sect. 4 and some preliminary workshops have been conducted [28], the practical implementation of the game is still in its early stages. As a result, the authors acknowledge that the current evaluation is not comprehensive enough to draw any firm conclusions about the effectiveness of the game. To address this limitation, the authors have initiated structured evaluation of the game, which is currently underway. This evaluation involves a more thorough examination of the game's design, mechanics, and gameplay, as well as testing its efficacy in achieving the intended learning outcomes.

References

1. Gronau, N.: Managing Knowledge in a Process-Oriented Way: Method and Tools for Using Knowledge as a Competitive Factor in Companies. Oldenbourg-Verlag, München (2009). (in German)
2. Peffers, K., Tuunanen, T., Rothenberger, M.A., Chatterjee, S.: A design science research methodology for information systems research. J. Manag. Inf. Syst. **24**(3), 45–77 (2007)

3. Nonaka, I., Takeuchi, H.: The Knowledge-Creating Company: How Japanese Companies Create the Dynamics of Innovation. Oxford University Press, New York (1995)
4. Nonaka, I.: A dynamic theory of organizational knowledge creation. Organ. Sci. **5**(1), 14–37 (1994)
5. Johnson-Laird, P.: Mental Models. Erlbaum, Hillsdale, N.J (1983)
6. Landers, R.N.: Developing a theory of gamified learning: linking serious games and gamification of learning. Simul. Gaming **45**(6), 752–768 (2014)
7. Banfield, J., Wilkerson, B.: Increasing student intrinsic motivation and self-efficacy through gamification pedagogy. CIER **7**(4), 291–298 (2014)
8. Breuer, J.S., Bente, G.: Why so serious? On the relation of serious games and learning. Eludamos: J. Comput. Game Cult. **4**(1), 7–24 (2010)
9. Depura, K., Garg, M.: Application of online gamification to new hire onboarding. In: 2012 Third International Conference on Services in Emerging Markets, pp. 153–156 (2012)
10. Fernandes, J., Duarte, D., Ribeiro, C., Farinha, C., Pereira, J.M., da Silva, M.M.: iThink: a game-based approach towards improving collaboration and participation in requirement elicitation. Procedia Comput. Sci. **15**, 66–77 (2012)
11. Arai, S., Sakamoto, K., Washizaki, H., Fukazawa, Y.: A gamified tool for motivating developers to remove warnings of bug pattern tools. In: Proceedings - 2014 6th International Workshop on Empirical Software Engineering in Practice, IWESEP 2014, pp. 37–42 (2014)
12. Csikszentmihalyi, M.: Flow and the Foundations of Positive Psychology: The Collected Works of Mihaly Csikszentmihalyi. Springer, Netherlands, Dordrecht (2014)
13. Deterding, S., Dixon, D., Khaled, R., Nacke, L.: From game design elements to gamefulness: defining "gamification". In: Proceedings of the 15th International Academic MindTrek Conference: Envisioning Future Media Environments, Tampere Finland, pp. 9–15 (2011)
14. Huizinga, J.: Homo ludens: a study of the play-element in culture. First Beacon Press, Paperback Edition. Beacon Press, Boston, Massachusetts (1955)
15. Toda, A., et al.: Analysing gamification elements in educational environments using an existing Gamification taxonomy. Smart Learning Environments **6** (2019)
16. Huotari, K., Hamari, J.: Defining gamification - a service marketing perspective. In: Proceeding of the 16th International Academic MindTrek Conference (2012)
17. Caponetto, I., Earp, J., Ott, M.: Gamification and education: a literature review. In: European Conference on Games Based Learning; Reading, pp. 50–57. Academic Conferences International Limited (2014)
18. Teichmann, M., Ullrich, A., Knost, D., Gronau, N.: Serious games in learning factories: perpetuating knowledge in learning loops by game-based learning. Procedia Manufact. **45**, 259–264 (2020)
19. Abt, C.C.: Serious Games. University Press of America (1987)
20. Michael, D., Chen, S.: Serious games: games that educate, train and inform. Thomson Course Technology, Boston, Mass (2006)
21. Bellotti, F., Berta, R., de Gloria, A., Ott, M., Arnab, S., de Freitas, S., Kiili, K.: Designing serious games for education: from pedagogical principles to game mechanisms. In: Proceedings 5th Euopean Conference on Game-Based Learning, pp. 26–34 (2011)
22. Teichmann, M.R., Ullrich, A., Kotarski, D., Gronau, N.: Facing the demographic change – recommendations for designing learning factories as age-appropriate teaching-learning environments for older blue-collar workers. In: SSRN Electronic Journal (2021)
23. Bioeconomy Council: Further development of the "National Research Strategy Bioeconomy 2030" (2016). (in German)
24. Urmetzer, S., Schlaile, M.P., Bogner, K., Mueller, M., Pyka, A.: Knowledge for change - knowledge-theoretical foundations of a sustainable bioeconomy policy. In: Konrad, W., Scheer, D., Weidtmann, A. (eds.) Bioökonomie nachhaltig gestalten, pp. 73–105. Springer Fachmedien Wiesbaden, Wiesbaden (2020) (in German)

25. The Federal Government of Germany. National German Bioeconomy Strategy (2020). (in German)
26. Scheer, D., Konrad, W.: The future discourse bioeconomy in the mirror of the current topic landscape. In: Konrad, W., Scheer, D., Weidtmann, A. (eds.) Bioökonomie Nachhaltig Gestalten, pp. 43–69. Springer Fachmedien Wiesbaden, Wiesbaden (2020) (in German)
27. The Federal Government of Germany. Bioeconomy as social change. Concept for the promotion of socio-economic research for the research for the bioeconomy (2014). (in German)
28. Gronau, N., Weber, E., Wander, P., Ullrich, A.: A regional remanufacturing network approach - modeling and simulation of circular economy processes in the era of industry 4.0. In: Plapper, P. (ed.) Digitization of the Work Environment for Sustainable Production, pp. 145–170. GITO Verlag (2022)

Enterprise Modeling with Conventions

Stef Joosten[1,2]([✉])([iD]) and Ella Roubtsova[1]([✉])([iD])

[1] Open University of the Netherlands,
Valkenburgerweg 177, Heerlen 6419, AT, The Netherlands
{stef.joosten,ella.roubtsova}@ou.nl
[2] Architecture Department, Ordina, Ringwade 1,
Nieuwegein 3439, LM, The Netherlands
stef.joosten@ordina.nl

Abstract. This paper investigates the use of modeling conventions for enterprise models. With the help of Archi, a tool supporting the Archi-Mate standard, we have enhanced the enterprise modeling process with semantic modeling conventions that support assessment of enterprise models during their design. For enterprise architects who want more from ArchiMate than just drawing pictures, this paper proposes to use a language and a tool, Ampersand, to impose and verify modeling conventions in ArchiMate models. Unlike informal languages, Ampersand allows enterprise architects to signal where an ArchiMate model violates their own modeling conventions, so they can fix the model accordingly. It allows enterprise architects to enhance their ArchiMate models with semantic modeling conventions that are verified by Ampersand. This paper contains a case study that demonstrates the approach. The authors also share their experience with modeling with semantic conventions.

Keywords: Modeling Convention · Ampersand · ArchiMate · Automated Constraint Verification · Enterprise Model · Relation Algebra

1 Introduction

The quality of a designed enterprise model goes beyond a syntactically and semantically correct model. An architecture team may have enterprise specific modeling conventions, which existing enterprise modeling tools will not verify because all of them are general purpose tools.

The authors have used a tool, Ampersand [14], alongside of ArchiMate [20] to check the modeling conventions of an architecture team. It enhances ArchiMate with a checker for enterprise specific modeling conventions.

In previous studies [1,7], it was found that business documents rarely contain business rules that can become modeling conventions. The existing natural modeling process and enterprise modeling tools do not invite modelers to document and verify modeling conventions.

B. Shishkov (Ed.): BMSD 2023, LNBIP 483, pp. 56–73, 2023.
https://doi.org/10.1007/978-3-031-36757-1_4

In this paper, we skip the elicitation of modeling conventions from documents. We propose a modeling process where the architects are invited to formulate conventions and use the ArchiMate checker whenever they want during the modeling. We also demonstrate the proposed modeling process with a number of modeling conventions formulated for evolving modeling views. Being verified these modeling conventions have caused corrections and refinement of modeling views. In other words, we propose a new iterative modeling process called "Enterprise Modeling with Conventions", where the formulating, documenting, verifying, and discussing of conventions is woven into the natural modeling process. The result of this revised process is an enterprise model with verified and documented quality features.

Section 2 gives an overview of the related work. It covers enterprise modeling with ArchiMate, the tool Ampersand, and it addresses modeling conventions found in the literature. Section 3 reports a case study that introduces and illustrates the enterprise modeling process with modeling conventions. Section 4 discusses the results of the proposed enterprise modeling process with verified conventions. Section 5 concludes the paper and draws on future work.

2   Related Work

As ArchiMate and Ampersand are starring in this paper, we discuss each of them in a separate section.

The third section discusses related work on modeling conventions, since the contribution of this paper is to enrich enterprise modeling with automatically checked modeling conventions.

2.1   ArchiMate

ArchiMate [20] is an enterprise modeling language. It is available to enterprise architects for visualizing and sharing ideas. ArchiMate gives its user maximal freedom in modeling, because it imposes hardly any restrictions. An enterprise architect can express almost anything in the elements and relationships provided by ArchiMate. She can even stretch that further by defining graphical aliases and providing relationships with names. This is nice for an individual who just wants to visualize an idea in her own way.

Throughout this paper we use the word "model" in the meaning used by ArchiMate, which contains a collection of views. Each view is one diagram. So, an ArchiMate model contains a collection of diagrams (views) as opposed to the more conventional meaning in which a model refers to one diagram only. In each single view, ArchiMate shows a set of boxes presenting instances of elements and lines between those boxes, presenting instances of relationships. The architect draws and perceives every view as a graphical diagram (the central part in Fig. 1) that shows details of the entire ArchiMate model. Each view is used by an enterprise architect to visualize one idea, such as an enterprise layer, a subsystem or a pattern [10].

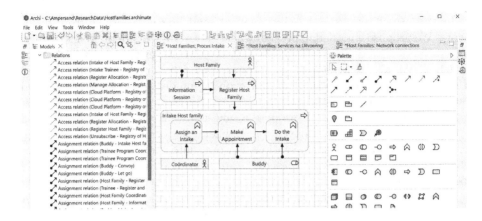

Fig. 1. How an architect works in ArchiMate

In the realm of tools available for ArchiMate, we have used Archi[1] [2] because it is open source, free, and popular. Figure 1 shows a screenshot of this tool. The internal data structure in Archi (shown in the panel on the left hand side of Fig. 1) contains

- a collection of instances of elements,
- a collection of instances of relationships, and
- a collection of views in which the instances of elements and relationships are shown.

Each element and each relationship has its own shape, to be picked by the modeler from a limited set of shapes, in the palette on the right hand side of Fig. 1. Each shape reflects the type of the element or relationship. The meaning of each shape is described in natural language in the ArchiMate reference document [20].

An attractive characteristic of ArchiMate is that different views can share the same instances of elements and relationships. One element instance can even have different shapes in different views, but still be the same instance. The notion of "the same" is not defined in the ArchiMate reference document [20], but ArchiMate tools typically use an internal key to identify elements. A useful consequence is that changing a name of an element or a relationship in one view is immediately reflected in all other views as well.

There are only a few rules in ArchiMate, allowing the architect to visualize her enterprise models in a variety of ways. This freedom of expression has a downside: ArchiMate cannot enforce the modeling conventions shared by enterprise architects. Unless they explicate their modeling conventions and find a way to test them against their enterprise model in ArchiMate.

This verification is possible because ArchiMate has a well-published meta-model [9]. Every ArchiMate model constitutes a "population" that is structured

---

[1] https://www.archimatetool.com/downloads/archi/Archi User Guide.pdf.

by the ArchiMate metamodel, much like data in a database is structured by a data model.

The ArchiMate metamodel offers a set of elements from different enterprise domains: business objects, roles, technological components, services, processes and their relationships. Elements are "used to define and describe the constituent parts of Enterprise Architectures and their unique set of characteristics" [20].

Listing 1.1 shows a fragment of this metamodel.

Listing 1.1. A fragment of the ArchiMate metamodel

```
RELATION  triggering  [ BusinessEvent ∗ BusinessProcess ]
RELATION  triggering  [ BusinessActor ∗ ApplicationFunction ]
RELATION  realization  [ BusinessFunction ∗ BusinessService ]
RELATION  serving  [ BusinessFunction ∗ ApplicationFunction ]
RELATION  type  [ Relationship ∗ Text ]  [ UNI ]
RELATION  name  [ ApplicationFunction ∗ Text ]  [ UNI ]
```

The fragment reveils relationships that represent connections between source and target elements. Every element in an ArchiMate model has a name and a type. To make verification possible, we assume that graphical elements with the same name and type are identical, i.e. have the same internal identifier.

Summarizing, the fixed metamodel of ArchiMate enables the verification of modeling constraints. This offers the perspective of a modeling process with built modeling conventions.

2.2   Assessment of ArchiMate Models with Ampersand

In this paper, we verify modeling conventions on ArchiMate models. The verification is supported by the tool Ampersand developed at the Open University of the Netherlands.

From an ArchiMate model, Ampersand derives the part of the ArchiMate metamodel needed to structure the data that constitutes the enterprise model. The Ampersand compiler "understands" ArchiMate files and reads an ArchiMate model as a populated model. Every relationship in an ArchiMate model is interpreted as a pair in the corresponding relation of the metamodel in Ampersand. Ampersand also derives the "population" of relations between concepts from the model. Ampersand refers to the set of all pairs of a relation as its "population". Listing 1.2 shows a fragment of the internal representation of an ArchiMate model generated by Ampersand. The long numbers are unique keys, internal to the ArchiMate tool, that represent instances of ArchiMate concepts (i.e. elements, relationships, and views). After compilation, each relation contains all pairs from all views. So, the scope of each relation in Ampersand comprises the entire ArchiMate model.

Listing 1.2. Populated model

```
POPULATION  realization  [BusinessFunction*BusinessService]
CONTAINS
[("37d64852-3ed1-466e-99d7-22a64c36516d",
                "77c76f36-6b0c-4ab4-8a8b-aa2ad81db69f")
,("823b1d78-3424-4ab7-b677-b4d9e4d4af5a",
                "867688b0-b7c1-4807-b3ed-5cb0346ad19c")
,("fa69bf84-a264-4d38-bf96-04a0dfd34644",
                "9b8bad05-1f66-48db-95a5-958ae088d96e")
,("77bb5f5f-c55c-4bc4-987f-2fa63554dace",
                "3f39d8e9-dddb-4cb0-97a9-3cbdbbf816ef")]
```

The Ampersand provides a language to formulate modeling conventions. The language Ampersand [6] is a syntactically sugared version of the Relation Algebra, which is also called Calculus of Relations [12,17]. It is similar to Alloy [5] and RelView [19]. The reason to formalize modeling conventions in Ampersand is that ArchiMate's metamodel consists of relations. Relation algebra is particularly well suited for manipulating relations, which are the building blocks of the ArchiMate metamodel.

A user defines each modeling convention as a rule in Ampersand, which is recognizable by the keyword RULE. Each rule is expressed using relations, concepts, and populations in a text file called an Ampersand script. The Ampersand compiler [6] checks all rules against the population of all relations in a script.

The Archi tool has a specific XML-format that is different from the Open Group ArchiMate Model Exchange File Format. The Ampersand compiler has been enhanced with a parser [4] to read the model from the Archi tool directly. The Ampersand team has plans to support the Open Group ArchiMate Model Exchange File Format in the future, to improve interoperability.

We want to emphasize that Ampersand derives the metamodel directly from the ArchiMate model. This approach is different from another existing approach [1] which creates its own metamodel for ArchiMate. Generating the meta-

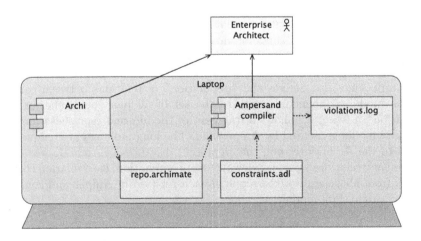

Fig. 2. A toolset for an enterprise architect [7].

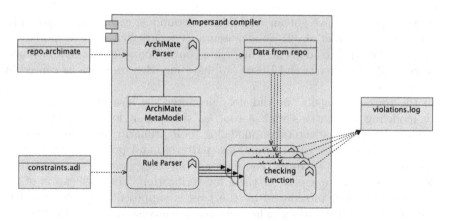

Fig. 3. Under the hood of the Ampersand compiler.

model (Listing 1.2) directly from the ArchiMate model ensures that there can be no discrepancy between the metamodel and the data from the ArchiMate model.

There are two tools serving the enterprise architect: an ArchiMate modeling tool and the Ampersand compiler (Fig. 2). The ArchiMate modeling tool (Archi) allows to produce an ArchMate model "repo.archimate" and modeling conventions "constraints.adl". Figure 3 shows that the Ampersand compiler parses the ArchiMate model and uses the elements and relationships to populate the relations in the ArchiMate metamodel. Modeling conventions are parsed according to the same metamodel, so the tool "knows" where to find the data to be checked. For each convention, a checking function is generated that can compute violations with respect to that convention. All violations found by the Ampersand compiler are emitted to the "violations.log".

The ArchiMate modeling tool and the Ampersand compiler with the built-in ArchiMate parser, are the predecessors of the new enterprise modeling process with conventions.

2.3   Modeling Conventions

Modeling conventions come from different perspectives and reflect different concerns. Many of conventions are design patterns known from software development. However, enterprise models also include new enterprise patterns that relate business process elements and their implementation by roles and technical components.

Many modeling convention reflect design policies and principles.

For example, Korman et al. [8] report modeling conventions caused by five existing access policies.

Tepandi et al. [18] present architectural patterns for the EU Once-Only Principle to ensure that citizens and businesses have to supply the same information only once.

Security policies have got an ArchiMate metamodel extension proposed by Mayer et al. [11]. Zhi et al. [21] model assurance security cases in ArchiMate.

Law regulations introduce new modeling conventions. For example, Blanco-Lainé et al. [3], Roubtsova and Bosua [13] have modeled conventions caused by privacy policies.

In the reviewed papers, we did not encounter the idea of using a tool to verify modeling conventions with a tool, as this paper does. The authors of the reviewed papers see enterprise modeling tools primarily as a way to model, and not as a way to verify conventions, patterns, and policies. The authors clearly feel the need to express conventions, but they describe them in their models rather than implementing them for verification. The verification of the modeling conventions introduced by the laws is supposed to be delegated to auditing or control institutions. This delegation is inconsistent with the practice and requirements for companies to self-assess their compliance with laws and policies.

3   Enterprise Modeling with Conventions

Considering the needs of enterprises in self-assessment and the existence of the predecessor tools that can support self-assessment, we propose a new enterprise modeling process, such that each enterprise model (a view or a set of views) is stamped with a set of modeling conventions, formulated and verified for the model.

This modeling process invites the modelers to think and agree on conventions, patterns and used regulations. The result of this new enterprise modeling process is an enterprise model with noted quality features.

3.1   Research Method

In this paper we use a case study as a research method. The case study is derived from an actual real-world situation, but it has been harnessed a little to respect the anonymity of the organization.

A case study is used for exploring the new enterprise modeling process. It illustrates the iterative refinement of the model using five modeling conventions. The five conventions cover the relations of the business process with its implementation and its infrastructure. The need of each modeling convention is explained. Each convention is precisely formulated, formalized and verified. Two conventions are visualized in ArchiMate. The research data have been carefully documented and can be found in the dataset HostFamilies [15]. The produced enterprise model and its noted quality features are discussed and evaluated.

3.2   A Case Study: Host Families

The hostfamily application is an information system that supports the placement of international trainees with host families throughout the country.

To ensure the success of each placement, each situation asks for careful matching process of trainees with host families. This matching is done by a volunteer organization, whereas responsibility of the placement lies with the national trainee programme organization. Some two dozen factors are matched (by hand), varying from languages spoken, to disabilities, allergies, and many more. The choice of the important factors has resulted in the business process shown in Fig. 4.

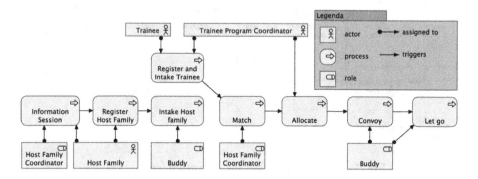

Fig. 4. Matching and allocating trainees with host families

There are different stakeholders in this business process. The organization that recruits host families is a volunteer organization that is entirely separate from the organization that sends out the trainees. Both organizations do their own intake, so there is ample knowledge about the trainees and about the host families to get a good match. The volunteer organization assigns buddies (also volunteers) to convoy the host families. A buddy provides a familiar face, a phone number to call, a listening ear, and practical assistance for any issues that might occur. Matching is done by a host family coordinator, who spends (on average) 4 h to find the right host family and make all the final arrangements. Typically, it takes just a few days for a trainee to apply for a host family until the moment of actual placement. For this reason, the host family organization holds a larger number of host families in a register.

The hostfamily application is used by a trainee program coordinator, a host family coordinator and buddies. The only thing a host family and a trainee can do in the system is to register themselves. Parts of the software runs on client nodes in an office, which are virtual PCs. Parts of the software also runs on mobile devices. For the sake of this presentation, we distinguish only two environments: Mobile and Client nodes. The actual registration of data is done in the cloud, making all services essentially stateless. So if something happens with the client hardware, the data is still safe.

Figure 5 shows which application services are serving which business processes. We have used ArchiMate's application services to model microservices of the hostfamily application. It also shows on which platforms which services are running.

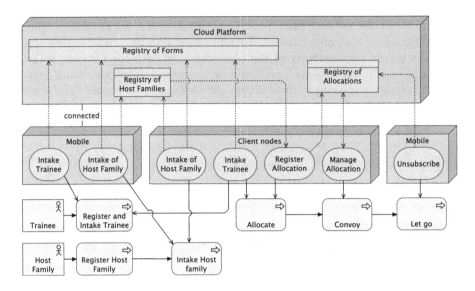

Fig. 5. Business processes aligned with microservices

In this paper, we show five modeling conventions relating the business process and implementation services. These convention have been accepted by enterprise architects and verified on the model. The file containing the conventions [16]² is called "hostfamilies.adl". Each of the following subsections applies one convention to the ArchiMate model. The modeling conventions allow to correct models by identification of forgotten or unnecessary concepts or relations. The verified modeling conventions note a quality feature of the model. If Ampersand detects no violation of a modeling convention, that convention is proven for the verified model.

3.3 Modeling Convention 1

The first modeling convention is that every business process must be served by at most one microservice. If microservices are not equal, than the processes are not equal. This convention simplifies maintenance of the system.

In the First Order Logic this constraint looks as follows:

$$\forall p, p' \in Business\ Process,\ \forall a, a' \in Application\ Service:$$

$$a\ serving\ p \land a'\ serving\ p' \land a \neq a' \rightarrow p \neq p'.$$

In the Ampersand language, this modeling convention is encoded in the Relation Algebra:

$$serving^{\smile}\ ;\ -I[ApplicationService]\ ;\ serving \vdash -I[BusinessProcess].$$

---

² https://github.com/AmpersandTarski/ampersand-models/tree/master/ ArchiChecker/ResearchData/hostfamilies.adl.

The Ampersand specification of the convention and its violation is the following:

```
RULE Maintainable microservices :
     serving~;-I[ApplicationService];serving |- -I [BusinessProcess]
VIOLATION ( TXT "Business Process "
          , SRC name
          , TXT " is served by multiple microservices: "
          , SRC serving~;name)
```

The transformation between the First Order Logic and the Relation Algebra is explained in [12].

The Ampersand compiler responds with:

```
There is one violation of RULE "Maintainable microservices":
Business Process "Allocate" is served by multiple microservices:
{"Register Allocation", "Intake Trainee"}
```

Indeed, we can see the misalignment in Fig. 5. The architects recognized this as a modeling mistake. Removing the serving relation between application service "Intake Trainee" and business process "Allocate" solves the problem.

However, the most important is that the model produced with this check has a quality feature: "every business process is served by at most one microservice".

3.4   Modeling Convention 2

The second modeling convention is aimed to prevent forgotten functionality. The purpose is to ensure that every step is supported by a service in the hostfamily application, unless there is a conscious decision to the contrary.

The modeling convention is that every business process should be served by a microservice. In the First Order Logic it is formulated as

$$\forall p \in Business\ Process\ \exists a \in ApplicationService : a\ serving\ p.$$

In the Relation Algebra it looks as follows:

$$I[BusinessProcess] \vdash, serving \smile; I[ApplicationService]; serving.$$

The Ampersand specification of its violation is:

```
RULE Coverage:
   I[BusinessProcess] |- serving~; I[ApplicationService];serving
   VIOLATION ( TXT "Business Process "
             , SRC name
             , TXT " is not served by any microservice.")
```

The Ampersand compiler responds with:

```
There are 4 violations of RULE Coverage:
Business Process "Information Session" is not served by any microservice.
Business Process "Match" is not served by any microservice.
Business Process "Register Host Family" is not served by any microservice.
Business Process "Register and Intake Trainee" is not served by any
microservice.
```

This response of the Ampersand compiler helps an architecture team to spot omissions. A reader looking at Fig. 5 might wonder how the system knows about business processes that are not mentioned in this figure? This is the case for business processes "Information Session" and "Match". The answer is that Ampersand makes its assessments over all views together, i.e. the entire ArchiMate model. So, Ampersand has also seen that business processes "Information Session" and "Match" (from Fig. 4) lack a serving relationship with application services.

From these violations, the design team can draw its conclusions. Let us assume they want to include the missing application services into the model, except for the business process "Information Session" because it requires no support.

The model has the noted quality feature: "business process is always served by a microservice".

3.5   Modeling Convention 3

The enterprise modeling covers not only business concepts and relations but those in infrastructure. The third modeling convention is about infrastructure. It says that if one wants to access a data object on another platform, the infrastructure needs to be in place. This convention can be modeled by itself (Fig. 6). The purpose of this modeling convention is to ensure that the required connections are visualized in the ArchiMate model of our case study.

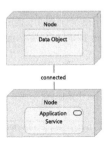

Fig. 6. Modeling convention 3 depicted in ArchiMate

The formulation of this convention in the First Order Logic is:

$$\forall a \in ApplicationService, \forall d \in DataObject, \forall n \in Node :$$

$$a\,access\,d \,\wedge\, n\,realization\,a \,\rightarrow$$

$$\exists n' \in Node : (n' = n \,\vee\, n'\,connected\,n \,\vee\, n\,connected\,n') \wedge (n'\,realisation\,d)).$$

The formulation of this convention in the Relation Algebra is:

$$access \vdash realization^{\smile} \setminus (I \,\cup\, connected \,\cup\, connected^{\smile}); access.$$

Ampersand specifies the constraint and its violation:

```
RULE Infra1 :
    access |- realization \ (I\/connected\/connected~);access
    VIOLATION ( TXT "ApplicationService ", SRC name
              , TXT " on node "
              , SRC realization~;
              ((I-connected;connected~)-connected~;connected);name
              , TXT " cannot access data object: ", TGT name
              , TXT " on node ", TGT access[Node*DataObject]~;name
              , TXT ".")
```

The Ampersand compiler responds with:

```
There are 6 violations of RULE "Infra1":
ApplicationService "Intake of Host Family" on node "Client nodes"
cannot access data
object: "Registry of Host Families" on node "Cloud Platform"
ApplicationService "Intake of Host Family" on node "Client nodes"
cannot access data
object: "Registry of Forms" on node "Cloud Platform"
ApplicationService "Intake Trainee" on node "Client nodes"
cannot access data object:
"Registry of Forms" on node "Cloud Platform"
ApplicationService "Register Allocation" on node "Client nodes"
cannot access data
object: "Registry of Allocations" on node "Cloud Platform"
ApplicationService "Register Allocation" on node "Client nodes"
cannot access data
object: "Registry of Host Families" on node "Cloud Platform"
ApplicationService "Manage Allocation" on node "Client nodes"
cannot access data object:
"Registry of Allocations" on node "Cloud Platform"
```

In Fig. 5, we see that precisely those services that run on the Client nodes cannot communicate with the Cloud. This implies that we need a connection between the Client nodes and the Cloud Platform. After we added an association called "connected" between the two, no violations remain and the problem is solved (Fig. 7).

Notice that this modeling convention is used only in situations where infrastructure is relevant. For example, an application that is distributed over different platforms may benefit from an explicit modeling of infrastructure. So, the person proposing a modeling convention must be able to judge whether the modeling of the infrastructure has value for her architecture team.

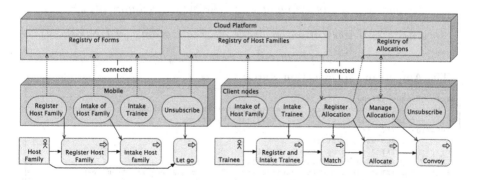

Fig. 7. Business processes aligned with application services

Also, the business process has changed, as shown in Fig. 8.

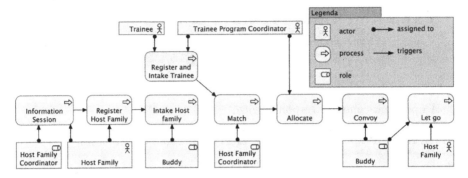

Fig. 8. Business processes after verification with new insights

3.6 Modeling Convention 4

The hostfamily application has many users. The purpose of the fourth constraint is to ensure convenience for users. A user should be able to finish subsequent process steps without switching devices. This makes the hostfamily application more user-friendly.

The fourth modeling convention is: If a business role or a business actor is assigned to two subsequent process steps that are being serviced, these steps must be realized by application services on the same node or device.

The convention, written in the First Order Logic, reads:

$$\forall p, p' \in BusinessProcess:$$

$$(p \ triggering \ p' \ \wedge \ \exists r \in Role: r \ assignment \ p \ \wedge \ r \ assignment \ p' \rightarrow$$

$$\forall a, a' \in ApplicationService: a \ serving \ p \ \wedge \ a' \ serving \ p' \ \wedge$$

$$\exists n \in Node: n \ realization \ a \ \wedge \ n \ realization \ a').$$

The convention in the Relation Algebra is:

$$triggering_{p,p'} \ ; \ assignment\breve{}_{r',p'} \ ; \ I[Role]_{r,r'} \ ; \ assignment_{r,p} \vdash$$

$$serving\breve{}_{a,p} \ ; \ \neg I[ApplicationService]_{a,a'} \ \wedge \ realization\breve{}_{n,a'} \ ; \ I[Node]_{n,n'} \ ;$$

$$realization_{n',a'} \ ; \ serving_{a',p'}.$$

The Ampersand specification states:

```
RULE SubsequentSteps:
    triggering[BusinessProcess] /\ serving~;V;serving /\ assignment~;assignment
    |- serving~;realization~;I[Node];realization;serving
VIOLATION ( TXT "If a "
         , SRC assignment~;name
         , TXT " performs step ", SRC name
         , TXT " on ", SRC serving~;realization~;name
         , TXT ", then she must switch to ", TGT serving~;realization~;name
         , TXT " for step ", TGT name
         , TXT "." )
```

The Ampersand compiler responds with:

```
There is one violation of RULE SubsequentSteps:
If a "Buddy" performs step "Convoy" on "Client nodes",
then she must switch to "Mobile" for step "Let go".
```

Interpreting this message with Fig. 5, we notice that the microservice "Unsubscribe" should run on mobile devices as well as on client nodes. Experimentation shows that this solution will resolve the issue.

However, some discussion among the developers revealed a more fundamental issue. They see the triggering relationship between steps "Convoy" and "Let go" as a modeling error, because the step of resigning as a host family is triggered by the host family. So the decision is made to remove the triggering relationship between steps "Convoy" and "Let go". That too resolves the violation. The decision is to do both: implement "Unsubscribe" on client nodes and make the host family trigger their own departure.

This discussion illustrates the relevance of this modeling convention. It signaled a problem without imposing a solution. As always, there are multiple solutions to a problem and it is up to architects themselves to propose the right one.

Figure 7 shows the result of applying the proposed changes in ArchiMate for all four modeling conventions discussed up to this point:

When checking the new model (Fig. 7), there is only violation left: Business process "Information Sessions" is not served by any application service. This is precisely what the architects want.

Inspection of Fig. 7 reveals that the application service "Unsubscribe" on the Mobile platform has no serving relationship with business process "Let go", whereas the same application service on the Client nodes does. In this situation, the architect has made clever use of ArchiMates aliasing mechanism; she has made both instances of the application service "Unsubscribe" aliases of each other. They are in fact one and the same application service. So a relationship with one of these shapes counts for both. Likewise, the application services "Intake Trainee" from Client nodes the same service from Mobile are aliases too. So, the serving relationship to "Register and Intake Trainee" is valid for both shapes, even though it is drawn from just one of them. In ArchiMate, this may be confusing. Two shapes of the same type with the same name may be the same (i.e. have the same internal ArchiMate identifier) but they may also be different (i.e. have different internal ArchiMate keys).

For this reason we advise architects to ensure that they identify all shapes with the same name and type as the same ArchiMate object. Ampersand can work with both alternatives, but the results of constraint verification may be somewhat unpredictable when the architect makes no clear choice. The choice we advise has the attractive property that fewer relationships need to be drawn, which saves on clutter in the diagrams.

3.7   Modeling Convention 5

The existing conventions can be also refined by other conventions. So let us refine the connectivity from modeling convention 3. The reader might already have noticed that the association called "connected" is somewhat gratuitous. Just adding a link does not say much about the infrastructure that is needed between the different nodes. At the very least, we should identify the networks that are used to connect these nodes.

For this reason we add a convention that says that "every connection requires that there is a network to connect both ends".

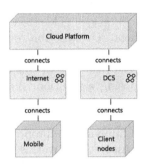

Fig. 9. Adding networks to describe the communication

Since this modeling convention only constrains the relationship "connected", none of the existing constraints is affected. In this way we have added detail about infrastructure (or any other subject) incrementally.

Writing this convention in the First Order Logic yields:

$$\forall n, n' \in Node, \exists w \in Network :$$

$$n \; connected \; n' \rightarrow n \; connects \; w \land n' \; connects \; w.$$

Writing it in the Relation Algebra gets the following look:

$$connected \vdash connects; I[w]; connects \smile .$$

Specification in Ampersand gives:

```
RULE "Network Connections":
   connected |- connects; I[w];connects~
VIOLATION ( TXT "Node "
         , SRC name
         , TXT " has no network to connect with node "
         , TGT name
         , TXT ".\n To resolve this, please use association "
         , TXT "connect[Node*Network] to connect "
         , TXT " these nodes to the same network.")
```

The Ampersand compiler responds with:

```
There are 2 violations of RULE "Network Connections":
Node "Cloud Platform" has no network to connect with node "Mobile".
To resolve this,please use association connect[Node*Network]
to connect these nodes to the same network.
Node "Client nodes" has no network to connect with node "Cloud Platform".
To resolve this, please use association connect[Node*Network]
to connect these nodes to the same network.
```

To describe the communication in terms of networks, we have created a new ArchiMate view (Fig. 9).

After adding this view, the Ampersand compiler is satisfied.

The addition of this extra modeling convention now means that we can make an extra claim: "Every connection between nodes in the ArchiMate model has a network assigned to it."

4   Discussion the Enterprise Modeling with Conventions

Having checked five modeling conventions and made changes accordingly, we can now make the following claims:

1. Every business process in the ArchiMate model is being served by at most one microservice.
2. Every business process except "Information Session" is being served by an application service.
3. Every application service in the ArchiMate model is connected to the registries from which it takes data objects.
4. Every person can perform subsequent steps in the process on the same device.
5. Every connection between nodes in the ArchiMate model has a network assigned to it.

The conventions 1 and 2 concern with maintainability of microservices implementing the business process. The convention 3 and 5 concern with connections with infrastructure and availability of data. The convention 4 is about usability of the application built for the business process.

Two conventions 3 and 5 have been added to the enterprise model as graphical views to simplify the model. The graphical representations of conventions 1, 2, and 3 do not express their specifics.

The architects can state that modeling conventions have been formally checked and verified by the Ampersand compiler, so now it is up to the builders of the hostfamily application to make a faithful implementation of the design. The proposed enterprise modeling with conventions is a process that stimulates enterprise modelers to create conventions and use patterns. The verified modeling conventions become noted model features, like quality stamps. This is an added value of the proposed modeling process.

5   Conclusion and Future Work

The need for modeling conventions has been demonstrated in related research (Sect. 2.3). However, their use is not a part of the standard enterprise modeling process. This is a missed opportunity to obtain models with known quality characteristics expressed as modeling conventions.

This paper proposes and investigates a novel enterprise modeling process where the documentation, formalization and verification of conventions are woven into the natural process of creating model views. The proposed process allows architects to verify their modeling conventions automatically. It works by deriving a metamodel from any ArchiMate model, and checking the modeling conventions on that metamodel. An architect specifies her modeling conventions and the Ampersand identifies the violations of those conventions or signals the model completeness with respect to those conventions. This process promises to increase the correctness and completeness of enterprise models.

This research has shown that this new modeling process with available tool-checker stimulates the formulation and verification of modeling conventions. On the one hand, the modeling process becomes more labor-intensive, but on the other hand it includes the self-assessment of the enterprise-specific quality conventions.

The proposed modeling process aims to improve enterprise modeling skills by making architects more aware of their modeling conventions. By making their modeling conventions explicit and checking their ArchiMate model accordingly, one would expect the entire group of architects to discuss and nurture their enterprise modeling skills. This is a topic for future research that examines modeling practices with and without automated verification. Another future work is to study the reusability of modeling conventions. We don't know (yet) whether there are modeling conventions that emerge in multiple situations, or if modeling conventions are largely enterprise-specific.

References

1. Babkin, E.A., Ponomarev, N.O.: Analysis of the consistency of enterprise architecture models using formal verification methods. Business Inf. **41**(3), 30–40 (2017)
2. Beauvoir, P., Sarrodie, J.: Archi user guide. The Open Group (2013)
3. Blanco-Lainé, G., Sottet, J.-S., Dupuy-Chessa, S.: Using an enterprise architecture model for GDPR compliance principles. In: Gordijn, J., Guédria, W., Proper, H.A. (eds.) PoEM 2019. LNBIP, vol. 369, pp. 199–214. Springer, Cham (2019). https://doi.org/10.1007/978-3-030-35151-9_13
4. Filet, P., van de Wetering, R., Joosten, S.: Enterprise architecture alignment. researchgate.net. Department of Information Sciences, Open University of the Netherland (2019)
5. Jackson, D.: Software abstractions: logic, language, and analysis. The MIT Press (2006)
6. Joosten, S.: Relation Algebra as programming language using the Ampersand compiler. J. Logical Algebr. Methods Programm. **100**, 113–129 (2018). https://doi.org/10.1016/j.jlamp.2018.04.002

7. Joosten, S., Roubtsova, E., Haddouchi, E.M.: Constraint formalization for automated assessment of enterprise models. In: Proceedings of the 24th International Conference on Enterprise Information Systems - Volume 2: ICEIS, pp. 430–441. SciTePress (2022)

8. Korman, M., Lagerström, R., Ekstedt, M.: Modeling enterprise authorization: a unified metamodel and initial validation. Complex Syst. Inf. Model. Quart. **7**, 1–24 (2016)

9. Lankhorst, M.M., Proper, H.A., Jonkers, H.: The architecture of the Archimate language. In: Halpin, T., et al. (eds.) BPMDS/EMMSAD -2009. LNBIP, vol. 29, pp. 367–380. Springer, Heidelberg (2009). https://doi.org/10.1007/978-3-642-01862-6_30

10. Lankhorst, M.M., Proper, H.A., Jonkers, H.: The anatomy of the ArchiMate language. Int. J. Inf. Syst. Model. Design (IJISMD) **1**(1), 1–32 (2010)

11. Mayer, N., Aubert, J., Grandry, E., Feltus, C., Goettelmann, E., Wieringa, R.: An integrated conceptual model for information system security risk management supported by enterprise architecture management. Softw. Syst. Model. **18**(3), 2285–2312 (2019)

12. Nakamura, Y.: Expressive power and succinctness of the positive calculus of relations. In: Fahrenberg, U., Jipsen, P., Winter, M. (eds.) RAMiCS 2020. LNCS, vol. 12062, pp. 204–220. Springer, Cham (2020). https://doi.org/10.1007/978-3-030-43520-2_13

13. Roubtsova, E., Bosua, R.: Privacy as a service (PraaS): a conceptual model of GDPR to construct privacy services. In: Shishkov, B. (ed.) BMSD 2021. LNBIP, vol. 422, pp. 170–189. Springer, Cham (2021). https://doi.org/10.1007/978-3-030-79976-2_10

14. Stef Joosten: AmpersandTarski GitBook project. Documentation of Ampersand. [GitHub]. https://ampersandtarski.gitbook.io/documentation/. Accessed 1 Oct 2022

15. Stef Joosten: HostFamilies. [GitHub]. https://github.com/AmpersandTarski/ampersand-models/tree/master/ArchiChecker/ResearchData/HostFamilies. archimate. Accessed 1 Oct 2022

16. Stef Joosten: HostFamilies. Constraints. [GitHub]. https://github.com/AmpersandTarski/ampersand-models/tree/master/ArchiChecker/ResearchData/hostfamilies.adl. Accessed 1 Oct 2022

17. Tarski, A., Givant, S.R.: A formalization of set theory without variables, vol. 41. American Mathematical Soc. (1988)

18. Tepandi, J., et al.: Towards a cross-border reference architecture for the once-only principle in Europe: an enterprise modelling approach. In: Gordijn, J., Guédria, W., Proper, H.A. (eds.) PoEM 2019. LNBIP, vol. 369, pp. 103–117. Springer, Cham (2019). https://doi.org/10.1007/978-3-030-35151-9_7

19. Berghammer, R., Neumann, F.: RelView – an OBDD-based computer algebra system for relations. In: Ganzha, V.G., Mayr, E.W., Vorozhtsov, E.V. (eds.) CASC 2005. LNCS, vol. 3718, pp. 40–51. Springer, Heidelberg (2005). https://doi.org/10.1007/11555964_4

20. The Open Group: Archimate 3.1 Specification. https://pubs.opengroup.org/architecture/archimate3-doc/. Accessed 1 Oct 2022

21. Zhi, Q., Yamamoto, S., Morisaki, S.: IMSA-Intra Model Security Assurance. J. Internet Serv. Inf. Secur. **8**(2), 18–32 (2018)

Business Modeling and (Human) Context Awareness

Coen Suurmond[(✉)] [ID]

Cesuur B.V., Velp, The Netherlands
coen@cesuur.info

Abstract. Business is a social endeavour, performed by humans, requiring flexibility and adaptation to a dynamic environment. Efficiency and stability in business processes require standardisation. IT systems, are highly efficient and important tools for business. At the same time, business processes must be capable of adapting to unforeseen circumstances. This requires human awareness, both in making sense of the situation and in finding solutions. The challenge is how to combine the computer world and the human world for the best results in the business world. This requires a distinction between two types of information, strongly coded such as computer data (which allows for automated processing) and weakly coded such as conveyed by natural language (which allows for a much more accurate representation of complex circumstances).

The paper will discuss these issues in two parts. The first part is theoretical and analytical, discussing theories relating to the business world, the computer world and the human world. The second part analyses practical issues of information in business and business processes and the role of context awareness in business processes. The paper ends with making a case for considering business information systems in a broader perspective than is common practice, founding business modelling on the human world of perception and action (Merkwelt and Wirkwelt).

Keywords: Theory of the Firm · Semiotics · Sign Systems · Context Awareness

1 Introduction

The paper analyses the differences and tensions between business as a social endeavour (fulfilling promises in a human world) and computer-based information systems as logical machines (characterised by a conceptual state space and transitions between states). It goes without saying that IT is indispensable in business today, but concepts in the computer (as in a conceptual data model) are different from concepts in natural language (which are often not crisp but are "frayed at the edges"). IT-concepts do not coincide with natural language concepts. IT concepts are fixed, abstract and idealised definitions to be used in formal procedures, while natural language concepts are based on their usage in social contexts, with meaning dependent on circumstances and evolving in time.

The paper has two objectives: to provide a theoretical insight in the fundamental differences between the formal world of IT and the human/social world of business,

B. Shishkov (Ed.): BMSD 2023, LNBIP 483, pp. 74–91, 2023.
https://doi.org/10.1007/978-3-031-36757-1_5

and to discuss some consequences of these differences. The paper should contribute to a reduction of reductive thinking in the IT community, taking a smooth and logical IT model as capturing ideal business behaviour. IT systems should support and not govern the business. Essentially, this paper is about an analysis of the (mis) fit of the computer world and the human world and its impact on business.

The paper makes a case for working with a dual view on operational information in business: the mainstream focus in information system development on structured and strongly coded information as processed by IT systems should be supplemented by a view on equally important weakly coded information. The latter is required for adapting business processes to non-standard circumstances and strongly interdependent with human awareness of their physical and social environment. It is both about being aware of that "something is out of the ordinary", and making aware of the need of adapted behaviour.

The paper will start with first a big picture and then more detailed discussion of the characteristics of the business world, computer world, and human world. The second part of the paper analyses general and contextual information in business and business processes, followed by the discussion of consequences for information systems design.

2 The Big Picture

Business is a social endeavour, constituted by institutional structures and habitual patterns. Business transactions are enacted in speech acts in natural language. Human behaviour is based on the way our world is perceived and acted upon (Merkwelt and Wirkwelt [1]), capabilities which are embedded in our physiological and neurological structures. The brain's inner workings are not well understood today, but at least it is clear that from the smallest level of neurons and neuronal groups up to high level systems such as our visual systems (plural!) its functioning is embedded in highly complex interrelationships. On the highest neurological level, our perceptual and cognitive capabilities are developed by interacting with the physical and social environment (again: Merkwelt and Wirkwelt). We perceive and think in general forms (which includes natural language) that are continuously challenged by new perceptions, hence general forms will change over time. We are sensitive to patterns, to contextual information, and we are able to notice that in a given situation "something is out of the ordinary". Doing business is about spotting challenges and possibilities in the environment, and acting upon it in a creative way.

Business transactions are about fulfilling mutual promises. Executing business processes is in a large part repetitive behaviour under standardized conditions (cause-and effect), thus contributing to business goals. To reliably achieve business goals, however, business processes must be able to adapt to unforeseen circumstances.

IT systems are logical machines, based on formal sign systems with fixed types and properties and operating in a state space predefined by types, properties and transactions. When developing information systems, our social sign systems (such as natural language) cannot be reduced to the formal sign systems of the IT world. Therefore, modelling business processes should be regarded as designing a (logical) machine that can serve business goals. Part of the design of IT systems should be the issue of who is in control of the outcomes of business processes. A related issue is where the control of the operational behaviour of the (logical) machine lies: with the operator or the designer? This is especially important when the IT system is used under unforeseen circumstances and business interests might require intervention in standard procedures.

Within the IT world, it is common to talk about context awareness in relation to IT systems, witnessed by the following Gartner definition: "**Context-aware comput-ing** is a style of computing in which situational and environmental information about people, places and things is used to anticipate immediate needs and proactively offer enriched, situation-aware and usable content, functions and experiences." [2] However, what should be emphasised is that it is the designer of the IT system who makes the computer system "aware" by supplying it with input channels that supply the software with data about the environment, which are taken (by the designer!) to represent explicit or latent needs of the user. We could designate this as programmed context awareness, representing the anticipation and interpretation of the designer of the context in which the IT system is expected to be applied. For now context-aware computing seems more relevant in the personal sphere than for business processes. Side remark: possible AI-generated anticipation could be feasible and could be designated as "context awareness by induction" as it is based on analysis of patterns from the past; it is not about new future states but about repeating past states.

Context awareness in the human world is different and richer. It is not only about being aware of a situation by projecting past experiences and applying routines and patterns, but it is also about making sense of the current situation in light of what is meant to be (where to go, what to achieve). Another fundamental difference is that human awareness encompasses "reading other people's minds": what do they expect, how will they act and react, what is acceptable behaviour and what not? It is this latter property of human awareness that is so critical in our social Merkwelt and Wirkwelt.

To summarize:

- Business is about exchanging promises about future transactions. It is based on human commitments and expectations, embedded in social institutions. Awareness of developments in the business environment is crucial for survival of the business.
- Humans are social animals, defined by their Merkwelt and Wirkwelt. Natural language is a constitutive part of the social world. Interpretation and sense making ("what is going on here?") is a crucial capability in the human world.
- IT systems are logical machines, very powerful in programmed behaviour, and fun-damentally lacking sense making capability (the computer as such is just shifting meaningless bits). In its functional behaviour, IT systems can take situational and environmental information into account, provided that the behaviour is prescribed by the programmer and provided that the environmental information is available as formalised, structured data.

In the next sections this big picture will be fleshed out. First by discussing theories about the business world, the computer world and the human world and then by discussing the role of different types of information in the three worlds.

3 Business World

3.1 A Story

The glossary of Daft's textbook defines organisations as "social entities that are goal-directed, deliberately structured activity systems linked to the external environment" [3]. This suggests that you could find out about the workings of an organisation by examining organisational structures. Such organisational theory did not help me to understand what I saw in practice, where I observed a great deal of informal "unstructured" adjustment in food processing industry. To put all such undocumented phenomena away under the header "informal aspects of the organisation" was unsatisfactory. Informal seemed to imply non-rational, and it was left to sociology and psychology to explore the drivers of such non-rational behaviour in organisations. I simply would not accept such a lazy escape to assumed irrationality of human behaviour in organisations.

In the early 1990s, a concrete experience changed my views on organisation. At the time, we worked on a project for a company producing prepackaged meat for retailers. The director-owner of this company (about 100–150 employees) was a very outspoken and dominant figure, his staff had very little to say. My question in this project: while it seems that everything and everyone is directly controlled by the owner, it was also inevitable that the operational behaviour required low level coordination. The company was successful in a dynamic and difficult market, so its business processes were doing OK. It was certainly not the case that people only dared to make safe decisions out of fear of the owner. The breakthrough for me was a question asked by a seasoned colleague over coffee on a test run in the weekend: "Why do you think Mr X (the owner) needs this IT system for his warehouse?". This changed my perspective, I suddenly recognised our system as an instrument to enhance the service level of the company towards its customers. Later on, I found theoretical underpinnings of this insight in the metaphor of the company as an organism (Sect. 3.4), contract theory in law (Sect. 3.3) and the theory of the firm (Sect. 3.2).

From that moment on I looked at business processes (and their supporting systems) as result-oriented functional elements to serve markets with products, instead as isolated mechanisms for transforming inputs to outputs. The daily rhythm of customer ordering defined the patterns in the business processes of distribution $\rightarrow$ packaging and pricing $\rightarrow$ preparing the meat $\rightarrow$ production planning $\rightarrow$ purchasing. Indeed, in order to understand the processes you had to start at the last process, and go backwards. Because the first processes would have to start before all customers had ordered (due to short lead times!), they would start based on prognosis, and adapt when required. Mutual adjustment was indeed highly informal, but also highly rational and understandable. Coordination was based on an understanding of the business values of the owner, and acting accordingly. And, of course, the fact that the director-owner could be quite intimidating when something went wrong, kept everyone on their toes.

3.2 Theory of the Firm

John Kay emphasised the central role of the set of relationships of a firm with its environment in his analysis of corporate success. He wrote "The firm is defined by its contracts and relationships. Added value is created by its success in putting these contracts and relationships together, so it is the quality and distinctiveness of these contracts that promote added value" [4]. Corporate success cannot be reduced to what the company does; how the company does it is often as important.

In the example above, it was the combination of niche products for large supermarket chains and standard products for niche retailers that defined the company. The project in the story was about strengthening the already strong position of the company in its niche markets. The driver of the project was reducing order lead times (for customers) and improving yield on hours and material (for the company). Adding an innovative automated warehousing for semi-finished products was a means to these ends.

Coase's analysis of transaction costs contributes to the understanding why the set of contracts and relationships are so important for corporate success as discussed above [5]. He asked in his 1937 article a very simple but consequential question: if markets are the solution for efficient economic transactions, why do companies exist? His equally simple answer was that classical economic theory had erroneously presumed the free availability of all relevant market information for the economic actor. Even if perfect markets and rational economic man would exist, this economic man would still have to expend part of his scarce resources to acquiring 'all' relevant market information. Which is why collective transactions are much cheaper, witnessed by the existence of companies with their employment contracts with employees and their relational contracts for recurring transactions with other companies.

By analogy, a similar argument can be made for information in business processes. Providing full information for a task in a business process is a fiction. Part of the required information for doing the task is 'frozen' into standard operating procedures (either designed or emerged), part is provided by training, part by mutual adjustment and part by task-specific information. Part of the information is provided by IT systems, part by human communication. Transaction cost theory would require an analysis which informational transactions are 'better' done by IT systems, and which by human communication ('better': considering both efficiency or less costs and effectiveness or achieving the intended result). Standard operation procedures rigidly frozen in IT systems can be highly efficient for foreseen situations, but generate high transaction costs in case of disruption.

3.3 Relational Contracts

Market transactions are governed by contract law. Black's Law Dictionary gives as the first of eight meanings for 'contract': "an agreement between two or more parties creating obligations that are enforceable or otherwise recognizable by law"; and as the second meaning: "the writing that sets forth such an agreement" [6]. Calamari and Perillo observed "The term 'contract' is also used by the lay person and lawyers alike to refer to a document in which the terms of a contract are written. Use of the word in this sense is by no means improper so long as it is clearly understood that rules of law utilizing the concept 'contract' rarely refer to the writing itself. Usually, the reference is to the agreement; the writing being merely a memorial of the agreement" [7] This distinction by itself is important, as it differentiates between the agreement between the contracting parties (reciprocal promises) and the written representation of the agreement. McNeil analysed how relational contracts are embedded in a commercial, institutional and social context. Business partners will meet again, reputation matters in business [8].

Doing business means maintaining relations with your environment, and business contracts are embedded in those relations. As discussed above, John Kay considered this as a defining the identity of a company. Coase's theory of transaction costs helps to explain why establishing longer lasting relationships with reliable business partners drives transaction costs down (but might drive prices up, which is positive when buying and negative when selling). The story provides a good illustration of such social, economic, and legal aspects of a company's behaviour.

3.4 The Living Company

As a business school student in the early 1950s, De Geus was taught about the 'economic company' as rational, calculable and controllable. [9] Later on, after working a lifetime at the Shell company, he realised "that the economic company is an abstraction with little to do with the reality of corporate life. … Companies could act according to the economic definition of success when managers felt that they were in control of their world. But rare is the manager who feels in control of today's turbulent environment. Therefore, to cope with a changing world, any entity must develop the capability to shift and change, to develop new skills and attitudes: in short, the capability to learn." De Geus observed that Piaget's concept of 'learning through accommodation' was applicable to companies, "to change one's internal structure to remain in harmony with a changed environment". Hence, De Geus coined the designation 'the living company' for long-lasting companies (such as Shell), characterized by sensitivity to its environment, a strong cohesion and identity, the ability to build constructive relationships with other entities, and the ability to govern its own growth and evolution effectively.

The tension between short term efficiency and long term adaption is addressed by Michaud and Thoenig. They observed that the internal organization of a company often is oriented towards short term goals and cost-efficiency. Strategy, however, is oriented towards "exploring different avenues from its current routines" [10]. Difficulties can arise from short-term optimization when simple static structures are not well suited to handle longer term dynamics of change. They write: "Those firms that survive in the economic battle are the ones that know how to reconcile the logic of exploitation and that of regeneration". Balancing short term and long term interests in business can require a high degree of context awareness!

To recapitulate: doing business is to maintain trustworthy relations, hence being sensitive to challenges and opportunities in the environment. The rationale of business processes is to fulfil the business transactions, even under internal or external disturbances. In its business processes a company must be aware both of its short term and longer term context, its actual and its future position in its social environment.

4 Computer World

4.1 Structured Computer Organisation (Tanenbaum)

My view on IT systems as formal sign systems is grounded in early encounters with the world of computing and computers in the late 1970's/earlier 1980's, both in practical first steps and from studying the literature. Writing an invoicing program in assembly language for an office computer with 2 KB primary memory makes you very much aware of the elementary logical operations of the internal processor. Witnessing how a friend was manipulating the behaviour of a (very, very) small computer system by connecting the interrupt line of its microprocessor to the outside world by soldering a tiny wire to it also contributed to my awareness of low-level computing. Literature provided me with background knowledge about digital electronics with AND and NAND gates, the internal building blocks of the microprocessor.

An essential step in the development of my thinking about computing and computers came by the book Structured Computer Organization by Andrew Tanenbaum, more specifically by his concept of the computer as a multilevel machine [11]. Tanenbaum describes a digital computer as "a machine that can solve problems for people by carrying out instructions to it. ... The electronic circuits of each computer can recognize and directly execute a limited set of simple instructions into which all its programs must be converted before they can be executed". Next, Tanenbaum describes the multilevel machine. On the lowest level 1 we find the actual computer M1 with machine language L1, capable to directly executing the instructions in its electronic circuits. Each next level n is a virtual computer with machine language Ln, programs written for the virtual machine Mn in language Ln are either interpreted by an interpreter on a lower machine, or translated to the machine language of a lower machine. The reciprocal relation between machine Mn and language Ln is that "each machine has some machine language, consisting of all the instructions that the machine can execute. In effect, a machine defines a language. Similarly, a language defines a machine – namely, the machine that can execute all programs written in that language.". This concept of a multilevel machine together with the core instruction set of the processor on level 1 implies that all software is ultimately executed on level 1, in elementary digital logic. As Dijkstra wrote: "Computing and computer science unavoidably emerge as exercises in formal mathematics or, if you wish an acronym, as an exercise in VLSAL (very large scale application of logic)" [12].

It should be remarked that the reduction of software to basic instructions does not imply faultless reduction, on the contrary. In fact, only a few programming languages are formally defined (think of Algol, Pascal, Modula) and many languages are implicitly defined by the behaviour of the compilers or interpreters written for those languages. This might result that it is not possible to be sure of the behaviour of software written in such ill-specified languages, and even that the behaviour may change because of a new version of the compiler without any change in the program written in that language.

4.2 Domains and Types: Relational Model for Database Management (Codd)

After getting acquainted with Tanenbaum's concepts about the computer as a multilevel system executing instructions in digital logic, I studied the work of Codd on databases.

Like the work of Tanenbaum, what appealed to me was the fundamental and simple character of the basic concepts and the approach. As Codd wrote in the preface of his book The Relation Model for Database Management, Version 2 [13], two of his primary concerns were the preservation of integrity in a commercial database and precision ("The relational model intentionally does not specify how a DBMS should be built, but it does specify what should be built, and for that it provides a precise specification"). Within the relation model, Codd defines the fundamental concept of the domain. According to Codd, a domain could be considered as an extended data, "conceptually similar to a basic data type found in many programming languages" but "intended to capture some of the meaning of the data" ("if … two semantically distinguishable types of real-world objects or properties happen to be represented by values of the same basic data type, the user nevertheless assigns distinct names to these types and *the system keeps track of their type distinction*").

Side remark: The concept of 'domain' in relational database theory could be compared to the concept of enumerated type in programming (but the two concepts are not identical!). As De Brock and Smedinga show in a recent paper, many relevant language-constructs of a relational database are not implemented in our common programming languages. It is quite peculiar that such a gap exists between the two worlds of databases and programming [14].

5 Human World

5.1 Two Pairs of Concepts

Let me start with Von Uexkülls biological twin concepts of Merkwelt and Wirkwelt: "everything a subject perceives belongs to its *perception world* [*Merkwelt*], and everything it produces, to its *effect world* [*Wirkwelt*]. These two worlds, of perception and production of effects, form one closed unit, the *environment*" [1]. Von Uexküll contrasted the biological view on the behaviour in animals ("what is it for?"), with the physiology point of view ("how does it work?"). He observed that the same physiological process (such as the contraction of a muscle) can be part of several functional cycles, each cycle existing to do something in the world (Wirkwelt) and initiated by some perception (Merkwelt). The world of a physiologist is about machinery which behaviour is caused by triggers and machine states. The world of a biologist is about organisms which behaviour is caused by purposes or final causes. Humans as (self) conscious organisms exhibit intentional behaviour that explains their actions (of course humans are also bound to physical causal laws and human routine behaviour is mostly cause-and-effect). Humans, as all organisms interact with their environment and are at the same time formed by and forming their environment. The Merkwelt and Wirkwelt of the computer is quite different, as it is 'living in' a logical space world of predefined concepts and categories.

A second conceptual pair is formed by essentialist (typologic) thinking as opposed to population thinking. In the words of the evolution biologist Ernst Mayr: "The ultimate conclusions of the population thinker and the typologist are precisely the opposite. For the typologist, the type (*eidos*) is real and variation an illusion, while for the populationist the type (average) is an abstraction and only the variation is real" [15]. When the composition of a population changes over time, or when individuals in a population adapt over time to a changing environment, so will the type (meaning, species) change. As indicated in the passage about the Merkwelt and Wirkwelt of the computer above, the world of the computer is an essentialist world of fixed logical state space of predefined concepts, categories and transitions.

5.2 Language and Semiotics

Language as a System

Wittgenstein wrote "The limits of my language mean the limits of my world" [16]. Understanding language is key to understanding the world as we experience it, our life-world. De Saussure made a distinction between language ('langue') and speech ('parole'), the first term designating language as an abstract system of rules and conventions, the latter term designating the use of language, or speech. Linguistics studies both language as a system (syntax and semantics) an in use (pragmatics). Because for the individual the system must precede the use, and because "speech is many sided and heterogeneous; straddling several areas simultaneously – physical, physiological, and psychological – it belongs both to the individual and to society; we cannot put it into any category of human facts, for we cannot discover its unity", de Saussure posits "from the very outset we must put both feet to the ground of language and use language as the norm of all other manifestations of speech" [17].

The distinction between language as a system and language in use is also found in the highly influential work of Chomsky, who distinguished between competence (knowledge about language) and performance (actual use of language). Chomsky noted in his Aspects of the Theory of Syntax "Linguistic theory is concerned primarily with an ideal speaker-listener, in a completely homogeneous speech-community, who knows its language perfectly and is unaffected by such grammatically irrelevant conditions as memory limitations, distractions, shifts of attention and interest, and errors (random or characteristic) in applying his knowledge of the language in actual performance" [18].

Charles Morris distinguished between semantics or "the relations of signs to the objects to which the signs are applicable", pragmatics or "the relation of signs to interpreters", and syntax or "the formal relation of signs to one another" [19]. This triad of concepts is nowadays commonly used. However, the views on the three aspects and their interrelationships have shifted considerably. Especially the view on pragmatics has changed. Scientists like De Saussure and Chomsky considered pragmatics as a collection of peripheral phenomena beyond the realm of proper linguistics, later on pragmatics became the starting point for understanding language.

Language in Use: Pragmatics

In traditional linguistics, pragmatics "studies how speakers use context and shared information to convey information that is supplementary to the semantic content of what they say, and how hearers make inferences on the basis of this information. ... pragmatics has ... restricted itself to a mere description of fragmentary issues" [20]. In the latter half of the 20th century the so-called ordinary language philosophers (Austin, Grice, Strawson) studied how language is embedded in social contexts with its habits, patterns and conventions. This school of thought, studying how language is actually used, led to the development of speech act theory (first by Austin [21], later extended by Searle [22] and to the postulation of Conversational Maxims by Grice [23].

Later on, in The Construction of Social Reality, Searle noted that "there are portions of the real world, objective facts in the world, that are only facts by human agreement. In a sense there are things that exist only because we believe them to exist. I am thinking of things like money, property, governments, and marriages" [24]. This led to his claim that "language is essentially constitutive of institutional reality".

Language as Use: Pragmatism

"The uses of words are woven into the tapestry of human life. ... We are what we are and can do those things that characterize us as human beings, because we are language users" wrote Baker and Hacker about Wittgenstein's later theory of language [25]. Knowing the meaning of a word is knowing how to use the word in a language game, and language games are learned in practice.

In his book 'Living Words' Ludlow develops "a dynamic theory of the nature of language and the lexicon ... that reject[s] the idea that languages are stable abstract objects that we learn and then use; instead, human languages are things that we build on a conversation-by-conversation basis" [26]. Lexical meaning is always underdetermined, "the meaning of the term can shift between conversations and even within a conversation". The combination of conversational context and 'static lexical meaning' determines the actual meaning of a term. At the same time, in learning how to use a language, "language conveys to the individual an already prepared system of ideas, classifications, relations" [21]. Being part of a language community implies following the conventions of the language, and the conventions are both strengthened and adapted in actual use on a conversation-by-conversation basis.

Semiotics

Both Peirce and De Saussure are often considered to be founding fathers of modern semiotics, the science of the (use of) signs. However, the two represent quite different strands of semiotics. De Saussure was focussed on the linguistic sign "which exists in the speaker's mind as a paring of *significant* (sound pattern) with *signifié* (concept)" and insisted that language as a linguistic system "be studied as synchronic phenomenon (i.e. without reference to the passage of time" [27]. In contrast, for Peirce a sign could be anything: "a sign, or *representamen*, is something which stands to somebody for something in some respect or capacity" [28]. As Short has analysed, in Peirce's later theory "the purposefulness of semiosis is rooted in the interpreter, not in signs or their objects ... The sign's 'action' therefore depends on its relevance to the purposes of an agent; only so does it have an effect" [29]. De Saussure is looking into static linguistic structures, Peirce is analysing semiosis as an action, as the purposeful interpretation of some representamen as sign in a context.

Like Peirce's theories, Van Heusden's semiotic theory is embedded in a general theory of cognition, and more specific "about the cognitive mechanisms of human culture" [30]. He distinguishes between memorised/generalised form and actual percept, which will never be identical. In routine cases the difference is negligible and the perception will be treated as a specimen of the general form and will trigger the associated habitual reaction. In other cases, however, you experience the difference, you are aware of the form not being adequate for your actual perception, and you have "to find, choose or make meaning". To borrow an example from Piaget [31]: for a young child the form "bird" may first be associated with the individual familiar canary at home. Later on, it will experience the same form being used for another canary and learn to distinguish "this bird" from other "birds". Still later, it will learn to extend the form to species (not all of them capable of flight!). In other words: in the cognitive mind forms (words, terms, concepts) develop over time as a consequence of interacting with the outside physical and social world.

In 1866, the mathematician and population thinker (before the term existed) John Venn observed about recurring events in the world: "the series we actually meet will show a changeable type, and the individuals of them will sometimes transgress their licensed irregularity. They have to be pruned a little into shape, as natural objects *always* have before they are capable of being accurately reasoned about. The form in which the series emerges is that of a series with a fixed type, and with its unwarranted irregularities omitted. This imaginary or ideal series is the basis of our [inferences]" (citation from Verburgt's biography [32]). Venn's metaphor is nice, individual occurrences have to be pruned a little bit into shape to fit in a general form. There is no such thing as lossless reduction of the particular to the general, but as long as the variability of the individual is within the limits of their 'licensed irregularity' we are just fine. It is only when the individual transgresses that boundary when we are aware of a not-negligible difference and semiosis occurs.

5.3   Perception and Cognition

Now, the question is "what do we know about our Merkwelt and Wirkwelt?" (or, as a requirements engineer might put it: "please tell me exactly what you use for input information, and what you do with that information"). The psychologist Selz, a contemporary of Von Uexküll, objected against the predominant passive and mere causal view of perception [33, 34]. According to Selz, perception is an active process, constrained by our physiological structures and controlled by the task-on-hand and anticipation. In the 1930s De Groot founded his study of chess thinking on the theoretical work of Selz and found: "The chess player is concerned with moves on the board, with movements and maneuvers, with spatial relationships, and with the dynamics of captures, threats, and control – all of which can be objects of perception, imagination, and thought, without any dependence on verbal formulations and concepts. ... the choice of a good move rests largely on *foreseen possibilities* for action and on the evaluation of their *foreseen results*." [35]. Perception and thinking are oriented towards answers, actions, results; not passive causal responses to sense data. His findings also match the general notion of signs or forms in semiotics, not limited to 'verbal formulations and concepts'.

The approach of Selz and De Groot is corroborated by modern neurological research in perception and cognition [36, 37] The distributed character of processing visual information in the brain is described by Weiszkrantz in his analysis of 'blindsight' (a phenomenon where people who are functionally blind are still capable of residual visual perception): "the major target of the eye in its connection to the brain lies at the back of the brain ... in a region of the cortex known as 'striate cortex' or 'V1' ... but it is not the only pathway ... In fact, the eye connects in parallel to 9 other targets in the brain aside from V1, although of course these pathways interact with each other + via other connexions." [37]. So, the sensoric-motoric functional cycles as posited by Von Uexküll, Selz and De Groot are embedded in highly distributed, interrelated and non-linear processes in the brain. Next question: how are such capabilities developed in the individual?

The neuroscientist Edelman applies in his theory of neuronal Darwinism the principles of variation and selection on the development of the brain. "The theory of neuronal group selection was formulated to explain a number of apparent inconsistencies in our knowledge of the development, anatomy, and physiological function of the central nervous system. Above all, it was formulated to explain how perceptual categorization could occur without assuming that the world is prearranged in an informational fashion or that the brain contains a homunculus ... the theory proposes that the key principle governing brain organization is a populational one and that in its operation the brain is a selective system." [38] The brain organises itself by a process of variation and selection of neuronal groups.

Eve Marder has shown that even on the level of the individual neuron its behaviour can be quite complex and variable: "each cell type has a repertoire of possibilities that are expressed under different conditions of neuromodulation" [39]. Her research has shown that a tiny group of 30 neurons (with 13 different cell types) exhibits staggering complex behaviour, which shows that the picture of the brain based on neurons as simple and stable functional units is much too simple.

6 Information in Business and Business Processes

6.1 Information in Business

Being recognisable and not faceless is important in business: why should your customer do business with you and not with your competitor? Individuality matters, as witnessed by Kay's concept of distinctive capabilities. All the same, a business transaction has many general and standardised elements, partly regulated by commercial law, that can be converted easily into predefined IDs and quantities in an IT system: Who? (customer, supplier, transporter, sales agent, ...); Where? (loading address, unloading address, invoice address, visiting address, ...); What? (item codes, this might already be a bit tricky); When? (at what date/time will the product be delivered, less clear in case of services); How much? (quantity of product, 'quantity of service'); what price (price, unit-of-pricing). Specifying the "what?" can be tricky because expectations and actual delivery may differ (was the battery included or not?). In some cases, the product or service has some variability, e.g. specific product characteristics (for fresh fish: how fresh? How fat? What size?) or delivery time (what is the bandwidth? Perhaps an agreement was made to provide a notification prior to arrival?). Such information about mutual expectations between business partners is much more in the realm of social sign systems. Recall that patterns of behaviour might first result in expectations and later taken tacitly as business commitments (the order for customer P is always prepared before the order for customer F, as a consequence customer P gets the better service level).

Elements of business transactions as viewed by classical contracts are mostly general and fit well in IT systems. Distinctive capabilities of a company which establish its competitive position are about mutual expectations based on patterns and on behaviour under incidental adverse circumstances. Such relational information does not fit in IT systems; more than that, they often cannot even be fully written down in natural language. It is about organisational culture, how things are done and how problems are dealt with. Newcomers in the organisation need time to grow into it, tuning their Merkwelt and Wirkwelt to their new environment. To use a neurological metaphor: similar to the not fully understood but significant way neurohormones modulate neural behaviour, organisational culture modulates staff behaviour.

6.2   Information in Business Processes

In business processes ("a set of activities that are performed in coordination in an organizational and technical environment … jointly realizing a business goal" [40]) individual cases are mostly processed in standardised shape, to make processes efficient, reliable, flexible, fast. Working with 'individual cases pruned a little into shape' ('forms', 'signs') is a capability of humans and computers alike. This is foundational for both human reasoning and for information processing in IT systems. Working with fixed types (standardised forms, shapes) makes business processes efficient. It makes IT very powerful in processing routine cases in business processes.

However, that is not the complete story. The other part is about the task of pruning real-world individual cases into the shape of general types, a task for the user when inputting data. Most of the time, this pruning into shape is not a problem, it is just a routine act. However, sometimes the concrete situation at hand simply does not fit into the shapes or general forms offered by the IT system, or it fits into several forms simultaneously and the user has to choose one. An example might be a property named "transaction-date". Imagine a factory where the night shift runs from 11PM – 7AM. The changeover to a new production order is scheduled at around 11:45 PM. A transaction with a time stamp of 11:34PM belongs to the night shift of the new date but the production order of the previous date. A transaction with a timestamp of 11:53PM has both a shift date and a production date of the next day, different from the date of the timestamp. The date used to calculate the expiry date might change at yet another moment. As always in IT, once you explain a problem clearly, someone will explain how this should have been foreseen and solved in the IT system. But that is not the point. The point is that in operational business processes the user will meet situations that do not fit neatly into the available fixed shapes offered by the IT system. To what extent will the IT system allow for and support the user in finding non-standard solutions to resolve such mismatches in the interest of the business? When "lossless" pruning into shape is not possible, and the IT system forces the user to make a choice, what are the consequences for the business?

Users working with the output of IT systems have a kind of mirror problem: how to apply the standardised information provided by the IT system to the concrete situation at hand? In the example above, what does 'scheduled changeover time: 11:45PM' mean for the supervisor's work on the shop floor? Without IT, the planner could have told the line supervisor "the next order will start shortly before midnight" (or perhaps: "is expected to start", which provides different information to the supervisor). It will not be an exact time, but how much leeway is allowed? What is normal variability, what is a significant deviation that should be reported (and to whom)? It all depends on the context, in one situation a deviation of 45 min might be irrelevant (because of the excess processing capacity available further down the line), in another situation 8 min might be critical. Users need other information to interpret such data adequately, and that other information can be found in general habits or protocols, or in specific information for that particular changeover by memos or face-to-face communication. Supervisors are also expected to use their senses (literally!), their expertise and their judgment to interpret the combination of concrete situation and data in a standardised 'context-free' form.

One additional remark: the rationale of business processes is to serve business, to fulfil the commitments of commercial business transactions. Sometimes processes have to be flexible in order to get required results. Every production plant knows about tensions between sales, logistics, planning and the shop floor. Flexibility and improvisation are important in solving such tensions, bureaucratic responses are generally not helpful. Human creative capability to "prune a little into shape" in irregular situations is important for getting results here. This was a clear competitive capability of the company in the story above.

6.3 Information Analysis in Business Processes

In order to analyse general properties of information Boisot has developed the concept of the three-dimensional Information Space. Its three axes represent the degree of abstraction, the degree of codification, and the degree of diffusion of information. "Codification and abstraction, often working in tandem, both reduce the data-processing load on an agent, whether individual or organizational. They also facilitate communication processes and hence the diffusion of information whether inside or across boundaries" [41] All important aspects of information are present in this concept. Standardisation is about both abstraction and codification and facilitates diffusion. Personal knowledge and experience, on the other hand, is much more concrete, non-codified and much harder to communicate. With the exception of craftsmen, most businesses today will heavily depend on highly codified information processed by IT systems (being a formal sign system), combined with more ad hoc concrete information that travels either up and down the organisational hierarchy or laterally in the form of mutual adjustment (using social sign systems such as natural language, pictures, drawings, etc.). I will designate the first kind as strongly coded information, and the second kind as weakly coded information, the designations to be understood as indicative for two sides on a continuum rather than as a rigid opposition. In other words: the twin designations are by itself an example of weakly coded information.

Fundamental to analysis of information in business processes are two simple questions:

– What information does an actor (either a human, a physical machine or a control system) need in order to do a proper job?
– What information does an actor (see above) need to make available so that actors in downstream processes can do their jobs properly?

The two questions are about all relevant information, regardless whether strongly or weakly coded. For order fulfilment the amount to be delivered is an example of strongly coded information, allowable under- or overshoot is often weakly coded. When the customer asks for "all you have got" of an article, the ordered quantity is weakly coded.

Later on, the delivered quantity will be strongly coded (a precise quantity), the service level in this case can be argued about but cannot be calculated. Generally speaking, the understanding of "doing a proper job" in a concrete case will depend on an interpretation of the situation on hand.

6.4 Information Systems: Two Views

To exemplify the issues about kinds of information discussed above, think of a production company with three main types of processes in its daily operational affairs: doing business (sales), planning and control, and shopfloor (primary processes). The three groups can be visualised as layers (Fig. 1). Sales orders (actual or expected) are the basis for the planning of shop floor jobs, the planning itself based on complicated algorithms taking into account delivery times, lead times, resources, capacities and other constraints. This type of view on information systems is focused on strongly coded information and has a strong emphasis on IT solutions.

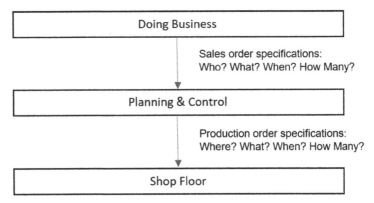

Fig. 1. Information System Type I: Strongly structured processes and information

However, this is not the full story of information in an organisation. Shop floor processes will be executed against background knowledge of how to understand the strongly coded and precise data about date, time, article, quantity. Shop floor staff must know about tolerances, margins, slack. The other way round, sales staff must have background knowledge about production and production costs in order to do their job properly. Based on this background knowledge, sales will occasionally provide additional information to draw attention to specific requirements of certain orders, products or customers. The shop floor will give feedback to sales about actual production results and provide explanation why some results were not according to expectations. Such information flows will be partly based on strongly coded information along the lines depicted in Fig. 1, and partly based on a second view on information systems based on mutual adjustment by exchanging weakly coded information in the triangle sales – planning & control – shop floor as depicted in Fig. 2.

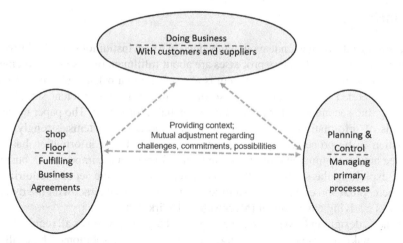

Fig. 2. Information System Type II: weakly structured processes and information

In companies, both structures will be present simultaneously: strongly structured standardised business processes connected by strongly coded information, and complementary coordination/adjustment structures for exchanging supplementary weakly coded information. Organisations that focus too much on the first structures are in danger of being rigid at the expense of flexibility, organisations that rely too much on informal mutual adjustment are in danger of being too dependent on personal knowledge and might have a lower efficiency.

In business modelling it is important to keep an eye on both Type I and Type II structures, and to find the right balance between strongly coded and weakly coded information in business processes. Software design will be about the design of the logical machine for processing strongly coded information. Between business modelling and software design there should be an intermediate step of information system design, where higher level design decisions are made about (1) what information is best strongly coded and what weakly coded, (2) how to combine the two types of information in actual operations.

One of the major risks of IT projects in organisations is that it implies a shift from weakly coded to strongly coded information for which the organisation was not prepared. This might result in disturbance of operational processes because of missing information (a consequence of reduction to strongly coded information), or a lack of coherence between information in the IT system and the information in the physical and social world of the IT users (a consequence of disregarding their Merkwelt and Wirkwelt).

A final point about awareness: some weakly coded information is not about giving specific instructions but rather about "please be aware of the following circumstances". As a consequence of such messages, staff will be aware of both situation and of the intentions of colleagues, which will have an impact on their Merkwelt and Wirkwelt. This is the crucial difference between the behaviour of an IT system (or a perfect bureaucrat) and a committed human.

7 Conclusion

Business is a goal-oriented endeavour, embedded in social institutions, and sensitive to a dynamic environment. Business processes are about fulfilment of business agreements. Designing a business information system is about striking a balance between strongly and weakly coded information. The first kind is important for efficient standardised processing, the second kind for providing contextual information. The paper discusses two kinds of information relevant for business information systems, strongly coded information to be processed by IT systems and weakly based information based on form-free human communication. Both kinds of information are important in business, the first exploiting the strengths of the computer world and the second requiring the human perceptual and cognitive capabilities of interacting to interact with the dynamic and always evolving environment (Merkwelt and Wirkwelt).

Business, designing IT systems and controlling business processes all require human awareness, making sense of the challenges and finding viable solutions. The challenge in business is how to use the capabilities of the computer world in combination with the human capabilities of sense making and of dealing with conflicting norms. The paper makes the case for information system development based on two views on information processes, processing different kinds of information and using different structures of communication. Future work will focus on further researching this notion of the dual structure in information system development.

References

1. Von Uexküll, J.: A Foray into the Worlds of Animals and Humans. University of Minnesota Press, Minnesota (2010)
2. Gartner Glossary. https://www.gartner.com/en/information-technology/glossary/context-aware-computing-2. last accessed 16 May 2023
3. Daft, R.L.: Organization Theory and Design, 7th edn. South-Western College Publishing, Cincinatti (2001)
4. Kay, J.: Foundations of Corporate Success. Oxford University Press, Oxford (1993)
5. Coase, R.: The Nature of the Firm. In: Williamson, O.E., Winter, S.G. (eds.) The Nature of the Firm. Oxford University Press, Oxford (1993)
6. Garner, B.A. (ed.): Black's Law Dictionary, 8th edn. Thomson West, St. Paul (2004)
7. Calamari, J.D., Perillo, J.M.: Contracts, 2nd edn. West Publishing Co. St. Paul (1977)
8. MacNeil, I.R.: The New Social Contract. Yale University Press, New Haven (1980)
9. De Geus, A.: The Living Company. Nicholas Brealey Publishing, London (1997)
10. Michaud, C., Thoenig, J.C.: Making Strategy and Organization Compatible. Palgrave, Basingstoke (2003)
11. Tanenbaum, A.S.: Structured Computer Organization. Prentice Hall International, London (1976)
12. Dijkstra, E.W.: The tide, not the waves. In: Denning, P.J., Metcalfe, R.M. (eds.) Beyond Calculation – The Next Fifty Years of Computing. Springer Verlag, New York (1997). https://doi.org/10.1007/978-1-4612-0685-9_4
13. Codd, E.F.: The Relational Model for Database Management, Version 2. Addison Wesley, Reading (1990)
14. De Brock, E.O., Smedinga, R.: Creating an OO Specification from a Conceptual Specification (in Press)

15. Mayr, E.: What Evolution Is. Basic Books, New York (2001)
16. Wittgenstein, L.: Tractatus Logico-Philosophicus. Translated from the German by Ogden, C.K.. Routledge, Oxon (2005, original edition by Routledge 1922)
17. De Saussure, F.: Course in General Linguistics. McGraw-Hill, New York (1966)
18. Chomsky, N.: Aspects of the Theory of Syntax. MIT Press, Cambridge (1965)
19. Morris, C.: Writings on the General Theory of Signs. Mouton, The Hague (1971)
20. Bianchi, C.: Semantics and pragmatics: the distinction reloaded. In: Bianchi, C. (ed.) The Semantics/Pragmatics Distinction. CSLI Publications, Stanford (2004)
21. Austin, J.L.: How to Do Things with Words, 2nd edn. Harvard University Press, Cambridge MA (1978)
22. Searle, J.R.: Speech Acts. Cambridge University Press, Cambridge (1969)
23. Grice, P.: Studies in the Ways of Words. Harvard University Press, Cambridge (1989)
24. Searle, J.R.: The Construction of Social Reality. Allen Lane, London (1995)
25. Baker, G.P., Hacker, P.M.S.: Wittgenstein Understanding and Meaning – Part I Essays, 2nd edn. Wiley-Blackwell, Chichester (2009)
26. Ludlow, P.: Living Words. Oxford University Press, Oxford (2014)
27. Cobley, P.: The Routledge Companion to Semiotics. Routledge, London (2010)
28. Hartshorne, C., Weiss, P. (eds.): Collected Papers of Charles Sanders Peirce. Thoemmes Press, Bristol (1998)
29. Short, T.L.: Peirce's Theory of Signs. Cambridge University Press, Cambridge (2007)
30. Heusden, B.P.: The Trias Semiotica (in Press)
31. Piaget, J.: The Psychology of Intelligence. Routledge & Kegan Paul Ltd, London (1950)
32. Verburgt, L.M.: John Venn – A Life in Logic. The University of Chicago Press, Chicago (2022)
33. Selz, O.: Wahrnehmungsaufbau und Denkprozeß – ausgewählte Schriften. Verlag Hans Huber, Bern (1991)
34. Selz, O.: Zur Psychologie des produktiven Denkens und des Irrtums. Verlag Friedrich Cohen, Bonn (1922)
35. De Groot, A.D.: Thought and Choice in Chess. Mouton, The Hague (1965)
36. Milner, A.D., Goodale, M.A.: The Visual Brain in Action. Oxford University Press, Oxford (1995)
37. Weiszkrantz, L.: Consciousness Lost and Found. Oxford University Press, Oxford (1997)
38. Edelman, G.M.: Neural Darwinism. Basic Books, New York (1987)
39. Nassim, C.: Lessons from the Lobster – Eve Marder's Work in Neuroscience. MIT Press, Cambridge (2018)
40. Weske, M.: Business Process Management. Springer Verlag, Heidelberg (2007). https://doi.org/10.1007/978-3-540-73522-9
41. Boisot, M.H.: Knowledge Assets. Oxford University Press, Oxford (1998)

Incorporating Trust into Context-Aware Services

Boris Shishkov[1,2,3]([⊠]), Hans-Georg Fill[4], Krassimira Ivanova[1], Marten van Sinderen[5], and Alexander Verbraeck[6]

[1] Institute of Mathematics and Informatics, Bulgarian Academy of Sciences, Sofia, Bulgaria
b.b.shishkov@iicrest.org, kivanova@math.bas.bg

[2] Faculty of Information Sciences, University of Library Studies and Information Technologies, Sofia, Bulgaria

[3] Institute IICREST, Sofia, Bulgaria

[4] Digitalization and Information Systems Group, University of Fribourg, Fribourg, Switzerland
hans-georg.fill@unifr.ch

[5] Faculty of Electrical Engineering, Mathematics and Computer Science, University of Twente, Enschede, The Netherlands
m.j.vansinderen@utwente.nl

[6] Faculty of Technology, Policy, and Management, Delft University of Technology, Delft, The Netherlands
a.verbraeck@tudelft.nl

Abstract. Enabling technologies concerning hardware, networking, and sensing have inspired the development of context-aware IT services. These adapt to the situation of the user, such that service provisioning is specific to his/her corresponding needs. We have seen successful applications of context-aware services in healthcare, well-being, and smart homes. It is, however, always a question what level of trust the users can place in the fulfillment of their needs by a certain IT-service. Trust has two major variants: policy-based, where a reputed institution provides guarantees about the service, and reputation-based, where other users of the service provide insight into the level of fulfillment of user needs. Services that are accessible to a small and known set of users typically use policy-based trust only. Services that have a wide community of users can use reputation-based trust, policy-based trust, or a combination. For both types of trust, however, context awareness poses a problem. Policy-based trust works within certain boundaries, outside of which no guarantees can be given about satisfying the user needs, and context awareness can push a service out of these boundaries. For reputation-based trust, the fact that users in a certain context were adequately served, does not mean that the same would happen when the service adapts to another user's needs. In this paper we consider the incorporation of trust into context-aware services, by proposing an ontological conceptualization for user-system trust. Analyzing service usage data for context parameters combined with the ability to fulfill user needs can help in eliciting components for the ontology.

Keywords: Context awareness · Trust · Data analytics

B. Shishkov (Ed.): BMSD 2023, LNBIP 483, pp. 92–109, 2023.
https://doi.org/10.1007/978-3-031-36757-1_6

1   Introduction

Many service-based IT systems interact with the user in a pre-defined manner to execute their tasks [1–3]. This is a reflection of a fixed set of corresponding user needs that are hence considered "static", at least for the particular servicing time frame [4]. Nevertheless, user needs may be highly dynamic and are often evolving over time. **Context awareness** improves IT services, by the development of *systems that adapt their servicing to the situation and/or needs of the user* [5–9] – this conceptual vision has been conceived in the 1990s [16, 17]. Still, it took one decade since then for enabling technologies to become available, namely developments in *hardware*, such as device miniaturization combined with low power consumption, in *networking*, such as high-bandwidth wireless communication and positioning-related capabilities, and in *sensing*, such as miniaturized sensors for many different phenomena and the availability of sensor networks [2, 10].

When using a service, the user wants to have a certain *guarantee* in advance that the service "will offer what it promises". Said otherwise, the service is expected to be able to *satisfy the user needs in the relevant contexts*. We can call this the **trust** *of the user in the service and/or in the system*. Two concepts of trust exist: policy-based, where a reputable organization provides guarantees about the fitness-for-purpose of the service, and reputation-based, where other users share their experiences with the use of the service with new users [11, 12]. *Policy-based trust* and *reputation-based trust* are used in different types of environments. Services that are accessible only to a small and defined set of users, such as back-office services and services for critical infrastructures, typically use *policy-based trust* only. *Reputation-based trust* would not make sense here, since the group of users is small, and users usually do not have a choice whether to use the service or not. Services that are open to a large and more heterogeneous group of users, such as commercial services offered through Web platforms, can make use of *reputation-based trust*, usually combined with some form of *policy-based trust*. Examples why *policy-based trust* is still needed when *reputation-based trust* is present, are issues with faking the reputation scores, e.g., by buying clicks, showing fake reviews, or manipulating reputation scores shown to the users. Hence, a good reputation score combined with trust in the organization offering the score, established through *policy-based trust*, helps in addressing these issues.

Nevertheless, a problem emerges when **combining either of the two types of trust with context awareness** since neither the *policy-based*, nor the *reputation-based trust* concept can give the guarantee of fulfilling the user needs anymore. With servicing adapting to the user *context*, applying *policy-based trust* may be challenging because the "envelope" of that *context* would often appear to be unknown or ill-defined. Hence, the *context* could go out-of-bounds to address a contextual situation that was not foreseen at design time. For *reputation-based trust*, the fact that the *reputation* was excellent in *context A* of using a service does not mean that when the service adapts to *context B*, it would also be excellent. Thus, we argue that trust, in a sense, assumes a constant and stable service offering, whereas context-aware services can adapt to the context, thereby "breaching" the assumptions on which that trust was based.

Policy-based trust is about restricting access and confining usability, because of its assumptions for rigorous designs that constrain the service within the boundaries of what was specified beforehand. Hence, this may substantially hamper the use of *context-aware* servicing principles and a question to answer is: ***How can we allow for context awareness in services governed by a policy-based trust principle***?

Further, for systems governed by *reputation-based trust*, *context awareness* causes two types of "surprises": (i) The wider use of a service as a result of *context awareness* may lead to situations that have not been anticipated at design time; (ii) The broader access to services would reduce *trust* because it is often unclear in what *context* the existing *reputation* score has been obtained. Users would become dissatisfied if the service does not satisfy their need in their specific *context* in spite of the fact that the *reputation* scores (based on other *contexts*) suggest otherwise. This leads to a second question to answer: ***How can reputation-based trust be implemented in a context-aware service***?

The first research question takes the *policy-based trust* as a given and looks at solutions in terms of how to implement *context awareness* in a more rigorously governed service system. In contrast, the second research question takes *context awareness* as a given and looks at what strategies for *reputation-based trust* would be effective for *context-aware* systems. The solution direction proposed in this paper concerns an **ontological conceptualization** that carefully defines elements of *context* and elements of *trust*, using the same ontological base, allowing for reasoning across the involved technical areas. We claim that this conceptualization could work to address the issues in both research questions, since they both address the integration of *context awareness* and the two dominant *trust* models.

This way of modeling can be assisted by *data analytics* concerning the service usage – based on historic data, user entities can be clustered and *context* situations can be predicted, as well as *trust*-related attitudes and the user perception of service quality. Service performance indicators can help in making such predictions [33]. *Machine learning* [13] (for example: *Bayesian modeling*) and *covering/clustering algorithms* can then partition the *context-aware* usage space into sub-spaces for which different *trust* levels would apply, and provide suggestions for boundaries for the *context* parameters, outside of which the service should not be used when a minimum *trust* level should be attained. Of course, one should be careful with fully automating these predictions, as a future situation might differ significantly from those described by historic data.

Note that in addition to *user-system* trust (the user's trust in the system), three other forms of trust exist: *system-user* trust (the system's trust in the user), *user-user* trust (trust that users of a system have in each other), and *system-system* trust (trust of systems in other systems on which they are dependent). In this work, we just focus on user-system (or user-service) trust.

The remainder of the current paper is structured as follows: Sect. 2 presents a conceptual model of context awareness, applying a functional perspective and taking into consideration related work. Section 3 provides rigorous definitions of trust concepts and the dimensions of trust strategies. In Sect. 4 we present our proposed ontology-driven conceptualization, partially justified by an example as well as by a discussion addressing some benefits and limitations of our propfosal (Sect. 5). We conclude the paper in Sect. 6.

2   Context Awareness

Among what has inspired us in considering *context awareness* are works and discussions of Albrecht Schmidt, such as [15] and our previous work, such as [3]. What determines the notion of *"context awareness"*? In our view, this is innate with regard to our smart human behavior, for example: a person would navigate his/her way around without being familiar with the place; or: a teacher would switch his/her phone to silent mode when in class. In contrast, any machine or computer device is "blind" for the *context*, for example: a mobile phone would ring whether or not the owner is busy; or: a laptop may be forced to restart no matter if this is convenient for the user or not. Hence, human beings are *context-aware* by nature and one would not even notice this, while to date many computer systems do not have such capabilities. For this reason, it is necessary that we DESIGN computer systems in such a way that they are capable of *perceiving the real world and acting upon what they interpret from it*. We have inspiring examples in this direction from the years since the new millennium: (i) The navigation system of a smart phone is an example of *context awareness* since the GPS-receiver of the phone allows for its "knowing" where it is and guiding the user; (ii) Related to the previous example concerning a smart phone: a driver could be diverted to avoid a "sensed" traffic jam, counting on the phone's location data and broader *context* that is captured (and used); (iii) There are house lighting systems, counting on sensors for establishing whether it is dark *and* somebody is moving (i.e., present) in the house. Of course, one can go from a *"context-aware"* mode to an *"explicit use"* mode - for example: one would fix the lighting to "on" if there are maintenance works in the building. Hence, *context awareness* is about making the usage of technology easier, by *freeing users from doing things that the system can do as well*. The above examples show that some useful realizations of this are currently present. Nevertheless, they stem from ideas that point back to the early 1990s, when the inspiring scientist and visioner Mark Weiser stated (in his '91 essay entitled "The Computer for the 21st Century", further reflected in [16]) that "specialized elements of hardware and software, connected by wires, radio waves and infrared, will be so ubiquitous that no one will notice their presence". This has paved the way to a discipline, labelled "ubiquitous computing" that in turn pushed towards what is currently labelled as *"context-aware computing"* or *"context awareness"*, as explicitly used by Bill Schilit already in 1995 [17]. All those concepts have been carefully addressed by relevant scientists in 2009 [18] where Anind Dey summarized what was widely agreed upon by then [19]:

- Since situational information, such as facial expressions, emotions, past and future events, the existence of others around, and relationships to them are crucial for humans to understand what is occurring, it is necessary to improve the "language" that humans can use to interact with computers.
- It is also necessary to increase the amount of situational information, or *context*, that is made available to computers.
- *Context* is defined as: any information that can be used to characterize the situation of an entity.

- A system is *context-aware* if it uses *context* to provide relevant information and/or services to the user, where relevancy depends on the user's task.

Considering this, we have introduced *three categories* of *context-aware* systems, with regard to adaptive service delivery [14], where the following adaptation perspectives are possible: serving *user needs*; *system needs*; and *public values*.

We argue that the abovementioned scientists (namely: Weiser, Schilit, Dey, and Schmidt) are the pioneers in the area of *context-aware computing*. In addition, other relevant works (authored by them and other scientists) have helped to further improve our understanding of the notion of *context* and to make serious progress in the development of *context-aware applications* [1, 5, 20, 21]. Finally, we have considered relevant R&D *context awareness* projects, such as CyberDesk [22], AWARENESS [2, 23], and SECAS [24] to get further insight. Our observation is that most projects follow bottom-up (*technology-driven*) developments (as opposed to *user-centric* developments); we consider this a serious obstacle with regard to adequately conceptualizing *context awareness*.

Other relevant literature contains for instance the useful survey of Alegre et al. [7] that is mainly focused on the development of *context-aware applications* as well as on the consideration of *public values*. The same holds for the works of Alférez and Pelechano [8] – they consider the dynamic evolution of *context-aware systems*, the development itself, and the relation to *web services*. The latter holds also for the *service-orientation perspective* as proposed by Abeywickrama [9]. In line with the abovementioned observation, all these works take a primarily *technology-driven perspective* and are less concerned with the *user perspective*. The same holds for other works touching upon the *adaptive delivery of services*, always considered in a bottom-up perspective, featuring *decision-making* [25], *safety* of stakeholders [26], and *routing* [27]. The technology-driven perspective is also visible in the *systematic literature review* in the doctoral thesis of Van Engelenburg [28].

We therefore conclude the following: As it concerns the *conceptual perspective*, not much has been added after Mark Weiser - 1991. As it concerns the *1991–2023 developments*, they mainly concern *enabling technologies* and their successful relevant implementations. We see **room for improvement concerning the user perspective** and the **alignment between context awareness and data analytics**, for the sake of providing **new ways of context gathering** that also concerns a possible *prediction of context situations and/or user preferences/attitudes*.

As already mentioned, *users* often have *needs evolving over time* that relate to corresponding *context situations*. *Context-aware systems* are expected to be providing **context-specific services to users in accordance with their context-dependent needs**. When delivering services, the *system* would interact with the *context*. Hence, not only *collecting data on the context* is important but also *delivering a service* that *matches* the *context*. The fact that the *service* is delivered to a *user* means that the user is part of the *context*; *context-aware* service delivery concerns the connection between what the *context* is and what a *user* needs. Hence, considering the above from a functional perspective gives two key processes that often go one after another, namely **situation determination** and **behavior adaptation**, as suggested by Fig. 1.

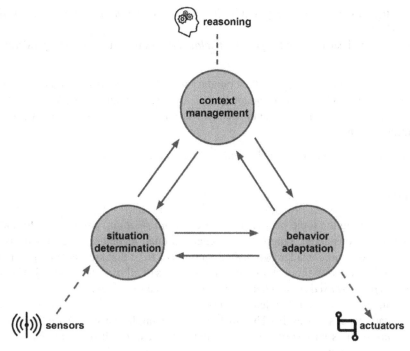

Fig. 1. Context awareness – a functional perspective

As shown in the figure: (a) *Situation determination* is often supported by *sensors*; we assume this in the current paper, acknowledging nevertheless that there may be also other ways of determining the (user) situation, for example: supported by *data analytics* and *predictive modeling* [13, 33, 34]. Hence, the (user) situation is determined using incoming sensor data, by *inferring higher-level context information*. (b) *Behavior adaptation* is needed such that *service delivery* is *aligned* with the *context situation* and corresponding *(user) needs*. This has effect on what the system is "doing", materialized by *actuators*. (c) *Context management* is needed to align incoming (sensor) data and the corresponding system behavior adaptation. This assumes *reasoning*, as illustrated in the figure, that is two-fold: (c$_1$) When a situation is determined, it should be established to which corresponding (user) needs it points and when this is not straightforward (because of precision-related and/or other issues) then the "*context manager*" may "ask" for more interpretation "attempts" (that is why the arrows between *situation determination* and *context management* are in both directions). (c$_2$) When the actual (user) needs are established, the "*context manager*" would "ask" the system to adapt its servicing accordingly and when the *behavior adaptation* requires more and/or more precise information, then the system would ask the "*context manager*" to provide more information (that is why the arrows between *context management* and *behavior adaptation* are in both directions).

Finally, there are arrows in both directions between *behavior adaptation* and *situation determination*, to indicate that implementing a behavior adaptation may require *real-time sensor data* (for example: concerning an actual location) and sometimes refining data featuring the (user) situation may require *information concerning actuators' operation being updated.*

As mentioned earlier in the paper, *trust-related issues* referring to *context awareness* are:

- The system could adapt beyond the boundary where it can be trusted and user-system trust before and after behavior adaptation of the system could be different.
- *Reputation* scores can have been provided for other *contexts* than the one the user is currently facing.

The next section provides an elaboration concerning *trust*.

3 Trust

When approaching the topic of *trust* in the area of *information systems*, a multitude of aspects can be considered, ranging from organizational, technical to legal aspects. In the following we will consider two main directions of *trust* that are essential pillars for many current systems without claiming exhaustiveness of all *trust* aspects [11]. The first direction is **policy-based trust** where access to information or services is regulated via some technical means and thus leads to *trust* by restricting the access to information to particular (groups of) users. This includes for example the use of *authentication mechanisms* such as passwords or digital signatures. The result of *policy-based trust* is the issuance of a permission to access a resource or the denial of that access. More fine-grained variants may be defined, e.g. for further detailing the types of permissions issued and also non-functional aspects – e.g. whether data is secure – could be added.

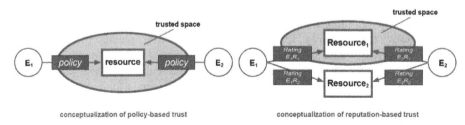

Fig. 2. Policy-based trust vs reputation-based trust

For conceptualizing this relationship, we can describe two *entities* (E_1 and E_2) that have access to a *resource* via a common *policy*. The *trusted space* is thus defined through this policy that is the same for all entities, see Fig. 2 – left.

The second direction is denoted as **reputation-based trust**. Here, the level of *trust* into a resource is calculated based on some kind of *reputation* assigned by other entities - either of the same or a different kind. Examples include *rating systems* for resources such as websites, documents, or products - either *explicitly* (via ratings by users) or *implicitly* (via references). The result of *reputation-based trust* is thus not a binary decision but rather a gradual description of how much *trust* can be placed in some resource, see Fig. 2 - right.

This can be conceptualized as follows: Two *entities* E_1 and E_2 which access *resources* R_1 and R_2 each conduct a *rating* of each *resource*, i.e. Rating E_1R_1 indicates that entity E_1 has rated resource R_1 with some numerical value. The combination of all ratings for a resource R_i from all entities E_i then defines the *trusted space*. The combination of the ratings may either be defined *centrally*, e.g. by the provider of the resource, or in a *decentralized fashion*, i.e. by each entity.

We can further distinguish between different **trust strategies** [12]. In an *optimistic strategy*, it is assumed that trustful resources are the default. Only if a violation or deviation occurs, further actions are needed. In a *pessimistic strategy*, trust is restricted unless a reason is given for not doing so. The *centralized strategy* proposes to use central organizations in which trust is placed. The *investigative strategy* requires entities to conduct their own investigations for deciding about their trust in resources. In a *transitive strategy*, delegation to other entities for determining trust in a resource is assumed. Finally, for the sake of exhaustiveness, we would like to mention the extreme example where the user would distrust anything unless rules indicate trust in a resource can be granted – we refer to this as *"zero-trust strategy"* [35].

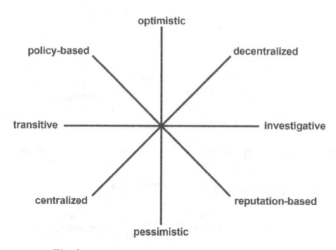

Fig. 3. An example of combining trust strategies

To briefly exemplify the above, we consider earth observations in different countries: (i) When they are governed by a state organization and concern everyday-life-related prognoses/warnings, earth observation centers would count on monolithic architectures, leaning towards {centralized, policy-based, transitive, pessimistic} trust strategies, for instance: NESDIS [40] and JMA [41]. (ii) When observations stem from agreements of independent organizations, such as universities, companies, and so on, they would usually count on federated structures, leaning towards {decentralized, policy-based, transitive} trust strategies, for instance: EPOS [42]. (iii) Finally, when open environmental data is created, counting on community-based infrastructures, such as Sensor. Community [43], one would lean towards {decentralized, reputation-based, investigative, optimistic} trust strategies.

These five strategies may be combined as different dimensions, as exemplified in Fig. 3. If we would be combining a *policy-based strategy* with the *investigative* and the *pessimistic* strategy, then: access to resources is restricted by policies and we in general assume that *trust* is only established if the result of the policy leads to a positive outcome; in addition, we employ the *investigative strategy* whereby we can inspect ourselves whether *trust* can be placed in a resource or not, thereby probably assuming a *pessimistic* outcome first. A prerequisite for the *investigative strategy* is that all necessary information is transparently available. A typical technological solution for this latter case would be *blockchains* [44].

4   Proposed Ontology-Driven Solution Directions

Starting from a general consideration of *service provisioning*, we provide in this section *conceptual views* concerning *context awareness* and *trust*. We also consider their alignment as well as possible added value of *data analytics*.

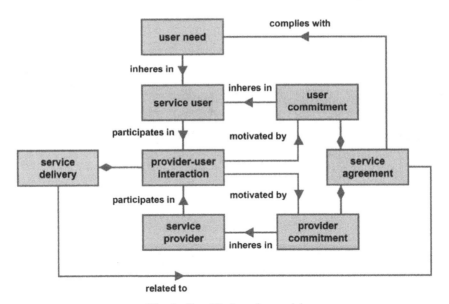

Fig. 4. Simplified service model

We are essentially focused on analyzing and/or designing enterprise information systems and in this we stick to the way of modeling suggested by Shishkov [10], which builds upon the ontological views of Dietz [31] that are in turn stemming from the systems-related views of Bunge [36]. From this perspective, we should have a **SYSTEM** under consideration, that is composed of entities interacting with other entities. Further, those entities that do not belong to the *system* but are interacting with entities of the *system* comprise the *system* **ENVIRONMENT**. Finally, instead of considering the (human) entities themselves as composition elements of a *system/environment*, we consider the **ROLES** in which they appear. Otherwise, it would be confusing considering some entities who may appear in different *roles*, including nontypical ones. With regard to *service provisioning*, we argue that two essential *roles* are **SERVICE PROVIDER** and **SERVICE USER**; each of them can be fulfilled not only by a human entity but also by an IT *system*. We are particularly interested in *service provisioning* because we claim that a **SERVICE MODEL** is needed as a basis for reasoning about **CONTEXT AWARENESS** and **TRUST**. We propose such a model (a simplified one) based on previous work [29, 30], see Fig. 4.

As seen from the figure, we focus on *service delivery*; we acknowledge that for a full account of the *service* concept, *service offering* + *service negotiation* also need to be considered. *Service delivery* starts after a *service user* and a *service provider* have reached a *service agreement*, which is composed of **COMMITMENTS** (from the side of the *service provider* and from the side of the *service user*). The *service agreement* complies with the **NEEDS** of the *service user*, assuming the *service user* has agreed upon *commitments* regarding *service delivery*, where *service delivery* consists of the execution of *provider-user interactions* aimed at fulfilling the *commitments* established in the *service agreement*.

This view is consistent with the *Language-Action Perspective* reflected in the *transaction* concept considered in the works of Dietz [31] and Shishkov [10], where interactions between parties are presented in terms of *commitments* and *negotiations* that are expressed and communicated by means of *elementary communicative acts*, such as *request*, *promise*, *state*, *accept*, and so on.

Taking all this into account and referring to our previous work - [14] (see Fig. 5 on p. 197, featuring our proposed meta-model) and [3] (see Fig. 1 on p. 122, featuring our *context awareness* conceptualization), we propose a **CONTEXT AWARENESS – TRUST CONCEPTUALIZATION** – see Fig. 5. As the figure suggests: One (human) *entity* may fulfill one or more **ROLES**, and types of *roles* (depending on the viewpoint) are **SERVICE PROVIDER / SERVICE USER, SENSOR/ACTUATOR, PROCESSOR, TRUSTOR / TRUSTEE**, and so on. One *role* is restricted by one or more **RULES** and one **REGULATION** comprises one or more *rules*; one or more *roles* are subject of one *regulation*. Going back to *entities*, they are the *composition elements* not only of our **SYSTEM** under consideration but also of its corresponding **ENVIRONMENT** (any *entity* that does not belong to a *system* but interacts with *entities* belonging to the *system* is considered part of the *system environment*; we certainly have the broader notion of **UNIVERSE-OF-DISCOURSE** to cover also *entities* that belong neither to the considered *system* nor to its *environment*). Finally, one or more *systems* are subject of a *regulation*.

Narrowing the discussion to **CONTEXT AWARENESS**, we consider the *role type* **SERVICE USER** and the *system type* **CONTEXT-AWARE SYSTEM**. A *service user* may consume one or more **SITUATION-SPECIFIC SERVICES** and one *context-aware system* is offering one or more such *services*. Then, what is the essence of a *context-aware* service delivery? It concerns the *situation-specific service* being delivered, that should fulfill a particular **NEED** of the *service user* who in turn has one or more *user needs*. Concerning this servicing, the *service user* is part of a broader **CONTEXT** that has one or more **CONTEXT SITUATIONS**. Finally, in its delivering a *situation-specific service* for the benefit of the *service user*, the *context-aware system* should be capable of detecting

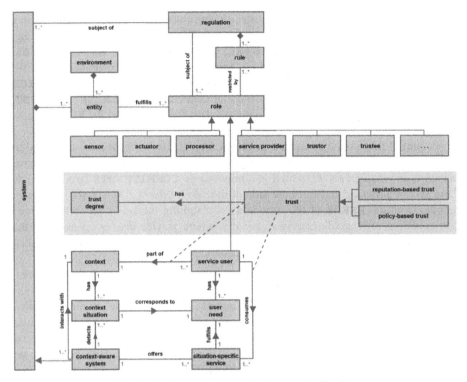

Fig. 5. Context awareness – trust conceptualization

the relevant *context-situation(s)* and this is what makes the servicing *situation-specific*, as an essential feature of *context awareness*.

How would we project *trust* in this? We have done this using the *association class* **TRUST** in two directions (see the dashed red lines in Fig. 5):

- [*service user – context* association] When a *service user* is consuming a *service*, it is to be taken into account what is his/her **TRUST DEGREE** with regard to the *context* in which (s)he is consuming the *service*.
- [*service user – situation-specific service* association] Concerning the above, it is also to be taken into account what is the **TRUST DEGREE** of the *service user* with regard to the *service* itself.

Related to this is the **TRUST DEGREE** class, as represented in the figure (actually, the quantitative perspective of *trust* may be represented using this class). We have also represented the two types of *trust* considered in the current paper, namely **POLICY-BASED TRUST** and **REPUTATION-BASED TRUST**.

And in the end, the *trust relationship* exists at the ROLE level but is driven by a corresponding ENTITY attitude. Said otherwise, it makes difference WHO is fulfilling the *service user* role. We will illustrate in Sub-Sect. 5.1 that different persons fulfilling a *role* would act differently because of different *trust attitudes* both as it concerns the *context* and the particular *service* being consumed.

In this discussion, we are taking a *viewpoint* featuring mainly the **SERVICE USER** *role* type, and it is possible to also take other relevant *trust-related viewpoints*, including a *viewpoint* featuring the **TRUSTOR** and **TRUSTEE** *role* types assuming that the *service user* is (overlaps with) the *trustor role type* and the service providing *system* is a *trustee*. Further, we consider *trust* as a complex mental state (concerning a *trustor* and a *trustee*) that is related to *beliefs* about the *capabilities* and *vulnerabilities* of the *trustee*, and of *intentions* of the *trustor* regarding a *goal* for which (s)he needs *actions* (or absence of *actions*) from the *trustee* – see Fig. 6. In considering this, we refer to related work [32].

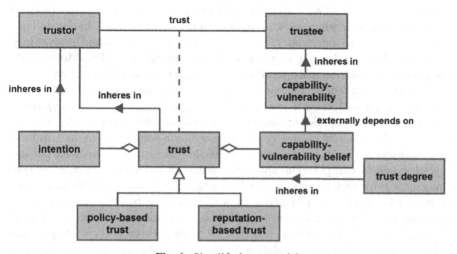

Fig. 6. Simplified trust model

Hence, in **linking trust to context-aware service delivery**, we would also consider identifying: (i) the **CAPABILITIES** and **VULNERABILITIES** of the *system* involved in the *context-aware service delivery*; (ii) how *vulnerabilities* of the *system* can be manifested by **THREAT EVENTS** that potentially cause *loss*, and how *actions* of the *service user* – motivated by the *service user's intentions* and based on his/her *trust* in the *service provider* – bring about *situations* that can trigger *threat events*.

In this regard, we have identified three challenges as follows:

- Aspects, such as *trust attitude* and *intention*, would be hard to capture by means of *sensors*, as in most *context-aware* systems (see Sect. 2).
- Reasoning about *vulnerabilities* is not always in technical terms and may concern aspects, such as *behavior patterns* and *preferences* – those are also hard to capture by means of *sensors*.
- Assuming *service provisioning* that covers very many *service users* would make it "hard-to-implement" arranging *sensor* facilitation for all, guaranteeing for technically solid and unbiased sensing feedback.

Inspired by those challenges, Shishkov and Van Sinderen [4, 33] have considered alternative ways to capture the *user situation* and other aspects concerning the *user*, emphasizing the relevant strengths of *data analytics*. Why is data analytics considered adequate in this regard? Because: (i) It is not physically restricted to sensor facilitation and hence has the potential of scaling up; (ii) Recent big-data-related developments concern many possibilities to easily, reliably and at low cost provide relevant data; (iii) Counting on historic (training) data allows for applying powerful statistical approaches and algorithms, for the sake of making predictions; (iv) Beyond this, other machine-learning related techniques could be applied for achieving classifications, clustering, and so on; (v) One could often apply in combination data analytics and sensors, for example: capturing emotion via sensors but using the sensor data in combination with data derived by training-data-driven "conclusions"; and so on.

Hence, we argue that **DATA ANALYTICS** can play an important role in the processes of **building user *trust* when working with *context-aware* systems**. The realization of this can be seen in two directions: (1) Using data analytics to **collect and analyze large amounts of data** for the sake of **ensuring better servicing.** (2) **Providing greater transparency of the system's operation**, which leads to **building greater *trust*.**

Regarding the <u>first direction</u>, big data collection tools are considered relevant with them allowing for analyses that aim at *personalizing user experience and preferences.* This could be usefully applied in *context-aware recommendation systems.* What is relevant here would span from *classical collaborative filtering algorithms* to state-of-the-art methods using *auto-encoders* to capture the complex interactions between the potential suggestions and the user [37]. This also concerns data analytics aiming at *monitoring the system security* by *tracking its activity* and potential *security threats.* In this way, *vulnerabilities* can be identified and addressed accordingly, thereby building greater user *trust.* Regarding the <u>second direction</u>, methods to make the system more *transparent* would often focus on *data collection processes, data processing*, and subsequent *interpretation.*

Further, the main *channels of data collection* in current *context-aware* systems can be divided into two main groups – the vast array of *IoT (Internet-of-Things) devices* [38], as well as the various *media channels*, especially social media. Such an increased data consumption requires special attention on *how to manage trust in the collection, storage and transmission of this data.* In [38], *trust* requirements have been identified, concerning IoT big data systems, such as interoperability-related requirements, security-related requirements, privacy-related requirements, and so on; also, state-of-the-art frameworks, models, and methods for an information-centric *trust* have been discussed, featuring IoT big data systems.

Finally, in terms of *information processing* and further *interaction with the service user*, the ability of the *system* to show the explainability of the decisions made is considered crucially important. In many cases *context-aware systems* use *machine learning models*, with *decision-making processes* that often appear as "black boxes" for the *service user*. This lack of *transparency* may lead to a *trust gap* between the *service user* and the *system*. A possible way to increase the *trust degree* is to explicitly show the *system accuracy* (as in [39]); another possibility would be to provide clear *explanations concerning the underlying logic and reasoning* that have gone into the *system's decision-making process.*

5   Evaluation

The current section presents an example that illustrates our *context awareness – trust* conceptualization and afterwards we discuss some benefits and limitations of our proposal.

5.1   Illustrative Example

Let's consider a system called "**TA**" (*Travel Assistant*), and also **Alice, John, Sara,** and **Richard** who are "*entities*" not belonging to **TA**. Imagine that each of them can fulfil the *role* "**BT**" (*Business Traveler*) that concerns the *role type* **user**. Then **BT** is part of context "**T**" (*Traveling*) that in turn has a number of *context situations*. Examples would be "**P**" (*Preparation*) - when **BT** needs travel arrangements, such as tickets and accommodation reservations; "**TIP**" (*Transport to Intermediate Point*) - when **BT** is in a process of reaching a bus station or an airport, or a highway (border) point, etc.; and "**O**" (*Orientation*) - when **BT** is in an unknown place and needs location-specific information/services. Imagine that the supportive system detects *context situation* **P** and hence provides to **BT** the *situation-specific service* "***accommodation arrangement***" to fulfil **BT**'s *need* for an accommodation reservation. Let us now consider the two *trust relations* as presented in Fig. 5 (see the dashed red lines):

- **BT is part of context T**: Here, a *trust relationship* exists at a *role level* but is driven by a corresponding *entity attitude*. In our example, the *role* **BT** can be fulfilled by **Alice, John, Sara,** and **Richard**. Imagine that: (i) **Alice** has no resistance for using any IT systems in any situation; (ii) **John** would always prepare everything beforehand such that he would not need any servicing during his business traveling; (iii) **Sara**, among other things, is involved in an intelligence project focusing on international crime, and for this reason she can only use services that are explicitly authorized by a particular person in the intelligence project; (iv) **Richard** is a brand-driven person who would only go for particular brands during travel. Therefore, the **TRUST ATTITUDE** of the particular *entity* (*person*) who is fulfilling the **BT** *role* (as it concerns *context* **T**) is important.
- When it comes to the **provision of the situation-specific service "*accommodation arrangement*"**, the *trust relationship* concerns the *service* itself. Again, the *entity attitude* is essential. In our example: (a) **Alice** would have a *high-level of trust* with regard to receiving *services* and would not mind using the *service* from **TA** in any way; (b) **John** would like to receive *extra guarantees* from the *system* that the accommodation is confirmed, pre-paid, and cannot be cancelled by the owner; (c) **Sara** would only consume **TA**'s *service* if the *recommendations* would be consistent with a received *authorization* for her project; (d) **Richard** would only consume a *service* from **TA** if the suggested accommodation is one of several selected *brands*. Therefore, again the **TRUST ATTITUDE** of the particular *entity* (*person*) who would be consuming the "***accommodation arrangement***" *service* is important.

5.2 Discussion

We argue that our proposed *ontological conceptualization* helps to sharply describe the relation between *context, service provision,* and *trust.* The *conceptualization* has both **strengths** and **limitations**.

One of the *strengths* of the proposed *conceptualization* is that it has been methodologically derived from context-awareness-specific and trust-specific concepts that have been *superimposed* for the sake of achieving an adequate *conceptual alignment.* A particular strength is that we have combined them in one ontological meta-model that establishes the *right restrictions* when either considering *trust* from a *context awareness* perspective or when considering *context awareness* from a *trust* perspective. The *derivation of concepts* stems from *well-focused state-of-the-art studies* featuring *context awareness* and *trust,* reflected in Sect. 2 and Sect. 3, respectively.

Another *strength* of the proposed *conceptualization* is that it is generic in the sense that it is *neither coupled to a specific use case nor is it narrowed to a particular application domain* and is *not restricted in methodological and/or notation terms.*

Limitations of our work are three-fold:

- The proposed conceptualization is still at high level and needs to be specified in more concrete terms;
- It is insufficiently discussed/researched if *policy-based trust* and *reputation-based trust* exhaustively cover the trust "space";
- The illustrative example and this discussion provide only partial justification of the proposed conceptualization and it is still in need of more solid validation (proof-of-principle or proof-of-concept).

6 Conclusions

This paper has considered the incorporation of *trust* in services delivered by *context-aware* (IT) systems, particularly addressing the *user's trust in the system.* We have conceptually aligned *context-aware computing* and concepts from *policy-* and *reputation-based trust.* Two research questions were formulated in the Introduction of the paper: *(i)* How can we allow for *context awareness* in services governed by a *policy-based trust* principle? *(ii)* How can *reputation-based trust* be implemented in a *context-aware service?* Our approach to these research questions was three-fold: First, we have presented a conceptual *context awareness* model, taking a functional perspective, rooting this model in key notions stemming from the evolution of *context-aware computing* in the 1991–2023 period and referring to the key state-of-the-art achievements. Second, we have presented conceptualizations of *policy-based trust* and *reputation-based trust,* and we have outlined possible *trust* strategies. Finally, we have methodologically derived an ontological conceptual meta-model that combines concepts of both *context awareness* and *trust,* also providing insight in the relevant strengths of *data analytics* for predictions of *context* situations and user attitudes, and for users clustering.

We have partially evaluated the conceptual meta-model, by considering an illustrative example and discussing some strengths and limitations of the model.

In future research, we plan to: (a) Consider a larger example and use it to fully validate our proposed conceptual model; (b) Reflect on our proposed conceptualization in the light of Enterprise Architectures (EA), and study the effects of combining *context awareness* and *trust* in EA.

Acknowledgement. This work was partially supported by: (i) Contract "NGIC – National Geoinformation Center for monitoring, assessment and prediction of natural and anthropogenic risks and disasters" under the Program "National Roadmap for Scientific Infrastructure 2017–2023", financed by the Bulgarian Ministry of Education and Science; (ii) Digitalization and Information Systems Group - University of Fribourg; (iii) Faculty of Electrical Engineering, Mathematics and Computer Science – University of Twente; (iv) Faculty of Technology, Policy, and Management – Delft University of Technology.

References

1. Dey, A., Abowd, G., Salber, D.: A conceptual framework and a toolkit for supporting the rapid prototyping of context-aware applications. Hum.-Comput. Interact. **16**(2–4), 97–166 (2001)
2. Wegdam, M.: Awareness: a project on context aware mobile networks and services. In: Proceedings of the 14th Mobile & Wireless Communications Summit. EURASIP (2005)
3. Shishkov, B., van Sinderen, M.: Towards well-founded and richer context-awareness conceptual models. In: Shishkov, B. (ed.) BMSD 2021. LNBIP, vol. 422, pp. 118–132. Springer, Cham (2021). https://doi.org/10.1007/978-3-030-79976-2_7
4. Shishkov, B., van Sinderen, M.: On the context-aware servicing of user needs: extracting and managing context information supported by rules and predictions. In: Shishkov, B. (ed) Business Modeling and Software Design. BMSD 2022. Lecture Notes in Business Information Processing, vol. 453. Springer, Cham (2022). https://doi.org/10.1007/978-3-031-11510-3_15
5. Dey, A.K., Newberger, A.: Support for context-aware intelligibility and control. In: Proceedings of the SIGCHI Conference on Human Factors in Computing Systems. ACM, USA (2009)
6. Bosems, S., van Sinderen, M.: Models in the design of context-aware well-being applications. In: Meersman, R., et al. (eds.) OTM 2014. LNCS, vol. 8842, pp. 37–42. Springer, Heidelberg (2014). https://doi.org/10.1007/978-3-662-45550-0_6
7. Alegre, U., Augusto, J.C., Clark, T.: Engineering context-aware systems and applications: a survey. J. Syst. Softw. **117**, 55–83 (2016). https://doi.org/10.1016/j.jss.2016.02.010
8. Alférez, G.H., Pelechano, V.: Context-aware autonomous web services in software product lines. In: Proceedings of the 15th International SPLC Conference. IEEE, CA, USA (2011)
9. Abeywickrama, D.B., Ramakrishnan, S.: Context-aware services engineering: models, transformations, and verification. ACM Trans. Internet Technol. J. **11**(3), 1–28 (2012). ACM
10. Shishkov, B.: Designing Enterprise Information Systems, Merging Enterprise Modeling and Software Specification. Springer, Cham (2020). https://doi.org/10.1007/978-3-030-22441-7
11. Bonatti, P., Duma, C., Olmedilla, D., Shahmehri, N.: An integration of reputation-based and policy-based trust management. Networks **2**(14), 10 (2007)
12. O'Hara, K., Alani, H., Kalfoglou, Y., Shadbolt, N.: Trust strategies for the semantic web. In: Proceedings of the 2004 International Conference on Trust, Security, and Reputation on the Semantic Web - Volume 127 (ISWC'04). CEUR-WS.org, Aachen, DEU, pp. 42–51 (2004)
13. Han, J., Kamber, M., Pei, J.: Data Mining: Concepts and Techniques, 3rd edn. Morgan Kaufmann Publ. Inc., San Francisco, CA, USA (2011)
14. Shishkov, B., Larsen, J.B., Warnier, M., Janssen, M.: Three categories of context-aware systems. In: Shishkov, B. (ed.) Business Modeling and Software Design. BMSD 2018. Lecture Notes in Business Information Processing, vol. 319. Springer, Cham (2018). https://doi.org/10.1007/978-3-319-94214-8_12

15. Knittel, J., Shirazi, A.S., Henze, N., Schmidt, A.: Utilizing contextual information for mobile communication. In: CHI '13 Extended Abstracts on Human Factors in Computing Systems (CHI EA '13). ACM, New York, NY, USA (2013)

16. Weiser, M.: The Computer for the 21st century. SIGMOBILE Mob. Comput. Commun. Rev. **3**(3), 3–11 (1999). ACM, New York, NY, USA

17. Schilit, B.N.: A system architecture for context-aware mobile computing. Ph.D. dissertation, Columbia University, New York, USA (1995)

18. Krumm, J. (ed.): Ubiquitous Computing Fundamentals. Taylor and Francis Group, LLC (2009)

19. Dey, A.: Chapter 8 - Context-Aware Computing. In: Krumm, J. (ed.) Ubiquitous Computing Fundamentals. Taylor and Francis Group, LLC (2009)

20. Schilit, B., Adams, N., Want, R.: Context-aware computing applications. In: First Workshop on Mobile Computing Systems and Applications, pp. 85–90. IEEE (1994)

21. Harter, A., Hopper, A., Steggles, P., Ward, A., Webster, P.: The anatomy of a context-aware application. Wirel. Netw. **8**, 187–197 (2002)

22. Dey, A.K.: Context-aware computing: the cyberdesk project. In: AAAI Spring Symposium on Intelligent Environments, AAAI Technical Report SS-88-02, pp. 51–54 (1998)

23. van Sinderen, M., van Halteren, A., Wegdam, M., et al.: Supporting context-aware mobile applications: an infrastructure approach. IEEE Commun. Mag. **44**(9), 96–104 (2006)

24. Chaari, T., Laforest, F., Celentano, A.: Adaptation in context-aware pervasive information systems: the SECAS project. Int. J. Perv. Comput. Commun. **3**(4), 400–425 (2007)

25. Borissova, D., Cvetkova, P., Garvanov, I., Garvanova, M.: A framework of business intelligence system for decision making in efficiency management. In: Saeed, K., Dvorský, J. (eds.) CISIM 2020. LNCS, vol. 12133, pp. 111–121. Springer, Cham (2020). https://doi.org/10.1007/978-3-030-47679-3_10

26. Garvanova, M., Garvanov, I., Kashukeev, I.: Business processes and the safety of stakeholders: considering the electromagnetic pollution. In: Shishkov, B. (ed.) BMSD 2020. LNBIP, vol. 391, pp. 386–393. Springer, Cham (2020). https://doi.org/10.1007/978-3-030-52306-0_28

27. Dimitrova, Z., Dimitrov, V., Borissova, D., Garvanov, I., Garvanova, M.: Two-stage search based approach for determination and sorting of mountain hiking routes using directed weighted multigraph. Cybern. Inf. Technol. **20**(6), 28–39 (2020). Print ISSN 1311-9702 Online ISSN 1314-4081. https://doi.org/10.2478/cait-2020-0058

28. Van Engelenburg, S.: Designing context-aware architectures for business-to-government information sharing. Ph.D. thesis. TU Delft Press (2019)

29. Nardi, J.C., et al.: Towards a commitment-based reference ontology for services. EDOC, pp. 175–184 (2013)

30. Nardi, J.C., et al.: A commitment-based reference ontology for services. Inf. Syst. **54**, 263–288 (2015)

31. Dietz, J.L.G.: Enterprise Ontology, Theory and Methodology. Springer, Heidelberg (2006)

32. Amaral, G., Sales, T.P., Guizzardi, G., Porello, D.: Towards a reference ontology of trust. In: Panetto, H., Debruyne, C., Hepp, M., Lewis, D., Ardagna, C.A., Meersman, R. (eds.) OTM 2019. LNCS, vol. 11877, pp. 3–21. Springer, Cham (2019). https://doi.org/10.1007/978-3-030-33246-4_1

33. Shishkov, B.: Tuning the behavior of context-aware applications. In: Shishkov, B. (ed.) BMSD 2019. LNBIP, vol. 356, pp. 134–152. Springer, Cham (2019). https://doi.org/10.1007/978-3-030-24854-3_9

34. Muff, F., Fill, H.-G.: A framework for context-dependent augmented reality applications using machine learning and ontological reasoning. In: Proceedings of the '22 Spring Symposium on Machine Learning and Knowledge Engineering for Hybrid Intelligence. AAAI-MAKE 2022. Stanford University Press, Palo Alto, CA (CEUR Workshop Proceedings) (2022)

35. Kindervag, J.: No More Chewy Centers: Introducing the Zero Trust Model of Information Security. Forester (2010)
36. Bunge, M.A.: Treatise on Basic Philosophy, vol. 4, A World of Systems. D. Reidel Publishing Company, Dordrecht (1979)
37. Abinaya, S., Alphonse, A.S., Abirami, S., et al.: Enhancing context-aware recommendation using trust-based contextual attentive autoencoder. Neural Process. Lett. (2023). https://doi.org/10.1007/s11063-023-11163-x
38. Ahmed, U., Raza, I., Hussain, S.A.: Information-centric trust management for big data-enabled IoT. Big Data-Enabled Internet of Things **2020**, 411–432 (2020)
39. Antifakos, S., Kern, N., Schiele, B., Schwaninger, A.: Towards improving trust in context-aware systems by displaying system confidence. In: MobileHCI '05: Proceedings of the 7th International Conference on Human Computer Interaction with Mobile Devices & Services
40. NESDIS: National Environmental Satellite, Data, and Information Service (2023). https://www.nesdis.noaa.gov
41. JMA: Japan Meteorological Agency (2023). https://www.jma.go.jp/jma
42. EPOS: European Plate Observing System (2023). https://www.epos-eu.org
43. Sensor. Community: Sensor Community (2023). https://sensor.community/en
44. Mendling, J.: Towards Blockchain Support for Business Processes. In: Shishkov, B. (ed.) Business Modeling and Software Design. BMSD 2018. Lecture Notes in Business Information Processing, vol. 319. Springer, Cham (2018). https://doi.org/10.1007/978-3-319-94214-8_15

VR-EvoEA+BP: Using Virtual Reality to Visualize Enterprise Context Dynamics Related to Enterprise Evolution and Business Processes

Roy Oberhauser[1(✉)] ⓘ, Marie Baehre[1], and Pedro Sousa[2,3]

[1] Computer Science Department, Aalen University, Aalen, Germany
`{roy.oberhauser,marie.baehre}@hs-aalen.de`
[2] Instituto Superior Técnico, University of Lisbon, Lisbon, Portugal
`pedro.manuel.sousa@tecnico.ulisboa.pt`
[3] Link Consulting, Lisbon, Portugal

Abstract. Enterprise digitalization results in an evolving and dynamic IT landscape of digital elements, relations, knowledge, content, activities, and business processes (BPs), which are spread across disparate enterprise IT systems, repositories, and tools. To be relevant, useful, and actionable, Enterprise Architecture (EA) relies on comprehensive documentation based on underlying information corresponding to reality. Yet current diagram-centric 2D visualizations for EA and BP models are too limited in scope to express reality (intentionally simplifying), are typically static (and not kept up-to-date), and cannot express and integrate the changing complexities of the enterprise context. This misalignment with reality and a changing enterprise misinforms and constrains the context-awareness and perception of EA and BP for stakeholders, impeding analyses, management, and holistic insights into the enterprise digital reality. This paper contributes our nexus-based Virtual Reality (VR) solution concept VR-EvoEA+BP to support comprehensive enterprise context visualization in conjunction with EA and model evolution and BP mining and analysis. Portraying an organic, evolving, and dynamic enterprise while supplementing static enterprise structure depictions, our implementation demonstrates its feasibility. A case study based on enterprise analysis and BP scenarios exhibits its potential.

Keywords: Virtual Reality · Enterprise Architecture · Business Processes · Context-Awareness · Enterprise Evolution · Process Mining · Enterprise Architecture Management · Enterprise Modeling · Visualization

1 Introduction

"Everything moves on and nothing is at rest," ascribed by Plato to Heraclitus [1] and reformulated by others in numerous ways, expresses change as the only constant. What is assumed to be stable and static in our perceived (enterprise) reality is often not, particularly the complex digital reality on which today's enterprises rely, which necessarily

© The Author(s), under exclusive license to Springer Nature Switzerland AG 2023
B. Shishkov (Ed.): BMSD 2023, LNBIP 483, pp. 110–128, 2023.
https://doi.org/10.1007/978-3-031-36757-1_7

evolves and adapts to market and technological disruptions. This may be especially true for Enterprise Architecture (EA), which comprises the structural and behavioral aspects needed for an enterprise to function and adapt in alignment with some vision. Hence, EA seeks to provide a comprehensive set of cohesive models describing the enterprise structure and functions, while logically arranging individual models to provide further detail about an enterprise [2]. Yet digitalization implies a growing set of digital elements, relations, and associated IT complexity, with EA information spanning disparate silos of repositories across organizations and systems. Operationally, BPs represent the structured activities of an organization towards achieving its business goals, and their execution represent a critical part of the dynamics of an enterprise. In particular, EA evolution and business processes (BPs) are key dynamic aspects of a "living" enterprise, and their visualization, especially concomitantly with their associated enterprise context, presents a challenge.

Many EA methods and diagrams assume static structures, yet the underlying digital reality an EA attempts to depict is increasingly dynamic. EA representations are an enterprise asset that must be governed [3], yet the effort required to maintain architectural views that are current is very high in organizations [4]. This is primarily due to the organization's structure being the result of an asynchronous, distributed, and heterogeneous process, producing representations in various languages and notations, at different levels of detail, and with different tools at different timepoints. Furthermore, current, EA and BP models are not readily accessible to all enterprise citizens or stakeholder groups, hindering the ability to exploit "grassroots modeling" [5] and ensure the validity, practicality, and optimization of EA or BP models. Furthermore, due to their lack of capability to visualize the enterprise reality, EA Management (EAM) methods and tools oversimplify and cannot convey the real associated enterprise context for any representation. Yet as enterprises evolve, explicit knowledge of and insight into the EA becomes indispensable for enterprise governance, compliance, maintenance, etc. Thus, for correct model perception, a valid and accurate depiction and comprehension of enterprise context is vital, yet not feasible with current EAM methods and tools. Moreover, inaccurate or missing context depiction impairs EA comprehension, resulting in misguided EA-related decisions and additional risk.

To address these challenges, the unlimited space of Virtual Reality (VR) could be leveraged to visualize an enterprise's digital reality as well as the context surrounding enterprise elements, while providing an immersive experience accessible to hitherto excluded stakeholder groups. In support of using VR, Müller et al. [6] investigated VR vs. 2D for a software analysis task, finding that VR did not significantly decrease comprehension and analysis time, yet improved the user experience, being more motivating, less demanding, more inventive/innovative, and more clearly structured. In our view, VR could similarly benefit EAM without incurring significant liabilities.

Our VR-related prior work includes VR-EAT [7] for dynamically-generated Atlas EA diagrams; VR-BPMN [8] for Business Process Model and Notation (BPMN) [9]; VR-ProcessMine [10]; and VR-EA+TCK [11], which integrates EA tool, Knowledge Management Systems (KMS), and Enterprise Content Management System (ECMS) capabilities. This paper describes VR-EvoEA+BP, our nexus-based VR solution concept, which contributes an enterprise context-enhanced visualization of 1) enterprise model evolution, and 2) mined BP and BP variant execution dynamics. An organic, evolving, and dynamic enterprise can be holistically portrayed with each element's context and relations, while supplementing further enterprise structure and content depiction (such as diagrams and media). Our implementation demonstrates its feasibility, while a case study exhibits its potential based on enterprise analysis scenarios.

This paper is structured as follows: Sect. 2 discusses related work while Sect. 3 provides background on Atlas. Our solution concept is described in Sect. 4. Section 5 details our prototype implementation. The evaluation is described in Sect. 6, followed by a conclusion.

2 Related Work

EA visualization work in the area of XR includes Rehring et al. [12], who posit from literature that VR or Mixed Reality (MR) offer affordances that can positively influence EAM decision-making quality and effectiveness. Rehring et al. [13] concluded that EAM with Augmented Reality (AR) can improve EA comprehension. The survey of EA visualization tools by Roth et al. [14] makes no mention of XR or VR, nor does the systematic review by Jugel [15]. Non-XR EA visualization work includes Naranjo et al. [16], who describe PRIMate, a 2D graph-based enterprise analysis framework containing a graph, treemap, and 3D visualization of an the archiSurance ArchiMate model [17]. Rehring et al. [18] used an 3D city metaphor to conceptualize an EA using districts for EA analysis scenarios and streets for processes. Work related to visualizing EA evolution includes Roth & Matthes [19], who use a 2D multi-layer interactive drill down paradigm to visualize EA model differences. Atlas [4, 20] includes EA evolution visualization support using a 2D browser (our solution integrates Atlas to support our VR-based evolution visualization). Beyond our own prior work, we are unaware of work applying VR to the EA area, specifically integrating EA tools, multi-EA-diagram support, heterogenous EA models (ArchiMate, BPMN, UML), ECMS and KMS integration, and a nexus-based visualization.

As to BP visualization in conjunction with enterprise context, the systematic literature review by Dani et al. [21] mentions techniques that augment BP models with additional information, yet context is not explicitly mentioned, with the only XR work mentioned being our own VR-BPMN [8]. AR approaches integrating enterprise context with BPs include: our own (as global context) [22, 23], Muff & Fill [24], and Grum & Gronau [25]. As to context-awareness support in BPM methods, Denner et al. [22, 26] assessed the degree of context-awareness in extant BPM methods, finding: support for goal exploration rare; very few methods account for process, organization, and environment dimensions; and the process dimension seldom supports the context factors knowledge-intensity, creativity, interdependence, and variability. As to BP variant analysis techniques in the area of process mining, the survey by Taymouri et al. [27] found the area fragmented, and while certain visualization techniques were discussed, no XR techniques are mentioned. Our previous work VR-ProcessMine [10] visualizes BP variants and enactments in VR, but lacks an enterprise context. In contrast, VR-EvoEA+BP depicts BPs and their mined processes in their entire enterprise context comprehensively, showing holistic relations to roles, people, and other relevant enterprise elements; visualizes BP variants; enables stepping through a BP variant or trace sequentially with complete enterprise context; augments any BP activity with additional real content, documentation, and knowledge; and depicts Atlas-generated (current and non-stale) BPMN model diagrams in 3D in VR.

3   Background on the EA Tool Atlas

Atlas is an enterprise cartography solution [4, 20, 28] that can support fast-changing organizations, creating and maintaining up-to-date architectural models and views spanning a large set of view types (see Fig. 1). Offering a fully configurable metamodel with a consolidated repository, it dynamically generates fully configurable views that can depict any timepoint with each element shown in its corresponding lifecycle state. It minimizes the effort to produce consolidated architectural views relative to any timepoint and the evolution of an architecture over time can be viewed.

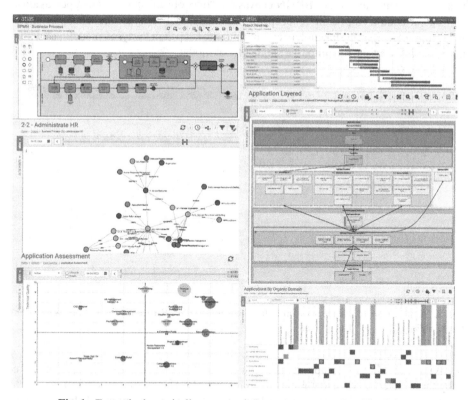

Fig. 1. Example dynamically generated diagram types supported by Atlas.

Support for temporal navigation and gap analysis is a unique feature of Atlas and, in our experience, fundamental to reducing the effort of maintaining architectural views in large organizations. In Atlas, all views have a time bar that allows the view contents to change according to the time bar position, from the past to the future. A view can depict the gap analysis between any two dates, as presented in the application organic view in Fig. 2. Elements marked with red are in production today but will be decommissioned at the future date. Elements marked in green are planned to be in production at a future date, while the those in yellow are expected to remain in production but changed in structure between the two dates.

Atlas also supports generated views of BPMN models as shown in the upper left in Fig. 1. As with all views, a unique feature of Atlas is its ability to generate and support temporal navigation in these views also. The BPMN design canvas is built on top of the BPMN.IO library to support the graphical aspects of BPMN. However, the semantics of each BPMN symbol remains configurable, allowing different mappings against the metamodel, each of which is also user-configurable. For example, in an Atlas metamodel referencing The Open Group Architecture Framework (TOGAF) Content Metamodel (CMM) [29], one BPMN canvas may map a "data object" to be an "Entity" in the metamodel, while in another BPMN canvas the "data object" could be mapped against a "Logical Data Component" concept in the metamodel. This is one example where Atlas supports different stakeholder communities to keep their "way-of-modeling," while mapping different models into to a single global model.

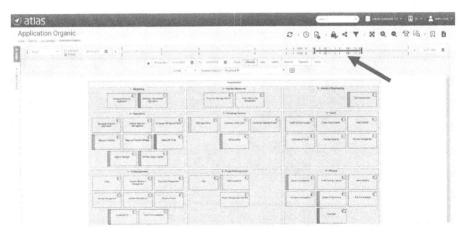

Fig. 2. Application landscape view in Atlas showing time bar gap analysis (red arrow). (Color figure online)

With ArchiMate [17], supported by Atlas, this different "ways-of-modeling" problem is by far more common and complex than for BPMN. This is due not only to the much larger set of concepts, but also because the notation has evolved significantly from version 1.0 to version 3.2, requiring support for importing models from different ArchiMate versions. For example, if the user configures the relationships of the type "is responsible for" and "uses" between an actor and a component application in the Atlas metamodel, when importing an Archimate models that contains relationships between actors and applications (having a different set of relation types between actors and applications), it should configure mapping the rules between them. This mapping can be defined in each instantiation of the drawing canvas.

The possibility to configure and instantiate multiple design canvases, each with a specialized mapping with the Atlas defined metamodel, enables mapping different ontologies for provisioning and viewing within the organization. Given the multiple and different internal views the different communities have of their organization, the external view plays a very significant role, and it stands as an independent view, against whom internal communities map their models and ontologies.

To mitigate the complexity of managing different architectural models, Atlas also supports modeling gap analysis, indicating what is common and distinctive to each model set. E.g., the gap between applications (modeled as an applications store) can be viewed in business-owned BPMN models, while IT uses its application catalog.

4 Solution Concept

Our solution approach leverages the unlimited space VR offers for visualizing the growing and complex set of EA models and their interrelationships simultaneously in a spatial structure. Furthermore, besides unlimited visualization, the VR environment provides an ability to immersively "experience" EA to explore and comprehend the "big picture" for structurally and hierarchically complex and interconnected models, diagrams, content, documentation, and digital elements in a 3D space viewable from different perspectives by various stakeholders with heterogeneous interests.

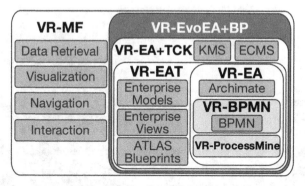

Fig. 3. Solution concept map showing VR-EvoEA+BP (blue) in relation to other concepts. (Color figure online)

Since EA is a broad topic with many facets, we have developed various solutions concepts, a map of which is shown in Fig. 3. Our generalized VR Modeling Framework (VR-MF), described in [30], provides a domain-independent hypermodeling framework addressing key aspects for modeling in VR: visualization, navigation, interaction, and data retrieval. Using this, VR-EA [30] provides specialized direct support and mapping for EA models in VR, including both ArchiMate as well as BPMN via VR-BPMN [8]. VR-ProcessMine [10] supports process mining in VR. VR-EAT [7] extends this to our enterprise repository integration solution, exemplified with Atlas integration, visualization of IT blueprints, and interaction capabilities. VR-EA+TCK [11] expands this further, integrating KMS and ECMS capabilities in VR.

Having this EA foundation for static models, diagrams, knowledge, and content is one thing, but how do we make EA "come alive"? We thus developed our solution concept VR-EvoEA+BP for expressing and conveying the "living enterprise," which, in our opinion, offers a vast set of possible scenarios and potential. To capture our intent and demonstrate the concept concretely, two scenarios where chosen that, in particular, provide for visualizing and experiencing EA *in conjunction with contextual dynamics*: 1) enterprise evolution / change / adaptation, explicitly bringing and visualizing the dimension of time into VR space, and 2) contextualized BP execution, leveraging process mining (or simulation) to not just see theoretical BP models, but comprehending and experiencing BP dynamics operationally in the enterprise with all their associated context. To achieve these objectives, our solution concept necessitates enterprise data integration and VR visualization, navigation, and interaction capabilities, which are addressed as follows:

Enterprise Data Integration. As a representative EA tool and repository, Atlas provides access to diverse EA-related data in a coherent repository and meta-model and is not restricted to certain standards or notations. VR-EAT details our integration with Atlas. Atlas blueprints (diagrams) are necessarily limited in scope to address some stakeholder concern, which is necessary and helpful for stakeholders to avoid information overload. Yet the larger picture of the entire digital enterprise and all of its elements and

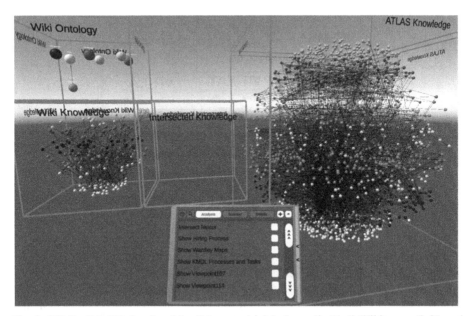

Fig. 4. VR-EvoEA+BP showing Atlas EA nexus (right), Semantic MediaWiki nexus (left), and VR-Tablet (foreground) in Analysis mode.

relations cannot be easily conveyed via such single 2D diagram views. Furthermore, second degree relations and elements (beyond the diagram) or not readily perceived. Thus, certain insights or missing elements, relations, or aspects may not be readily detected. Furthermore, any models retained in a repository are typically limited in scope to that repository, and inter-repository relations (such as between Atlas and an ECMS or KMS, addressed via VR-EA+TCK [7]) are usually not obvious or discovered.

Visualization. As there are many possible relations between digital elements, a spherical nexus was chosen to visualize all elements and relations in a repository (see Fig. 4). To provide some initial ordering, layering within the sphere is available as a grouping mechanism based on similar element types using the color assigned to that type, resulting in a sphere with colored layers (intra-layer element placement is random). The default (customizable) node color scheme is loosely based on KMDL® [31], e.g., actor {white}, role {yellow}, information object {red}, task/conversion {green}, knowledge object {pink/purple}, requirement {orange}. To assist with orientation and make interaction more intuitive by providing a context for what a model represents, labeled glass boxes readable from any angle contain a nexus based on the model of a repository (ECMS, KMS). To show inter-relations between nexuses or models, we found directly drawn additional lines between nexus spheres to lead to a large crisscross of associations, making analysis difficult. A dynamically-generated nexus can show the intersection between nexus models (see [7]). As 2D-based views and diagrams remain a primary form of EA documentation, they are visualized (such as those from the EAT Atlas) as 3D hyperplanes in proximity to its nexus for contextual support. In summary, intangible digital elements or digital twins are made visible and related to one another across the enterprise spectrum.

Navigation. To support immersive navigation in VR while reducing the likelihood of potential VR sickness symptoms, two navigation modes are supported in the solution concept: the default uses gliding controls, enabling users to fly through the VR space and get an overview of the entire model from any angle they wish. Alternatively, teleporting permits a user to select a destination and be instantly placed there (i.e., moving the camera to that position), potentially reducing the probability of VR sickness when moving through a virtual space.

Interaction. Interaction in VR is supported primarily via the VR controllers and our VR-Tablet concept. Views consisting of diagrams (blueprints in Atlas terminology) stacked as hyperplanes, with corresponding objects highlighted in the Nexus or diagram with the other object is selected. Our VR-Tablet paradigm provides: interaction support, detailed information regarding a selected element, browser-based multimedia content, browsing, filtering, and searching for nexus nodes. For time-machine-like interaction and navigation, a timepoint slider is offered on the VR-Tablet that correspondingly adjusts the visualization to that timepoint.

5 Realization

The logical architecture used by our realization of VR-EvoEA+BP is shown in Fig. 5. Our foundational VR modeling framework VR-MF addresses visualization, navigation, interaction, and data integration, and realization aspects and details are described below.

Enterprise Data Integration. The Data Hub (Fig. 5 center) is based on .NET and provides data integration, data storage via MongoDB 5 as BSON (shown at the bottom), with data retrieval via JSON. Atlas integration (Fig. 5 top left) is cloud-based, including repository data and service access via REST queries, which retrieves Atlas blueprint diagram data as JSON. Data is loaded into the Data Hub is saved to MongoDB as BSON based on an internal schema format that enables us to transform and annotate the data as needed for VR. A command line extension (Fig. 5 left) provides helper functions for configuration, mapping, and data loading for the Data Hub. For demonstrating ECMS/KMS integration, the Semantic MediaWiki (SMW) (shown on the bottom right, purple) was integrated, consisting of MediaWiki with PHP and SMW within a Docker container, and with MariaDB running in a separate container. The MediaWiki Ontology is exported via the SWW script dumpRDF and parsed with dotNetRDF. Further multi-model integration – independent of the Data Hub and direct with Unity – is shown (upper right, green,), and includes ArchiMate (VR-EA) and BPMN (VR-BPMN).

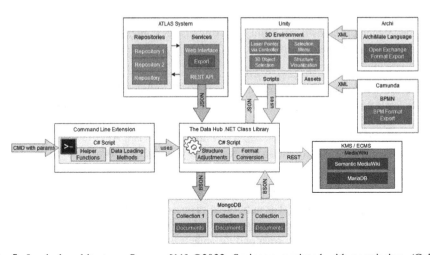

Fig. 5. Logical architecture. Source: [11] ©2022, Springer, reprinted with permission. (Color figure online)

Visualization. VR-MF uses Unity (Fig. 5 top center) with the OpenVR XR Plugin. For digital element type and relational analysis support in VR, a glass meta-layer above any nexus represents all node types as spheres, with the type differentiated by color, and size conveying the relative number of instances (largest having most). Selecting a type at the meta-layer indicates all instances of that type within the nexus via a glow, while ghosting all non-related nodes. Selecting an element instance in a nexus highlights its corresponding type at the meta-layer, while first-degree neighbors and relations remain visible and all other elements are ghosted to reduce visual distractions (by unselecting, all become visible again).

To support evolution visualization in the nexus, colored glows represent the object state at a selected timepoint (Fig. 6). Following the color scheme of the legend for lifecycles in Atlas, elements marked with a red glow are in production at the chosen timepoint, but will be decommissioned at some future date. Elements marked in green are planned to be in production at a future date, while the those in yellow are expected to remain in production but changed in structure between the two dates. Since it would be trivial to provide a second button on the slider to support time gap analysis, it was deferred to focus on BP capabilities.

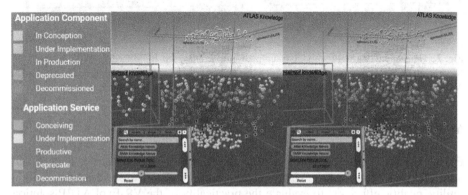

Fig. 6. Atlas timepoint lifecycle state legend (left) with correspondingly colored halos shown in the Nexus for 2008 (center) and 2022 (right). (Color figure online)

Interaction. For evolution support, a timepoint slider was integrated on the VR-Tablet (Fig. 6) that enables timepoint interaction and navigation, adjusting the VR visualization accordingly. To support unified interaction between Atlas diagrams and the nexus in VR, a blueprint diagram stack is positioned in proximity to the nexus. If an element on a blueprint is selected, that corresponding node in the nexus is highlighted and the rest are ghosted, while the dynamic blueprint stack on the right is updated to show all blueprints that include that element. If all elements in a blueprint are selected, then all nodes in the nexus are highlighted with a different colored glow and the rest are ghosted. Besides supporting interaction, the VR-Tablet provides details about a selected nexus or diagram object. In Browser Mode, if the object has associated content, knowledge, or a web address (e.g., wiki), the VR-Tablet dynamically displays the content, exemplified in Fig. 13.

Multi-model Analysis. Immersive heterogeneous multi-model analysis can be supported by loading multiple models in VR. This is depicted in Fig. 7, where a ECMS/KMS Wiki Knowledge Nexus, an EA Atlas Nexus, one Atlas Blueprint, and an ArchiSurance Archimate model is shown.

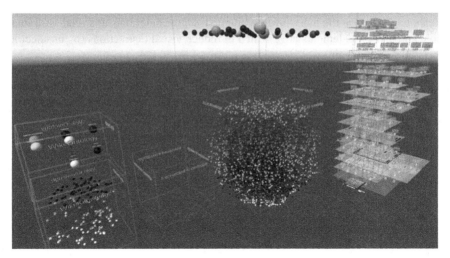

Fig. 7. Heterogeneous multi-model visualization and analysis: ECMS/KMS Wiki Knowledge Nexus (left), EA Atlas Nexus (center), Atlas Blueprint (right bottom, blue), and the ArchiSurance Archimate model (far right). Source: [11] ©2022, Springer, reprinted with permission.

6 Evaluation

For the evaluation of our solution concept, we refer to the design science method and principles [32], in particular, a viable artifact, problem relevance, and design evaluation (utility, quality, efficacy). To evaluate the practicality of the VR-EvoEA+BP solution concept and realization, a case study is used focusing on support for two illustrative analysis scenarios related to conveying the dynamics of enterprises: 1) an Enterprise Evolution Scenario, and 2) a Business Process, Variants, and Process Mining Scenario.

Enterprise data is highly sensitive, from a competitive, business, regulatory, and security standpoint among others. Thus, we relied on a simulated base. The enterprise data consisted of an Atlas repository that contained 66 sample core blueprints, and, via parameter choices, is capable of generating 7843 different blueprints diagrams across all selection combinations. This results in a total of 2034 nodes (unique entity instances) in the Atlas nexus, with 43 types and 2357 intra-nexus relations between element instances.

6.1 Enterprise Evolution Scenario

Our evolution scenario focuses on visualizing enterprise change over time for a stakeholder while offering element and relational context. While one knows enterprises evolve, it is difficult to comprehensively describe exactly what changed when, since often scarce comprehensive visualization capabilities regarding enterprise evolution in EA tools, especially since Atlas uniquely provides this support but not at a full visualization level. What exactly is evolving how over time, from the past to the present, and from the present to the future, and not at an overly abstract level or just a single diagram context, but with regard to the enterprise in its entirety, i.e., all enterprise objects. This limitation is partially a result of 2D modeling lacking a viable diagram type with sufficient granularity and visual space to comprehensively convey the enterprise at any given timepoint. If a specific context is known and diagrams obvious, Atlas uniquely offers lifecycle state and time gap analysis on a per diagram basis (see Sect. 2), which we incorporate in VR via our blueprint diagram stack.

To address a comprehensive evolution view, our nexus visualization concept leverages VR to depict in a condensed space all known enterprise objects and their relations at once, while capable of hiding objects and relations of no interest. Since Atlas retains the timepoint state of all objects, we utilized this data for our Nexus to convey the enterprise evolution at the full Nexus scale as shown in Fig. 8. Notice that in 2008 (see a and b) many nodes (e.g., meta-layer at the top of the Nexus and throughout) have a white halo (representing "in conception"), whereas in 2022 (see c and d), most nodes have a green halo (representing "in production"). In 2022 some nodes have a red halo representing "decommissioned" (seen in d). All ghosted nodes and relations had no associated time-point state data, so, as their state at any given timepoint is unknown, they were ghosted (ghosting can be toggled). Hence, an animated evolution of the enterprise from the past to the planned future can be visualized using the time slider, while holistically depicting the enterprise context around an element. While our focus here was visualizing evolution, a separate nexus-centric time-gap analysis is also readily feasible by including an additional reference timepoint on the slider.

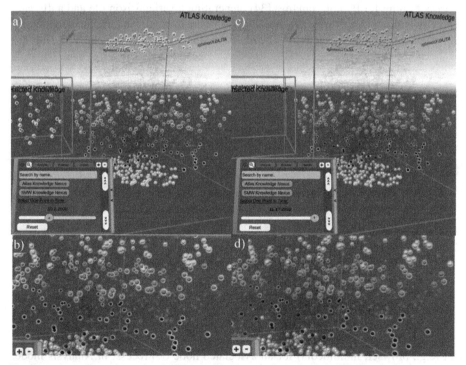

Fig. 8. Nexus object states as colored halos at timepoints: a) 2008 (top left) and b) enlargement (bottom left), and c) 2022 (top right) and d) enlargement of 2022 (bottom right).

In summary, a time-machine-like immersive enterprise time transport becomes viable for EA, allowing stakeholders to "move" to any timepoint in the past or the future of the enterprise, (since our visualization controls what is depicted and can be perceived). Dynamically moving the slider allows one to see an animated "movie" of the evolution of the enterprise.

6.2   Business Process, Variants, and Process Mining Scenario

As automation, efficiency, and productivity pressures increase, analyzing business processes (BP) becomes critical for enterprises. This includes assessing the activities involved in a BP, the sequencing of these activities, and the BP variants that occur during process enactment. For the BP evaluation scenario we used a Hiring Process example from our Atlas repository, depicted as seen in Atlas as a generated blueprint in Fig. 9 and modeled in BPMN in Fig. 10. The VR equivalent Atlas blueprint diagram is shown in Fig. 11 with the Atlas Nexus visible nearby on the left.

To provide sufficient trace and variant data, BP and BP variant simulation data was generated, since we did not receive permission to use actual enterprise process data. Following the event log XES file structure of 'running-example.xes' from the Process Mining book material [33], a Hiring Process.xes was manually created based on the Atlas Hiring Process structure. This XES file (see Fig. 12) was then processed by Process Mining for Python (pm4py) [34], generating a variants.json file and a dfg.json (Directly Follows Graph or DFG), wherein roles were manually incorporated to identify the responsible role for an activity. The files were then imported into our Data Hub.

Fig. 9. Hiring Process as depicted in Atlas as a generated blueprint.

Fig. 10. Hiring Process modeled in BPMN.

As shown in Fig. 13, Browser mode on the VR-Tablet offers context-specific content (e.g., browser, multimedia) for an associated node or process. In Analysis mode, selecting the Hiring Process highlights the involved nodes and connections in the Atlas Nexus, while ghosting all other nodes and connections. Start and end nodes are explicitly labeled as such to help with process navigation. Connections are annotated with their

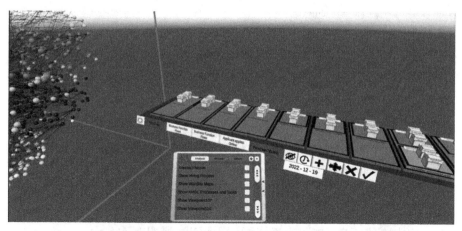

Fig. 11. VR-EvoEA+BP Hiring Process as a VR Atlas blueprint (right) with Atlas Nexus (left).

total number of occurrences in BP logs. For variant analysis, selecting a variant in the VR-Tablet highlights those nodes and connections with a colored glow (see Fig. 14). Automated navigation of that BP variant is supported via the VR-Tablet; a play button automates fly-through navigation to the next sequential node following the connection trace; a pause permits the user to stop the automation; and step back and forward buttons are provided as well. Further event details for a specific trace within a variant could be accessed via the VR-Tablet in Browser mode.

Besides BP variant analysis support, VR-EvoEA+BP provides additional contextual information for BP. E.g., below the BP graph white nodes can be seen (Fig. 14), which are associated roles and people involved in the BP activities. Figure 15 provides a closeup, a left node representing the Hiring Committee and a node on the right the Interview Committee, whereby committee member names are seen in the foreground. This can help with responsibility and authority determination with regard to BPs, and from there, additional contextual analysis spanning BPs and enterprise areas could be considered, since BPs are embedded within the entire enterprise.

BP Contextualization. BPs can be considered the heart of an enterprise. VR-EvoEA+BP supports the contextual integration of related knowledge or enterprise content (e.g., documentation, checklists, training videos, etc.) with a BP activity. This is often missing and not "experienced" when stakeholders view or analyze BP models or perform process mining related tasks. Furthermore, BP analysis can contextually combine the other analyses described in more detail in VR-EA+TCK [11], such as the ECMS/KMS coverage analysis, knowledge chain analysis, Wardley Map value chain analysis, and risk and governance analysis, ensuring that these important BPs consider all relevant aspects. By explicitly showing all elements, a stakeholder could potentially determine what is missing, what is desirable, what should be adapted in the enterprise structure, or what has become irrelevant and should be removed. These aspects might potentially be buried deep within certain diagrams and not be otherwise perceived without the comprehensive, holistic visualization offered by VR-EvoEA+BP.

```xml
<?xml version='1.0' encoding='UTF-8'?>
<log xes.version="1849-2016">
 <string key="origin" value="csv"/>
 <extension name="Concept" prefix="concept" uri="http://www.xes-standard.org/concept.xesext"/>
 <extension name="Organizational" prefix="org" uri="http://www.xes-standard.org/org.xesext"/>
 <extension name="Cost" prefix="cost" uri="http://www.xes-standard.org/cost.xesext"/>
 <extension name="Time" prefix="time" uri="http://www.xes-standard.org/time.xesext"/>
 <trace>
    <string key="concept:name" value="1"/>
    <event>
      <string key="concept:name" value="Applicant applies online"/>
      <date key="time:timestamp" value="2010-12-30T11:02:00.000+01:00"/>
      <int key="cost:total" value="50"/>
      <string key="org:resource" value="Pete"/>
      <int key="@@index" value="14"/>
    </event>
    <event>
      <string key="concept:name" value="HR receives application"/>
      <date key="time:timestamp" value="2010-12-31T10:06:00.000+01:00"/>
      <int key="cost:total" value="400"/>
      <string key="org:resource" value="Sue"/>
      <int key="@@index" value="15"/>
    </event>
    <event>
      <string key="concept:name" value="HR releases application to Interview Committee"/>
      <date key="time:timestamp" value="2011-01-05T15:12:00.000+01:00"/>
      <int key="cost:total" value="100"/>
      <string key="org:resource" value="Mike"/>
      <int key="@@index" value="16"/>
    </event>
    <event>
      <string key="concept:name" value="Conduct Interview/Make recommendations"/>
      <date key="time:timestamp" value="2011-01-06T11:18:00.000+01:00"/>
      <int key="cost:total" value="200"/>
      <string key="org:resource" value="Sara"/>
      <int key="@@index" value="17"/>
    </event>
```

Fig. 12.   Snippet from the Hiring Process XES file.

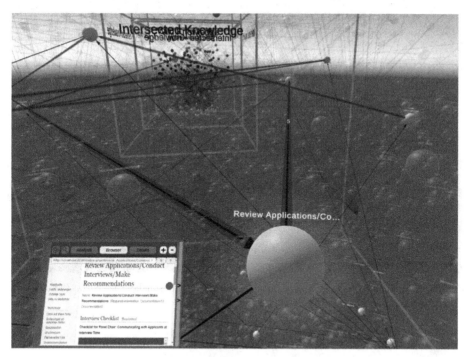

Fig. 13. BP activities and connections highlighted as nodes and relations in the Atlas Nexus; VR-Tablet shows content; associated roles can be seen as the small white nodes bottom right.

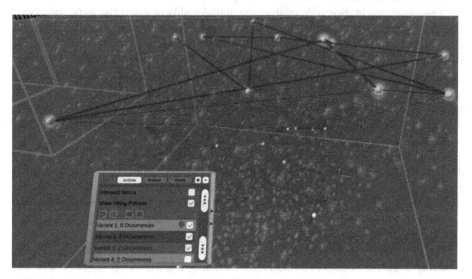

Fig. 14. Selecting any BP variant adds its color halo to its subset of nodes and connections.

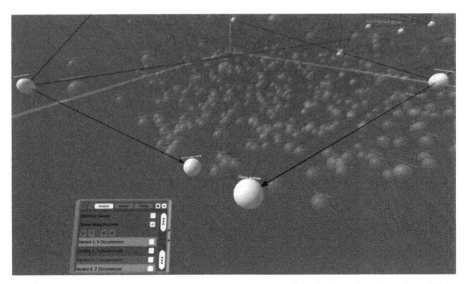

Fig. 15. Closeup of roles and people associated with BP activities in the Atlas Nexus (here Hiring Committee, Interview Committee members).

7 Conclusion

Comprehensive visualization of the dynamics of enterprises, exhibited primarily in the evolution (both past and planned future changes) of the EA as well as the activities structured and executed in their BPs, enables the digital reality of enterprise to be perceived. The growing scale and complexity of the IT landscape makes VR an ideal medium for scaling beyond single EA diagrams to depict the associated enterprise context. VR-EvoEA+BP contributes a unique nexus-based VR visualization solution concept, providing comprehensive integration, visualization, and synthesis of heterogenous enterprise entities and their relations, models, and diagrams together with their enterprise context. Related enterprise knowledge and content is accessible via the browser-capable VR-Tablet. Our implementation demonstrated its feasibility, while the evaluation case study showed its potential to incorporate enterprise context in practical EAM analysis scenarios, specifically: evolution, time, and gap analysis between timepoints (past to the future planned states), as well as BP model, process mining, BP variant, and BP trace support. With our VR solution concept, EAM activities including analysis, discovery, inquiry, reasoning, decision-making, synthesis, and assessment becomes accessible for additional stakeholder groups to support inclusive "grass-roots modeling" with the associated validation and optimization benefits.

Future work includes enhancing the interactive, informational, analytical, and modeling capabilities of VR-EvoEA+BP, including force-directed layout, additional visualization alternatives, and a comprehensive empirical study.

References

1. Robinson, J.M.: An Introduction to Early Greek Philosophy: The Chief Fragments and Ancient Testimony, with Connecting Commentary, p. 90. Advanced Reasoning Forum, Fragment 5.14 (2021)
2. Jarvis, B.: Enterprise Architecture: Understanding the Bigger Picture – A Best Practice Guide for Decision Makers in IT. The UK National Computing Centre (2003)
3. Hoogervorst, J.: Enterprise Governance and Enterprise Engineering. Springer, Heidelberg (2009). https://doi.org/10.1007/978-3-540-92671-9
4. Sousa, P., Leal, R., Sampaio, A.: Atlas: the enterprise cartography tool. In: 18th Enterprise Engineering Working Conference Forum, vol. 2229. CEUR-WS.org (2018)
5. Sandkuhl, K., et al.: From expert discipline to common practice: a vision and research agenda for extending the reach of enterprise modeling. Bus. Inf. Syst. Eng. **60**(1), 69–80 (2018). https://doi.org/10.1007/s12599-017-0516-y
6. Müller, R., Kovacs, P., Schilbach, J., Zeckzer, D.: How to master challenges in experimental evaluation of 2D versus 3D software visualizations. In: 2014 IEEE VIS International Workshop on 3Dvis (3Dvis), pp. 33–36. IEEE (2014)
7. Oberhauser, R., Sousa, P., Michel, F.: VR-EAT: visualization of enterprise architecture tool diagrams in virtual reality. In: Shishkov, B. (ed.) BMSD 2020. LNBIP, vol. 391, pp. 221–239. Springer, Cham (2020). https://doi.org/10.1007/978-3-030-52306-0_14
8. Oberhauser, R., Pogolski, C., Matic, A.: VR-BPMN: visualizing BPMN models in virtual reality. In: Shishkov, B. (ed.) BMSD 2018. LNBIP, vol. 319, pp. 83–97. Springer, Cham (2018). https://doi.org/10.1007/978-3-319-94214-8_6
9. Object Management Group: BPMN Specification 2.0.2 (2014). https://www.bpmn.org
10. Oberhauser, R.: VR-ProcessMine: immersive process mining visualization and analysis in virtual reality. In: The Fourteenth International Conference on Information, Process, and Knowledge Management (eKNOW 2022), pp. 29–36. IARIA (2022)
11. Oberhauser, R., Baehre, M., Sousa, P.: VR-EA+TCK: visualizing enterprise architecture, content, and knowledge in virtual reality. In: Shishkov, B. (eds.) Business Modeling and Software Design (BMSD 2022), pp. 122–140. LNBIP, vol. 453. Springer, Cham (2022). https://doi.org/10.1007/978-3-031-11510-3_8
12. Rehring, K., Hoffmann, D., Ahlemann, F.: Put your glasses on: conceptualizing affordances of mixed and virtual reality for enterprise architecture management. Multikonferenz Wirtschaftsinformatik (2018)
13. Rehring, K., Greulich, M., Bredenfeld, L., Ahlemann, F.: Let's get in touch – decision making about enterprise architecture using 3D visualization in augmented reality. In: Proceedings of 52nd Hawaii International Conference on System Sciences (HICSS), pp. 1769–1778. IEEE (2019)
14. Roth, S., Zec, M., Matthes, F.: Enterprise architecture visualization tool survey. Technical Report, Sebis, Technical University Munich (2014)
15. Jugel, D., Sandkuhl, K., Zimmermann, A.: Visual analytics in enterprise architecture management: a systematic literature review. In: Abramowicz, W., Alt, R., Franczyk, B. (eds.) BIS 2016. LNBIP, vol. 263, pp. 99–110. Springer, Cham (2017). https://doi.org/10.1007/978-3-319-52464-1_10
16. Naranjo, D., Sánchez, M., Villalobos, J.: Towards a unified and modular approach for visual analysis of enterprise models. In: Proceedings of EDOCW 2014, pp. 77–86. IEEE (2014)
17. The OpenGroup: The ArchiMate® Enterprise Architecture Modeling Language (2016)
18. Rehring, K., Brée, T., Gulden, J., Bredenfeld, L.: Conceptualizing EA cities: towards visualizing enterprise architectures as cities. In: Twenty-Seventh European Conference on Information Systems (ECIS2019), Stockholm-Uppsala, Sweden (2019)

19. Roth, S., Matthes, F.: Visualizing differences of enterprise architecture models. In: International Workshop on Comparison and Versioning of Software Models at Software Engineering (2014)

20. Sousa, P.: Enterprise cartography. In: Enterprise Architecture and Cartography: From Practice to Theory; From Representation to Design, pp. 141–156. Springer, (2022). https://doi.org/10.1007/978-3-030-96264-7_5

21. Dani, V., Freitas, C., Thom, L.H.: Ten years of visualization of business process models: a systematic literature review. Comput. Stand. Interfaces **66**, 103347 (2019)

22. Grambow, G., Hieber, D., Oberhauser, R., Pogolski, C.: A context and augmented reality BPMN and BPMS extension for industrial internet of things processes. In: Marrella, A., Weber, B. (eds.) BPM 2021. LNBIP, vol. 436, pp. 379–390. Springer, Cham (2022). https://doi.org/10.1007/978-3-030-94343-1_29

23. Grambow, G., Hieber, D., Oberhauser, R., Pogolski, C.: ARPF - an augmented reality process framework for context-aware process execution in industry 4.0 processes. Int. J. Adv. Intell. Syst. **15**(1 & 2), 49–59 (2022)

24. Muff, F., Fill, H.G.: A framework for context-dependent augmented reality applications using machine learning and ontological reasoning. In: AAAI-MAKE 2022 (2022)

25. Grum, M., Gronau, N.: Process modeling within augmented reality. In: Shishkov, B. (ed.) BMSD 2018. LNBIP, vol. 319, pp. 98–115. Springer, Cham (2018). https://doi.org/10.1007/978-3-319-94214-8_7

26. Denner, M.-S., Röglinger, M., Schmiedel, T., Stelzl, K., Wehking, C.: How context-aware are extant bpm methods? - Development of an assessment scheme. In: Weske, M., Montali, M., Weber, I., vom Brocke, J. (eds.) BPM 2018. LNCS, vol. 11080, pp. 480–495. Springer, Cham (2018). https://doi.org/10.1007/978-3-319-98648-7_28

27. Taymouri, F., La Rosa, M., Dumas, M., Maggi, F.M.: Business process variant analysis: survey and classification. Knowl.-Based Syst. **211**, 106557 (2021)

28. Sousa, P., Lima, J., Sampaio, A., Pereira, C.: An approach for creating and managing enterprise blueprints: a case for IT blueprints. In: Albani, A., Barjis, J., Dietz, J.L.G. (eds.) CIAO!/EOMAS - 2009. LNBIP, vol. 34, pp. 70–84. Springer, Heidelberg (2009). https://doi.org/10.1007/978-3-642-01915-9_6

29. The OpenGroup: The TOGAF® Standard, Version 9.2 (2018)

30. Oberhauser, R., Pogolski, C.: VR-EA: virtual reality visualization of enterprise architecture models with archimate and BPMN. In: Shishkov, B. (ed.) BMSD 2019. LNBIP, vol. 356, pp. 170–187. Springer, Cham (2019). https://doi.org/10.1007/978-3-030-24854-3_11

31. Pogorzelska, B.: KMDL® v2.2 a semi-formal description language for modelling knowledge conversions. In: Gronau, N. (ed.) Modeling and Analyzing Knowledge Intensive Business Processes with KMDL, pp. 87–192. GITO mbH Verlag (2012)

32. Bichler, M.: Design science in information systems research. Wirtschaftsinformatik **48**(2), 133–135 (2006). https://doi.org/10.1007/s11576-006-0028-8

33. van der Aalst, W.M.P.: Process Mining. Springer, Heidelberg (2011)

34. Berti, A., van Zelst, S.J., van der Aalst, W.M.P.: Process mining for Python (PM4Py): bridging the gap between process-and data science. In: Proceedings of ICPM Demo Track 2019, International Conference on Process Mining (ICPM 2019), pp. 13–16 (2019) http://ceur-ws.org/Vol-2374/

Past Achievements and Future Opportunities in Combining Conceptual Modeling with VR/AR: A Systematic Derivation

Fabian Muff[(✉)] and Hans-Georg Fill

University of Fribourg, Research Group Digitalization and Information Systems,
Fribourg, Switzerland
{fabian.muff,hans-georg.fill}@unifr.ch

Abstract. Despite the increased interest in virtual and augmented reality in recent years, they are not yet mainstream technologies for everyday use in industry. We argue that a promising approach to facilitate the application of virtual and augmented reality is to combine it with conceptual modeling. In this paper, we thus conducted a systematic literature review on the combination of conceptual modeling with virtual and augmented reality within the last two decades. For this purpose, we reverted to a manual literature search, computational topic modeling, and an expert-driven classification process. This analysis highlights the areas in which such a combination of virtual and augmented reality and conceptual modeling already exists, as well as the aspects that are not yet covered or that would offer opportunities for further research.

Keywords: Bibliometric Analysis · Augmented Reality · Virtual Reality · Conceptual Modeling · Latent Dirichlet Allocation

1 Introduction

Throughout the last years, the application of virtual reality (VR) and augmented reality (AR) technologies to business scenarios has been increasingly studied by the research community [37]. In VR, the user's perception is based entirely on *virtual* information in a *virtual* world. In AR, computer-generated information is provided to the user in addition to data collected from real life, enhancing the user's perception of *reality*. Due to the recent technological progress [42], affordable and mobile VR and AR devices became widely available and enabled the broad application of the technology in industrial scenarios such as for maintenance tasks or training [16]. A study from PwC estimates that VR and AR will deliver an enormous boost to the global economy until 2030 [13]. Further, a recent study from 2022 indicates that a majority of U.S. executives are highly interested in exploring AR and VR as a foundation for the Metaverse [31].

However, the development of such applications still requires considerable technical know-how. Thus, the provision of *systematic* and at the same time

© The Author(s), under exclusive license to Springer Nature Switzerland AG 2023
B. Shishkov (Ed.): BMSD 2023, LNBIP 483, pp. 129–144, 2023.
https://doi.org/10.1007/978-3-031-36757-1_8

flexible approaches for *designing* VR and AR applications is regarded as a pre-requisite for a more widespread adoption, cf. [41]. Conceptual modeling, e.g., as used in enterprise modeling, may serve as a solution for both aspects [35]. On the one hand it aims to reduce complexity by structuring a particular domain for improving human understanding [8,28]. This may involve the use of novel technologies, e.g., in three-dimensional space [2]. On the other hand, the knowledge made explicit in such models may be processed algorithmically, e.g., as found in model-driven engineering for easing the creation of software applications [7] or for fueling knowledge into existing applications [14].

This leads us to propose two main directions for virtual and augmented reality in relation to conceptual modeling. First, the use of functionalities of VR and AR for modeling itself. We will denote this as *VR/AR-assisted modeling*. Second, the incorporation of information from the model space into VR or AR applications, which we will denote as *knowledge-based VR/AR*. This second direction includes both design-time and run-time aspects, i.e., the modeling and model-driven generation of VR/AR applications as well as the fueling of model contents into existing VR/AR applications.

The paper at hand aims to explore the multitude of approaches proposed in academic research for combining conceptual modeling with virtual and augmented reality. Despite numerous contributions, no structured analysis of them has been undertaken so far to the best of our knowledge. Therefore, we conducted a systematic literature review on the combination of conceptual modeling with VR and AR within the last two decades. Further, we employed a computational content analysis to identify distinct research streams that have been explored in this field. Finally, we analyzed and refined the results of our analysis with the help of expert classification. The contribution of this study is to provide a comprehensive understanding of the main contributions for combining conceptual modeling with virtual and augmented reality, identify the main topics that have been studied in the past, and highlight the areas that require further research.

The remainder of the paper is structured as follows. In Sect. 2, we will describe the research methodology used for the review. Section 3 will describe the literature search results, which were used as input for Latent Dirichlet Allocation to computationally derive a first set of topics. Further, it will be shown how these topics have been refined using expert classification and the allocation of papers to the final set of topics. Finally, we will discuss the results of the analysis and derive points for future research in Sect. 4, as well as related work in Sect. 5.

2   Research Methodology

The methodology that we followed in this study is mainly based on the recommendations by Kitchenham [19] for conducting systematic literature reviews. This includes the three phases *Planning, Conducting*, and *Reporting*. The planning phase includes the identification of the need of the review as described above, as well as the definition of a research protocol, as shown in Fig. 1. The research protocol describes each step of the review process according to Booth et al. [5]. For the conduction phase, we further reverted to the guidelines by Webster and Watson [39], who recommend in particular the screening of dedicated outlets and the application of forward- and backward searches. In addition, we performed a computational literature analysis followed by an expert classification for deriving the topics of the different research streams.

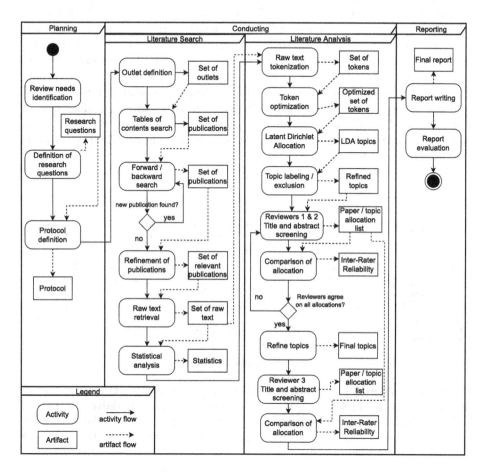

Fig. 1. Description of the research protocol. The protocol is divided into the three main areas as proposed by Kitchenham [19]. The process shows the undertaken steps together with the resulting artifacts.

2.1 Aims and Scope of the Study

The aim of this work is to identify the main research topics that combine conceptual modeling with virtual and augmented reality. Further, the study shall give detailed insights on the proposed concepts of *VR/AR-assisted modeling* and *knowledge-based VR/AR*. The investigated time frame includes academic papers

that have been published between the years 2000 and the first half of 2022, with
the goal to show the most recent research developments in these areas.

2.2 Literature Collection

For identifying the main research contributions on combining conceptual modeling with VR/AR, we reverted primarily to the method proposed by Webster and
Watson [39] to determine an initial set of relevant sources. We describe in the
following the steps as shown in the *Literature Search* section of the research protocol in Fig. 1. We first identified the nine most important outlets in the field of
conceptual modeling, based on a recent review by Härer and Fill [17]. According
to this source, many topics in conceptual modeling are strongly related to enterprise modeling. For example, business/business process models, or data models
and schemas. In addition, we added five outlets in the area of *Business Informatics* and *Information Systems* with potentially relevant contributions (*Outlet
definition*) - see Fig. 2.

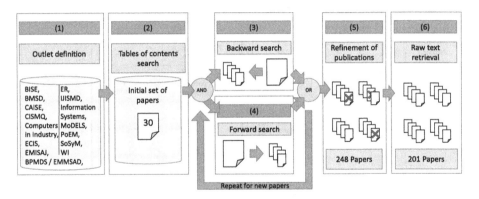

Fig. 2. Data collection process following Webster & Watson [39]: (1) Identification of
the relevant outlets. (2) Screening of tables of contents. (3 and 4) Iterative forward- and
backward search, based on the newly added relevant papers. (5) Selection refinement
by a more profound inspection of the selected papers, resulting in 201 relevant papers
of which the raw texts were retrieved (6).

We analyzed the tables of contents of the outlets to identify relevant contributions (*Tables of contents search*). For each of the found contributions, we
applied a forward- and backward search, i.e., finding for each paper relevant
cited and citing articles using *semanticscholar.org* and *google.scholar.com* (*Forward / backward search*). We repeated this step until no new papers were found.
We then reviewed the set of papers for excluding wrongly selected papers (*Refinement of publications*). Finally, we retrieved the raw texts of the papers for further
analysis (*Raw text retrieval*), and calculated quantitative indicators of the set
of relevant papers (*Statistical analysis*). A detailed description of the results of
this literature search will follow in Sect. 3.1.

2.3   Content-Based Data Analysis

To derive the research contribution in terms of previously studied topics, we conducted a computational analysis and complemented it with an expert-driven classification of relevant papers into distinct topical domains. The following steps refer to the *Literature Analysis* section in the research protocol as defined in Fig. 1.

Computational Data Analysis: For the compilation of an initial set of topics describing the main directions in the papers of the literature analysis, we resorted to the technique of *topic modeling*. This required the tokenization of the raw text of each document and preliminary tasks such as minimal stemming, stopword filtering, case transformation, synonym replacement, and single character filtering (*Raw text tokenization* and *Token optimization*). On this basis, we performed an LDA (*Latent Dirichlet Allocation*), which is an established method in computational topic modeling that has been successfully applied in previous literature reviews [17,27]. For the LDA, we used an iterative approach, which tries to optimize the hyperparameters for the topic generation, i.e., the number of topics, alpha and beta heuristics, as well as some evaluation measures like the topic coherence and the topic perplexity [23]. At the end of this iterative process, we decided on pursuing an analysis with ten topics. Details and results of this process will be described in Sect. 3.2.

Expert Analysis and Refinement: The topics proposed by the LDA were then labeled and refined manually by the authors and one external expert in an iterative procedure. By looking at the different words allocated by the LDA to the topics and by considering the list of the most probable allocated topic for each paper, we allocated labels to each topic (*Topic labeling/exclusion*). After this first topic labeling, the papers were manually allocated to one of the topics. As proposed by Vessey et al. [38], two experts allocated the papers independently from each other to exactly derive one topic by screening the titles of the papers. Then, each disagreement was discussed iteratively to find a consensus based on the abstracts of the contributions (*Title and abstract screening*).

For checking the reviewers' agreement, we calculated the inter-rater reliability (IRR) by using *Cohen's Kappa* (κ) [12] (*Comparison of allocation*). These steps were repeated until reviewers one and two reached an agreement on their allocation. Thereby, the topics could also be refined by renaming them or by merging similar topics, if found necessary, during the manual evaluation (*Refine topics*). This resulted in the final list of topics.

As an extension of the labeling process for two reviewers proposed by [38], a third reviewer manually assigned the papers to the final topics derived by reviewers one and two through a title and abstract screening (*Reviewer 3 Title and abstract screening*). The goal was to validate the reliability of the final assignment of reviewers one and two. Again, the IRR between the decision of the third reviewer and the joint assignment of reviewers one and two was calculated (*Comparison of allocation*).

3   Results

In this section, we describe the results obtained from the literature search process defined in Sect. 2.2, as well as of the content-based data analysis process described in Sect. 2.3.

3.1   Literature Search for Combining Virtual and Augmented Reality with Conceptual Modeling

As described in the methodology section above, we initially examined 15 outlets. We went manually through the outlets' tables of contents and searched for the terms *AR, VR, augmented reality, virtual reality,* and *3D.* The abstracts of the resulting papers were used to decide whether they are relevant for the analysis. A paper was considered relevant if it addressed at least one of the above areas, as well as conceptual modeling. In the context of this paper, we regard conceptual modeling in a broad sense, i.e., relating to the formal description of some aspect of the world around us based on a schema for the purpose of human understanding and communication [17,28]. The initial screening of these outlets led to a list of 30 relevant papers. The forward- and backward searches resulted in a list of 248 papers. Subsequently, a more detailed analysis of whether each paper indeed involved conceptual modeling was performed. Through a manual review of abstracts and/or full texts, we identified and excluded papers that are not based on a schema. This process resulted in a final list of 201 relevant papers. Due to space restrictions, the documentation of the whole process is available in the online Appendix A.

Regarding the number of publications over time, there is a clearly increasing trend in the number of published papers with a slope of $m = 0.4675$ when excluding the values from 2022 – see the right side of Fig. 3. In addition, the publications are distributed over many outlets. Only 30 out of the 201 relevant papers were published in one of the initially defined 15 outlets. In total, the 201 papers were published in 143 different outlets and only 12 of these outlets had three or more publications in the observed time span – see left side of Fig. 3. From the initial 15 outlets only *BMSD, CAiSE, ECIS* and *Computers in Industry* have three or more relevant publications.

3.2   Computational Topic Modeling

For the content-based analysis, we used computational topic modeling. Two common methods are LDA (Latent Dirichlet Allocation) [4] and NMF (Non-Negative Matrix Factorization) [36], which have been used for a long time. NMF is increasingly used for document collections with large noise, e.g., prepositions, abbreviations, or slang words. LDA can struggle with noise, but can be used in an iterative, semi-supervised way to produce a good ground truth of topics [11]. When the ground assumption of non-correlating topics does not hold, alternatives such as CTM (Correlated Topic Models) and STM (Structural Topic Models) may be used. CTM relaxes the assumption of independent topics [20].

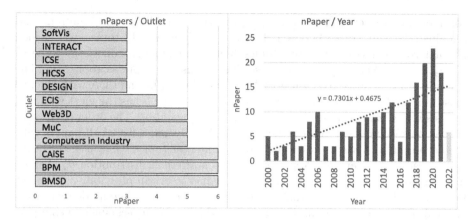

Fig. 3. Outlets with three or more relevant papers obtained from the literature search (left) and number of articles published per year with a linear trend line (right). The year 2022 was not considered since not all publications were yet available at the cut-off date of the analysis.

STM is a mixture model, in which each document can belong to a mixture of the specified k topics [34] and is often used for documents containing questionnaire data with open-ended questions. For datasets consisting mainly of short texts such as social media posts, specific methods have been developed, among others, SATM [33], or ETM [32]. Since our dataset consists exclusively of scientific papers, we decided to exclude the recent methods for short texts. We assumed that the topics in our analysis should be unique and independent. Further, we aimed to achieve the clearest possible assignment of a paper to a topic. Thus, we chose to exclude CTM and STM. Finally, we selected the traditional LDA as our basic methodology, which has been validated by several empirical studies as being capable of extracting semantically meaningful topics from texts and categorizing texts according to these topics [6,9,22,24].

We used MALLET (**MA**chine **L**earning for **L**anguag**E** **T**oolkit), as well as the LDA implementation that is part of RapidMiner Studio 9.5. As topic modeling is an unsupervised process, the evaluation of the results of an LDA presents some challenges. First, the quality of topics can be measured and compared by the *coherence value* of the topics [9,24]. It gives an overview of the semantic interpretability of the topics [24]. Second, *perplexity* measures of how well a probability model predicts a given sample. However, Chang et al. [9] showed, that human judgement and perplexity often do not correlate. Since the goal of our analysis was to get distinguishable topics that are human-interpretable, we focused on coherence rather than perplexity. Regarding the number of tokens assigned to each topic (topic size), there is no optimal topic value according to Mimno et al. [24]. However, smaller topics seem to be of better quality.

Based on this information, we performed different iterations of LDA for seven to thirteen topics and compared the corresponding average coherence values C_{UMass}. The values varied between -3.369 and -4.257, where lower values are considered as better [24]. Since C_{UMass} decreases rapidly at the beginning and remains relatively stable between the LDA with ten and 13 topics, we decided to analyze the model with ten topics having an average coherence value of $C_{UMass} = -4.203$. Further, we chose five tokens per topic as topic size. The left side of Fig. 4 shows the ten initial topics delivered by the LDA with the five most weighted words for each topic. For example, *Topic 0* has the most weighted terms *system, maintenance, context, user,* and *information.* The order of the topics has no specific meaning. Further, the LDA delivered a list of all papers with the according allocation probability to the different topics. Over a set of documents, each document d is represented by a statistical distribution θ_d over its different topics. That means, that each topic has a certain probability or weight for d, and for each topic k a distribution of words $\theta_{d,k}$ [3]. The hidden variables of the distributions are computed with the Gibbs sampling scheme by using parallel processing, where the weights per word are determined to maximize their probability of occurring in a given topic [29].

Only 27 (13%) papers had a most probable allocation to one of the ten topics of < 0.5. The remaining 174 papers had a most probable allocation of ≥ 0.5 and 101 papers (50%) had a most probable allocation of ≥ 0.7.

For our study, the LDA was intended as an objective ground truth for further analysis. For this reason, we do not elaborate further on the original topics of the LDA, but rather focus on the additional findings through the manual topic refinement and the paper assignment process in the next section.

3.3 Topics and Their Contribution

Since there is almost no human interference, LDA is a relatively objective process. The results of the LDA require however some interpretation and contextualization to increase their value. In this section, we therefore show the results of the labeling and revision of the ten initial topics through expert assessment, as well as the allocation of the different papers to these topics.

Refined Topics: For the labeling of the ten topics, the two authors considered the words allocated to the topics by the LDA together with the list of the most probable topic for each paper as defined by the *Literature Analysis* section of the research protocol visible in Fig. 1. Thereby, the most probable topic for each paper is the one to which the LDA assigns the paper with the highest probability.

We then decided commonly on a label for each LDA topic. Some topics required specific treatment: *Topic 8* consists of the terms *system, service, glass, smart,* and *information.* This indicates a focus on smart glasses, which have been explicitly researched in several of the selected papers. Since this is a hardware-specific category, it was decided to exclude this topic from the subsequent steps. Further, *Topic 7* and *Topic 9* were considered as similar in terms of their research area. The terms *sysml, uml, diagram,* and *visualization* were interpreted as related to software or system visualization. Thus, they were merged in one topic with the label *Software and System Visualization.* As shown in Fig. 4 (Refined Topics), out of the 10 LDA topics, eight topics were kept for the further analysis.

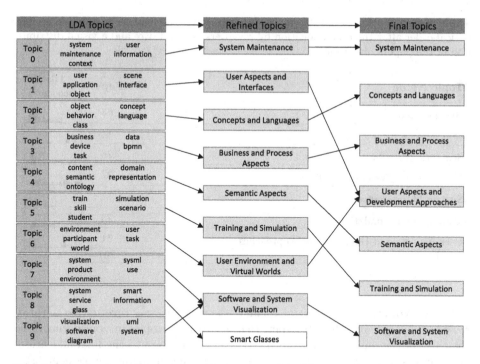

Fig. 4. Visualization of the topic evolution over the different refinement steps. **LDA Topics:** Initial topics delivered by the LDA analysis with the five most weighted words each. The order of the topics has no systematic ranking. **Refined Topics:** Topics according to the expert topic labeling. **Final Topics:** Final seven topics after the last refinement step.

Paper Allocation and Final Topics: After the initial topic labeling, the papers were manually allocated to one of the topics by the two authors to express the core focus of each paper through a single assignment. The resulting inter-rater reliability (IRR) in the form of *Cohen's Kappa* [12] was $\kappa = 0.617$ after the first allocation. According to Landis and Koch [21] values between 0.6 and 0.8 indicate a substantial agreement. After agreeing on the allocation of papers to the various topics, reviewers one and two discussed and refined the topics again. Thereby, the topics *User Aspects and Interfaces*, and *User Environment and Virtual Worlds* were merged into one topic entitled *User Aspects and Development Approaches*, which was regarded as a more suitable, common label when inspecting the underlying papers. This resulted in the final set of the seven topics visible in Fig. 4 (Final Topics).

As shown in Table 1, 63 papers (31.3%) were allocated to the topic *Business and Process Aspects*, followed by 37 papers (18.4%) allocated to *Software and System Visualization*, 31 papers to *User Aspects and Development Approaches* (15.4%), 26 papers to *Semantic Aspects* (12.9%), 23 papers to *Training and Simulation* (11.4%), 14 papers to *Concepts and Languages* (7%), and 7 papers to *System Maintenance* (3.5%). We will discuss the final topics and its main contributions in more detail in Sect. 4.

Table 1. Distribution of the 201 papers (nPapers) over the final seven topics in alphabetical order after the final allocation by reviewers one and two, and a visual distribution of the papers over time.

Topic Name	nPapers	Dist. 2000-2022
Business and Process Aspects	63	
Concepts and Languages	14	
Semantic Aspects	26	
Software and System Visualization	37	
System Maintenance	7	
Training and Simulation	23	
User Aspects and Development Approaches	31	
Total	201	

Quality Audit: For additional quality assurance it was reverted to a third reviewer who assigned the 201 papers to the final seven topics by considering only the titles of the papers. The resulting IRR in comparison to the final allocation of reviewers one and two was $\kappa = 0.520$, indicating moderate agreement [21]. Following the title screening, the third reviewer was then additionally presented with the abstracts of those papers to which he had not assigned the same topic as reviewers one and two, without revealing the assignments of the other reviewers to him. He could then decide whether to assign a different topic or maintain his selection. After this step, the resulting IRR in comparison to the final allocation of reviewers one and two increased to $\kappa = 0.655$, which indicates a substantial agreement [21].

4   Discussion

With the insights gained above, we can now advance to the discussion of our findings in regard to the initially proposed directions of *VR/AR-assisted modeling* and *knowledge-based VR/AR*. Further, we will highlight areas that have not yet been covered by research.

The main research contributions are the following: First, the research question on the main contributions of combining conceptual modeling with virtual and augmented reality can be answered directly in terms of the literature search (Sect. 3.1). The 201 relevant papers are distributed across many different outlets, with no outlet dominating. The research area reviewed in this paper shows a clearly increasing trend in publications, which is a promising sign for future research. Second, by discussing the results from Sect. 3.3 and by reflecting on possible application areas that would push research and industry forward, we can identify the main topics that have been studied in the past, and highlight the areas that require further research. Regarding the identification of the main topics, we need to consider the final topics, their interpretation, the allocation of the papers to these topics by the reviewers, as well as some exemplary contributions to these topics. It shall be noted that the labeling of the different topics is a subjective task and that other reviewers may allocate different labels. However, we tried to mitigate this subjective factor by conducting the objective LDA analysis as a ground truth for further investigation. Further, the labeling of the different topics was conducted by two reviewers in an iterative process and dissenting opinions were discussed. In the following, we discuss the final topics and their interpretation as well as some sample papers that the reviewers assigned to these topics.

Papers assigned to the topic *Business and Process Aspects* deal mainly with business process management. With regard to the traditional business process life cycle [40], Design/Analysis [R90, R169, R244][1], Configuration [R72, R193], and Enactment [R152, R173, R219] have been subject of research related to VR/AR. However, we could not yet discover research on the *Evaluation* of business processes related to VR/AR. This is surprising, since VR/AR devices provide a variety of sensor data that would be predestined for process evaluation. The areas *VR/AR-assisted modeling*, e.g., [R96] and *knowledge-based VR/AR*, e.g., [R1, R158] are both present in research.

Concepts and Languages contain contributions like languages for modeling VR/AR systems, or for authoring VR/AR content. Thereby, we could identify the three main streams: *content creation* [R88, R186], *metamodeling* [R147, R26], and *concepts for model-driven code generation* [R184, R119]. All these research streams can be related to *knowledge-based VR/AR*, either for design-time, or for run-time, i.e., real-time content creation. What seems to have not been covered so far is the combination of *knowledge-based VR/AR* and *VR/AR-assisted modeling* in a generic way, e.g., for allowing VR-based model-driven engineering of VR/AR applications, which could be useful for simulating the interaction with 3D environments in VR prior to their realization using AR.

For structuring the papers allocated to the topic of *Semantic Aspects*, we found that they can be related to the seven components of the semantic web framework derived in [15]. Considering these components, we found approaches for *Querying and Reasoning* [R4, R148, R206], *Ontology Engineering* [R41, R205], *Ontology Instance Generation* [R160, R208], and *Semantic Web Services* [R188]. The assignment to *VR/AR-assisted modeling* or *knowledge-based VR/AR* is not always clear. It depends on whether the semantic aspects are used for modeling ontology-driven VR/AR applications [R41], for semantic aspects such as reasoning for AR during run-time [R148], or for generating models by analyzing the sensor data of VR/AR devices. This last point seems to be missing so far in the found papers.

---

[1] For space reasons, references to articles from our literature analysis are linked in a separate document. Clicking on the [R] reference opens a web page showing the selected reference at the top.

In *Software and System Visualization* the focus lies on *requirement gathering and analysis, designing, coding, testing,* and *maintenance and support,* i.e., on the software development life cycle [18]. Most of the discovered papers deal with analyzing [R58, R142, R155, R156 R157] (*knowledge-based VR/AR*) and designing [R105, R177] (*VR/AR-assisted modeling*) software and systems. Only few addressed testing and maintenance of software and systems [R9, R85] and none addressed so far the coding phase.

System Maintenance is an area where VR/AR is used in relation to maintenance activities, e.g., modeling languages and VR/AR systems guiding maintenance processes on the basis of conceptual models [R78, R99]. This refers mainly to the area of *knowledge-based VR/AR* as described at the beginning of the paper. Looking at the different types of maintenance, e.g., *improving, preventing,* and *correcting* [25], all types are covered by the found approaches, since most of them are not bound to a particular maintenance type.

In the *Training and Simulation* topic, contributions focus mainly on training and simulation aspects, e.g., in business process training. Mostly we can refer here again to *knowledge-based VR/AR for design- or run-time.* Most research is conducted in training applications involving virtual worlds for desktop applications [R8, R34, R121] followed by VR training environments [R182, R234]. Very little research has been done in the area of AR training applications combined with conceptual modeling [R75, R228]. This is an area that should be explored further, as training in AR offers many potential application scenarios.

The topic *User Aspects and Development Approaches* is twofold. First, contributions focusing on the user, i.e., *user interaction* [R57], *user interfaces* [R29], and *collaboration* [R215]. Second, research focusing on development approaches, i.e., approaches investigating *content authoring* [R42, R102], *model-driven development* [R30, R46], and the development of *virtual worlds* [R25]. Both of these main streams primarily cover design-time aspects, and thus, belong to *knowledge-based VR/AR.* Only very few contributions dealt with pedagogic or learning aspects [R132]. This is surprising as there is a lot of ongoing research on general VR/AR learning approaches, as recently shown by Chen et al. [10].

From the above descriptions and the mentioned papers, it becomes clear that most of the contributions found in our analysis are positioned in the area of *knowledge-based VR/AR* where models are used as input for VR/AR applications. Currently, there exist very few approaches where modeling in VR/AR, or the automated elicitation of models is considered. Further, only some contributions focus on pedagogic and learning aspects in AR modeling. Regarding missing areas, some aspects are not covered at all by research yet. For example, approaches combining knowledge-based VR/AR and VR/AR-assisted modeling, allowing the interplay of these two areas. Further, we could not yet identify approaches on the evaluation of business processes using VR/AR and no approaches for the semantic elicitation of conceptual models during run-time, e.g., for generating conceptual models on the basis of the user context.

Further, in comparison to the most promising industry use cases as proposed by the *Augmented Reality for Enterprise Alliance (AREA)* [1], which acts under the umbrella of the Object Management Group (OMG), 11 out of the 13 use case areas are covered also by our analysis. Only the areas *remote assistance* and *marketing and sales* did not become apparent in our study. This large overlap illustrates the relevance of the topics researched in academia for industry.

5   Related Work

Based on the wide research and analysis that we conducted, we can confidently state that to date, there has been no literature review that systematically investigates the combination of conceptual modeling with VR and AR. While there has been a previous review in the field conducted by Poehler and Teutenberg [30], it is important to note that their focus was specifically on the application of VR for business processes, rather than conceptual modeling as a whole. Thus, our findings highlight the novelty and importance of our review in filling this gap in the existing body of literature.

6   Conclusion

In this paper we conducted a systematic literature review, a computational bibliometric study, as well as an expert driven classification of papers combining conceptual modeling with VR/AR. The analysis suggests that there is a clear upward trend in the number of publications in this research area. There are no specific venues for this area so far, but the contributions are rather spread across many different outlets. The elaborated research areas include research in both VR/AR-assisted modeling, as well as knowledge-based VR/AR. However, the focus so far lies strongly on knowledge-based VR/AR. Only few publications deal with VR/AR-assisted modeling.

Despite the large number of publications that we reviewed, this study is however not without limitations. First, the initial selection of outlets for the literature search could have been extended to include further venues. However, since we performed a comprehensive forward- and a backward search for each paper, we are confident that we found most relevant papers. Second, we performed a computer-assisted content analysis using only unigrams. We did not consider bi-grams or n-grams, as this would have increased the complexity. This could be considered for an extension of the study in the future. Third, we only allowed papers to be allocated to one single topic. This follows the proposal of Vessey et al. [38]. However, this could be extended to multiple allocations, thereby permitting greater insight into the overlap of topics.

The results of our study offer valuable insights into the combination of conceptual modeling with virtual and augmented reality, which we believe will be of great interest to both the research community and industry practitioners. We hope that our findings will stimulate discussions and lead to further research in this evolving field. Moreover, we plan to standardize our process and share our insights with other members of the AR modeling community, which will help to advance the field and drive future innovation, e.g., in AR-related enterprise modeling, like the use cases derived in [26].

Appendix A   Dataset of the Review Process

The bibliographies of the document corpora [R1-R248], as well as the various lists [T1-T8] documenting the whole process shown in Fig. 1 are available as HTML files online[2]. In particular, we provide lists with the initial papers [T2], all papers [T3], papers per journal [T4], the most probable topics per paper [T5], as well as the assignments of the reviewers during the review process [T6, T7, T8, T9].

References

1. AREA: AREA AR use case descriptions. Technical report, Augmented Reality for Enterprises Alliance (AREA) (2022). https://thearea.org/wp-content/uploads/2022/05/AR-Use-Case-Descriptions-and-Examples.pdf. Accessed 07 Nov 2022
2. Betz, S., et al.: 3D representation of business process models. In: Modellierung betrieblicher Informationssysteme. LNI, vol. P-141, pp. 73–87. GI (2008). https://dl.gi.de/20.500.12116/23619
3. Blei, D.M.: Probabilistic topic models. Commun. ACM **55**(4), 77–84 (2012). https://doi.org/10.1145/2133806.2133826
4. Blei, D.M., Ng, A.Y., Jordan, M.I.: Latent dirichlet allocation. J. Mach. Learn. Res. **3**, 993–1022 (2003)
5. Booth, A., Sutton, A., Papaioannou, D.: Systematic approaches to a successful literature review, 2nd edn. Sage (2016)
6. Boyd-Graber, J., Mimno, D., Newman, D.: Care and Feeding of Topic Models: Problems, Diagnostics, and Improvements. CRC Handbooks of Modern Statistical Methods, CRC Press (2014)
7. Brambilla, M., Cabot, J., Wimmer, M.: Model-Driven Software Engineering in Practice. Morgan & Claypool (2017). https://doi.org/10.2200/S00751ED2V01Y201701SWE004
8. Cabot, J., Vallecillo, A.: Modeling should be an independent scientific discipline. Softw. Syst. Model. **21**(6), 2101–2107 (2022). https://doi.org/10.1007/s10270-022-01035-8, https://doi.org/10.1007/s10270-022-01035-8
9. Chang, J., Boyd-Graber, J., Gerrish, S., Wang, C., Blei, D.M.: Reading tea leaves: how humans interpret topic models. In: NIPS 2009 Conference, pp. 288–296 (2009)
10. Chen, P., Liu, X., Cheng, W., Huang, R.: A review of using augmented reality in education from 2011 to 2016. In: Innovations in Smart Learning. LNET, pp. 13–18. Springer, Singapore (2017). https://doi.org/10.1007/978-981-10-2419-1_2
11. Churchill, R., Singh, L.: The evolution of topic modeling. ACM Comput. Surv. (2022). https://doi.org/10.1145/3507900
12. Cohen, J.: A coefficient of agreement for nominal scales. Educ. Psychol. Meas. **20**(1), 37–46 (1960). https://doi.org/10.1177/001316446002000104
13. Dalton, J., Gillham, J.: Seeing is believing (2019). https://www.pwc.com/gx/en/industries/technology/publications/economic-impact-of-vr-ar.html. Accessed 07 Nov 2022
14. Fill, H.-G., Härer, F., Muff, F., Curty, S.: Towards augmented enterprise models as low-code interfaces to digital systems. In: Shishkov, B. (ed.) BMSD 2021. LNBIP, vol. 422, pp. 343–352. Springer, Cham (2021). https://doi.org/10.1007/978-3-030-79976-2_22

---

[2] https://doi.org/10.5281/zenodo.7794278.

15. García-Castro, R., Gómez-Pérez, A., Muñoz-García, Ó., Nixon, L.J.B.: Towards a component-based framework for developing semantic web applications. In: Domingue, J., Anutariya, C. (eds.) ASWC 2008. LNCS, vol. 5367, pp. 197–211. Springer, Heidelberg (2008). https://doi.org/10.1007/978-3-540-89704-0_14

16. Grambow, G., Hieber, D., Oberhauser, R., Pogolski, C.: A context and augmented reality BPMN and BPMS extension for industrial internet of things processes. In: Marrella, A., Weber, B. (eds.) BPM 2021. LNBIP, vol. 436, pp. 379–390. Springer, Cham (2022). https://doi.org/10.1007/978-3-030-94343-1_29

17. Härer, F., Fill, H.-G.: Past trends and future prospects in conceptual modeling - a bibliometric analysis. In: Dobbie, G., Frank, U., Kappel, G., Liddle, S.W., Mayr, H.C. (eds.) ER 2020. LNCS, vol. 12400, pp. 34–47. Springer, Cham (2020). https://doi.org/10.1007/978-3-030-62522-1_3

18. Khan, N.A.: Research on various software development lifecycle models. In: Arai, K., Kapoor, S., Bhatia, R. (eds.) FTC 2020. AISC, vol. 1290, pp. 357–364. Springer, Cham (2021). https://doi.org/10.1007/978-3-030-63092-8_24

19. Kitchenham, B.: Procedures for performing systematic reviews. Technical report (2004)

20. Lafferty, J., Blei, D.: Correlated topic models. In: Advances in Neural Information Processing Systems, vol. 18, pp. 147–154. MIT Press (2005)

21. Landis, J.R., Koch, G.G.: The measurement of observer agreement for categorical data. Biometrics **33**(1), 159 (1977). https://doi.org/10.2307/2529310

22. Lau, J.H., Newman, D., Baldwin, T.: Machine reading tea leaves: automatically evaluating topic coherence and topic model quality. In: Conference of the European Chapter of the Association for Computational Linguistics, pp. 530–539. ACL (2014). https://doi.org/10.3115/v1/E14-1056

23. McCallum, A.K.: Mallet: a machine learning for language toolkit (2002). http://mallet.cs.umass.edu. Accessed 07 Nov 2022

24. Mimno, D., Wallach, H.M., Talley, E., Leenders, M., McCallum, A.: Optimizing semantic coherence in topic models. In: EMNLP 2011, pp. 262–272. ACL (2011)

25. Mobley, R.: Maintenance Fundamentals. Plant Engineering, Elsevier Science (2011). https://doi.org/10.1016/b978-0-7506-7798-1.x5021-3

26. Muff, F., Fill, H.: Use cases for augmented reality applications in enterprise modeling: A morphological analysis. In: Shishkov, B. (ed.) BMSD 2022. LNCS, vol. 453, pp. 230–239. Springer, Cham (2022). https://doi.org/10.1007/978-3-031-11510-3_14

27. Muff, F., Härer, F., Fill, H.: Trends in academic and industrial research on business process management - a computational literature analysis. In: HICSS, pp. 1–10. ScholarSpace (2022). http://hdl.handle.net/10125/80215

28. Mylopoulos, J.: Conceptual modelling and Telos. In: Conceptual Modeling, Databases, and Case: An Integrated View of Information Systems Development, pp. 49–68. Wiley (1992)

29. Newman, D., Asuncion, A.U., Smyth, P., Welling, M.: Distributed algorithms for topic models. J. Mach. Learn. Res. **10**, 1801–1828 (2009). https://doi.org/10.5555/1577069.1755845

30. Pöhler, L., Teuteberg, F.: Closing spatial und motivational gaps: virtual reality in business process improvement. In: European Conference on Information Systems, AIS (2021). https://aisel.aisnet.org/ecis2021_rp/151

31. PricewaterhouseCoopers: Us metaverse survey: Build a metaverse strategy to deliver sustainable business outcomes (2022). https://www.pwc.com/us/en/tech-effect/emerging-tech/metaverse-survey.html. Accessed 07 Nov 2022

32. Qiang, J., Chen, P., Wang, T., Wu, X.: Topic modeling over short texts by incorporating word embeddings. In: Kim, J., Shim, K., Cao, L., Lee, J.-G., Lin, X., Moon, Y.-S. (eds.) PAKDD 2017. LNCS (LNAI), vol. 10235, pp. 363–374. Springer, Cham (2017). https://doi.org/10.1007/978-3-319-57529-2_29

33. Quan, X., Kit, C., Ge, Y., Pan, S.J.: Short and sparse text topic modeling via self-aggregation. In: Joint Conference on Artificial Intelligence, pp. 2270–2276. AAAI (2015). http://ijcai.org/Abstract/15/321

34. Roberts, M.E., et al.: Structural topic models for open-ended survey responses. Am. J. Pol. Sci. **58**(4), 1064–1082 (2014). https://doi.org/10.1111/ajps.12103

35. Sandkuhl, K., et al.: From expert discipline to common practice: a vision and research agenda for extending the reach of enterprise modeling. Bus. Inf. Syst. Eng. **60**(1), 69–80 (2018). https://doi.org/10.1007/s12599-017-0516-y

36. Shahnaz, F., Berry, M.W., Pauca, V.P., Plemmons, R.J.: Document clustering using nonnegative matrix factorization. Inf. Process. Manag. **42**(2), 373–386 (2006). https://doi.org/10.1016/j.ipm.2004.11.005

37. de Souza Cardoso, L.F., Mariano, F.C.M.Q., Zorzal, E.R.: A survey of industrial augmented reality. Comput. Ind. Eng. 139 (2020). https://doi.org/10.1016/j.cie.2019.106159

38. Vessey, I., Ramesh, V., Glass, R.L.: Research in information systems: an empirical study of diversity in the discipline and its journals. J. Manag. Inf. Syst. **19**(2), 129–174 (2002). https://doi.org/10.1080/07421222.2002.11045721

39. Webster, J., Watson, R.T.: Analyzing the past to prepare for the future: writing a literature review. MIS Q. **26**(2) (2002)

40. Weske, M.: Business Process Management - Concepts, Languages, Architectures, 3rd edn. Springer, Cham (2019). https://doi.org/10.1007/978-3-662-59432-2

41. Wild, F., Perey, C., Hensen, B., Klamma, R.: IEEE standard for augmented reality learning experience models. In: IEEE International Conference on Teaching, Assessment, and Learning for Engineering, TALE 2020, pp. 1–3. IEEE (2020). https://doi.org/10.1109/TALE48869.2020.9368405

42. Yin, K., He, Z., Xiong, J., Zou, J., Li, K., Wu, S.T.: Virtual reality and augmented reality displays: advances and future perspectives. J. Phys. Photon. **3**(2) (2021). https://doi.org/10.1088/2515-7647/abf02e

FaaSOnto: A Semantic Model for Enabling Function-as-a-Service Platform Selection

Stijn van Geene[1,2], Indika Kumara[1,2(✉)], Geert Monsieur[1,3],
Willem-Jan van Den Heuvel[1,2], and Damian Andrew Tamburri[1,3]

[1] Jheronimus Academy of Data Science, Sint Janssingel 92, 5211 DA
's-Hertogenbosch, North Brabant, The Netherlands
{s.vangeene,i.p.k.weerasinghadewage,
w.j.a.m.vdnHeuvel}@tilburguniversity.edu
[2] Tilburg University, Warandelaan 2, 5037 AB Tilburg, North Brabant,
The Netherlands
[3] Eindhoven University of Technology, Groene Loper 3, 5612 AE Eindhoven,
North Brabant, The Netherlands
{g.monsieur,d.a.tamburri}@tue.nl

Abstract. Serverless computing shifts the responsibilities of provisioning and managing cloud infrastructure resources from developers to cloud service providers, allowing developers to focus solely on their applications. Function-as-a-Service (FaaS) is a serverless computing approach that enables developers to develop their applications as event-driven functions. There are many FaaS platforms available through public cloud providers or open-source distributions. Understanding the differences in these platforms and keeping up to date with their latest developments is challenging. Hence, it is necessary to systematically model the information about FaaS Platforms to allow practitioners to select the platform most suited for realizing their use cases. This paper presents the *FaaSOnto* ontology, a semantic model that represents the characteristics of FaaS platforms. We developed the ontology systematically following the NeOn methodology. We fully implemented the ontology using OWL2 and created a knowledge base with information about ten different FaaS platforms. The knowledge base is semi-automatically populated. On top of the knowledge base, we developed a minimal decision support system to enable the sorting and filtering of FaaS platforms based on their characteristics to facilitate an interactive platform selection process.

Keywords: Function-as-a-Service · FaaS · Serverless Computing · Ontology · Cloud Platform Selection · Knowledge Graph

1 Introduction

Serverless computing is increasingly gaining attention from practitioners and researchers [1]. For example, a recent survey from the Cloud Native Computing

S. van Geene and I. Kumara—Contributed equally to this work.

Foundation (CNCF) found that 39% of respondents have adopted serverless technology [2]. The serverless model enables developers to build and run applications faster by eliminating the need for them to provision or manage infrastructure. In particular, Function-as-a-Service (FaaS), a specific serverless model, allows the developers to create software functions in a cloud environment and automatically execute them in response to events or requests. According to CNCF, the adoption of FaaS has grown steadily since its introduction in 2016 [2].

FaaS platforms constantly evolve, leading to challenges for practitioners to compare and select the platforms most suited for implementing their applications [2,3]. Open source and commercial FaaS platforms exist, e.g., OpenFaaS, AWS Lambda, Google Cloud Functions, and Microsoft Azure Functions [2]. These platforms do not use a coherent vocabulary to describe their characteristics. This results in ambiguity around the characteristics of FaaS platforms, making it hard to compare them accurately [3].

The work presented in this paper seeks to address the FaaS selection decision-making challenge and is guided by the following research question:

How can we systematically model the characteristics of FaaS platforms to enable their selection by non-experts?

Several studies have attempted to address the problem of the FaaS platform selection. In particular, Marcin *et al.* [4] created a benchmark suite to evaluate the performance of FaaS platforms. Vladimir *et al.* [3] built a classification framework that uses various organizational and technical characteristics for comparing FaaS platforms. Similarly, Jinfeng *et al.* [5] created a taxonomy of features of serverless computing platforms. However, the information in the frameworks in these studies is in natural languages, which may not be precise and unambiguous, making searching for, auto-updating, and integrating such information problematic.

This paper presents a semantic-enabled framework that represents the knowledge necessary for selecting the FaaS platform using an ontology, namely *FaaSOnto*, to address the aforementioned limitations of the existing studies. We systematically developed *FaaSOnto* by applying the NeOn ontology engineering methodology [6]. *FaaSOnto* was fully represented using OWL2 Web Ontology Language. Furthermore, we developed a knowledge-based system using *FaaSOnto* on Amazon Cloud and used it to realize different knowledge-capturing and exploration scenarios for evaluating *FaaSOnto*'s capabilities to compare and select the FaaS platforms based on different criteria. We also developed the techniques to semi-automatically populate and update the knowledge base using publicly available information, such as release notes, GitHub repository data, and Stack Overflow data. Moreover, we created a minimum viable product of a decision support system to assess the practicability of using the *FaaSOnto* knowledge base to support an interactive platform selection process for end-users.

This paper is structured as follows. Section 2 describes the ontology development methodology, including the requirements and competency questions of *FaaSOnto*. Then, in Sect. 3, we present *FaaSOnto* in detail. Section 4 describes

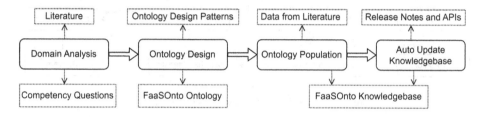

Fig. 1. Schematic Representation of Ontology Development Methodology

the implementation of the *FaaSOnto* knowledge base and the decision support system that uses the *FaaSOnto* ontology. Finally, Sect. 5 reviews the related work, and Sect. 6 concludes the paper.

2 Ontology Development Methodology

We applied the NeOn methodology [6] to develop the *FaaSOnto* ontology. We mainly used scenario 7 in NeOn, which focuses on using ontology design patterns [7] to ensure the reusability and extensibility of the developed ontology. Figure 1 shows the workflow of our methodology. In the rest of this section, we briefly discuss each phase in the workflow.

We primarily use the related FaaS literature (*e.g.*, [3,5]) to identify the criteria for comparing FaaS platforms and the competency questions (CQs) for the *FaaSOnto* ontology. We formulated CQs as question templates that can be instantiated to create multiple question instances.

- CQ1: What characteristics does FaaS platform A have?
- CQ2: Which FaaS platforms support characteristic B?
- CQ3: Which FaaS platforms satisfy condition C for characteristic D?
- CQ4: What is the equivalent of FaaS platform E's characteristic F on FaaS platform G?
- CQ5: Which FaaS platform has the [highest/lowest] value for numerical characteristic H?

We used the DOLCE+DnS Ultra Lite (DUL) ontology[1] as the foundational ontology. The DUL is based on ontology design patterns [7]. We designed *FaaSOnto* by adopting and extending the DnS (Descriptions and Situations) design pattern [8] from the DUL. The DnS pattern enables modeling high-level descriptions and situations that can be used in various domains. We implemented *FaaSOnto* using OWL2 Web Ontology Language.

We deployed the OWL-based implementation of *FaaSOnto* into the AWS Neptune graph database service. To populate the ontology, we semi-automatically extracted the data from the related literature [3,5]. Moreover, we also used the release notes of FaaS platforms, GitHub APIs, and the Stack

---

[1] http://ontologydesignpatterns.org/wiki/Ontology:DOLCE+DnS_Ultralite.

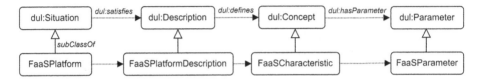

Fig. 2. *FaaSOnto* Ontology Conceptual Model

Overflow APIs to update the information in the *FaaSOnto* knowledgebase regularly and automatically. To assess the expressiveness of *FaaSOnto*, we used multiple instances of CQs. We implemented CQs using the SPARQL query language. Moreover, throughout the *FaaSOnto* development process, we used the ontology evaluation tool OOPS (i.e., Ontology Pitfall Scanner) [9] to assess and improve the ontology continuously.

3   FaaSOnto Ontology

This section presents the *FaaSOnto* ontology in detail. We first introduce the high-level conceptual model of *FaaSOnto* and then explain the modeling of each characteristic of a FaaS platform.

3.1   Conceptual Model

We adopted the core concepts of the DUL ontology, such as Situation, Description, and Concept, to model the key concepts of FaaS platforms (similar to the approach taken in [10]). Figure 2 shows the top-level concepts of *FaaSOnto*. A *DUL Situation* consists of entities and relationships among them. A *DUL Description* is an entity that represents a theory and can be interpreted by an *agent*. A *DUL Concept* classifies entities within a domain and describes how they should be interpreted in a particular situation. A *DUL Parameter* enriches a *DUL Concept* with additional descriptive context. We molded *FaaSPlatform* as a sub-class of *dul:Situation. FaaSPlatform* has a *FaaSPlatformDescription*, which is a sub-class of *dul:Description.* They are connected via the *dul:satisfies* relationship. A *FaaSPlatformDescription*is related to *FaaSCharacteristic* (sub-class of *dul:Concept*) through the *dul:defines* relationship. Finally, the *FaaSCharacteristic* class is related to *FaaSParameter* (sub-class of *dul:Parameter*) through the *dul:hasParameter* relationship.

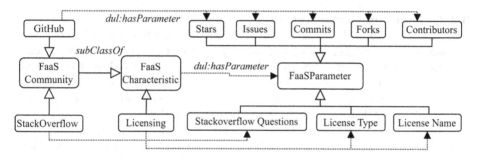

Fig. 3. Community and Licensing Characteristics

3.2 Modeling FaaS Characteristics and Parameters

The characteristics and parameters of FaaS platforms are modeled following the
DUL upper ontology. All characteristics are sub-classes of *FaaSCharacteristic*.
The sub-categories of a FaaS characteristic are also modeled as sub-classes of
the corresponding characteristic class. All parameters are sub-classes of *FaaS-Parameter*.

3.2.1 Community and Licensing

Figure 3 defines community and licensing characteristics. *FaaSCommunity*
describes the properties of the developer community surrounding the FaaS Platform. *Stackoverflow* criterion indicates how many questions were asked on Stack
Overflow about a FaaS platform over a certain period. *GitHub* captures data
on the GitHub repository, such as the number of stars, forks, and contributors,
which are only available for open-source FaaS platforms. *Licensing* represents
information about the license of the FaaS platforms. *License Type* and *License
Name* describe the type and name of the license under which a platform is
released, for example, types of permissive, public domain, and proprietary, and
names of Apache 2.0 and MIT.

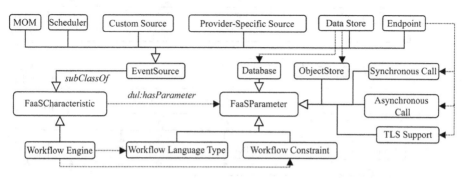

Fig. 4. Function Orchestration Characteristic

3.2.2   Function Orchestration

The events produced by cloud services, such as storage buckets, databases, and message brokers, trigger the executions of FaaS functions. For example, when a new file is added to an AWS S3 bucket, an event is generated, and that event can trigger one or more AWS Lambda functions. In addition to the event-driven execution of functions, workflow engines can also be used to orchestrate serverless functions, *e.g.,* AWS Step Functions and Google Workflows.

Figure 4 represents the function orchestration characteristic. *MOM (Message-Oriented Middleware)* represents message or event brokers that can trigger FaaS functions, *e.g.,* Google Pub/Sub and AWS Simple Queue Service. *Scheduler* indicates whether a given FaaS platform supports scheduled function invocation, which allows functions to be invoked periodically (*e.g.,* hourly, daily, or weekly). *Object Store* and *Database* are two main types of data storage services (*Data Store*) that can produce events. AWS S3 and GCP Storage are examples of object stores, and Azure CosmosDB and AWS Aurora are databases. A FaaS function can also be exposed as an API endpoint (*Endpoint*). *Synchronous Call* and *Asynchronous Call* define the function invocation through synchronous and asynchronous API requests. *Custom Source* is to model the support for integrating the third-party event sources, *e.g.,* using Rabbit MQ message broker to trigger AWS Lambda Functions. *Provider-Specific Source* represents the cloud platform-specific services that can trigger FaaS functions, *e.g.,* AWS Alexa or IBM Watson. Regarding workflow engines, they generally provide languages to define the order of the execution of functions, including function inputs and outputs. The language can be a standard workflow definition language or a custom DSL (Domain Specific Language). Workflow engines can also impose some constraints, *e.g.,* limits on control flow constructs, execution time, input size, and output size.

3.2.3   Development and Deployment

The features of the development and deployment tools (offered by FaaS platforms) affect developers' productivity and thus are essential to consider them in the platform selection process. Figure 5 represents development and deployment

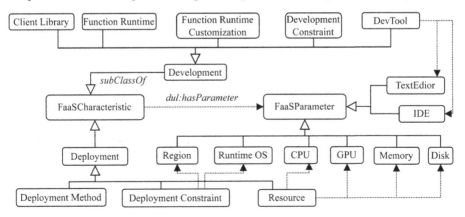

Fig. 5. Development and Deployment Characteristics

characteristics. Developers create functions using a programming language supported by the platform (*Function Runtime*). They typically use the libraries provided by the platform to develop, deploy and manage functions (*Client Libraries*). They also use IDEs and text editors, for which a given platform provides plugins(*IDE and Text Editor*). For example, a developer uses PyCharm IDE with AWS Toolkit installed to create a Python-based AWS Lambda function using the Python library *boto3*. FaaS platforms typically allow using a custom Docker image as the function runtime (*Runtime Customization*). They also impose various constraints on functions, *e.g.*, package or Docker image size and function execution duration. Once a function is successfully developed, it can be deployed using various methods,*e.g.*, source code and docker container (*Deployment Methods*). Developers can also generally specify the resources (*e.g.*, CPU, GPU, memory, and disk) and operating system to be used by the function. They can also choose the data center's location that hosts the function(*Region*).

3.2.4   Best Practices in Development and Deployment

FaaS platforms also support applying the best software engineering practices, such as the reuse and versioning of function code, testing and debugging of code, and application delivery automation. Figure 6 represents such platform characteristics. *Function Marketplace* indicates whether a given FaaS platform has function or application examples available through a marketplace, *e.g.*, Azure Marketplace or the OpenFaaS function store. *Code Sample Repository* indicates whether a given FaaS platform provides one or more repositories with code samples that developers can use as a starting point or reference for their application. *Application Versioning* and *Function Versioning* define a platform's support for versioning on the level of the whole application or individual functions. Developers can use CI/CD (Continuous Integration and Continuous Deployment) pipelines to automate the building, testing, and deployment of FaaS functions (*CI/CD Pipeline*). Some platforms also support using IaC (Infrastructure as Code) tools [11] for deploying functions (*IaC Blueprint*), *e.g.*, AWS CloudFormation for AWS Lambda. The source code of functions and applications must be tested and debugged before being deployed to production. *Testing* describes tools related to the various types of testing, such as functional (*e.g.*, unit testing) and non-functional (*e.g.*, load testing). *Debugging* defines tools used for debugging function code locally or remotely.

3.2.5   Installation and Usage

Figure 7 represents the characteristics related to the installation and usage of FaaS platforms. *Installation Type* indicates if the FaaS platform is installable, hosted as-a-service, or both. *Target Host* defines to which target hosts a platform can be installed. For example, the OpenFaaS platform can be deployed onto a Kubernetes cluster, and AWS Lambda is a hosted service. FaaS platforms offer different types of interfaces for developers to interact with them. *Interface Type* indicates which interfaces a given platform provides, such as GUI, CLI, and API. *Application Management* and *Platform Administration* define the types of operations supported by a given platform, *e.g.*, creation and deletion of applications

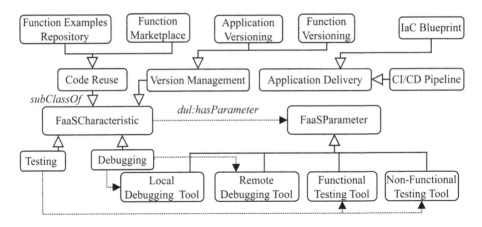

Fig. 6. Development and Deployment Best Practice Characteristics

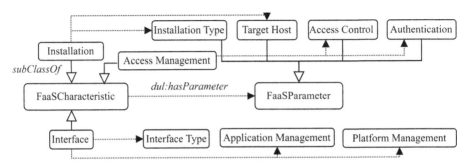

Fig. 7. Characteristics of Installation and Usage of FaaS Platforms

and deployment and configuration of platforms. *Access Control* and *Authentication* indicate whether a given platform provides access control and authentication mechanisms. For example, some FaaS platforms have features that support the authentication of users through their Google or Twitter accounts.

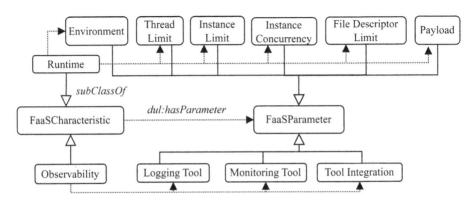

Fig. 8. Runtime and Observability Characteristics

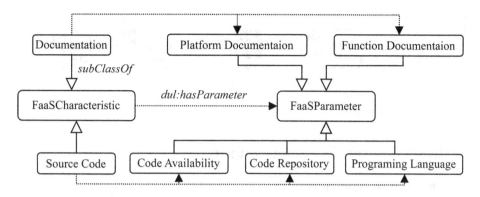

Fig. 9. Documentation and Source Code Characteristics

3.2.6   Platform at Runtime

Figure 8 represents the runtime characteristics of FaaS platforms. *Environment* defines the host environment a function instance runs on, for example, a lightweight VM such as Firecracker or a container-based environment like Docker. *Thread Limit* specifies the maximum number of threads allowed. *Instance Limit* defines the maximum number of instances created when a function is invoked. *Instance Concurrency* represents the maximum number of concurrent invocations a single function instance can process. *File Descriptors* describes the limit on file descriptors, which determines the maximum number of opened files. *Payload* specifies the size limit for a request message payload (in MB) when calling a function. FaaS platforms also enable developers to monitor functions, including their usage and logs generated. *Monitoring Tool* and *Logging Tool* indicate which monitoring and logging tools a given platform supports. *Tool Integration* specifies a platform's support for integrating logging and monitoring tools. A developer can use platform-native tools(*e.g.,* AWS CloudWatch) or 3rd party tools (*e.g.,* Prometheus).

3.2.7   Documentation and Source Code

The documentation and source codes of platforms are essential criteria for selecting platforms. Figure 9 represents these characteristics. *Functions Documentation* specifies the availability of documentation on developing and deploying functions. *Platform Documentation* indicates whether a given platform provides the documentation on how to use and extend it, including the platform's architecture. The source code category mainly distinguishes between open-source and closed-source FaaS platforms (*Code Availability*). Furthermore, *Programming Language* defines the primary implementation language of a given open-source platform. *Code Repository* specifies the repository provider, such as GitHub or BitBucket.

Fig. 10. Architecture of Ontology Population and Update

4   Implementation and Evaluation

4.1   FaaSOnto Knowledge Base

We fully implemented the *FaaSOnto* ontology using OWL2. We also developed a knowledge-based system using *FaaSOnto* on Amazon cloud services (AWS). The FaaSOnto GitHub repository[2] includes the artifacts the implementation uses, including OWL files, python scripts, and data.

We deployed the ontology in the graph database on AWS Neptune and partially automated the population of the ontology. Figure 10 shows the architecture of the ontology population and update. The data from multiple sources are automatically extracted and analyzed to generate triples containing subject, predicate, and object. These triples are sent to the (REST) API Gateway on AWS, which is connected to an AWS Lambda function that translates the triples into SPARQL INSERT DATA queries. The Lambda function executes the queries by sending requests to the SPARQL HTTP API of the AWS Neptune instance.

We used the FaaS platform data from the FaaStener project [3] and the publication of Jinfeng *et al.* [5] to instantiate the knowledge base. First, we programmatically extracted the data from the FaaStener GitHub repository and converted it to triples. However, the data from Jinfeng *et al.* [5] is not available in a public GitHub repository, and thus we manually translate the data extracted from the corresponding publication into triples.

To keep the *FaaSOnto* knowledge base up to date, we used multiple approaches suited to different categories of information. For GitHub and Stack-Overflow metrics of FaaS Platforms, we queried the GitHub API and the Stack-overflow API on a scheduled basis through AWS Lambda functions. The triples are generated in the Lambda functions and sent to the API Gateway, where they are inserted into the knowledge base. We employed the approaches proposed by the existing research studies to extract the relevant information via APIs. For example, the number of Stackoverflow questions per platform has been determined by querying the Stackoverflow API by tag, as in [12].

To update the rest of the information in the knowledge base, we rely on the release notes of the FaaS platforms. The three leading public cloud providers (GCP, AWS, and Azure) publish the release notes of their FaaS platforms as public RSS (Really Simple Syndication) feeds. We first automatically retrieve the RSS feeds and parse them as XML. Next, the regex patterns are used to extract the words that contain the relevant information. The Natural Language

---

[2] https://github.com/IndikaKuma/FaaSOnto.

Table 1. Examples of Competency Questions and their Answers in SPARQL

CQ Instances	SPARQL Query
What are the available hosted FaaS platforms?	SELECT ?platform WHERE { ?platform faas:hasFeature faas:as-a-service }

What runtimes does AWSLambda support?	SELECT ?runtime
	FROM faas:AWSLambda
	WHERE {
	?runtime rdfs:subClassOf faas:FunctionRuntime .
	faas:AWSLambda faas:hasFeature ?runtime .
	}

What message queue solutions can be used to trigger functions on each platform?	SELECT *
	WHERE {
	?s rdfs:subClassOf faas:MessageQueue .
	?plt faas:hasFeature ?s .
	}

How many GitHub stars does ApacheOpenwhisk have?	SELECT *
	FROM faas:ApacheOpenwhisk
	WHERE {
	faas:GitHubStars dul:hasDataValue ?o
	}

Does AWSLambda support runtime customization?	ASK {
	aas:AWSLambda faas:hasFeature
	faas:RuntimeCustomization
	}

Processing (NLP) package *spaCy* is used to process these pieces of text further. Similar to [13], we first tokenize the text and then apply techniques such as Part-of-Speech (POS) tagging and lemmatization. The output of the text processing is used as input to pre-trained models in *spaCy*. In particular, we used spaCy's similarity models to predict the similarity between two pieces of text using word vectors (multi-dimensional representation of words). For each candidate entity, the similarity between the relevant section in the release notes and all the descriptions of the characteristics from the *FaaSOnto* ontology (stored as *rdfs:comment*) has been computed. The three classes with the highest similarity are returned as possible super-classes for a given entity. The platform features that can potentially become sub-classes of a super-class are identified based on their POS tags, following the approach in [14]. The results of the release note processing are shown in the interface of the decision support system (DSS), where the users of the DSS can select the correct features and super-classes (see Sect. 4.3). The corresponding triples are generated and added to the knowledge base when a user submits the selection of the features and super-classes.

4.2   Ontology Evaluation

We evaluated the *FaaSOnto* ontology by answering the competency questions (CQs), providing standard ontology metrics, and checking for common mistakes in the ontology using the Ontology Pitfall Scanner [9].

156   S. van Geene et al.

Table 2. A Summary of OWL2 Representation of FaaSOnto

Metric	FaaSOnto (Including DUL)	DUL
Axiom	4164	1549
Logical axiom count	1482	605
Declaration axioms count	778	202
Class count	404	79
Object property count	114	112
Data property count	5	5
Individual count	244	0
Annotation Property count	9	9

We created multiple examples (instances) of CQs and answered them using SPARQL queries. Table 1 shows a subset of those questions (instances) and their answers in SPARQL.

Table 2 provides an overview of the OWL2 implementation of *FaaSOnto*. We extracted these metrics using the Protégé tool[3], a widely-used ontology editor. Figure 11 visualizes part of the *FaaSOnto* knowledge base. It shows the event sources that can be used with AWS Lambda FaaS functions.

To evaluate the *FaaSOnto* ontology and check for common mistakes, the Ontology Pitfall Scanner was used. It is a web application that can detect com-

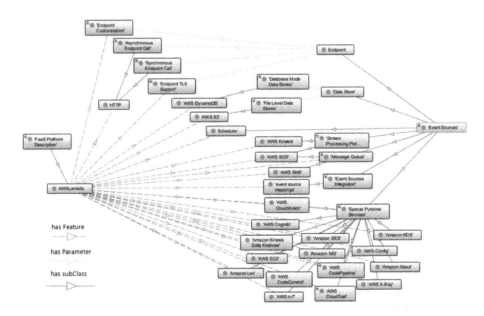

Fig. 11. AWSLambda and its Characteristics related to Event Sources

---

[3] https://protege.stanford.edu/.

[Expand All] | [Collapse All]

Results for P08: Missing annotations.	11 cases | Minor ⌒
Results for P11: Missing domain or range in properties.	1 case | Important ⊘
Results for P13: Inverse relationships not explicitly declared.	3 cases | Minor ⌒
Results for P22: Using different naming conventions in the ontology.	ontology* | Minor ⌒
Results for P34: Untyped class.	5 cases | Important ⊘
Results for P41: No license declared.	ontology* | Important ⊘

Fig. 12. Results from the Ontology Pitfall Scanner (Screenshot)

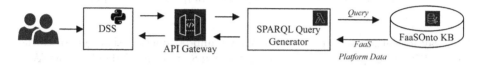

Fig. 13. Architecture of the DSS (Decision Support System)

mon issues based on three levels of importance: critical, important, and minor. For example, a missing annotation is considered a minor pitfall, and an object- or data property missing its domain or range is an important pitfall. Critical pitfalls hinder the correct functioning of ontology. Figure 12 shows the results for the *FaaSOnto* ontology. No critical pitfalls have been discovered. The important pitfalls are related to the DUL ontology, not the FaaSOnto ontology.

4.3   Decision Support System

On top of the *FaaSOnto* Knowledge Base, we created a decision support system (DSS) to evaluate the feasibility of performing the FaaS platform selection using our knowledge base. The DSS was built in Python using the open-source Dash and Plotly libraries. Figure 13 presents its architecture. The DSS front-end retrieves the data via the REST API deployed on AWS API Gateway. The API

FaaS Decision Support System

Use the interactive table below to sort and filter the data.

⇕	FaaS Platform ⌃	Installation Type ⇕	Runtime Customization ⇕	Github Stars ⇕	Stackoverflow questions
	filter data...		Indicates the number of stars the GitHub repository a FaaS platform has		>100
	AWS Lambda	As-a-service			16800
	Google Cloud Funtions	As-a-service	no		12386
	Microsoft Azure Functions	As-a-service	yes		7200
	Apache OpenWhisk	Installable	yes	4800	198

Fig. 14. Example of Filtering and Sorting Data with the DSS (Screenshot)

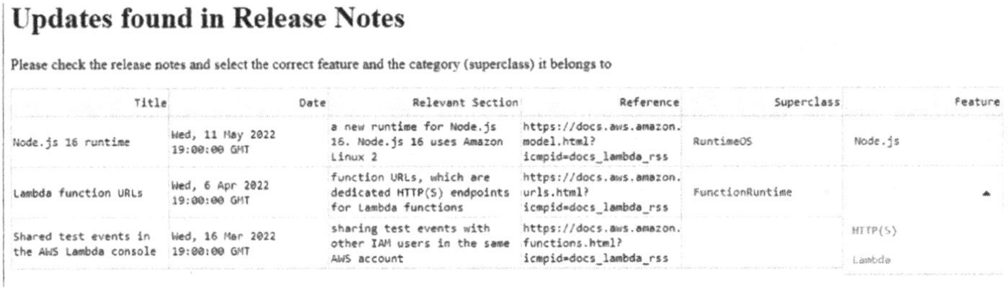

Updates found in Release Notes

Please check the release notes and select the correct feature and the category (superclass) it belongs to

Title	Date	Relevant Section	Reference	Superclass	Feature
Node.js 16 runtime	Wed, 11 May 2022 19:00:00 GMT	a new runtime for Node.js 16. Node.js 16 uses Amazon Linux 2	https://docs.aws.amazon.model.html? icmpid=docs_lambda_rss	RuntimeOS	Node.js
Lambda function URLs	Wed, 6 Apr 2022 19:00:00 GMT	function URLs, which are dedicated HTTP(S) endpoints for Lambda functions	https://docs.aws.amazon.urls.html? icmpid=docs_lambda_rss	FunctionRuntime	▲
Shared test events in the AWS Lambda console	Wed, 16 Mar 2022 19:00:00 GMT	sharing test events with other IAM users in the same AWS account	https://docs.aws.amazon.functions.html? icmpid=docs_lambda_rss	HTTP(S) Lambda	

Fig. 15. Screenshot of the DSS: Update Information Section

Gateway forwards the request to an AWS Lambda function that generates the correct SPARQL query and sends it to the *FaaSOnto* knowledge base on AWS Neptune. The response is returned to the API Gateway, which forwards it to the DSS. Finally, the returned data is transformed into the correct format for presentation in the DSS as a Dash *DataTable*.

The layout of the DSS is an interactive table that displays the data from the knowledge base. The column data can be sorted by clicking the arrows on the left side of the column header, which sorts the values alphabetically for textual data and numerically for numeric columns. Additionally, the values can be filtered by typing in the box below the header. The filtering criteria can be logical statements, for example, >100, indicating a numeric value for a given characteristic has to be greater than 100. The tooltips of the column headers are used to show the descriptions of the corresponding characteristics when the mouse hovers over the column headers. Figure 14 shows the use of the DSS UI to sort the platforms based on installation type and filters for platforms with at least 100 Stack Overflow questions. The mouse hovers over the column header of GitHub *Stars* at the moment of the screenshot, which shows the description of the GitHub *Stars* characteristic.

The results of the release notes processing are also similarly presented to users using an interactive table. In this case, however, the cells in the table are editable via a drop-down menu that shows the most likely values for the characteristic and super-class columns. Figure 15 provides a screenshot of the release note processing. The small downward-facing triangle indicates a drop-down selection possible for that cell. The users can select the values to modify the results of the release note processing and can submit the updated results to be added to the knowledge base.

5   Related Work

This section reviews the studies on the classification of FaaS platforms, ontologies representing cloud services, cloud ontologies leveraging NLP, and decision support systems for cloud service selection.

Vladimir *et al.* [3] created a classification framework (*FaaStener*) for FaaS platforms by incorporating their technical and business aspects. They reviewed the academic literature about FaaS and the official documentation of the commercial and open-source platforms. The business view includes properties such as licensing, source code availability, and community metrics that can help to assess the level of market adoption of a given FaaS platform. The technical view includes properties such as function execution runtimes, function triggers, and CI/CD pipelines. Jinfeng *et al.* [5] created a taxonomy of FaaS characteristics from the developer's perspective. These characteristics are modeled at a more detailed level compared to the work of Vladimir *et al.* For example, the taxonomy includes numerical features of FaaS platforms, such as the maximum size of the memory a function can use and the maximum execution time for a function.

Francesco *et al.* [15] designed the mOSAIC ontology, a first step towards standardizing cloud service concepts and semantics. Eleni *et al.* [16] developed the Cloud4SOA ontology, which focuses on the standardization and interoperability of cloud providers. Le *et al.* [17] created a fuzzy ontology to enable cloud service selection using MCDM (Multi-Criteria Decision Making) methods. More recently, Mustafa *et al.* [18] developed a comprehensive cloud service ontology that classifies services based on their functionality. In [19,20], we also presented an ontology that can represent the deployment models of cloud applications. We used it to detect various quality issues in the descriptions of deployment models. Finally, Nick *et al.* [10] developed the PaaSport ontology that semantically represents the characteristics of PaaS (Platform as a service) offerings and requirements of applications built on a PaaS platform. The PaaSport ontology is designed to facilitate the PaaSport Marketplace, a platform that aims to improve the interoperability of cloud platforms and the portability of applications.

Ontologies can be learned from natural language texts by leveraging text-mining techniques [21]. Ganapathy *et al.* [14] applies ontology learning techniques to the cloud computing domain. They automatically extract the information in the service level agreements of cloud service providers using various NLP techniques and use the extracted data to generate an ontology.

Farshidi *et al.* [22] created a decision support framework based on MCDM methods for enabling technology selection. They have applied their framework in several domains, including Blockchain platforms [23], cloud service providers [24], and programming languages [25]. With the DSS, users can indicate what features and criteria are important to them through the MoSCoW prioritization technique [26]. For each feature of technology, a user can indicate that it is a "Must have", "Should have", "Could have" or "will not have." An inference engine analyses the data provided by the users and gives detailed recommendations for selecting particular technologies.

Table 3 summarizes and compares the related studies with our work. Compared with the related work, we created an ontology representing the information necessary for FaaS platform selection. We also created a knowledge base using our ontology and developed the support for populating and updating the knowledge base semi-automatically. We also created a minimal decision support system that enables the end-users to explore the information in the knowledge base interactively.

Table 3. Analysis of Related Work

Study	Focus	Ontology-based	Knowledge Auto-Update	Decision Support System
PaaSport	PaaS	Yes	No	+
CloudFNF	Full Cloud	Yes	No	−
FaaStener	FaaS	No	No	−
Farshidi *et al.*	Cloud Provider	No	No	++
FaaSOnto	FaaS	Yes	Semi-Automated	+

6 Conclusion and Future Work

In this paper, we presented a semantic model, namely the *FaaSOnto* ontology, that can systematically describe the characteristics and features of FaaS platforms to facilitate practitioners to select and compare FaaS platforms accurately. We implemented the ontology using OWL2. Moreover, a knowledge base system that employs the *FaaSOnto* ontology was developed using AWS cloud services. The knowledge base can be semi-automatically populated and updated using the data from release notes of FaaS platforms, GitHub API, and Stack Overflow API. Finally, a minimal decision support system was built upon the knowledge base to demonstrate the feasibility of our approach to enable practitioners to easily select the FaaS platform(s) most suited to support their applications.

We identified several research directions for future work. First, we plan to improve the automated data extraction in our framework using advanced text-mining techniques. Next, we aim to extend the *FaaSOnto* ontology to capture information such as business factors and platform performance data published in the research papers. Finally, we will improve the decision support system by incorporating MCDM methods.

Acknowledgments. This research has received funding from the Dutch government under the SENTINEL project and the European Union's Horizon research and innovation program under the grant agreement No 101097036 (ONCOSCREEN).

References

1. Castro, P., Ishakian, V., Muthusamy, V., Slominski, A.: The rise of serverless computing. Commun. ACM 62(12), 44–54 (2019)
2. Foundation, C.N.C.: CNCF Annual Survey 2021 (2021). https://www.cncf.io/reports/cncf-annual-survey-2021/. Accessed 22 May 2022
3. Yussupov, V., Soldani, J., Breitenbücher, U., Brogi, A., Leymann, F.: FaaSten your decisions: a classification framework and technology review of function-asa-Service platforms. J. Syst. Softw. **175**, 110906 (2021)
4. Copik, M., Kwasniewski, G., Besta, M., Podstawski, M., Hoeer, T.: SEBS: a serverless benchmark suite for function-as-a-service computing. In: Proceedings of the 22nd International Middleware Conference, pp. 64–78 (2021)

5. Wen, J., Liu, Y., Chen, Z., Chen, J., Ma, Y.: Characterizing commodity serverless computing platforms. J. Softw. Evol. Process **n/a**(n/a), 2394 (2021)
6. Suárez-Figueroa, Mari Carmen, Gómez-Pérez, Asunción, Fernández-López, Mariano: The neon methodology for ontology Engineering. In: Suárez-Figueroa, Mari Carmen, Gómez-Pérez, Asunción, Motta, Enrico, Gangemi, Aldo (eds.) Ontology Engineering in a Networked World, pp. 9–34. Springer, Heidelberg (2012). https://doi.org/10.1007/978-3-642-24794-1_2
7. Gangemi, Aldo, Presutti, Valentina: Ontology design patterns. In: Staab, Steffen, Studer, Rudi (eds.) Handbook on Ontologies. IHIS, pp. 221–243. Springer, Heidelberg (2009). https://doi.org/10.1007/978-3-540-92673-3_10
8. Gangemi, A., Mika, P.: Understanding the semantic web through descriptions and situations. In: OTM Confederated International Conferences on the Move to Meaningful Internet Systems, pp. 689–706. Springer, Berlin, Heidelberg (2003)
9. Poveda-Villalón, M., Suárez-Figueroa, M.C., Gómez-Pérez, A.: Validating ontologies with oops! In: Teije, A., et al. (eds.) Knowledge Engineering and Knowledge Management, pp. 267–281. Springer, Berlin, Heidelberg (2012)
10. Bassiliades, N., Symeonidis, M., Gouvas, P., Kontopoulos, E., Meditskos, G., Vlahavas, I.: PaaSport semantic model: an ontology for a platform-as-a-service semantically interoperable marketplace. Data Knowl. Eng. **113**, 81–115 (2018)
11. Kumara, I., et al.: The do's and don'ts of infrastructure code: a systematic gray literature review. Inf. Softw. Technol. **137**, 106593 (2021)
12. Wen, J., et al.: An empirical study on challenges of application development in serverless computing. In: Proceedings of the 29th ACM Joint Meeting on European Software Engineering Conference and Symposium on the Foundations of Software Engineering, pp. 416–428. ACM, Athens Greece (2021)
13. Fawei, B., Pan, J.Z., Kollingbaum, M., Wyner, A.Z.: A semi-automated ontology construction for legal question answering. New Gen. Comput. **37**(4), 453–478 (2019)
14. Ganapathy, D.N., Joshi, K.P.: A semantically rich framework to automate cloud service level agreements. IEEE Trans. Serv. Comput. **16**(1), 53–64 (2023)
15. Moscato, F., Aversa, R., Di Martino, B., Fortiş, T.-F., Munteanu, V.: An analysis of mosaic ontology for cloud resources annotation. In: 2011 Federated Conference on Computer Science and Information Systems (FedCSIS), pp. 973–980 (2011)
16. Kamateri, E., et al.: Cloud4SOA: a semantic-interoperability PaaS solution for multi-cloud platform management and portability. In: Lau, Kung-Kiu., Lamersdorf, Winfried, Pimentel, Ernesto (eds.) ESOCC 2013. LNCS, vol. 8135, pp. 64–78. Springer, Heidelberg (2013). https://doi.org/10.1007/978-3-642-40651-5_6
17. Sun, L., Ma, J., Zhang, Y., Dong, H., Hussain, F.K.: Cloud-FuSeR: fuzzy ontology and MCDM based cloud service selection. Future Gen. Comput. Syst. **57**, 42–55 (2016)
18. Al-Sayed, M.M., Hassan, H.A., Omara, F.A.: CloudFNF: an ontology structure for functional and non-functional features of cloud services. J. Parallel Distrib. Comput. **141**, 143–173 (2020)
19. Kumara, I., et al.: Towards semantic detection of smells in cloud infrastructure code. In: Proceedings of the 10th International Conference on Web Intelligence, Mining And Semantics, pp. 63–67. ACM, Biarritz France (2020)
20. Di Nitto, E., Gorroñogoitia Cruz, J., Kumara, I., Radolović, D., Tokmakov, K., Vasileiou, Z.: Deployment and Operation of Complex Software in Heterogeneous Execution Environments: The SODALITE Approach. Springer, Cham, Gewerbestrasse (2022)

21. Wong, W., Liu, W., Bennamoun, M.: Ontology learning from text: a look back and into the future. ACM Comput. Surv. **44**(4) (2012)

22. Farshidi, S., Jansen, S., Jong, R., Brinkkemper, S.: A decision support system for cloud service provider selection problem in software producing organizations. In: 2018 IEEE 20th Conference on Business Informatics (CBI), vol. 01, pp. 139–148 (2018)

23. Farshidi, S., Jansen, S., Espa na, S., Verkleij, J.: Decision support for blockchain platform selection: three industry case studies. IEEE Trans. Eng. Manage. **67**(4), 1109–1128 (2020)

24. Farshidi, S., Jansen, S., Jong, R., Brinkkemper, S.: A decision support system for software technology selection. J. Decis. Syst. **27**(sup1), 98–110 (2018)

25. Farshidi, S., Jansen, S., Deldar, M.: A decision model for programming language ecosystem selection: Seven industry case studies. Inf. Softw. Technol. **139**, 106640 (2021)

26. DSDM Consortium, R., et al.: The DSDM agile project framework handbook. Ashford, Kent, UK: DSDM Consortium (2014)

Development of a Capability Maturity Model for Organization-Wide Green IT Adoption

Victor Brand[(✉)], Maryam Razavian, and Baris Ozkan

Department of Industrial Engineering and Innovation Sciences,
Eindhoven University of Technology, Eindhoven, The Netherlands
victor.brand@live.nl, {m.razavian,b.ozkan}@tue.nl

Abstract. Although organizations aim to become more sustainable, they have faced challenges in creating a clear path to reshape their capabilities in line with the adoption of Green IT. Therefore, they need guidance from a holistic viewpoint to facilitate in their business model adaptation. This paper proposes a maturity model to assist organizations by providing current Green IT maturity determination and guidance in the creation of a roadmap for improvement. We adopt a design science research methodology for developing and evaluating the maturity model. Our model is based on a review of existing Green IT maturity models and is thereafter iteratively developed and refined through a Delphi study. The evaluation of the Green IT model reveals that the model is applicable for identifying the organizational-level capabilities that contribute to Green IT adoption, and to enable organizations to assess their current state of Green IT adoption.

Keywords: Green IT adoption · organizational capabilities · capability maturity model

1 Introduction

As society aims at reducing the environmental impact, many organizations envision adopting sustainable practices. Although Information Technology (IT) holds the potential to play a pivotal role in a sustainable future [1,2], it can have a substantial negative impact [3]. This impact has evolved into a critical area of focus and led to the development of Green IT [4,5], considered to positively impact environmental performance and ecosystems, *'either directly by reducing physical and energy inputs in their production, use, disposal, and recycling; or indirectly through their wider application and use in other equipment and systems'* [5, p. 58]. In short, Green IT can be considered to reduce the direct negative impacts of IT as well as to enhance the indirect positive impacts of IT [6]. While organizations aim to adopt Green IT, they face challenges in creating a clear path to reshape their capabilities and adapt their business model accordingly. As the mere intention to adopt Green IT does not necessarily translate to the capability to do so [7], organizations need guidance from a holistic viewpoint.

© The Author(s), under exclusive license to Springer Nature Switzerland AG 2023
B. Shishkov (Ed.): BMSD 2023, LNBIP 483, pp. 163–179, 2023.
https://doi.org/10.1007/978-3-031-36757-1_10

Maturity models have been suggested as a means of offering such guidance, as they can embody domain knowledge and can reveal the strengths and areas for improvement within an organization [8]. Accordingly, these models can offer support in identifying improvement activities that have the potential to reshape the capabilities of an organization [9]. Although some Green IT maturity models have been presented in the literature (e.g., [7,10,11]), they tend to lack support on the capabilities required for organization-wide adoption. These existing models focus on areas within organizations where Green IT can be applied, but overlook the high-level capabilities that are crucial to widespread adoption. This is why there is a need for a maturity model that defines and structures these contributing capabilities, as Green IT adoption requires a systemic approach from the organization [12]. As such, the objective of this paper is to develop a Green IT capability maturity model (CMM) to support the organization-wide adoption of Green IT by enabling them to assess and improve on their capabilities. This CMM is developed by capturing domain knowledge from the literature and enhancing and refining it through a Delphi study.

Our Green IT CMM guides organizations in developing, assessing, and improving the capabilities required for Green IT adoption. To offer guidance, CMMs are generally suggested, as they provide a set of related capabilities and indicate levels of maturity for these capabilities [13,14]. Therefore, our CMM should identify the capabilities an organization should have for Green IT adoption. Furthermore, by defining maturity levels for each capability, our CMM should enable organizations in assessing their current state of Green IT adoption and should support them in defining a roadmap to improve.

The remainder of this paper is structured as follows: Sect. 2 discusses the research methods we used; Sect. 3 outlines the development of our CMM; Sect. 4 presents our CMM and its use in practice; Sect. 5 elaborates on the evaluation of the model; and, lastly, Sect. 6 presents the conclusion and discussion.

2   Research Method

The development of our CMM was conducted utilizing the design science research methodology (DSRM) as proposed by Peffers *et al.* [15]. A visual representation of our DSRM project approach is provided in Fig. 1. The six research activities associated with the DSRM approach are briefly discussed below.

(1) Identify Problem and Motivate. The problem was identified through interviews with practitioners and a snowballing literature review to explore existing Green IT models and frameworks [16]. The protocol and comprehensive results of this literature review can be found in [17].

(2) Define Objectives of a Solution. The objectives of a solution were defined based on the suggested functionalities of a CMM. These objectives were aligned with the research objectives and are detailed in Sect. 3.

(3) Design and Development. The design and development of the artifact (i.e., Green IT CMM) was carried out through a Delphi study [13]. The initial version

of the artifact was created by aggregating existing Green IT models and frameworks. This initial version was then subjected to a three-round Delphi study involving twelve domain experts. The Delphi development process is described in Sect. 3.2.

(4) Demonstration. In each Delphi round, the model was demonstrated to the participating domain experts, and interviews were conducted to allow for suggestions on the latest iteration of the artifact. This feedback from the experts was used to further develop the artifact until a consensus was reached after the third Delphi round. This resulted in the final artifact after three iterations between the design and development and the demonstration activities.

(5) Evaluation. The final artifact was evaluated together with practitioners from both in-house and consultancy industries, as it was anticipated that practitioners from both perspectives would use the model in practice. Group interviews were conducted to evaluate the artifact and assess its utility in practice. This evaluation research is discussed in Sect. 5.

(6) Communication. The proposed artifact was communicated through the writing of this paper, which elaborates on our conducted research.

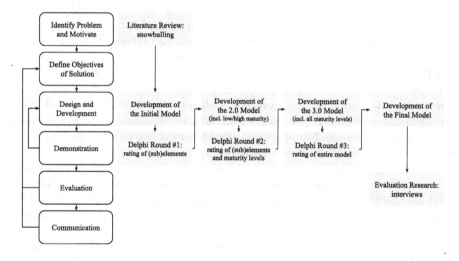

Fig. 1. DSRM Project Design

3   Development of the Artifact

In the development of our CMM, we adhered to the guidelines proposed by Becker *et al.* [13]. Prior to developing the artifact, we established three solution objectives (SO) to serve as evaluation criteria for the final iteration of our CMM. These objectives are:

(SO1) The artifact should identify organization-wide capabilities that contribute to Green IT adoption.
(SO2) The artifact should enable organizations to assess their current state of Green IT adoption.
(SO3) The artifact should support organizations to define a roadmap to improve their Green IT adoption.

3.1   Development of the Initial Model

In order to develop a theoretical underpinning for our initial version of the artifact, we conducted a literature review by utilizing the snowballing method [16] (protocols and results are elaborated in [17]). The objective of this literature review was to identify and review the maturity models and capability frameworks that currently exist in the field of Green IT. Through this snowballing process, we first identified a set of relevant literature reviews on Green IT adoption, such as [18–22]. These reviews enabled us to assemble a pool of existing Green IT models and frameworks that identify Green IT adoption capabilities (i.e., [7, 10, 11, 18, 20, 23–25]). We utilized this collection of literature to construct our initial model, which we built upon by combining all the identified Green IT adoption capabilities as mentioned. For this, we followed the categorization proposed by Curley *et al.* [10]. Table 1 summarizes the identified capabilities and serves as the theoretical foundation of our model.

A visual representation of our initial model is presented in Fig. 2. This model was created by consolidating the identified capabilities, and its structure was based on the Process and Enterprise Maturity Model (PEMM) proposed by Hammer [26]. PEMM identifies contributing characteristics that are distributed across several domains. In our model, we identified 14 contributing characteristics across four capability domains. Furthermore, we formulated definitions for each characteristic by synthesizing the definitions provided in the literature. The initial model served as the starting point for further artifact development through the application of a Delphi study.

Table 1. Overview of Green IT Adoption Capabilities

CATEGORY	CAPABILITY	DEFINITIONS
Strategy & Planning	Objectives	Define the Green IT objectives for the IT function [10]
		Define and agree on sustainability objectives for ICT [23]
	Alignment	Align Green IT objectives between IT function and the rest of the business [10]
		Define and execute the ICT sustainability strategy to influence and align to business sustainability objectives [23]
		Defined as 'Strategic Intent': The alignment between IT and organizational objectives examines the relationship between such alignment and Green IT adoption [20]
	Innovation	The resources and skills associated with the firm's encouragement of innovation and reinforcement of innovative resources [18]
	Top Management Support	Support from the organization's top managers or champions who recognize the values of an innovation and support its development and implementation [20]
Process Management	Operations and Life Cycle	Source/design, operate and dispose of IT systems in an environmentally sensitive manner [10]
		Source, operate, and dispose of ICT systems to deliver sustainability objectives [23]
		Defined as 'Practice': To what extent an organization has translated its concerns and policies into actions [7,25]
	Technology-Enhanced Business Processes	Identify IT solutions that enable environmentally sensitive business operations [10]
		Defined as 'ICT-enabled Business Processes': Create provisions for ICT systems that enable improved sustainability outcomes across the extended enterprise [23]
		Defined as 'Technology': The extent to which more environmentally effective technologies are acquired and solutions are developed to support enterprise-wide green initiatives [7,25]
	Performance and Reporting	Demonstrate progress against objectives for Green IT concerning the IT function or technology-enabled solutions across business operations [10]
		Report and demonstrate progress against ICT-specific and ICT-enabled sustainability objectives, within the ICT business and across the extended enterprise [23]
	Green Standards and Metrics	Required for promotion, comparison and benchmarking of sustainability initiatives, products, services and practices [24]
People & Culture	Language	Define, communicate and use language and vocabulary for Green IT that are understood by all stakeholders [10]
		Define, communicate, and use common sustainability language and vocabulary across ICT and other business units, including the extended enterprise, to leverage a common understanding [23]
	Adoption	Promote principles and behaviours that support Green IT [10]
		Embed sustainability principles across ICT and the extended enterprise [23]
	Attitude	The extent to which both IT and business are aware and interested about the economical, strategic, regulatory, environmental and social concerns related to the use of IT [7,25]
		Defined as Emotional Management: The extent of emotional appeal towards environmental impact upon convincing the organizational social system to act green [18]
		Defined as 'Greening of Organizational Culture': Green IT, which also pursues economic and environmental values, is highly consistent with green organization culture [20]
	Learning	The extent to which the organization facilitates the diffusion of IT in terms of technology acceptance and organizational encouragement [18]
Governance	Regulatory Compliance	Enable and demonstrate compliance with external standards and regulations concerning the environmental impact of computing and business operation activities [10]
		Defined as 'External Compliance': Evangelize sustainability successes and contribute to industry best practices [23]
	Corporate Policies	Establish corporate policies to support a Green IT strategy [10]
		Enable and demonstrate compliance with ICT and business sustainability legislation and regulation. Require accountability for sustainability roles and decision-making across ICT and the enterprise [23]
		Defined as 'Policy': The extent to which green and sustainability policies are developed throughout an organization and permeate the value chain [7,25]
		Defined as 'Green Strategies and Policies': Effective and actionable strategies and policies that add value and focus on both long and short-term benefits [24]

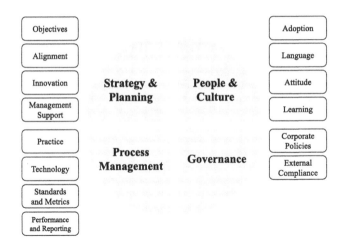

Fig. 2. Green IT CMM - Initial Model

3.2 Delphi Study

This section outlines the methodology of the Delphi study, including the selection of the Delphi panel and the evolution of the model over the course of the Delphi study.

Delphi Study Setup. The Delphi study was chosen as the method of inquiry due to its suitability for exploratory studies, as highlighted in previous literature [8]. Given the limited knowledge available in our field of research, the Delphi study was considered an effective means of contributing to this incomplete state of knowledge [27]. A Delphi study is a group facilitation process that seeks to obtain consensus on the opinions of a group experts through rounds of individual interviews [28]. Following this Delphi method, our artifact was gradually developed with a panel of relevant domain experts (i.e., the Delphi panel) [29]. We decided to set up a Delphi study of three rounds in order to sufficiently observe convergence among experts [30,31]. The first two rounds of the Delphi study were exploratory in nature, allowing for the addition of new elements to the model. The third round was confirmatory, with no possibility for the addition of new elements. During each round, the interviews were conducted individually and were moderated by the researcher.

During each expert interview, the expert reviewed the latest iteration of the artifact with the help of a corresponding questionnaire. The questionnaire served as a guide for reviewing all elements of the model, with experts given the option to vote for *stay, change,* or *go* for each element. Additionally, open-ended questions were posed to elicit the rationale behind the feedback received. Based on the obtained feedback after each round of interviews, the next iteration of the model was developed. A consensus for *stay* was considered to have been reached if the fraction of votes was no less than two-thirds for a specific element. If this threshold was not met, the element was either changed or removed from the model.

Delphi Panel Selection. The aim was to identify and gather a diverse group of experts to participate, as heterogeneity among the Delphi panel is crucial to obtaining a broad range of insights [32]. As such, the experts were purposively sampled [33], targeting both practitioners and academics. Practitioner experts were selected based on their experience in Green IT and IT capability assessments, while academic experts were selected based on their involvement in research related to Green IT and CMM development. In total, 12 experts joined the Delphi panel as detailed in Table 2. The Delphi rounds took place over a period of approximately two months, from June to August 2022. Expert participation in each round was dependent on availability, with no specific assignment to rounds. Nevertheless, every effort was made to involve as many participants as possible in each round. As detailed in Table 2, each Delphi round can be considered valid, as a minimum of eight participants per round was deemed sufficient.

Table 2. Overview of the Delphi Panel and Involvement

#	Role	Area of Expertise	Years of Expertise	Delphi Rounds		
				#1	#2	#3
(1)	Professor and Researcher	Green IT	35 in academia	✓	✓	✓
(2)	Specialist Director	Sustainability in IT	30 in consultancy	✓	✓	✓
(3)	Director	Sustainability in IT, and CMMs	30 in consultancy & industry	✓	✓	✓
(4)	IT Architect and Manager	IT and Sustainability	15 in industry & consultancy	✓	✓	
(5)	Project Coordinator and Postdoc Researcher	Green IT	15 in academia	✓	✓	✓
(6)	Professor and Researcher	CMMs	14 in academia	✓	✓	
(7)	Manager	CMMs and IT Operating Models	10 in consultancy		✓	✓
(8)	Manager	IT Capability Assessments	10 in consultancy	✓	✓	✓
(9)	Data & Analytics Lead and Postdoc Researcher	Sustainability of Software and IT Systems	9 in industry & academia		✓	✓
(10)	Postdoc Researcher	Sustainability within Software Design	6 in academia	✓	✓	✓
(11)	Manager	Sustainability in IT	5 in consultancy		✓	
(12)	Senior Consultant	IT Capability Assessments	4 in consultancy	✓	✓	✓
				$n = 9$	$n = 12$	$n = 9$

Delphi Model Development. As our artifact development was an iterative process, our artifact evolved over the course of the Delphi study. Through the rounds of interviews with the Delphi panel, the artifact gradually developed, eventually resulting in our proposed artifact: the Green IT CMM (presented in the subsequent section). The suggestions and corresponding changes during the three Delphi rounds are briefly discussed below. An extensive elaboration on the model development can be found in [17].

- *Round #1.* Considering the domains, it was suggested to split *Strategy & Planning* into two separate domains: *Vision & Strategy* and *Planning.* Furthermore, it was suggested to redefine *Process Management* to *Process & Technology.* Considering the characteristics, it was suggested to split some characteristics. Furthermore, it was suggested to add four new characteristics to the model, as some were considered to be missing Finally, we were able to define the lowest and highest maturity levels for each characteristic based on the feedback acquired during this round.
- *Round #2.* Considering the domains, it was suggested to make two changes. First, *Process & Technology* was split up into two domains: *Technology & Data* and *Process.* Second, *Planning* was redefined to *Planning & Execution* and was visualized in the center of the model to stress its overarching character. Considering the characteristics, it was suggested to merge several characteristics and add three new characteristics, as some were still considered to be missing. Finally, we were able to define all the maturity levels (i.e., *low, moderate, high, top*) based on the feedback acquired during this round.
- *Round #3.* Considering the domains, a consensus was reached so no additional changes were made. In terms of the visualization, it was suggested to put *Vision & Strategy* at the center of the model, surrounded by *Planning & Execution,* to represent the translation from strategy to action. As such, the overarching character of both domains is clearly visualized and the remaining four domains are represented by four quarters around the two central domains. Considering the characteristics, it was not suggested to add, remove, merge, or split any characteristics; only to redefine and move some. This final iteration represents the consensus among the Delphi experts and concludes our final model: the Green IT CMM.

4   Artifact and Its Use in Practice

Our proposed Green IT CMM is a comprehensive framework and stands out from existing Green IT models as it explicitly focuses on organizational capabilities, which, therefore, supports the widespread adoption of Green IT within an organization. Our proposed model identifies the critical organizational capabilities that are necessary to initiate or improve the adoption of Green IT. Therefore, the model can serve as a guide for organizations to facilitate discussions on Green IT, and to identify actions for further adoption. Furthermore, the model defines maturity levels for each of the identified capabilities, enabling organizations to perform self-assessments to evaluate their current state [26].

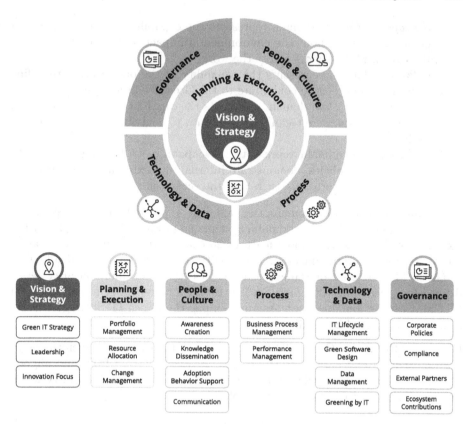

Fig. 3. Green IT Capability Maturity Model

4.1 The Green IT Capability Maturity Model

Figure 3 visualizes our proposed Green IT CMM. As depicted in the top figure, the model identifies six capability domains where a baseline competence is required to adopt Green IT [26]. In here, *Vision & Strategy* and *Planning & Execution* are depicted as central domains, where *Vision & Strategy* is at the heart, surrounded by *Planning & Execution*. The latter domain is considered to be relevant to all other domains and plays a crucial role in translating the strategy into action. Lastly, the model includes definitions for each of these six capability domains, as provided below.

- The *Vision & Strategy* domain represents the capability of the organization to define, align, and promote a Green IT vision and strategy within the organization.
- The *Planning & Execution* domain represents the capability of the organization to support the planning and execution of Green IT projects and initiatives successfully, and guide on the associated changes.

- The *People & Culture* domain represents the capability of the organization to create awareness about the environmental impact of IT and stimulate to embed Green IT behaviors across the workforce.
- The *Process* domain represents the capability of the organization to define and optimize processes to contribute to the Green IT objectives.
- The *Technology & Data* domain represents the capability of the organization to optimize and leverage technology and data to contribute to the Green IT objectives.
- The *Governance* domain represents the capability of the organization to define Green IT policies, demonstrate internal and external compliance and collaborate with external partners and the ecosystems.

Within each capability domain, the model identifies contributing characteristics to that specific capability domain, as depicted in Fig. 3. Distributed over the six different domains, the model features 20 characteristics where each characteristic represents an organizational capability that contributes to the adoption of Green IT. For each of these characteristics, there are four maturity levels defined (i.e., *low, moderate, high, top*). A total overview of our proposed Green IT CMM can be found online[1]. As an example, the Green IT Strategy characteristic is elaborated in detail below.

Green IT Strategy. Green IT Strategy refers to the extent to which the organization defines and agrees on a Green IT strategy, derived from and aligned with its organizational vision and strategy. The corresponding maturity levels for this characteristic are defined in Table 3.

Table 3. Green IT Strategy - Maturity Levels

LOW	MODERATE	HIGH	TOP
There is no or a limited Green IT strategy defined	There might be some Green IT vision, strategy or objectives defined, but these are not complete or not in line with the organizational vision and strategy	There is a defined and agreed Green IT strategy including vision, strategy, and objectives; aligned with the organizational vision and strategy	There is a defined and agreed Green IT strategy including vision, strategy, and objectives; aligned with the organizational vision and strategy. This strategy is continually reviewed and improved

---

[1] Green IT CMM online: https://gitcmm.gitbook.io/.

4.2   Using the Artifact in Practice

Our proposed model can be used by organizations that are adopting or intending to adopt Green IT within their operations. The model provides a means of self-assessment for organizations to determine their current state of Green IT adoption. Based on the feedback obtained from the Delphi experts, the following guidelines were established for effectively conducting the assessment and correctly interpreting its results.

(G1) *Organize a workshop with multiple stakeholders.* For conducting a reliable assessment, it is suggested to organize the assessment in a workshop with various stakeholders involved. The model can then be used to facilitate group discussions. For this workshop, it is suggested to invite a diverse base of employees involved in sustainability topics around IT, as it is important to involve multiple perspectives of various organizational functions [34].

(G2) *Ask stakeholders to prepare for the workshop.* In preparation for the workshop, it is suggested to ask the participants to get familiar with the structure and content of the model. Optionally, the participants can already try to self-assess the organization from their perspective in advance and use their findings as input for the group discussion.

(G3) *Have the workshop facilitated by an expert.* To make sure the model works best, it is suggested to have an experienced facilitator involved. This can be either an internal or an external expert; as long as they are familiar with the Green IT CMM. As it is important to not consider the model as a standalone tool, it is valuable to have an expert involved to guide in conducting the assessment.

(G4) *Use the model to define directions for improvement.* In the end, the conducted self-assessment represents the current state and unveils where the organization excels and where it can improve. The gap between the current and desired state can indicate suggestions for improvement, so that an improvement path can be developed next. As such, the model can help the organization prioritize improvements and can provide input for defining a next steps.

5   Evaluation of the Artifact

To evaluate our proposed Green IT CMM, we discussed the utility of our model and the extent to which the model provides an improved solution for the defined problem [13]. In line with commonly used evaluation criteria for newly proposed models, we adopted the three quality criteria of the Technology Acceptance Model (TAM): *perceived usefulness*, *perceived ease-of-use*, and *intention-to-use* [35]. In here, our primary focus was on *perceived usefulness*, which was concluded by evaluating the model on its defined solution objectives (SO). The three evaluation questions that correspond with the TAM criteria are defined as follows:

- *Perceived usefulness:* To what extent does our proposed Green IT CMM meet its defined SO's?

– *Perceived ease-of-use:* To what extent is our proposed Green IT CMM considered to be easy to use?
– *Intention-to-use:* To what extent would the practitioners be interested to use our proposed Green IT CMM?

5.1 Selection of the Practitioners

The final artifact was evaluated together with practitioners from in-house and consultancy companies. To answer the defined evaluation questions, three evaluation interviews were organized, each with two Green IT practitioners participating, as shown in Table 4. From the in-house perspective, one interview was conducted with two practitioners from a Dutch bank in the process of adopting Green IT. We considered E-service organizations to be the primary beneficiaries of our model. As these organizations offer services that are *'produced, provided or consumed through the use of IT'* [36, p. 226], the adoption of Green IT can play a crucial role in achieving their sustainability objectives. Hence, we selected one of the larger financial institutions in the Netherlands. In recent years, this bank has initiated various sustainable initiatives to reduce the environmental impact of its IT and has successfully executed several Green IT projects.

From the consultancy perspective, two interviews were conducted with two Green IT consultants participating in each. We selected four experienced consultants involved in Green IT practices and familiar with maturity models, all employed by one of the larger consultancy organizations in the Netherlands.

Table 4. Participants for Evaluation Interviews

#	ROLE	TENURE	AREAS OF EXPERTISE
	Interview 1: In-house		
(1)	CIO - Domain Expert	25 years	Sustainable IT & IT Strategy
(2)	Internal Management Consultant	12 years	Sustainable IT & ESG
	Interview 2: Consultancy		
(3)	Director	30 years	Green IT & Digital Transformations
(4)	Manager	10 years	Green IT & Enterprise Architecture
	Interview 3: Consultancy		
(5)	Specialist Director	30 years	Green IT & IT Strategy
(6)	Manager	15 years	Green IT & IT Architecture

5.2 Evaluation Results

After conducting the evaluation interviews, we first transcribed the recordings and qualitatively analyzed the transcriptions. Based on this data, we were able to conclude the model in terms of the three TAM criteria. Firstly, concerning *perceived usefulness*, our results showed that the model was successful in identifying the organizational-level capabilities that contribute to Green IT adoption (SO1) and in enabling organizations to assess their current state of Green IT adoption (SO2). However, it was found that the model did not fully support organizations in defining a roadmap for future Green IT adoption (SO3).

In terms of *perceived ease-of-use*, the participants in the evaluation interviews reported that the model was relatively straightforward to use, especially when guided by an expert. Lastly, all practitioners expressed the *intention-to-use* the model in their practices, emphasizing its potential value as a tool for Green IT adoption.

6   Conclusion and Discussion

The objective of this research was to develop a CMM which enables organizations to assess their current state of Green IT adoption and supports them in defining a roadmap to improve their Green IT adoption capabilities. By combining literature insights, we developed an initial model which was used as a starting point for subsequent development through a Delphi study. This Delphi study comprised of three rounds of interviews with 12 domain experts, ultimately resulting in our proposed artifact: the Green IT CMM. To evaluate our artifact, we conducted three evaluation interviews. Our analysis revealed the artifact's projected utility in terms of perceived usefulness, perceived ease-of-use, and intention-to-use. To this end, we evaluated the model on its defined SO's, as illustrated in Table 5.

Table 5. Conclusion on Solution Objectives

(SO1)	*The artifact should identify organization-wide capabilities that contribute to Green IT adoption*
✓	Our Green IT CMM identifies relevant organization-wide capabilities that contribute to Green IT adoption, so we can conclude the first solution objective is met
(SO2)	*The artifact should enable organizations to assess their current state of Green IT adoption*
✓	Our Green IT CMM can enable organizations to assess their current state of Green IT adoption, so we can conclude the second solution objective is met
(SO3)	*The artifact should support organizations to define a roadmap to improve on their Green IT adoption*
~	Our Green IT CMM can indicate directions for improvement to support the development of a roadmap, yet to define an actual roadmap, additional resources are required. Therefore, we can conclude that the third solution objective is partially met

The evaluation research provided positive evidence supporting the attainment of SO1 and SO2. However, SO3 was only partially supported since the model does not provide a concrete roadmap. Nevertheless, the evaluation indicated that the model can provide directions to support the development of such a roadmap.

All practitioners valued the model and considered the model to be a significant contribution to guiding and supporting organizations in their adoption of Green IT. To their knowledge, there is no other model available that combines all the contributing capabilities to Green IT adoption in one model, and consequently enables an organization to assess its current state. Thus, we conclude our Green IT CMM makes a valuable contribution, as it can be used to facilitate the discussion on Green IT, assess the current state of Green IT adoption, and identify directions for Green IT improvement within organizations.

6.1   Contributions

Our main contribution to the field of Green IT lies in providing a comprehensive framework that identifies the capabilities organizations should have for Green IT adoption. As a result, our research makes contributions to both academia and practice.

Firstly, our research contributes to the academic literature on Green IT and Green IT adoption. As these fields of research are still emerging, there is limited empirical research available on organization-wide Green IT adoption. Our Green IT CMM combines literature insights and validated expert opinions into an overarching and comprehensive framework; which is non-existent in literature yet. As Green IT adoption requires a systemic approach from the organization, such a framework can provide an understanding of what organizational capabilities contribute to Green IT. Our framework can provide an understanding of how organizational capabilities contribute to the adoption of Green IT within an organization.

Secondly, our research contributes to practice as it has implications for Green IT practitioners as well. As organizations are challenged to adopt Green IT across their organization, they require a model or framework that can guide them. As concluded in the evaluation, our Green IT CMM can enable organizations to assess their current state of Green IT adoption. Hereby, the model can unveil where the organization excels and where it can improve; which can indicate directions for improvement. These insights can help to prioritize improvements and can partially support the development of a roadmap towards future Green IT adoption. As such, practitioners could use the model to sharpen their internal discussions (from an in-house perspective) or to guide organizations on their Green IT journey (from a consultancy perspective).

6.2   Limitations and Future Research

In this research, we were able to identify some limitations in combination with suggestions for future work. In a Delphi study, subjectivity and interpretation are involved during the model development, as the input is based on the opinions of experts. Based on the one-on-one interviews, we tried to identify a consensus view and iterate the model accordingly. Although we attempted to minimize our subjectivity as much as possible, there is still a potential bias when performing a Delphi study. Additionally, our model cannot be considered exhaustive since our input was limited to existing literature and the experts we selected. As the capabilities we identified will continue to evolve, future changes cannot be anticipated, and our proposed model should remain open for adjustments. Future work can be devoted to identifying more contributing capabilities.

Furthermore, we evaluated our proposed artifact by means of three evaluation interviews. As these interviews were evaluating the potential utility only, the complete model has not yet been tested in practice. A more extensive evaluation through applying the model to various industry case studies would provide useful insights into the strengths and weaknesses of the model. Only by applying the model to a real-life context, it is possible to evaluate the model's practical applicability. Furthermore, it would be valuable to empirically validate the model by performing maturity assessments of organizations and testing them in relation to their environmental impact of IT. While our model's identified capabilities are deemed to contribute to Green IT based on literature and expert opinions, it would be worthwhile to empirically test this claim. Only by demonstrating the model in practice, it is possible to empirically validate the extent to which the model contributes to the sustainability performance of an organization.

Finally, future work can be devoted to suggestions for future model development. For instance, by developing extensive guidelines on how to use the model in practice and whom to involve in the self-assessments. In addition, it is suggested to define a consistent approach to obtain reliable results. As these suggestions can support practitioners in facilitating the discussion and performing the assessment, it is expected that they will lead to more valuable insights.

Acknowledgement. We thank Deloitte and the participants of this study for their contributions. Providing feedback and suggestions helped us to improve and challenged us to develop a practical applicable artifact. We thank Eindhoven University of Technology for its support.

References

1. Bischoff, Y., van der Wiel, R., van den Hooff, B., Lago, P.: A taxonomy about information systems complexity and sustainability. Environ. Inform. 17–33 (2021)
2. Verdecchia, R., Lago, P., Ebert, C., De Vries, C.: Green it and green software. IEEE Softw. **38**, 7–15 (2021)
3. Lago, P., Koçak, S.A., Crnkovic, I., Penzenstadler, B.: Framing sustainability as a property of software quality. Commun. ACM **58**, 70–78 (2015)
4. Singh, M., Sahu, G.P.: Towards adoption of green IS: a literature review using classification methodology. Int. J. Inf. Manag. **54**, 102–147 (2020)
5. Vickery, G.: Smarter and greener? Information technology and the environment: positive or negative impacts?. Int. Inst. Sustain. Dev. 57–63 (2012)

6. Hilty, L.M., Arnfalk, P., Erdmann, L., Goodman, J., Lehmann, M., Wäger, P.A.: The relevance of information and communication technologies for environmental sustainability - a prospective simulation study. Environ. Model. Softw. **21**, 1618–1629 (2006)

7. Molla, A., et al.: E-readiness to g-readiness: developing a green information technology readiness framework. In: ACIS 2008 Proceedings, vol. 35, December 2008

8. De Bruin, T., Rosemann, M., Freeze, R., Kaulkarni, U.: Understanding the main phases of developing a maturity assessment model. In: Australasian Conference on Information Systems, pp. 8–19 (2005)

9. Lahrmann, G., Marx, F.: Systematization of maturity model extensions. Glob. Perspect. Des. Sci. Res. **5**, 522–525 (2010)

10. Curley, M., Kenneally, J., Carcary, M.: It capability maturity framework. Van Haren (2016)

11. Hankel, A., Oud, L., Saan, M., Lago, P.: A maturity model for green ICT: the case of the SURF green ICT maturity model. In: Proceedings of the 28th EnviroInfo 2014 Conference, pp. 33–40, September 2014

12. Hankel, A., Heimeriks, G., Lago, P.: Green ICT adoption using a maturity model. Sustainability **11** (2019)

13. Becker, J., Knackstedt, R., Pöppelbuß, J.: Developing maturity models for IT management. Bus. Inf. Syst. Eng. **3**, 213–222 (2009)

14. Tarhan, A., Turetken, O., Reijers, H.A.: Business process maturity models: a systematic literature review. Inf. Softw. Technol. **75**, 122–134 (2016)

15. Peffers, K., Tuunanen, T., Rothenberger, M.A., Chatterjee, S.: A design science research methodology for information systems research. J. Manag. Inf. Syst. **24**, 45–77 (2007)

16. Wohlin, C.: Guidelines for snowballing in systematic literature studies and a replication in software engineering. In: Proceedings of the 18th International Conference on Evaluation and Assessment in Software Engineering, pp. 1–10, May 2014

17. Brand, V.J.: Master thesis: development of a capability maturity model for organization-wide green IT adoption. Eindhoven University of Technology, November 2022

18. Abu Al-Rejal, H.M.E., Udin, Z.M., Hassan, M.G., Sharif, K.I.M., Al-Rahmi, W.M., Al-Kumaim, N.H.: Green information technology adoption antecedence: a conceptual framework. In: International Conference of Reliable Information and Communication Technology, pp. 1098–1108, November 2019

19. Buchalcevova, A.: Green ICT maturity model for Czech SMEs. J. Syst. Integr. **6**, 24–36 (2015)

20. Deng, Q., Ji, S.: Organizational green it adoption: concept and evidence. Sustainability **7**, 16737–16755 (2015)

21. Lautenschutz, D.L., et al.: A comparative analysis of green ICT maturity models. In: ICT4S 2018, vol. 52, pp. 153–167 (2018)

22. Patón-Romero, D.J., Baldassarre, M.T., Rodríguez, M., Piattini, M.: Maturity model based on CMMI for governance and management of Green IT. IET Softw. **13**, 555–563 (2019)

23. Donnellan, B., Sheridan, C., Curry, E.: A capability maturity framework for sustainable information and communication technology. IT Prof. **13**, 33–40 (2011)

24. Murugesan, S., Gangadharan, G.: Green it: an overview. In: Harnessing Green IT: Principles and Practices, pp. 1–21, September 2012

25. Philipson, G.: A Green ICT Framework: Understanding and Measuring Green ICT. Connection Research, New South Wales (2010)

26. Hammer, M.: The process audit. Harv. Bus. Rev. **85** (2007)
27. Murphy, M.K., et al.: Consensus development methods, and their use in clinical guideline development. Health Technol. Assess. **2** (1998)
28. Hasson, F., Keeney, S., McKenna, H.: Research guidelines for the Delphi survey technique. J. Adv. Nurs. **32**, 1008–1015 (2008)
29. Mahajan, V.: The Delphi method: techniques and applications. J. Mark. Res. **13**, 317 (1976)
30. Gallego, D., Bueno, S.: Exploring the application of the Delphi method as a forecasting tool in information systems and technologies research. Technol. Anal. Strateg. Manag. **26**, 987–999 (2014)
31. Linstone, H.A., Turoff, M.: The Delphi Method, Reading, pp. 3–12 (1975)
32. Delbecq, A.L., Van de Ven, A.H., Gustafson, D.H.: Group techniques for program planning: a guide to nominal group and Delphi processes (1975)
33. Rowley, J.: Conducting research interviews. Manag. Res. Rev. **35**, 260–271 (2012)
34. Van Looy, A.: An experiment for measuring business process maturity with different maturity models. In: ECIS 2015 Proceedings, pp. 1–12, June 2015
35. Davis, F.D.: Perceived usefulness, perceived ease of use, and user acceptance of information technology. MIS Q. **13**, 319–340 (1989)
36. Scupola, A.: E-services: definition, characteristics and taxonomy. J. Electron. Commerce Organ. **6** (2008)
37. Verdecchia, R., Ricchiuti, F., Hankel, A., Lago, P., Procaccianti, G.: Green ICT research and challenges. In: Advances and New Trends in Environmental Informatics, pp. 37–48, September 2016

From Conceptual Specification
to OO Specification

Bert de Brock[(✉)] and Rein Smedinga

University of Groningen, Groningen, The Netherlands
{e.o.de.brock,r.smedinga}@rug.nl

Abstract. Our earlier work showed how to improve the development path for an information system from *initial user wishes* via a *conceptual specification* (CS) to an *implementation design* in a systematic way. A CS should be implementation-independent. We generated implementations in a few directions, e.g., towards a relational DBMS using SQL. An *object-oriented (OO) implementation design* is another important direction.

This paper works out a systematic mapping towards an OO-implementation, by giving formal mapping rules or 'semi-automatic' guidelines. We also look at the differences between the OO-mapping and our earlier SQL-mappings. E.g., how to specify constraints: SQL has language constructs to specify constraints, e.g., (foreign) keys, but programming languages usually lack such constructs. How to deal with it in a systematic way? This is an essential issue in software development, but one which is systematically overlooked.

We start from a general analysis resulting in a CS and prove that we can create an OO-implementation out of it. Without any change in that CS, we also can create a Relational implementation.

We map a CS systematically towards an OO-implementation. We use the MVC-pattern and create a default class diagram (statics/data) and default methods (dynamics/processes) from a CS. Our *enhanced* class diagrams inherit the constraints from the CS, which are then worked out systematically into OO pseudo-code. We generate pseudo-code which an OO-programmer can easily transform into real code. We also compare it to the SQL-mapping. Being able to map our CSs to different software paradigms shows that our CSs are truly implementation-independent.

Keywords: Conceptual Specification · Implementation-Independence · Object-Oriented Mapping · Implementation Design · MVC-Pattern · Guarding Constraints · Comparing OO and SQL

1 Introduction

In earlier work we showed how to improve the development of an information system all the way from *initial user wishes* via a *conceptual specification* (CS) to an *implementation design* in a systematic manner [1]. A CS models a relevant part of an organization and should be implementation-independent. We illustrated this by generating subsequent

© The Author(s), under exclusive license to Springer Nature Switzerland AG 2023
B. Shishkov (Ed.): BMSD 2023, LNBIP 483, pp. 180–199, 2023.
https://doi.org/10.1007/978-3-031-36757-1_11

implementations in different directions, for an arbitrary CS. For instance, an implementation with parchment scrolls and slates [2] as well as a Relational implementation in SQL [3, 4]. In particular, we worked out in detail how to develop a CS and to map a CS towards a Relational implementation. Another important direction is to design an *object-oriented (OO) implementation*. These options are summarized in Fig. 1.

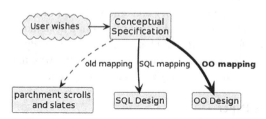

Fig. 1. Earlier work and current work

Essentially, the result of an RE-phase for a system to be developed is a *conceptual specification*, consisting of a description of the *statics*, describing the relevant *data* (structures), and of the *dynamics*, describing the relevant *processes*. Together, the statics and dynamics constitute a complete conceptual 'blue print' of the system to be developed:

System specification ≡ Statics (Data) + Dynamics (Processes)

In this paper, we work out how a CS can be mapped towards an OO implementation in a systematic manner: We give formal mapping rules and sometimes 'semi-automatic' general guidelines. So, no 'Theory-by-Example'. For an elaborate example, interested readers are referred to [5].

Moreover, we compare the OO-mapping to our earlier SQL-mapping. For instance, we show how constraints can be specified in both cases: The language SQL has language constructs to specify constraints, such as (FOREIGN) KEYs, but programming languages usually lack such language constructs to specify constraints. How to deal with that in a systematic way?

The OOPSLA conferences (http://sigplan.org/Conferences/OOPSLA/) include all aspects of OO programming languages and software engineering. Papers of for instance Coad & Yourdon [6, 7] and Jacobson and others [8, 9] start directly with an OO approach leading to an OO design and implementation and is, therefore, limited to an OO implementation. Our paper starts with a general language-independent approach where the analysis part results in a CS independent of any further possible implementation. We subsequently prove in this paper that one possibility is to create an OO implementation out of this. Without any change in that CS, we can create a Relational implementation in SQL; see our earlier papers. The current paper also shows the differences.

We work out how to map a CS towards an OO-implementation in a systematic way. We recall the MVC-principle and show how to separate *Model* from *View* and *Controller* and how to create a default class diagram (statics/data) and default methods (dynamics/processes) from a CS. In other words, from a black box (conceptual specification) via a grey box (MVC) to a white box (classes and methods).

Our initial class diagrams are actually *enhanced* class diagrams: They inherit the constraints specified in the CS. These constraints are subsequently worked out systematically in the OO-specification.

Moreover, we compare the OO-mapping to the mapping towards SQL. As an example, the language SQL has language constructs to specify constraints, e.g., PRIMARY KEY, FOREIGN KEY, and NULL/NOT NULL. Usually, (OO) programming languages lack such language constructs to specify constraints. Therefore, in our mapping towards an OO programming language, we take care of that in a systematic way. Our approach is such that the choice for a specific OO language (like Java or Python, for instance) can be postponed till later. We generate pseudo-code in such a way that a programmer in a specific (OO) language can easily transform this to real code.

Organization of the Paper

As elaborated in Sect. 2, we give the *statics* in the form of a *Conceptual Data Model* and the *dynamics* in the form of *textual SSDs* (*System Sequence Descriptions*). Together they form a *Conceptual Specification* of the system. Summarized in a 'formula':

> §2: Conceptual specification ≡ Conceptual Data Model + textual SSDs

Section 3 recalls the important, general MVC software design pattern, where MVC is an abbreviation of *Model-View-Controller*. There we split our (black box) system into a kernel and an interface:

> §3: System = Kernel + Interface

Section 4 recalls and summarizes how to map a conceptual specification to a *relational* specification, which consists of a *Relational Database* and *Stored Procedures*:

> §4: Relational specification ≡ Relational Database + Stored Procedures

Section 5 outlines how to map a conceptual specification to an *object-oriented* specification, consisting of a so-called *Enhanced Class Diagram* and *White Box SSDs*:

> §5: Object-Oriented specification ≡ Enhanced Class Diagram + White Box SSDs

2   Conceptual Specification

We recall that a conceptual specification (CS) consists of a Conceptual Data Model (Sect. 2.1) and a set of textual SSDs (Sect. 2.2).

2.1 Conceptual Data Model

A Conceptual Data Model (CDM) can partly be depicted by a *graph* of which each *node* represents a concept and each *arrow* represents a reference relevant for the application at hand. Each node also enumerates the relevant properties of that concept. Moreover, a CDM can contain constraints. In this paper, we concentrate on the important and ubiquitous constraints *non-optionality*, *uniqueness*, and *referential* constraints.

We will put a property for which a value is optional (i.e., no value required) between the brackets '[' and ']'. Each referencing property is indicated by a '^' in front. Within each concept, a uniqueness constraint is indicated by a '!' in front of the properties involved; i.e., each value of the property (combination) preceded by '!' is unique. If there is another uniqueness constraint within the same concept, that uniqueness constraint is indicated by another symbol (say '%') in front of the properties involved. (Alternatively, if there are several uniqueness constraints for the same concept, the properties involved could be preceded by 'UC1', 'UC2', 'UC3', etc.)

Concept B in Fig. 2 contains all these constructs: The property *B-id* is unique, just as the combination of *P1* and *P2*. There is a reference to the concept C, another required property *ReqProp* and an optional property *OptProp*. Such constructs can also be combined, e.g., the 'optional reference' to B in concept A, i.e., for which a value is optional.

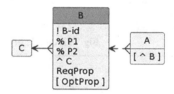

Fig. 2. Concept B has 2 uniqueness constraints, 1 reference, another 'required property', and 1 'optional property'

Figure 3 shows the kind of arrows (and their alternative names) we can distinguish.

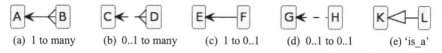

(a) 1 to many   (b) 0..1 to many   (c) 1 to 0..1   (d) 0..1 to 0..1   (e) 'is_a'

Fig. 3. Different kinds of arrows (references) and their alternative names

Explanation of the arrows in Fig. 3

(a) A B-instance refers to exactly 1 A-instance and
    each A-instance can be referred to by 0 or more B-instances
(b) A D-instance refers to at most 1 C-instance and
    each C-instance can be referred to by 0 or more D-instances
(c) An F-instance refers to exactly 1 E-instance and
    each E-instance can be referred to by at most 1 F-instance

(d) An H-instance refers to <u>at most 1</u> G-instance and
    each G-instance can be referred to by <u>at most 1</u> H-instance

(e) Each L-instance ***is a*** K-instance

Actually, (e) strengthens (c): (e) indicates that L represents a 'subset' of K.

In summary: a solid arrow indicates '<u>exactly 1</u>', a dashed arrow '<u>at most 1</u>', and the arrow head '◁' indicates a subset. If the tail of an arrow has a 'crow's foot' it indicates '<u>0 or more</u>' and otherwise '<u>at most 1</u>'.

Our running example concerns Courses with their Exams, Lecturers with their Teaching Activities, and Students with their Exam Enrolments and Exam Results.

A lecturer can have teaching activities for several courses and several lecturers can be involved in the same course. A student can enrol for several exams and an exam can have several enrolled students. There can be at most 1 result per exam enrolment. Furthermore, a phone number of a student *may be* known (but not necessarily) and a lecturer has a unique Employee ID and *maybe* a Social Security Number (SSN), which will be unique too in that case.

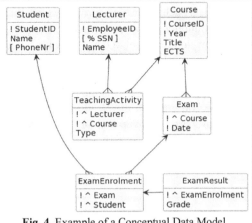

Fig. 4. Example of a Conceptual Data Model

2.2 (Textual) System Sequence Descriptions

A <u>System Sequence Description</u> (SSD) of a use case schematically depicts the interactions between the <u>primary actor</u> (user), the <u>system</u>, and its <u>supporting actors</u> (if any), including the <u>messages</u> between them. So, an SSD also specifies the actors involved. SSDs can constitute a bridge between the informal world and the formal world.

In this paper we use the following simple subset of our <u>grammar</u> (expressed in Backus-Naur Form) to specify *textual* SSDs:

```
A ::= P -> P: M
P ::= User | System | ...
S ::= A | S ; S | if C then S [else S] end | while C do S end | repeat S until C
    | perform N            /* represents an Include (or Call)
D ::= define N as S end
```

The terminals in the language are written in **bold**. The nonterminal A stands for 'atomic instruction', P for 'actor' (or 'participant'), M for 'message', S for 'instruction' (or SSD), C for 'condition', N for 'instruction name', and D for 'definition'.

Informally, 'X -> Y: M' means '*X sends M to Y*' for X ≠ Y, while 'X -> X: M' means '*X does M*'. The values (terminals) for the nonterminals C, P, M, and N are application dependent ('domain specific'), apart from **User** and **System** for P, and will appear during the development of the particular application.

In our example in Fig. 4, we might consider the elementary user wish *Enter a Grade*. Given our conceptual data model, the parameterized user wish will be something like:

Enter the grade of a given student for a given exam of a given course.

The textual SSD could be as shown below on the left. The graphical SSD (on the right) follows easily from the textual SSD (see [2] or [10]).

1. U -> S: Enter a Grade ;
2. S -> S: retrieve all courses (of this year) ;
3. S -> U: all courses (of this year) ;
4. U -> S: Course C1 ;
5. S -> S: retrieve all exams of C1 ;
6. S -> U: all exams of C1 ;
7. U -> S: Exam E1 ;
8. S -> S: retrieve all students enrolled for E1 ;
9. S -> U: all students enrolled for E1 ;
10. U -> S: Student S1 with Grade G1 ;
11. S -> S: EnterGrade(G1, S1, E1) ;
12. **if** successful
    then S -> U: "Done"
    else S -> U: reason(s) why not
    end

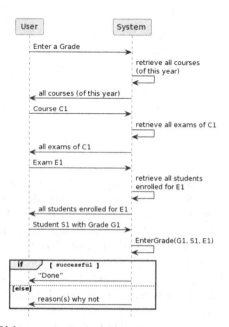

Hence, the system should be able to create an Exam Result having the retrieved values (Step 11) and to retrieve the following sets:

In Step 2: { c | c is a course (of this year) }
In Step 5: { e | e is an exam of Course C1 }
In Step 8: { s | s is a student enrolled for Exam E1 }

3 Interactions with a Software System

In the next sections we go from conceptual specification to (software) system design. The *system* (as a 'black box') can be split into an *interface* and a *kernel*, becoming a 'grey box'. The typical 'analysis-SSD' in Fig. 5 then transforms into the corresponding 'design-SSD' in Fig. 6, where the system is depicted as a grey box. The 1st step in the analysis-SSD is split into 2 steps in the design-SSD: From *user* to *interface* and from *interface* to *kernel*. Also the 3rd step in the analysis-SSD is split into 2 steps in the design-SSD: From the *kernel* back to the *interface* and from the *interface* back to the *user*.

This is in fact the general **Model-View-Controller** (MVC) design pattern, an important basic software design pattern that allows to separate internal representations of information from the ways information is presented to, and accepted from, the user [11].

Analysis-SSD

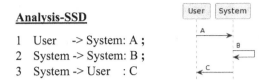

1 User   -> System: A ;
2 System -> System: B ;
3 System -> User   : C

Fig. 5. An 'analysis-SSD'

Design-SSD

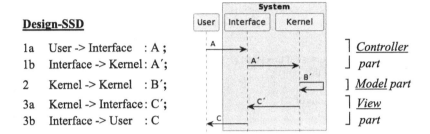

1a User -> Interface   : A ;   ⎤ *Controller*
1b Interface -> Kernel: A';   ⎦ *part*

2   Kernel -> Kernel   : B';   ⎤ *Model* part

3a Kernel -> Interface: C';   ⎤ *View*
3b Interface -> User   : C   ⎦ *part*

Fig. 6. A corresponding 'design-SSD'

For instance, the kernel could send error codes, while the interface can convert those error codes into human-understandable text. That text might even depend on the native language of the user at hand. Steps 1a and 1b in Fig. 6 are steps for the *Controller*, Step 2 for the *Model*, and steps 3a and 3b for the *View*.

What should A', B', and C' in Fig. 6 be? B' expresses what the kernel must do to realize B. Preferably, B' is a (stored) procedure call or method call in the kernel's language. A' could simply be something like '**do** B''' since the interface is supposed to address the kernel in the kernel's language. Finally, C' could be some machine-readable code, for instance, an (error) code with some parameters or a query-result expressed in Java or SQL. The interface must convert it into a user-readable message C and send it to the user. The user can be a human or a system. Here, the interface could even apply Native Language Support (NLS) to send the message in the native language of the user.

Sometimes the interface can handle things itself, e.g., checking whether a required property is indeed filled in. In that case, the arrows A', B', and C' in Fig. 6 are replaced by arrow B from Interface to Interface.

Each 'call' to the kernel must subsequently be worked out in detail (becoming a 'white box') in the programming language concerned, e.g., Java, Python, or SQL. The next sections in this paper concentrate on the kernel, not on the interface(s).

4   Relational Specification

We globally recall our approach in [3]. We recall that a Relational specification consists of a Relational Database (Sect. 4.1) and a set of Stored Procedures (Sect. 4.2).

4.1   From Conceptual Data Model to Relational Database

We recall the following rules from [3] to map a Conceptual Data Model to a Relational Database Model in SQL:

- First of all, each reference to a concept C is replaced by the primary key attribute(s) of C; some attributes maybe preceded by the name of C (for clarity)
- A declaration CREATE DATABASE <database name> is introduced
- Each concept becomes a *table*
- Each property of a concept becomes an *attribute* – a.k.a. *column* – in that table
- Each uniqueness constraint translates to a *primary key* constraint (exactly one per table) or a *unique* constraint, each specified by one or more attributes
- Each reference translates to a *foreign key* constraint
- An attribute for which a value is *optional* (i.e., no value required) can be 'NULL'; if a value is required then the attribute should be declared 'NOT NULL'
- Each extra attribute constraint or tuple constraint translates to a *check* constraint
- Because table names and attribute names should be one word and not contain '-', replace each space and '-' in them by, say, '_' or capitalize the next word and delete the space or '-' (as we already did beforehand in this paper)

Figure 7 shows the result for our running example. The database tables are indicated by the orange 'T'. Optionality is indicated by the informal hint '*(may be NULL)*'. Each uniqueness constraint translates to a *primary key* constraint (indicated by a '!' in front of its attributes), except the second one for Lecturer (SSN), which will translate to a *unique* constraint (indicated by a '%'in front of its attribute). Each reference to a concept C is crossed out and replaced by the primary key attribute(s) of C, indicated by attributes with a dot in front. For clarity, some attributes are preceded by the name of C.

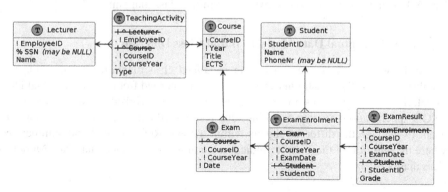

Fig. 7. Relational Model of our running example

4.2 From Textual SSDs to Stored Procedures

A textual SSD can lead to one or more interactions with the system. For instance, our textual SSD for the user wish *Enter a Grade* in Sect. 2.2 leads to four interactions with the system: Three retrievals (in steps 2/3, 5/6, and 8/9) and one modification (in Step 11). The retrievals could be (simple) SQL-statements of the form

```
SELECT * FROM <table> WHERE <condition>
```

which will be straightforward translations of the 3 specifications given earlier. The modification could be the following INSERT-statement, with 5 input parameters: @ci, @cy, @ed, @si, and @g, for CourseID, CourseYear, ExamDate, StudentID, and Grade:

INSERT INTO ExamResult(CourseID, CourseYear, ExamDate, StudentID, Grade)

VALUES(@ci, @cy, @ed, @si, @g)

Each interaction with the system might need one or more SQL-statements and can therefore be put in the form of a *stored procedure*: A *stored procedure* consists of a sequence of one or more SQL-statements mixed with language constructs for control-of-flow. A basic minimal syntax for a stored procedure, expressed informally:

```
CREATE PROCEDURE <procedure name> [<parameters>]
AS <SQL-statements mixed with control-of-flow constructs>
```

5 Object-Oriented Specification

An OO specification consists of a Class Diagram and a set of White Box SSDs. Sect. 5.1 outlines how to map a Conceptual Data Model stepwise to an initial Class Diagram, while Sect. 5.2 outlines how to map textual SSDs stepwise to White Box SSDs. Subsequently, Sect. 5.3 explains why and how to extend the initial class diagram.

5.1 From Conceptual Data Model to Initial Class Diagram

As will be worked out in Sect. 5.1.1, an *enhanced* class diagram is a class diagram that also mentions the constraints specified in (and inherited from) the Conceptual Data Model. Sectin 5.1.2 outlines how these constraints can be worked out systematically in the OO-specification. Section 5.1.3 introduces so-called *managers* in a class diagram, meant to manage the different objects within a class. Reformulated and summarized (where the addition of the green ⓒ indicates we move from Conceptual Data Model to Class diagram):

§5.1.1: V0.1 = CDM + ⓒ + empty methods-sections
§5.1.2: V0.2 = V0.1 + (standard) conditional modifications
§5.1.3: V0.3 = V0.2 + managers

5.1.1   Enhanced Class Diagram (V0.1)

Mapping a Conceptual Data Model to a full-fledged Class Diagram goes in a few steps. This section describes how to get a 'Version 0.1' of a Class Diagram and Sect. 5.1.2 how to get a 'Version 0.2'. These class diagrams are actually *enhanced* class diagrams: They inherit the constraints from the Conceptual Data Model. While the language SQL has all kinds of language constructs to specify and check constraints, such as PRIMARY KEY, FOREIGN KEY, NULL/NOT NULL, programming languages typically lack such constructs. Therefore, we have to incorporate the checking of constraints systematically in our mappings. We will treat this in Sect. 5.1.2.

Mapping a Conceptual Data Model to a 'Version 0.1' of a Class Diagram is simple:

o Each concept becomes a *class*
o Each property of a concept becomes an *attribute* (or *field*) in that class
o Each reference becomes a link to an instance of a class
o Each class has an initially 'empty' component, meant for its *methods* (or *operations*)

Figure 8 shows a fragment for our running example.

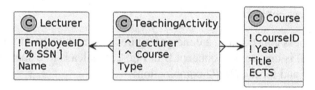

Fig. 8. Fragment of our Enhanced Class Diagram (Version 0.1)

Methods are used to implement the interactions with the system, e.g., those described earlier in SSDs. In the OO-tradition, method names start with a lowercase letter. Usually, this also holds for attributes, but in this paper we keep the already used capitals.

Over time, *derived fields* might be also useful to add, e.g., to improve performance. Derived fields are fields of which the values can be derived from the other data in the model. So, in principle, derived fields are superfluous, but they might be useful, e.g., when the computation of their value is very time-consuming and their value is needed frequently, while the underlying data changes only infrequently. However, the 'semantics' of a derived field must be defined clearly! Moreover, derived fields must be kept up-to-date. In our running example, for instance, a useful derived field for Student might be 'PointsEarned', defined as the sum of all the ECTS of the different (!) courses for which the student passed one of its exams, i.e., an exam for which the student earned a grade of at least 6. Derived fields are preceded by a '/'. E.g., for our example (Fig. 9):

5.1.2   Handling Constraints (V0.2)

When mapping a Conceptual Data Model to a Class Diagram, we have to incorporate the checking of constraints in our mappings, as explained earlier. Simple (datatype) constraints, such as INTEGER, [VAR]CHAR(n), and maybe enumeration types, can usually be expressed directly in the target programming language itself, using its datatypes. But,

Fig. 9. A class with a derived field

in general, this does not hold for all constraints. That implies that any straightforward modification statement must become a *conditional* modification statement. In particular, we work out the important (and ubiquitous) constraints mentioned in the beginning of Sect. 2: *non-optionality, uniqueness*, and *referential* constraints.

(1) Non-optionality constraints

For each property in a concept for which a value is required, 'null' is not allowed. For instance, for concept B in Fig. 2 this leads to 5 such constraints (that is, for all its properties except the property *OptProp*)

(2) Uniqueness constraints

Each uniqueness constraint in a concept requires that each value of that property (combination) is unique. For concept B in Fig. 2, this leads to 2 such constraints (i.e., for *B-id* and for the *P1-P2* combination)

(3) Referential constraints

Each referencing property in an object requires that the mentioned object must exist in the referenced concept. For concept B in Fig. 2, this leads to 1 such constraint (i.e., the reference to concept C). For the 'optional reference' to concept B in concept A (Fig. 2), it means that *if* an object is mentioned, that object must exist in B

When *adding* an object to a class, all these constraints apply. So, in that case the number of constraints to be checked is the number of its properties for which a value is required + the number of its uniqueness constraints + the number of its (outgoing) references.

Regarding *updates*, not all properties might be updateable. E.g., an update on Student in our running example might concern the Name and/or Phone Number, but a StudentID should probably not be updateable. In other words, some properties might not even be updated in *any* update. Typical candidates are properties participating in a uniqueness constraint. On the other hand, the property Date in the concept Exam might be updateable, e.g., when the envisaged date of a future Exam changes. But it is up to the customer to decide which properties should be updateable (and by which roles).

When *updating* an object in a class, the previously mentioned types of constraints apply to only the properties to be updated. E.g., the applicable constraints for an update of the Date of an Exam in our example are the non-optionality for Date and the uniqueness of the Course-Date combination. All in all, the number of constraints to be checked when updating an object in a class is the number of its 'required properties' to be updated + the number of 'involved' uniqueness constraints + the number of its (outgoing) references to be updated.

When *deleting* an object from a class, each reference to that class implies the constraint that there should not be objects referring to the object to be deleted. So, the number of constraints to be checked when deleting an object from a class is the number of its *incoming* references. For concept B in Fig. 2, there is one such constraint (i.e., the reference *from* concept A).

An alternative delete, per referential constraint, would be a *cascading delete*, which means that upon the deletion of the object all objects referring to that object should also be deleted. However, maybe (some of) those other objects might not be deletable (because of other constraints) or those objects might (recursively) trigger new cascading deletes again. This can lead to (very) complicated situations of which the effects might be hard to understand. It can also lead to (very) complicated *rollbacks*.

For our running example, Table 1 gives the number of constraints for a few concepts in case of *adding* or *deleting* an object (using the abbreviations Req for Required value, Uni for Uniqueness constraint, Ref out for Reference outgoing, and Ref in for Reference incoming):

Table 1. Number of constraints and type of modification for a few concepts

Modification → ↓ Concept	Adding				Deleting
	Req	Uni	Ref out	Total	Ref in
Exam	2	1	1	4	1
ExamEnrolment	2	1	2	5	1

Now we encounter some design questions: How should the required *conditional* modification behave? E.g., should it stop after the first constraint violation is found or should all violations be reported? And which (error) messages should be used in case of a violation? And how to do all this in a systematic way?

It turns out that it is more convenient for the user that all violations are reported at once, not one by one. So, we incorporate that in our 'design decisions'.

It leads us to the following general program structure, where the local variable *ec* stands for *error counter* and counts the number of errors found:

```
ec := 0 ;
if not <constraint₁> then ec := ec + 1 ; <send error message regarding constraint₁> end ;
  ⋮
if not <constraintₙ> then ec := ec + 1 ; <send error message regarding constraintₙ> end ;
if ec = 0 then <modification>; <final message1> else <final message2> end
```

<final message1> could be 'The modification has been completed successfully.' and <final message2> 'The modification could not be completed since there were errors.' In that case, the value of ec (the number of found errors) could also be mentioned.

The program structure in words: The error counter starts with the value 0. If a constraint is violated, the counter is increased by 1 and a proper error message is produced and sent. Finally, if there were no errors, the modification will take place and a proper message is produced; otherwise, another proper message is produced.

Note that this general program structure can also include constraints other than *non-optionality*, *uniqueness*, and *referential* constraints, for instance, if the allowed values for a property P are constrained to an enumeration type.

Furthermore, each kind of constraint violation can have its own general message structure. For instance, upon *adding* an object:

- if a value for a property P is required but not filled in, the error message could be something like: **'You should fill in the P.'** E.g.: **'You should fill in the** Grade.'
- if a uniqueness constraint for a concept C consists of a property P but is violated, the error message could be something like: **'A[n]** C **with that** P **already exists.'**
  For example: **'A** Student **with that** StudentID **already exists. '**
- if a uniqueness constraint for a concept C consists of, say, two properties P1 and P2, the error message could be: **'A[n]** C **with that** P1–P2 **combination already exists.'**
  For example: **'An** Exam **with that** Course-Date **combination already exists.'**
- if a reference to a supposed object in class C does not exist, the error message could be something like: **'That** C **is unknown to the system.'** E.g.: **'That** Student **is unknown to the system.'**

Upon *deleting* an object from a class B which is still referred to by another object from a class A (which might be class B itself), the error message can be something like:

'There are still As **belonging to this** B. '

For example: **'There are still** ExamEnrollments **belonging to this** Exam.'

From Table 1 we conclude that the concept Exam has all ingredients. Therefore we will use Exam as an example to show its textual and graphical SSDs.

The textual SSD for conditionally *creating* an Exam for Course c on Date d must check 4 constraints and will be as follows (where S stands for System and U for User):

```
DEFINE conditionallyCreateExam(c, d) AS
  S -> S: ec := 0 ;
  if c = null then S -> S: ec := ec + 1;  S -> U: 'You should fill in the Course. ' end ;
  if d = null then S -> S: ec := ec + 1;  S -> U: 'You should fill in the Date. ' end ;
  if that Course-Date combination already occurs in Exam
    then  S -> S: ec := ec + 1 ;
          S -> U: 'An Exam with that Course-Date combination already exists. '
  end ;
  if course c does not occur in Course
    then  S -> S: ec := ec + 1;
          S -> U: 'That Course is unknown to the system. '
  end ;
  if ec = 0
    then  S -> S:  createExam(c, d) ;
          S -> U: 'The modification has been completed successfully. '
    else  S -> U: 'The modification could not be completed since there were errors. '
  end
END
```

Following [10], the corresponding graphical SSD follows easily from the textual SSD:

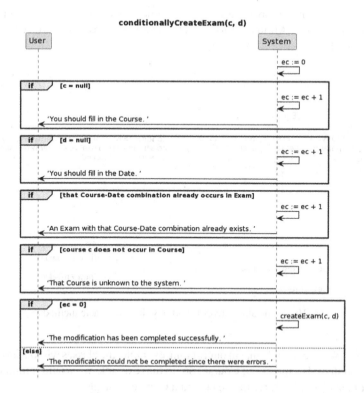

The textual and graphical SSD for conditionally *updating* an exam with, say, a new date are similar to those for conditionally *creating* an exam. Also the textual and graphical SSD for conditionally *deleting* an exam are similar. See [5] for the elaborations.

As a general principle, for each class E there should be 3 basic modification methods (for creating, updating, and deleting an E-object), each of which takes care of checking the applicable constraints. Let's name those methods conditionallyCreateE, conditionallyUpdateE, and conditionallyDeleteE.

5.1.3 Adding or Designating Managers (V0.3)

A method of a class E applies to an *existing* object of E and an object cannot kill itself ('no suicide'). Therefore, those three methods cannot be methods of class E itself (maybe except conditionallyUpdateE, e.g., when there are no constraints to check).

By adding a so-called *manager* class to class E, we can add those methods to the manager class. Such an 'E_manager' is meant to manage the different objects in E. If E has an *outgoing* arrow, i.e. refers to another class, say F, then class F could act as an E-manager. In this way, we get a 'Version 0.3' of the class diagram. The existence check regarding the F-object where the E-object is referring to might then be dropped. (As a further refinement, the methods could even be spread over several classes where class E is referring to.)

For each updateable property P of E we also need a separate method to update the P-value of an E-object. All in all, this leads to the alternatives in Fig. 10 (where e is an object in class E):

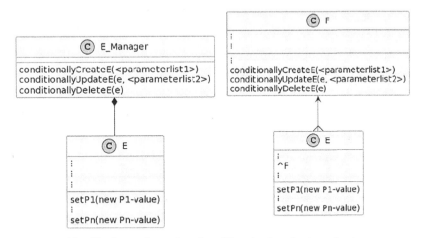

Fig. 10. Some alternatives for adding the three basic methods

From Fig. 4, we conclude that in our running example, the classes without an *outgoing* arrow are Student, Lecturer, and Course. So, in that example we would minimally need a Student manager, a Lecturer manager, and a Course manager.

5.2   From a Textual SSD to White Box SSDs

The condition in an **if**-, **while**-, or **repeat**-statement in an SSD must also be checked, which is in fact a separate step (usually done by the system). So, to make it explicit:

if C **then** S1 [**else** S2]	becomes	b := *C?* ; **if** b **then** S1 [**else** S2]
while C **do** S **end**	becomes	b := *C?* ; **while** b **do** S ; b := *C?* **end**
repeat S **until** C	becomes	**repeat** S ; b := *C?* **until** b

where the Boolean variable b gets the value of the check *C?* (so **true** or **false**). In the SSD we must still specify the actor that does that check.

As an example, for conditionallyCreateExam we get five explicit checks: *c = null?*, *d = null?*, *that Course-Date combination already occurs in Exam?*, *course c does not occur in Course?*, and *ec = 0?*

An important software design question is what should be done by the *interface* and what should be done by the *kernel* (see Sect. 3). Simple, local checks could be done by the interface, e.g., checking whether a required property is indeed filled in (for instance, *c = null?* and *d = null?*).

In general, the kernel is needed when persistent data are involved, e.g., in case of actual CRUD-operations (Create, Retrieve, Update, Delete) on the persistent data. But also when *checking* conditions that involve persistent data (e.g., *that Course-Date combination already occurs in Exam?*, and *course c does not occur in Course?*).

In our Exam-example, the interface can do the assignments to the local variable *ec* and the local checks *c = null?*, *d = null?*, and *ec = 0?*. The kernel must do the remaining checks and the actual Create, Update, and Delete.

Each individual interaction with the kernel must be worked out, leading to a so-called *white box*. For *conditionallyCreateExam* this results in the next interactions:

- The check b := *that Course-Date combination already occurs in Exam?* implies that the kernel must check whether the course the Exam belongs to already has an exam on that new date. So, the kernel could check the date of all the exams of that course.
- Similarly, the check b := *that course does not occur in Course?* implies that the kernel must check whether that course does not occur in Course yet.
- The interaction *createExam(c, d)* means that the kernel must create a new Exam-object with the given course and date.

In the black box SSDs, the System is a black box. In the grey box SSD, the kernel is a black box and the interface is used to transform information and requests from the user to the kernel and vice versa. Now we further develop the kernel. In the kernel, all persistent data have an object structure that is in line with the class diagram V0.3.

Using the principle of *separation of concerns*, the connection between the interface and the kernel must be as small as possible. This leads to an interface and kernel that are as independent of each other as possible. Since the interface needs to communicate with the object structure in the kernel, we will only use the Managers as introduced in Version 0.3 of the class diagram for this. With this approach, designers and programmers can change the internal structure of the objects in the kernel later on (e.g., when refactoring parts of the code), without the interface having to know this. This approach also means, that the interface does not (need to) know the references to internal objects within the kernel. Instead, we will use the key attributes of the objects to denote them.

The kernel contains the persistent data of the application, the interface contains data temporally (only during the session). For instance, after a user has logged in, the interface can ask the kernel what the rights of this user are. Once, the application stops and is restarted later on, the login information and rights are still available in the kernel. So, if the user logs in again, the interface can reconstruct the rights of the user.

In a white box we use the objects as they are known from the class diagram Version 0.3. Important is to find out which object is first responsible for handling the kernel request. In Larman [12], GRASP (General Responsibility Assignment Software Patterns) is used to establish the object that is best suitable to be the first responsible object.

Let's have a look at the kernel request

b := *that Course-Date combination already occurs in Exam?*

First we reformulate this request in such a way that it becomes a real method call:

b := searchForExamWith(c, d)

where c is the course we are investigating and d is the date (for a new Exam).

The responsible object for this request is the Course_Manager, which, in turn, knows the object c and can pass the request over to this object.

We will abbreviate the common pattern below to the notation next to it, both for a textual SSD and a graphical SSD (saying *I asks K for A and gets back the result in R*):

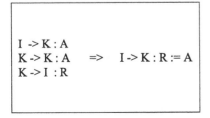
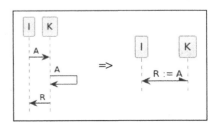

The complete white box SSD for b := *searchForExamWith(c, d)* in graphical form will then be as follows (where the '*' after e emphasizes that e is a *variable* in an iteration):

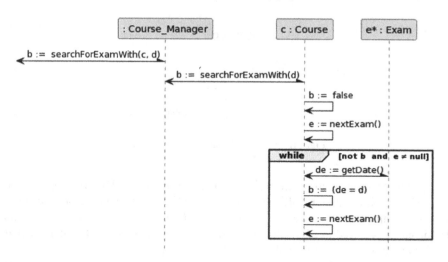

searchForExamWith(c, d)

If the interface itself already has the correct reference to the Course object c, the first step involving the Course_Manager can be skipped and the request can be sent directly to the Course c. However, since MVC expects the interaction between model and view/controller to be as independent as possible, we prefer to involve the Course_Manager here as first responsible object. In this case, we are more independent of later changes in, for instance, the requests internal objects in the kernel can handle. In fact, we are using the Façade design pattern here [12, 13].

For the updateExam-request and the deleteExam-request we can create similar white box SSDs, assuming the interface already knows the reference to the Exam under consideration. The further elaboration is in [5].

The white box SSDs show that the designer will provide a more or less complete design to be used by the programmer to code this in the preferred OO language.

In this design phase we do not yet bother to much about efficient code yet. In some situations, the programmer might refactor the given design in order to make the code faster, for instance. As an example, our *searchForExamWith* SSD has a while loop that loops over all Exams e of Course c until either no more Exams are found or an Exam is found with the given date. On the other hand, if the Exams are stored in the course ordered by date, a better and more efficient search algorithm to check for an exam with a given date can be used. Such refactorings and improvements in the code are left for the programmer.

In general: Consider a request y := X(aKey, parList) from the interface to the kernel in the grey box SSD and, according to GRASP, we conclude that class E is the best suitable one for receiving this request. The first step then is sending X(aKey, parList) to the E-Manager, the manager of all objects from class E, where aKey is the key value uniquely identifying the E-object. Next, the E-Manager object knows how to find that E-object from the aKey value and can send the request X(parList) to that E-object directly. Then it is up to that E-object to decide what to do next and how to deal with the request and how to determine the return value y.

In a graph this will look like (Fig. 11):

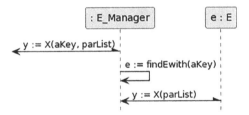

Fig. 11. Handling a request by a manager

Sending the request to the manager first is according to the Façade design pattern [12, 13]. Even if the design will change later on and object e may have other methods or another implementation, we can still first use E_Manager and only internally, within this manager, we need to adjust the further handling of the request. The interface does not need to know anything from this possible internal update.

In general, not each object will have its own manager, so we start with the most suitable manager available and redirect our request from that manager downwards to the object.

5.3 Extending the Initial Class Diagram

When white box SSDs have been created, we must extend the class diagram V0.3 as well, because an object then has more methods. [5] contains the result for our running example.

Once we have created white box SSDs for all grey box SSDs, this will result in a complete class diagram that can be used by the programmer, not only to see the structure of the used objects, but also to see all methods that need to be implemented.

6 Conclusion

We were able to systematically transform an implementation-independent *Conceptual Specification* of a system, consisting of a *Conceptual Data Model* (representing its *statics*) + a set of *textual SSDs* (representing its *dynamics*), into an *Object-Oriented* specification, consisting of an *Enhanced Class Diagram* + a set of *White Box SSDs*. Our *enhanced* class diagrams inherit the *constraints* from the Conceptual Specification. We worked out how to convert an *Enhanced Class Diagram* into a genuine *Class Diagram* with the proper constraints checking methods.

While a (4th generation) language such as SQL has language constructs to specify constraints, (3rd generation) programming languages usually lack such constructs. This is an essential issue in software development, one which is systematically overlooked. However, we showed how to deal with constraints towards an OO-implementation in a systematic way, giving formal mapping rules or 'semi-automatic' guidelines. Further research can be done on how to further automate creating code according to these guidelines. Using the general MVC software design pattern and splitting the (black box) system into a kernel and an interface, constraints are worked out systematically into OO pseudo-code. Since this pseudo-code is very simple and similar to Java-code, for example, an OO-programmer can easily translate that pseudo-code into real code.

We could also compare the OO-mappings with our earlier *Relational* mappings, i.e., from the same conceptual specifications towards a *Relational Database* + a set of *Stored Procedures*.

Being able to map our conceptual specifications to different software paradigms also shows that our conceptual specifications are truly implementation-independent.

References

1. de Brock, E.O.: An NL-based Foundation for Increased Traceability, Transparency, and Speed in Continuous Development of Information Systems. NLP4RE (2019)
2. de Brock, E.O.: Developing Information Systems Accurately - A Wholistic Approach. Springer, Cham (2023). https://doi.org/10.1007/978-3-031-16862-8
3. Brock, B.: From elementary user wishes and domain models to SQL-specifications. In: Shishkov, B. (ed.) BMSD 2021. LNBIP, vol. 422, pp. 97–117. Springer, Cham (2021). https://doi.org/10.1007/978-3-030-79976-2_6
4. de Brock, E.O.: Advantages of a formal specification of a case - from informal description via formal specification to realization. In: Shishkov, B. (ed.) BMSD'22. LNBIP, vol. 453, pp. 158–181. Springer, Cham (2022). https://doi.org/10.1007/978-3-031-11510-3_10
5. Smedinga, R., de Brock, E.O.: A development example: from conceptual specification to OO-specification. In: Shishkov, B. (ed.) BMSD'23. LNBIP, vol. 483, pp. xx–yy (2023)
6. Coad, P., Yourdon, E.: Object Oriented Analysis. Yourdon Press, Englewood Cliffs (1991)
7. Coad, P., Yourdon, E.: Object Oriented Design. Yourdon Press, Englewood Cliffs (1991)
8. Jacobson, I., et al.: Object-Oriented Software Engineering: A Use Case Driven Approach. Addison-Wesley, Reading (1992)
9. Jacobson, I., Booch, G., Rumbaugh, J.: The Unified Software Development Process. Addison-Wesley, Reading (1999)
10. de Brock, E.O.: On System Sequence Descriptions, NLP4RE (2020)
11. SWEBOK (Software Engineering Body of Knowledge). https://www.computer.org/education/bodies-of-knowledge/software-engineering. Accessed 5 May 2023
12. Larman, C.: Applying UML and Patterns: An Introduction to Object-Oriented Analysis and Design and Iterative Development, 3rd edn. Addison Wesley Professional (2004)
13. Gamma, E., et al.: Design Patterns - Elements of Reusable Object-Oriented Software. Addison Wesley, Reading (1995)

Short Papers

Architecting Agility: Unraveling the Impact of AI Capability on Organizational Change and Competitive Advantage

Rogier van de Wetering$^{(\boxtimes)}$ ⓘ, Petra de Weerd-Nederhof ⓘ, Samaneh Bagheri ⓘ, and Roger Bons ⓘ

Faculty of Science, Open University of the Netherlands, Valkenburgerweg 177, 6419 AT Heerlen, The Netherlands

`{rogier.vandewetering,petra.deweerd-nederhof,samaneh.bagheri,`
`roger.bons}@ou.nl`

Abstract. With the progressing developments of Artificial Intelligence (AI) in business and society, understanding the role of AI in enabling organizational change and agility has become an increasingly relevant area of inquiry. However, despite this interest, the specific effects of an AI architecture capability that helps firms design and deploy AI technologies in the organization on firms' dynamic change capability remains an underexplored area in the literature. To address this gap, we built upon the dynamic capabilities view and conducted an extensive survey of senior business and IT managers in the Netherlands. Based on a sample of 168 final respondents, we tested a research model with associated hypotheses using a composite-based structural equation modeling (SEM) approach. The analyses confirm the hypotheses and show that AI architecture positively enables the firm's change capability. Furthermore, the firm's change capability positively impacts operational agility. Hence, our work extends the current knowledge base of dynamic capabilities while offering various implications for practice. These practical recommendations could facilitate managers overcoming change capability and agility challenges.

Keywords: Artificial Intelligence (AI) · AI Architecture Capability · Change Capability · Dynamic Capabilities · Operational Agility · Composite-based structural equation modeling

1 Introduction

Today's market and technological trends are reshaping the competitive business ecosystem, making the organization's ability to change and adapt as crucial as its competitive strategy. Due to major market and technology disruptions, the competitive landscape is constantly changing, emphasizing the key role of a firm's ability to respond quickly to changing market demands [1, 2].

Artificial intelligence (AI) is one of several key technologies currently reshaping the business ecosystem. Therefore, it has gained considerable attention from both scholars

© The Author(s), under exclusive license to Springer Nature Switzerland AG 2023
B. Shishkov (Ed.): BMSD 2023, LNBIP 483, pp. 203–213, 2023.
https://doi.org/10.1007/978-3-031-36757-1_12

and business professionals [3, 4]. Various studies tried to understand the value and contribution of AI in relation to elements of organizational performance, e.g., improved operational effectiveness, enhanced customer satisfaction, and better financial performance [5, 6]. However, many of these contributions are atheoretical and remain conceptual without clear empirical evidence that unfolds how AI business value can be effectuated, so debates about AI's value remain. Moreover, many studies focus on AI (or, e.g., machine learning, neural networks) as a system, not embedding AI in organizational capabilities, so AI's broader organizational implications and architectural alignment are not considered [4, 6].

A capability concerns the aggregation of underlying elements that refer to tangible and intangible assets firms use to develop and implement the business strategy. AI is, therefore, a key resource to drive capabilities that facilitate strategic change.

Another stream of scholarship focuses more on the contribution of AI to the development of dynamic capabilities and a firm's ability to sense and capitalize upon environmental changes [1, 7, 8]. Dynamic capabilities are essential for modern-day firms to ensure the business can meet the needs of an increasingly complex environment. These capabilities enable firms to manage change and transformation efforts to yield superior returns while aligning organizations to accelerate strategic action [9]. AI can support these capabilities by identifying trends and customer insights, enhancing resource allocation, and developing new products and services [10]. However, despite the interest in AI, not all firms successfully capitalize upon their AI investments [4]. Moreover, it remains unclear how AI can be deployed to drive organizational 'dynamic' capabilities to manage and implement transformations [5, 7, 11–13]. As such, our understanding of this matter remains limited while there is a clear need to unravel further the AI value-creating mechanisms to enhance a firm's operational agility in a turbulent market.

Change capability is a key dynamic capability responsible for these organizational transformations [14]. With a change capability, firms can efficiently deliver processes and enable customized services under changing market conditions [14–16]. Therefore, it is important to understand how AI, as an organizational resource, can be designed, developed, and deployed within an organization's infrastructure to bolster firms' change capability [7, 11, 17].

This study addresses these current gaps in the literature. It proposes that AI architecture capability—an AI-based capability specifically focusing on deploying and using AI in processes—is an essential organizational capability that further drives change and contributes to operational agility [6, 14]. Therefore, this study enriches the previous literature in several ways. First, it expands upon the growing body of research investigating AI technologies as enablers of organizational agility [2, 8, 18]. Specifically, our work contributes to understanding how AI architecture and change capability interact and how these factors may facilitate or hinder the development of operational agility [7, 12]. Second, we position AI in a broader value network and contribute to the dynamic capabilities view [1, 7]. Finally, we also offer practical implications to organizations seeking to leverage AI.

This work addresses the following central research question: *"To what extent do a firm's AI architecture capability and change capability impact organizational agility?"*.

We structured the study as follows. In the next section, we develop the hypotheses and the research model. Section 3 outlines the methods and our survey approach. The results section follows. We end this paper by discussing the theoretical and practical implications, outlining the study's limitations, and offering avenues for future research.

2 Theoretical Framework and Hypotheses Development

2.1 Dynamic Capabilities View

The dynamic capabilities view (DCV) extends the resource-based view of the firm (RBV) that dominated management and strategy literature in the early 90s. The RBV argues that a firm's resources (e.g., IT, data, and human capital) provide it with a competitive edge. However, the RBV failed to account for market turbulence and changing industry conditions that might significantly affect a firm's competitiveness [19]. The DCV explains competitiveness better than RBV under these scenarios [1, 20]. Hence, this theory provides scholars and leaders with insights into how to adapt firms under turbulent conditions.

Dynamic capabilities, in general, can be defined as '...the firm's behavioral orientation constantly to integrate, reconfigure, renew and recreate its resources and capabilities and, most importantly, upgrade and reconstruct its core capabilities in response to the changing environment to attain and sustain competitive advantage.' [20]. As markets tend to evolve and technological disruption progresses fast, dynamic capabilities are even more relevant [21, 22].

Three broad dynamic capabilities can be synthesized from the academic literature, i.e., sensing, mobilizing, and transforming [1, 21]. The sensing capability concerns firms' ability to identify and spot business opportunities (and threats) and technological developments. The mobilizing, or seizing, capability concerns capitalizing upon sensed opportunities and mobilizing organizational resources. Finally, transforming capability concerns reconfiguring processes [9, 21]. A firm's change capability represents the transformational element of the above dynamic capabilities, which will be discussed next.

2.2 Change Capability as a Transformative Dynamic Capability

A firm's change capability is crucial to adapt to tumultuous business ecosystems as it specifically focuses on managing and implementing transformations [1]. Hence, firms that have developed their change capability can better identify inefficiencies in business processes, subsequently change and implement improvement to promptly address market and technological changes, and deliver flexible services and operations for customized demand [14–16]. In addition, change capability embraces a culture of change, learning, and improvements. As such, this could lead to developing new products and services, thereby contributing to the firm's overall performance. Finally, change capability is even more relevant in the context of networked businesses and services, so effective interfaces across organizational boundaries and fluid networks can be built and easily reconfigured when needed.

Thus, change capability enables firms to make high-impact action across widely distributed resources that support and advance the strategy and anticipate and respond to rapid, complex environmental changes.

2.3 Hypotheses Development

This study now argues that firms' AI architecture capability can positively shape their change capability. AI architecture capability concerns a firm's ability to integrate state-of-the-art AI tools, algorithms, models, and data management systems to facilitate decision-making processes, automation, and innovation [3]. Other than, for instance, IT or enterprise architecture (EA) capabilities, AI architecture capability particularly highlights the implementation and use of AI in business processes. While all these capabilities involve digital technologies, AI architecture capability focuses more on, e.g., the application of machine learning, deep learning, and natural language processing. IT and EA capabilities, on the other hand, focus more broadly on aligning digital technologies with the firm strategy [23]. As a core organizational resource, AI architecture capability enables firms to design and architect entire business units and processes based on these technologies and integrate core data assets across business solutions and applications [4, 17]. As such, this capability drives business units and departments to become AI-driven and process data more quickly, effectively, and with more insights, enhancing collaboration among colleagues and developing a product-focused mentality [3, 24]. Therefore, AI architecture capability is essential in responding to market changes, opportunities, and threats [7, 8, 13]. Furthermore, firms with a well-developed AI architecture capability are better equipped to acquire the necessary AI competencies and skills, govern AI projects, and proactively respond to environmental changes [4, 25]. As a result, firms with AI architecture capabilities are better positioned to shape and implement innovative solutions in response to changing market conditions, bolstering their change capability. Hence, we define the following:

Hypothesis 1 (H1): *AI architecture capability positively enables the firm's change capability.*

We argue that the greater the firms' change capability, the greater the operational agility, defined as the ability to rapidly and flexibly adjust its operations in response to changing market conditions and customer needs [26]. Operational agility is about efficiently delivering reliable services (and products) aligned with current market demands, and customer needs [2, 27]. Change capability enables firms to capitalize upon market and customer developments and trends and adjust their business processes accordingly [19]. So this way, firms can implement strategies to address market changes and reconfigure processes to stay ahead of the competition [14]. Also, firms with a mature change capability can engage productive employees, encourage communication among colleagues, efficiently (re)allocate organizational resources, and foster a culture of continuous improvement and innovation, further enhancing operational agility [2, 10, 16].

This also will eliminate possible business process inefficiencies leading to cost reduction, increased productivity, and faster response times [14]. Thus, the firm's change capability, driven by AI architecture capability, enables the firm to adapt and reconfigure processes to deliver high-quality services and offerings in the market. Hence, we define the following:

Hypothesis 2 (H2): *The firm's change capability positively impacts operational agility.*

3 Methods

3.1 Data Collection

To gather data, we conducted an online survey between September 19th and November 11th, 2022. To get descend response to our survey, we targeted C-level professionals like Chief Information Officers (CIOs), Chief Executive Officers (CEOs), and innovation, IT, and business managers that are typically responsible for digital and organizational transformation programs. Moreover, students[1] participating in an advanced strategic IT and architecture management course at a Dutch University were asked to distribute this survey into their network and snowball it to two experts from other firms in their respective professional networks.

We designed the survey using scales and constructs from empirically validated work (see Table 1) and pretested the survey on several occasions using expert input to ensure content validity. These experts included two academics and two business professionals. All items were measured using a 1–7 Likert scale ranging from strongly disagree to strongly agree. Apart from these constructs, data concerning the respondent's function, industry, firm size, and age were collected so we could control for possible confounding.

In total, 214 respondents started the survey, and we had 166 complete responses to all our questions. Two respondents only missed 1 question, so for those entries, the average was included, so we ended up with 168 respondents. Of those 168, 71% represent the senior management and directors (including CEO, CIO, IT, operations, and innovation managers), 26% are business/IT consultants and lead architects, and a small percentage (2%) have other functions.

3.2 Composite-Based Analyses

We used a composite-based approach of Structural Equation Modeling (SEM) to analyze the survey data [28]. Composite-based SEM allows to simultaneous assess both the measurement model (examining the relationship between items and constructs) and the structural model used to test the research model's associations [29]. This approach to SEM fits our work also due to its focus on prediction and its ability to model the.

complex relationships between AI architecture, change capability, and operational agility. Moreover, the approach is flexible concerning distributional assumptions and small sample sizes like the one used in this study [29].

However, before we can test hypotheses (by analyzing the structural model), we should ensure that the measurement model analyses show valid and reliable results.

---

[1] These are students who are studying in addition to their daily jobs and are, therefore, actually professionals.

Table 1. Constructs, items, and sources

Construct(s)	Items	Sources
AI architecture capability *CA: 0.89; CR: 0.91; AVE: 0.68*	We are capable of architecting business units on a new integrated foundation of data, analytics, and AI systems	*Own construct*
	We standardize and integrate data assets across a range of applications	Based on work by [24]
	We are capable of acquiring important AI competenties and skills	
	We have a product-focused mentality to get this done with AI	
	We have a multidisciplinary governance program for our AI	
Change capability *CA: 0.80; CR: 0.86; AVE: 0.53*	We change business processes in a timely manner	[14]
	We rapidly adapt business processes to competitive changes	
	We quickly reallocate resources among business processes	
	We effectively combine existing resources within business processes	
	We effectively change business processes	
	We effectively reconfigure business processes	
Operational agility *CA: 0.89; CR: 0.91; AVE: 0.62*	Reliability of our offerings (i.e., services and products) has increased	[27]
	Our day-to-day operations are flexible for customized demand	
	Our offerings are more cost-efficient than competitors	
	We accomplish greater speed in delivering our offerings	

(continued)

Table 1. (*continued*)

Construct(s)	Items	Sources
	Our response to market changes is very reliable	
	We have greater flexibility in our offerings to adopt market changes	
	We efficiently redesign our offerings to adopt market changes	

Hence, following guidelines by [29], we examined each construct's item loadings, assessed reliability metrics (Cronbach's alpha, CA, and composite reliability, CR), the average variance extracted (AVE), and finally evaluated discriminant validity tests (through cross-loading and the advanced heterotrait-monotrait ratio of correlations, HTMT assessment).

The reliability and validity statistics are included in Table 1 and show reliable and valid results [29]. Also, the discriminant validity tests indicated adequate discriminant validity. Therefore, based on the results, we can test the hypotheses using the structural model analyses. We used SmartPLS software v 4.0.9.2 for these analyses.

4   Study Findings

Figure 1 summarizes the structural model analysis results, illustrating the tested value paths, regression coefficients (Beta-values), t-values, R^2 values, and their corresponding predictive values, as indicated by Stone-Geisser's Q^2 value (a measure of predictive relevance). Hence, H1 posited that AI architecture capability positively enables the firm's change capability. The structural model outcomes supported this hypothesis ($\beta = 0.72$, $t = 16.71$, $p \leq 0.0001$). Furthermore, the explained variance (coefficient of determination) for change capability of 0.51 indicates that AI architecture capability can explain 51% of the variance in change capability. At the same time, the Q^2 value of 0.26 suggests a satisfactory predictive relevance of the model.

The structural analyses also hypothesis 2, i.e., change capability positively impacts operational agility ($\beta = 0.67$, $t = 6.82$, $p \leq 0.0001$). The explained variance for operational agility was 0.38 ($R^2 = 0.38$) with an associated Q^2 value of 0.22. These outcomes also support our models' predictive relevance.

We can further assess whether or not the direct relationship between AI architecture capability and operational agility was statistically significant. We followed meditation guidelines and a stepwise procedure by Carrión, Nitzl, & Roldán [30]. First, we assessed the significance of the indirect effect as we have done through testing the two hypotheses. Then, as a next step, we assessed the direct effect (AI architecture capability → operational agility) to determine the type of mediation (i.e., partial or fully mediated). The structural model outcomes reveal that this particular (direct) effect was insignificant ($\beta = -0.08$, $t = 0.77$, $p \leq 0.44$). Hence, it can be concluded that change capability fully mediates the effect of AI architecture capability on operational agility. Furthermore, the included control variables showed non-significant results. Therefore, no evidence has been found for the presence of confounding issues in the data.

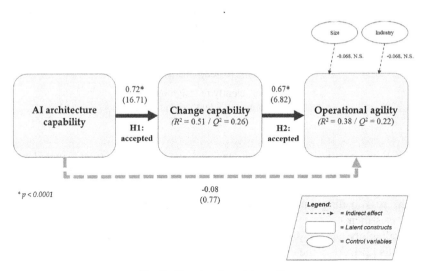

Fig. 1. Structural model results

5 Discussion and Conclusions

5.1 Theoretical Contributions

Our main study's objective was to unfold to what extent a firm's AI architecture capability and change capability impact organizational agility. We built upon the dynamic capabilities view, conceptualized a research model, and conducted a survey.

Through the analyses of a sample of 168 Dutch firms, we tested the two core hypotheses of this work. Hence, we showed that AI architecture capability positively enables change capability, a transformative dynamic capability. This outcome supports the idea that firms that efficaciously design, develop, and deploy AI technologies and systems within the organization, are better equipped to change and reconfigure business processes when responding to opportunities and threats and ultimately drive operational agility. These core results align with previous contributions [3, 18, 25] and extend current insights on the role and contribution of AI to organizations. Furthermore, the results showcase that the dynamic capabilities view is a fitting lens to investigate AI's value path and mechanism in firms. Therefore, we contribute to this view and extend work by [1, 7, 9, 13, 14] by offering empirical support for the crucial role of AI architecture capability as a critical resource and factor in developing dynamic capabilities. Also, our work concurs with [23, 31] in that AI, as a resource (similar to, e.g., IT or enterprise architecture), should be embedded in firms' capabilities to use, deploy and diffuse AI in processes and routines that drive change.

Moreover, we confirm that change capability fully mediates the impact of AI architecture capability on operational agility. Specifically, our work contributes to understanding how AI architecture and change capability interact and how these factors may facilitate or hinder the development of operational agility [7, 12]. Therefore, we extend the current literature [1, 2, 7, 10] and better understand the value path through which firms can capitalize upon their AI investments and project portfolio and drive competitiveness.

5.2   Practical Contributions

Our findings have several substantial managerial and practical implications. First, our work shows how investing in AI practices is important as it ultimately leads to operational agility. Hence, decision-makers and managers must invest in enhancing and developing an AI architecture capability. In doing so, firms can use the measurement items as a starting point to review the current practice and maturity. Then, further develop key aspects of the AI architecture capability (e.g., architecting business, standardizing and integrating data assets, multidisciplinary governance program, and portfolio). Firms can then better accelerate the development of a transformative change capability to ensure the business can meet the needs of an increasingly complex environment. Also, our work showcases the importance of developing dynamic capabilities, particularly a change capability. The current market and technological trends also demand that firms build such a capability to anticipate and respond to rapid environmental changes, change and reconfigure processes timely and adequately, and enable the free flow of resources (e.g., information, people, and people) resources across boundaries).

Firms with a well-developed change capability are more likely to produce long-term results and operational agility that contribute to the firm's evolutionary fitness and competitiveness. In practice, it is essential to develop a shared understanding regarding why change is necessary, what the actual change will be, and how it will affect each individual across the organization. Also, the management and leadership should ensure that different departments, teams, and individuals actively contribute to the increased effectiveness and efficiency of the firm.

5.3   Limitations and Future Work

This study has limitations that should be acknowledged. First, our current data is limited to firms from the Netherlands. This limits the generalizability of our findings. Future work could, therefore, focus on a more diverse and extensive approach, including survey data from other countries (e.g., in Europe, the US, or Asia). Second, we used a single-informant approach, which could lead to informant bias. A matched-pair approach could address this problem adequately. Also, the hypotheses testing was done using self-reported data, as obtaining objective measures is challenging. However, using self-reported data can still be defended as these data types have been shown to be strongly correlated with objective measures [32].

Nonetheless, the survey data can be complemented with publicly available data (secondary data) to strengthen the results further. The results can also be enriched with several case studies to gain more insights into the interplay between the focal constructs. Also, our study did not consider the types of AI tools and technologies firms use. Different

AI tools and technologies have varying degrees of complexity and scalability, so that they may require different levels of AI architecture capability. Future work could explore the impact of these tools and technologies on measuring AI architecture capability.

Acknowledgement. We want to thank all the respondents and organizations contributing to this research. This is much appreciated.

References

1. Teece, D.J.: Explicating dynamic capabilities: the nature and microfoundations of (sustainable) enterprise performance. Strat. Manag. J. **28**(13), 1319–1350 (2007)
2. Van de Wetering, R.: Understanding the impact of enterprise architecture driven dynamic capabilities on agility: a variance and fsQCA study. Pacific Asia J. Assoc. Inf. Syst. **13**(4), 2 (2021)
3. Brynjolfsson, E., Mcafee, A.: Artificial Intelligence, for Real. Harvard Business Review (2017)
4. Abou-Foul, M., Ruiz-Alba, J.L., López-Tenorio, P.J.: The impact of artificial intelligence capabilities on servitization: the moderating role of absorptive capacity-a dynamic capabilities perspective. J. Bus. Res. **157**, 113609 (2023)
5. Chui, M., Manyika, J., Miremadi, M.: Where machines could replace humans-and where they can't (yet) (2016)
6. Davenport, T.H.: From analytics to artificial intelligence. J. Bus. Anal. **1**(2), 73–80 (2018)
7. Drydakis, N.: Artificial Intelligence and reduced SMEs' business risks. A dynamic capabilities analysis during the COVID-19 pandemic. Inf. Syst. Front. **24**(4), 1223–1247 (2022)
8. Van de Wetering, R., Milakef, P., Dennehy, D.: Artificial intelligence ambidexterity, adaptive transformation capability, and their impact on performance under tumultuous times. In: Papagiannidis, S., Alamanos, E., Gupta, S., Dwivedi, Y.K., Mäntymäki, M., Pappas, I.O. (eds.) Conference on e-Business, e-Services and e-Society, pp. 25–37. Springer, Cham (2022). https://doi.org/10.1007/978-3-031-15342-6_3
9. Teece, D., Peteraf, M., Leih, S.: Dynamic capabilities and organizational agility: risk, uncertainty, and strategy in the innovation economy. California Manage. Rev. **58**(4), 13–35 (2016)
10. Pavlou, P.A., El Sawy, O.A.: Understanding the elusive black box of dynamic capabilities. Dec. Sci. **42**(1), 239–273 (2011)
11. Fountaine, T., McCarthy, B., Saleh, T.: Building the AI-powered organization. Harvard Bus. Rev. **97**(4), 62–73 (2019)
12. Weber, M., Engert, M., Schaffer, N., Weking, J., Krcmar, H.: Organizational capabilities for AI implementation—coping with inscrutability and data dependency in AI. Inf. Syst. Front. 1–21 (2022)
13. Wamba-Taguimdje, S.-L., Wamba, S.F., Kamdjoug, J.R.K., Wanko, C.E.T.: Influence of artificial intelligence (AI) on firm performance: the business value of AI-based transformation projects. Bus. Process Manage. J. (2020)
14. Torres, R., Sidorova, A., Jones, M.C.: Enabling firm performance through business intelligence and analytics: a dynamic capabilities perspective. Inf. Manage. **55**(7), 822–839 (2018)
15. Helfat, C.E., Peteraf, M.A.: Understanding dynamic capabilities: progress along a developmental path. Strat. Organ. **7**(1), 91–102 (2009)

16. Armenakis, A.A., Bedeian, A.G.: Organizational change: a review of theory and research in the 1990s. J. Manage. **25**(3), 293–315 (1999)
17. Van de Wetering, R.: Enterprise architecture resources, dynamic capabilities, and their pathways to operational value. In: Fortieth International Conference on Information Systems. Munich: AIS (2019)
18. Haenlein, M., Kaplan, A.: A brief history of artificial intelligence: on the past, present, and future of artificial intelligence. California Manage. Rev. **61**(4), 5–14 (2019)
19. Eisenhardt, K.M., Martin, J.A.: Dynamic capabilities: what are they? Strat. Manage. J. **21**(10–11), 1105–1121 (2000)
20. Wang, C.L., Ahmed, P.K.: Dynamic capabilities: a review and research agenda. Int. J. Manage. Rev. **9**(1), 31–51 (2007)
21. Van de Wetering, R.: The role of enterprise architecture-driven dynamic capabilities and operational digital ambidexterity in driving business value under the COVID-19 shock. Heliyon **2022**, e11484 (2022)
22. Van de Wetering, R., Roelens, B., de Langen, F.: Improvisational and dynamic capabilities as drivers of business model innovation: an enterprise architecture perspective. Pacific Asia J. Assoc. Inf. Syst. **15**(1), 1 (2023)
23. Van de Wetering, R.: Dynamic enterprise architecture capabilities and organizational benefits: an empirical mediation study. In: Proceedings of the Twenty-Eigth European Conference on Information Systems (ECIS2020) (2020)
24. Iansiti, M., Lakhani, K.R.: Competing in the Age of AI: Strategy and Leadership When Algorithms and Networks Run the World. Harvard Business Press (2020)
25. Daugherty, P.R., Wilson, H.J.: Human+ Machine: Reimagining Work in the Age of AI. Harvard Business Press (2018)
26. Sambamurthy, V., Bharadwaj, A., Grover, V.: Shaping agility through digital options: reconceptualizing the role of information technology in contemporary firms. MIS Q. **27**(2), 237–263 (2003)
27. Akhtar, P., Khan, Z., Tarba, S., Jayawickrama, U.: The Internet of Things, dynamic data and information processing capabilities, and operational agility. Technol. Forecast. Soc. Change. **136**, 307–316 (2018)
28. Henseler J. Composite-based structural equation modeling: analyzing latent and emergent variables. Guilford Publications; 2020
29. Hair Jr., J.F., Sarstedt, M., Ringle, C.M., Gudergan, S.P.: Advanced Issues in Partial Least Squares Structural Equation Modeling. SAGE Publications (2017)
30. Carrión, G.C., Nitzl, C., Roldán, J.L.: Mediation analyses in partial least squares structural equation modeling: Guidelines and empirical examples. In: Latan, H., Noonan, R. (eds.) Partial least squares path modeling, pp. 173–195. Springer, Cham (2017). https://doi.org/10.1007/978-3-319-64069-3_8
31. Wetering, R.: Dynamic enterprise architecture capabilities: conceptualization and validation. In: Abramowicz, W., Corchuelo, R. (eds.) BIS 2019. LNBIP, vol. 354, pp. 221–232. Springer, Cham (2019). https://doi.org/10.1007/978-3-030-20482-2_18
32. Wu, S.P.-J., Straub, D.W., Liang, T.-P.: How information technology governance mechanisms and strategic alignment influence organizational performance: insights from a matched survey of business and IT managers. Mis Q. **39**(2), 497–518 (2015)

Enterprise Architecture Artifacts' Role in Improved Organizational Performance

Frank Grave[✉] , Rogier Van de Wetering , and Rob Kusters

Open University, Valkenburgerweg 177, 6419 AT Heerlen, The Netherlands
{frank.grave,rogier.vandewetering,rob.kusters}@ou.nl

Abstract. The significance of enterprise architecture (EA) in strategic renewal, such as digital transformations, is evident and widely accepted. Firms rely on EA to support strategic renewal, especially digital technology-driven strategic renewal. EA artifacts are used to document and communicate decisions and facts about the EA's current, future, and transition states. They facilitate bridging the communication gap and alignment between business and IT stakeholders. However, despite extant research in the area of EA, its role in strategic renewal, and its contribution to improving organizational performance, EA artifacts' contribution mechanism is still unknown. Therefore, this research explores how EA artifact creation and use facilitate strategic renewal, such as digital transformations. Based on 29 interviews at 4 case firms, we found 17 different EA artifacts and 16 ways EA contributes to strategic renewal, i.e., 16 EA values. Moreover, we determined the interrelatedness of EA values and a model of how EA artifacts contribute to strategic renewal and improved organizational performance. The EA artifact value contribution mechanism described in this study is simple and universal and, thus, has significant implications for both practice and research.

Keywords: Enterprise Architecture · Organizational Performance · Enterprise Architecture Artifacts · Multiple Case Study

1 Introduction

Increasing pressure due to factors such as turbulence in contemporary markets and global technology trends, demand for close alignment of business, and information technology (IT) [1–3]. Global technology trends are digital technologies such as big data, the Internet of Things, artificial intelligence, and combinations. The resulting digital technology-driven strategic renewal of business models is often called digital transformation [3, 4].

Integrating new digital technologies into firms' existing technology, processes, roles, and responsibilities requires changes in the enterprise architecture (EA) [1, 2]. The EA capability defines the current and desirable organizing logic of people, processes, and IT and designs the roadmap for realizing the desired organizing logic [5, 6]. Artifacts that document these definitions and designs are EA artifacts. EA artifacts describe the EA from an integrated business and IT perspective, intending to bridge the communication

B. Shishkov (Ed.): BMSD 2023, LNBIP 483, pp. 214–224, 2023.
https://doi.org/10.1007/978-3-031-36757-1_13

gap between business and IT stakeholders and improve business-IT alignment [2, 7]. Moreover, enterprise architects create and use, or at least facilitate, the creation and use of EA artifacts. Thus, EA artifacts are created and used to facilitate digital transformations and prepare firms to be readily changeable and adaptable.

Recent empirical research on EA artifacts identified which EA artifacts facilitate digital transformation's strategic planning process, thereby expanding our knowledge of an EA capability facilitating the strategic planning process [2, 7–9]. However, how these EA artifacts contribute to improved organizational performance remains unclear. Hence, enterprise architects may have difficulties communicating the need to create and use EA artifacts. Especially in turbulent environments, where the rate and unpredictability of change are high [10], the creation and use of EA artifacts might be experienced as a document-heavy approach delaying the transformation process. Consequently, EA concerns related to the transformation might not be considered. Therefore, we want to explore the contribution of EA artifacts to improved organizational performance to add to existing studies on the EA capability. Our primary research question is: how do EA artifacts contribute to improved organizational performance?

This study proceeds as follows. First, this study outlines the theoretical background and related work. Then, we outline the research method. Section four presents the key results and our proposed EA artifact value contribution mechanism. Finally, in section five, we discuss the results of this study from the perspective of the current literature on EA, followed by our contribution to research and practice, a discussion on the limitations of this study, and we end with some concluding remarks.

2   Related Work

The EA capability has been found to contribute to numerous types of organizational value, such as reduced cost (e.g., [6, 8, 11–15]), increased agility (e.g., [5, 8, 14, 16, 17]), improved project delivery (e.g., [5–8, 11–17]), and competitive differentiation (e.g., [2, 5, 7, 12–14, 16, 17]). Furthermore, different types of more or less overlapping value-creation mechanisms have been researched (e.g., [1, 5, 8, 9, 11–13, 15, 17–20]).

For example, Van Steenbergen and Brinkkemper [18] developed a cause-and-effect-based network model that shows how EA practices contribute to business goals via organizational performance effects. E.g., an EA practice can improve strategic analysis by offering insight into new or altered business models or IT opportunities. The improved strategic analysis leads to improved organizational performance through an updated strategy. As a result, the updated strategy leads to the business goal of, for instance, improved market share.

Additionally, research by Haki and Legner [15] specifically investigated the mechanics of EA principles. They divided the mechanism into three related concepts: ways, means, and ends. The means are the required resources to achieve certain ends by following ways. That is, the resources are the EA principles, and the ways are procedures and inductors to achieve specific desired results. The way of principles resides in their limitational effect on the EA design space. Subsequently, enforcing the EA principles leads to appropriate EA outcomes and, finally, to desired organizational results.

Furthermore, EA value has been clustered in many different ways. For example, Shanks et al. [5] and Foorthuis et al. [13] cluster EA values into project and organization-wide benefits. Alternatively, Jusuf and Kurnia [21] cluster values into operational, managerial, strategic, IT infrastructure, and organizational benefits. Then again, Niemi and Pekkola [6] cluster the benefits into first-, second-, and third-level benefits.

These varying perspectives and aspects of EA value and EA value creation mechanisms offer various valuable views on EA's role in organizational performance. However, they also highlight the fragmented body of knowledge provided by EA scholars, lack the general role of EA artifacts, and do not fully explain how EA artifacts contribute to EA value and improved organizational performance.

3   Research Method

This study addresses a new view of the general mechanism of EA artifacts' contribution to improved organizational performance through the EA capability, making it exploratory research. Although preceding empirical research on the EA capability, EA artifacts, and EA value can be used as a basis for research purposes, no such study is available for the integral view we aim to investigate. We wanted to gain in-depth insights into the value contribution mechanism of EA artifacts, which warranted an exploratory case study as the research method. Furthermore, in the absence of established theories we could use as a basis for our research, we used an inductive approach.

We assume that the in-depth knowledge of the EA artifact value creation mechanism necessary to answer our research question is present in the people working at organizations undertaking digital transformations and who are involved in creating and using EA artifacts. Rather than choosing a single case study, we chose a multiple case study to gain the data for our research. A multiple case study enables comparisons between cases, thereby mitigating the idiosyncratic characteristics of a single case and providing a more substantial base for theory building [22]. The multiple-case approach enabled a broader exploration of the research question and yielded a more robust and generalizable theory.

We selected four case firms and conducted 29 interviews to base our results. The firms were selected based on having undertaken a digital transformation and permitting access to interviewees. For ethical reasons, we anonymized the firms' names to Alpha, Beta, Gamma, and Delta. Alpha is a large retail firm mainly selling furniture and interior decorations. They have around 4,000 employees and many physical stores spread over the Netherlands. Beta is a prominent Dutch local government with over 12,000 employees. Gamma is a large international financial services organization with more than 55,000 workers and is active in Asia, Europe, North America, South America, and Oceania. Finally, Delta is a Dutch government agency with nearly 3,000 employees across two locations. We selected interviewees who created or used EA artifacts for their digital transformation. We selected a wide range of employees from business to IT and strategic to tactical to get a broad view of the EA artifact value contribution mechanism.

We selected semi-structured interviews as the most appropriate research method [23]. All the interviews were held using an interview guide covering the topics: EA, EA artifacts, and EA and EA artifact value for digital transformations. All the interviews were recorded with the permission of the interviewees and then transcribed ad-verbatim for qualitative analysis.

Given the inductive nature of this explorative research, we started the analysis of the transcribed data with an initial coding cycle, followed by an axial coding cycle. We finished with a theoretical coding cycle [24]. In the initial coding cycle, we were motivated by the general components of EA artifacts, EA value, and the mechanics of value creation through EA artifacts. Therefore, we coded EA artifacts, EA value, and EA value mechanics throughout the transcriptions. Furthermore, we coded antecedents of EA-artifact value and EA-artifacts' value contributions recognized by the interviewees. And we also coded relationships among the elements when explicitly mentioned by the interviewees to increase the explanatory power of the results. Subsequently, we performed a cycle of axial coding to refine our coding scheme into a more manageable set of related themes. And finally, we completed a cycle of theoretical coding to integrate and refine the categories we identified in the previous coding cycle. Consequently, relating EA values and EA artifacts resulted in the model of an EA artifact value contribution mechanism that integrates the data from our analysis of the concepts and their central relationships from the interviews.

Based on suggestions from [22], we took several mitigating measures to improve the quality of our study. Hence, we monitored construct validity and generalizability by embedding the concepts we used, e.g., the solution overview EA artifact, in existing scientific literature. Furthermore, although the coding process of the interview was performed only by the first researcher, the second and third researchers reviewed this study for any anomalies in the use of concepts. For improved internal validity, we triangulated the interview results with the documents shown during the interviews. To ensure reliability, we maintained a case study database for this study, where we kept all our data. Finally, ethics were handled by anonymizing the interviewees and case firms, having the interviewees sign an informed consent form, and assuring our interviewees that they were free to stop participating in this research whenever they wanted.

4   Results

Our qualitative analysis of the interview data and EA artifacts that were shown to us identified 17 different EA artifacts and 16 EA values. These EA artifacts and values have been abstracted into a model of the role of EA artifacts in improved organizational performance. The values and the abstraction toward the contribution of EA artifacts are described below.

4.1   EA Artifacts and EA Value

We found a total of 17 different EA artifacts at our case firms. Although the names of the EA artifacts differed among the case firms, we generalized them and used the most logical name and thus distinguished 17 different EA artifacts. For example, Alpha mentioned a high-level design, and Delta mentioned a solution overview. Since the characteristics of these EA artifacts were the same, we generalized these EA artifacts into one EA artifact.

The values of EA have been studied extensively, e.g., [1, 5, 6, 11, 13, 14, 17, 21]. Despite these studies and the combined knowledge they provide us, we used explorative interview questions to stay open to new empirical insights. Additionally, we tried to keep an open mind during the interview data coding process [24]. This resulted in the list of values presented in Table 1.

Table 1. Values enabled or provided by the EA capability

Value	Alpha	Beta	Gamma	Delta
Improved agility	X	X		X
Improved business-IT alignment	X	X	X	X
Improved commitment	X	X		
Improved communication	X	X	X	X
Improved complexity control	X	X	X	X
Improved decision-making		X	X	X
Improved goal realization		X	X	X
Improved insights	X	X	X	X
Improved knowledge conservation				X
Improved prioritization and resource allocation	X	X		
Improved regulatory compliance			X	X
Improved reliability of the IT landscape			X	X
Improved resource effectiveness	X		X	X
Improved risk management				X
Lower cost of change	X		X	X
Shorter lead times				X

Following is a short description of the EA values found. Improved agility manifests when the enterprise architecture landscape design becomes more easily adaptable. Improved business-IT alignment occurs when business and IT strategies and operations align better. Improved commitment results from providing the information necessary to convince relevant stakeholders. When many people work together, it takes effort to communicate clearly. Defining concepts more sharply and visualizing complex situations through, for example, graphical models improves general communication within the organization and projects. Furthermore, firms get greater control over the complexity of their enterprise architecture landscape by systematically structuring it. The available information leads to better-informed decisions and, thus, better-quality decisions. Besides, the EA capability translates high-level goals into a high-level design of roles, processes, IT, guidelines, and principles. Doing so assures alignment between the high-level goals and the high-level EA design. Additionally, EA provides insight into aspects such as the current situation, the target situation, integration design, the impact of changes, necessary capabilities, and EA strengths, weaknesses, opportunities, and threats. Explicating knowledge in EA artifacts makes that knowledge available to current and future stakeholders. Improved prioritization and resource allocation are enabled by the insights provided by the EA capability. The EA capability considers legal requirements when making an architecture that supports legal compliance. EA artifacts facilitate the reliability and sustainability of the IT landscape, considering aspects such as scalability and availability. Deploying resources the way they are intended to be deployed improves through, for example, the reuse of resources. The structures and insights provided by EA explicate risks, enabling improved risk management. Improved communication and improved insights facilitated by EA artifacts allow a lower cost of change. And finally, a more easily adaptable firm can adapt to change in less time.

4.2 EA Artifacts and Organizational Performance

The description of EA value in the previous section already hints at the interrelatedness of EA values. E.g., it would help if you had insight into the EA to control its complexity, and a less complex EA landscape is more adaptable, making the firm more agile. Furthermore, an EA landscape that becomes easier to manage will lead to lower management effort, thus lowering the cost for the firm. Through an in-depth analysis of the interviews, we managed to infer the interrelatedness of EA values. Hence, we derived the relations between different EA values on empirical data from our interview results.

This study aimed to explore how EA artifacts contribute to improved organizational performance. We do so because the extant literature does not clarify EA artifacts' role in enabling value. Moreover, this gap leaves scholars with the practical inconvenience of being unable to clearly explain EA artifacts' value and justify creating and using them even in highly dynamic environments. After a thorough qualitative analysis of 29 interviews at four case firms and going back and forth through the data, we abstracted a mechanism of EA artifact role in organizational performance. We found that EA artifacts improve knowledge conservation and provide improved insights to its stakeholders, and creating these insights is not always obvious. The CIO of Delta described it: "This means that as an architect, you have to do work to make professional sketches because that is the explicitly formulated knowledge about the organization. And that is not self-evident." An additional quote from Alpha's project manager highlights the improved insights aspect of EA artifacts: "The direct value is more about how are we going to set up the organization and also somewhat directly who is responsible for what, what roles do you need in that. Then it also comes out of what is a transition; we have the as-is and to-be." In each case, it was apparent that EA artifacts, as instruments of knowledge conservation, provided improved insights into various aspects such as the current situation, desired situation, integration, and the impact of changes and their risks.

Furthermore, we found that EA artifacts enable improved communication. Beta's strategic IT consultant gave an example of how the explicated knowledge in EA artifacts is used: "People from HR will be needed to assess whether certain data may be passed on. This also requires investments on the part of HR. Sharing the design with them also ensures they are willing to participate in such a process." Another typical response on the creation and use of EA artifacts related to the communication aspect was given, for example, by Gamma's business owner: "So making an artifact and throwing it over the fence, then no one will ever use it. It's about the conversation and conviction." Independent of EA artifacts, communication was seen as a critical aspect of strategic renewal. For example, Alpha's business consultant said, "Those artifacts, yes, they are important. But even more important is the alignment, the talking, all being on the same wavelength, so to speak, the soft side of it."

We argue that by providing improved insight and enabling improved communication, EA artifacts contribute to improved decision-making. And likewise, the actual communication and insights provided through EA artifacts contribute to improved decision-making. Furthermore, EA artifacts were deemed essential for documenting decisions: "You have made decisions in the past, and you must continue to write them down [in EA artifacts]." [Gamma's Chief Architect] Additionally, many interviewees indicated that improved communication led to improved insights on new possibilities and vice versa, which we concluded from interview responses such as: "It's about the conversation and discovering new possibilities together" [Delta's business consultant].

Not surprisingly, our analysis revealed a cyclic dependency between improved knowledge conservation, insights, and communication. These three values depend on each other and thus mutually influence each other. In the remainder of this paper, we will refer to this cluster of values as the EA value fundament. Based on the cyclic nature of the components of the EA value fundament, we argue that EA artifacts, as instruments of improved knowledge conservation, provide improved insight and enable improved communication. And improved insight enables improved communications and improved knowledge conservation. Additionally, improved communication enables improved insight and improved knowledge conservation.

We also established sequentiality in EA value creation. Our analysis showed that the EA value fundament precedes improved decision-making and that improved decision-making influences all other improvements either directly or indirectly. For example,

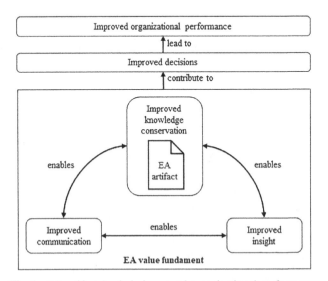

Fig. 1. EA artifacts' role in improved organizational performance

improved decisions about the target architecture design will impact business-IT alignment. Furthermore, when abstracting the improvements that sequentially come after improved decision-making into the general concept of improved organizational performance, we create a clear and straightforward view of the contribution of EA artifacts to improved organizational performance. Figure 1 shows the position of EA artifact's contribution to improved organizational performance.

5 Discussion, Contribution, Limitations, and Conclusion

5.1 Discussion

EA artifacts have received considerable attention in existing EA research. These studies aim to arrive at a point where a widely used standard exists for their form and function (e.g., [2, 7, 8, 19]). While these are all sound evidence-based studies analyzing the role of EA artifacts, the extent they arrive at well-established standards is low. For instance, Kotusev [7] identified solution overviews, landscape diagrams, and context diagrams as separate artifacts. However, several of our interviewees indicated that solution overviews contain landscape diagrams and that some landscape diagrams are context diagrams. Furthermore, Grave et al. [2] deviate from Kotusev [7] in multiple aspects. For example, they presented a strategic plan as an EA artifact. Although enterprise architects can provide valuable input for a strategic plan, it is in no way their accountability. Our research identified different EA artifacts, such as the architecture assessment and scenario plans. Interestingly, Grave et al. [2] subsequently denote "ambiguity surrounding the definition of EA artifacts." The ambiguity and diversity in the practical application of EA artifacts found in empirical studies and the fragmented body of knowledge provided by EA scholars seem to be an immaturity trait of the EA discipline.

Contrary to EA artifact research, we argue that EA value research is relatively convergent. We came across many of the values found in previous studies. We found apparent values such as improved business-IT alignment, improved agility, and a lower cost of change reported by many scholars before us (e.g., [6, 8, 14]). Nevertheless, we also identified two EA values that have not been reported by these three studies, i.e., improved commitment and improved regulatory compliance. Furthermore, Van de Wetering et al. [20] noted that an EA capability that drives dynamic capabilities enhances a firm's innovativeness. Our interviewees did not explicitly mention this EA value. Thus, although there are minor differences and probably improvements in establishing EA's value, we believe that research in this area is converging. Scholars seem to agree on its value generally.

Nevertheless, it remains challenging to clearly show the value of EA and EA artifacts in particular. Our elaboration on the relatedness of EA artifacts and organizational performance uncovers a mutually reinforcing value mechanism. EA values do not stand independently and, therefore, cannot be seen as separate goals to strive for. EA values are a complete package enabled by EA knowledge conservation, communication, and EA insights that lead to improved decisions. These improved decisions manifest themselves because they are better-informed decisions that ultimately improve organizational performance, such as enhanced agility and lowered costs. However, of course, it is still necessary to balance the level of investment in the EA capability with the benefits it may offer.

5.2 Contribution to Research and Practice

This study has various theoretical implications. First, our findings extend those of other EA artifact researchers (e.g., [2, 7, 8, 19]) in the empirical observation that the use of EA artifacts differs considerably among firms. The four case firms subject to our study again showed new artifacts compared to previous studies. Furthermore, this study unveiled a list of EA values experienced by case firm interviewees. We further ground the values of EA on empirical findings, and although we found several new values, we notice a strong convergence of these values in EA value research. More importantly, we established an empirically based analysis of EA values which provides insights into the relatedness of EA values. Moreover, improved knowledge conservation, communication, and insights are at the heart of all EA value opportunities. Finally, we established EA artifacts' role in improved organizational performance. I.e., EA artifacts, as an instance of knowledge conservation, together with the improved communication and insights they enable, lead to improved decisions and ultimately to improved organizational performance.

The first practical contribution is that this study offers an overview of EA values in natural, realistic settings. This may help other organizations reflect on their use of EA artifacts and the realization of EA value. Second, this study touches upon the values of an EA capability and the interrelatedness of these values. This understanding may help practitioners in their work and help them understand what they can do to realize as much EA value as possible for their organization. For example, they can explain how EA artifacts and improved communications and insights can help improve project prioritization decisions and complexity control. Finally, this study also describes how EA artifacts fit into the equation of EA value creation. This understanding allows practitioners to reflect on what to document and what not to document in EA artifacts. Primarily, it helps them use EA artifacts to improve communication and thus share insights, which might result in new insights followed by improved decisions by their management.

5.3 Limitations

Deriving the results from a multiple case study is an obvious limitation and might have caused bias. Furthermore, there are apparent geographical, industry, size, and maturity limitations. First, our case firms were all headquartered in the Netherlands. Second, we only investigated one firm in the retail industry, one local government, one financial services organization, and one government agency. Third, the specific sizes of our case firms might have influenced the results. Fourth, the case firms we explored had a certain maturity of their EA capability, and we did not conduct the same number of interviews in each firm which might have affected the results. We tried to mitigate external validity limitations by covering diverse firms. However, even with our varied set of firms, we still encountered a substantial degree of variety in the results.

5.4 Conclusion

This study explored EA artifacts' role in organizational performance in-depth using a multiple case study at four case firms with 29 semi-structured interviews. We identified 17 EA artifacts and 16 types of value associated with the EA capability. Furthermore, based on the interviews, we analyzed the interrelatedness of EA values. We touched upon how the different EA values influence and reinforce each other. Additionally, we conceptualized EA artifacts' role in organizational performance consists of five interrelated concepts. EA artifacts as instances of knowledge conservation, together with improved communication and improved insights, contribute to improved decision-making, ultimately leading to improved organizational performance. This study adds to an enhanced understanding of EA values and the mechanism of EA value creation and, hence, offers an important contribution to research and practice.

References

1. Van de Wetering, R., Kurnia, S., Kotusev, S.: The effect of enterprise architecture deployment practices on organizational benefits: a dynamic capability perspective. Sustainability **12**, 8902 (2020)
2. Grave, F., Van de Wetering, R., Kusters, R.J.: Enterprise architecture artifacts facilitating digital transformations' strategy planning process: a systematic literature review and multiple case study. IADIS Int. J. Comput. Sci. Inf. Syst. **16**, 46–62 (2021)
3. Hess, T., Matt, C., Benlian, A., Wiesböck, F.: Options for formulating a digital transformation strategy. MIS Quarterly Executive 15 (2016)
4. Vial, G.: Understanding digital transformation: a review and a research agenda. J. Strateg. Inf. Syst. **28**, 118–144 (2019)
5. Shanks, G., et al.: Achieving benefits with enterprise architecture. J. Strat. Inf. Syst. **27**, 139–156 (2018)
6. Niemi, E., Pekkola, S.: The benefits of enterprise architecture in organizational transformation. Bus. Inf. Syst. Eng. **62**(6), 585–597 (2019). https://doi.org/10.1007/s12599-019-00605-3
7. Kotusev, S.: Enterprise architecture and enterprise architecture artifacts: questioning the old concept in light of new findings. J. Inf. Technol. **34**, 102–128 (2019)
8. Kurnia, S., Kotusev, S., Shanks, G., Dilnutt, R., Taylor, P., Milton, S.K.: Enterprise architecture practice under a magnifying glass: linking artifacts, activities, benefits, and blockers. Commun. Assoc. Inf. Syst. **49**, 34 (2021)
9. Van den Berg, M., Slot, R., Van Steenbergen, M., Faasse, P.: How enterprise architecture improves the quality of IT investment decisions. J. Syst. Softw. **152**, 134–150 (2019)
10. Danneels, E., Sethi, R.: New product exploration under environmental turbulence. Organ. Sci. **22**, 1026–1039 (2010)
11. Ahlemann, F., Stettiner, E., Messerschmidt, M., Legner, C.: Strategic enterprise architecture management: challenges, best practices, and future developments (2012). https://doi.org/10.1007/978-3-642-24223-6
12. Ahlemann, F., Legner, C., Lux, J.: A resource-based perspective of value generation through enterprise architecture management. Inf. Manage. **58,** 103266 (2021)
13. Foorthuis, R., Van Steenbergen, M., Brinkkemper, S., Bruls, W.A.G.: A theory building study of enterprise architecture practices and benefits. Inf. Syst. Front. **18**, 541–564 (2016)
14. Frampton, K., Shanks, G.G., Tamm, T., Kurnia, S., Milton, S.K.: Enterprise Architecture Service Provision: Pathways to Value. ECIS 2015 Research-in-Progress Papers (2015)

15. Haki, K., Legner, C.: The mechanics of enterprise architecture principles. J. Assoc. Inf. Syst. **22**, 1334–1375 (2021)
16. Grave, F., Van de Wetering, R., Kusters, R.: How EA information drives digital transformation: a multiple case study and framework. In: IEEE 24th Conference on Business Informatics (CBI) (2022)
17. Tamm, T., Seddon, P.B., Shanks, G.: How enterprise architecture leads to organisational benefits. Int. J. Inf. Manage. **67**, 102554 (2022)
18. Van Steenbergen, M., Brinkkemper, S.: Modeling the contribution of enterprise architecture practice to the achievement of business goals. In: Papadopoulos, G.A., Wojtkowski, W., Wojtkowski, G., Wrycza, S., Zupancic, J. (eds.) Information Systems Development: Towards a Service Provision Society, pp. 609–618. Springer, US, Boston, MA (2010)
19. Niemi, E., Pekkola, S.: Using enterprise architecture artefacts in an organisation. Enterp. Inf. Syst. **11**, 313–338 (2017)
20. Van de Wetering, R., Hendrickx, T., Brinkkemper, S., Kurnia, S.: The impact of EA-driven dynamic capabilities, innovativeness, and structure on organizational benefits: a variance and fsQCA perspective. Sustainability **13**, 5414 (2021)
21. Jusuf MB, Kurnia, S.: Understanding the benefits and success factors of enterprise architecture. In: Proceedings of the 50th Hawaii International Conference on System Sciences (2017). https://doi.org/10.24251/HICSS.2017.593
22. Yin, R.K.: Case study research and applications: design and methods. Sage publications, Los Angeles, Sixth edit (2018)
23. Saunders, M.N.K., Lewis, P., Thornhill, A.: Research Methods for Business Students, 8th edn. Pearson, New York (2019)
24. Saldaña, J.: The coding manual for qualitative researchers, 3rd edn. SAGE Publications Ltd, London (2016)

A Semiotic Analysis of the Representativeness of BPMN Graphic Elements

Evelyne Batista Duarte[1], Rafael Batista Duarte[2] (iD), and Denis Silva da Silveira[1](✉) (iD)

[1] Federal University of Pernambuco, Recife, PE, Brazil
{evelyne.duarte,dsilveira}@ufpe.br
[2] University of Pernambuco, Recife, PE, Brazil
rbd@ecomp.poli.br

Abstract. Business Process Modeling (BPM) has been under considerable attention from business and information technology (IT) communities. It is an important asset in the quest to decrease the gap in communication between these two groups. To contribute to decreasing this gap, this paper presents the execution of a *quasi*-experiment to verify whether Business Process Modelling Notation's (BPMN) graphical elements are representative according to their semantics. Data collected with 89 participants, so far, through a semiotic analysis has shown that the notations' elements are based on symbolic signs, understood due to shared law, while participants showed preference for iconic signs, that have visual relation to the real object.

Keywords: Business Process Models · BPMN · Semiotics Analysis · *Quasi*-Experiment

1 Introduction

In this paper, we analyze the 14 most used BPMN's graphical elements [1, 2] to clarify whether they represent the intended object, besides how language and interpretation should be understood from a semiotics' point of view. Semiotics is revisited as a means to reduce the communication gap between stakeholders.

Business Process Models (BPM) have been implemented in organizations to promote improvements in strategies, obtain competitive advantages in the market [3], and elicit information systems requirements [4]. However, it has been known that there is some difficulty in the communication between the interested parties due to different aspects (*e.g.*, linguistic and social differences). It is paramount that the languages used to build these models are actually concerned with decreasing validation errors, when stakeholders mistakenly interpret representations in a diagram and accept specifications that do not meet the needs, which compromise implementing information systems, for instance. Thus, incurring in high costs for projects that do not adequately achieve their purpose [5, 6]. Therefore, it is essential to establish a vocabulary that can be understood by the majority of stakeholders.

B. Shishkov (Ed.): BMSD 2023, LNBIP 483, pp. 225–234, 2023.
https://doi.org/10.1007/978-3-031-36757-1_14

Business Process Model and Notation (BPMN) [7] has been the most used Business Process Modeling Language (BPML) among business professionals to describe business behavior [8]. It is also considered an expressly complex grammar, hence rich in symbology [9]. In the context of this paper, BPMN was the selected modeling language. Being this paper's aim to perform a semiotic assessment to verify whether the BPMN graphic elements are indeed representative of its semantics.

This paper is structured as follows: In Sect. 2 we give a brief overview of semiotics. In Sect. 3 we describe how this study was conducted. In Sect. 4 we discuss validity threats and mitigations. In Sect. 5 we present related work. Finally, in Sect. 6 we conclude the paper by suggesting possibilities for future work.

2 Background

Any modeling language is based in three characteristics [3]: (*i*) syntax (set of constructs and rules); (*ii*) semantics (meaning of the constructions defined in the syntax); and (*iii*) the notation (graphic elements' set, used in diagrams' representation). Hence, to comprehend the graphical elements represented users must be familiar with the modeling language used [10]. Since the main goal of languages is to present a comprehensible notation for all stakeholders, it is important to ensure that the graphic elements presented in this notation are indeed representative for the stakeholders. Semiotics is the science that studies visual and verbal signs, such as the graphic elements of a language. Therefore, to assess the representativeness of these signs, it is important to understand semiotics as summarized in this section.

Semiotics is the science that studies visual and verbal signs, such as BPMN's graphical elements. Therefore, to assess the representativeness of those signs it is important to understand semiotics, as summarized in this section.

2.1 Semiotics

Signs are anything that communicates a meaning, to the interpreter, that is not the object itself [11, 12]. They can be subdivided as follows: (*i*) an icon is a sign which refers to the object it represents by its proper characters. Whether it is an existing object or not, as long as a sign is similar to the object, it can be an icon (*e.g.*, the drawing of a tree); (*ii*) a symbol is a sign that, by virtue of a law, refers to the object it represents. It is usually an association of general ideas that leads to the symbol being interpreted as referring to that object. There must be instances of what the symbol denotes, even if it is in the realm of imagination (*e.g.*, skull with crossed bones symbolizes a poisonous area); (*iii*) an index is a sign that refers to the object by actually being affected by it. Its properties are what they are, independent of anything else. By being affected by the object, the index has a property in common with it (*e.g.*, seeing the footprint of a large animal and suspecting dinosaurs exist).

Graphic languages must make use of physical analogies, visual metaphors, common logical properties and cultural associations to make meanings accessible to all [13]. The goal is for signs to have visual similarities to their objects so that meanings can be easily understood. The design of signs needs to be carefully thought, because if it is not designed correctly, stakeholders may interpret a sign with the wrong meaning, leading to a misinterpretation of the process model.

3 Research Design

The *quasi*-experiment presented here was divided into four stages (adapted from [14]), namely: *scope, planning, operation* and *analysis and interpretation.* These stages are explained in more detail below.

3.1 Scope

This research was developed from the perspective of researchers, with the participation of subjects (students and professionals from the fields of business and IT) who answered questionnaires. Thus, the scope of this research was: to analyze which BPMN graphical elements are more or less representative for these participants and ask for suggestions for more representative signs for the less representative elements; collect and categorize this information to understand which new signs are most representative in the context of these participants.

3.2 Planning

A pilot application of the *quasi*-experiment occurred to make sure the models presented and the questionnaires had no mistakes to later present them to participants. A scale from 0–10 for the familiarity with BPMN was added after the pilots to make sure participants had been properly selected.

The instruments (used in two different phases) consisted in the first phase of (*i*) a consent letter; (*ii*) a BPMN model (Fig. 1) specially created in the laboratory to represent the process of a "*Property Appraisal*"; (*iii*) a questionnaire to illustrate the graphical BPMN elements and in the second phase of (*iv*) a model with new signs proposed by the participants (Fig. 2); (*v*) a questionnaire to check the understanding of the model with the proposed signs.

The research was accompanied by two phases of researcher interactions developed in controlled environments (*e.g.*, classrooms or meeting rooms). Participants were purposely selected and divided into two groups: those with prior knowledge of BPMN (first phase) and those who had no knowledge of BPMN (second phase). They were presented with the models and asked to rate the representativeness of the signals. The first phase evaluated the graphical BPMN elements, while the second phase analyzed the elements proposed in the first phase.

As in a *quasi*-experiment according to [14], this directed selection of participants is possible. We decided on two different profiles of participants. In the first phase, only those who had prior knowledge of BPMN, and in the second phase, only those who had not yet been formally introduced to the notation, in order to avoid any kind of bias in the results. However, all participants were working in business or IT.

For the time being, this study was conducted with 89 participants: 54 in the first phase and 35 in the second phase. These numbers already have statistical value [15], but we still intend to increase the sample. Then, the hypotheses are stated formally, including a null and an alternative hypothesis: (H_1) BPMN's graphical elements have representativeness according to their semantics; (H_0) BPMN's graphical elements haven't got representativeness according to their semantics.

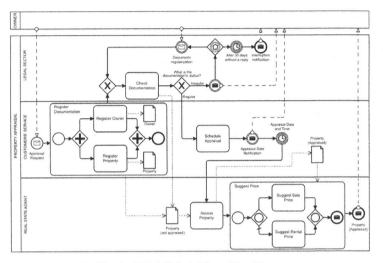

Fig. 1. BPMN Model from First Phase.

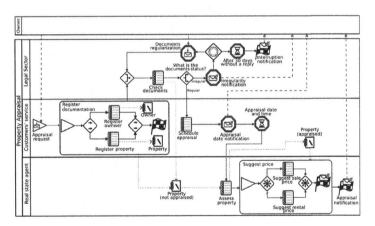

Fig. 2. Model with New Signs from Second Phase.

3.3 Operation

To understand how participants perceive the representativeness of BPMN signs' representativeness, we divided the operation into two phases: the first phase (Fig. 3) to understand how participants perceive the representativeness of BPMN signs and to collect different graphical elements proposed by them; and the second phase (Fig. 3) to test whether different graphical representations can influence representativeness.

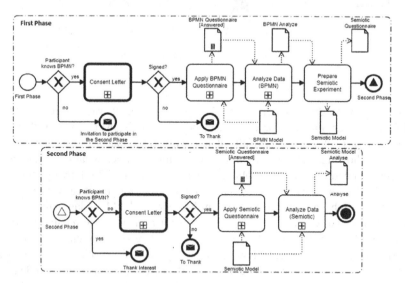

Fig. 3. Research Design.

3.4 Analysis and Interpretation

This section contains the analysis and interpretation of data collected during both phases of the operation. When asked to rate their familiarity to BPMN, during first phase, 49% of participants declared numbers from 6 to 10,46% from 0 to 5, and 2% did not reply. It can be seen that, even in the group of participants who had had previous formal training in the notation there is still a large number of participants who do not feel familiar with it. The analysis, after data collection from the first phase, consisted of separating the replies for each graphic element (sign) from all the participants, comparing the drawings, and separating them into semantic fields (*e.g.*, circles, squares, circles with letters).

Message (catch) event received in total 9 suggestions (Table 1), approximately 22.2% used arrows inside the graphical element to indicate the direction the notification is flowing in the process. Participants chose to keep the essence of a notification as a letter (icon), and the generalized idea of arrows to indicate direction (symbol). The average of representativeness from first phase to the second decrease from 8.74 to 7.11. The same happens to Message (throw), 16 suggestions, approximately 18.7% included checkmarks to indicate that a message is being sent (Table 1). Such symbol has become a routine in the lives of those who make use of messaging social networks, therefore this might be why it is engraved in the minds of participants. Its average went from 8.32 to 7.2.

Table 1. Messages, Start, End and Intermediate Events.

	Message (Catch)	Message (Throw)	Start Event	End Event	Intermediate Event
BPMN	✉	✉	○	○	◎
First Phase			▷	[END]	
	22.2%	18.7%	25.7%	25.6%	24.1%

As for Start, End and Intermediate Events, it was possible to see that BPMN elements are mostly characterized by being symbols. In other words, their meanings are arbitrarily chosen and lawfully stated, while participants chose to suggest more iconic items showing preference to seeing similarities between what is represented and the object intended to represent (Table 2). There were in total 35 drawings for Start Event, 25.7% of those were on the semantic field of gaming, specifically the start button of a joystick. Slight improvement of 0.2 in the average. BPMN's language, then, opts for a symbolic sign, while suggestions directed for an iconic one recalling a joystick start button. The End Event, 39 suggestions, 25.6% related to racing, mostly related to a Formula 1 finish line flag. It showed the most positive feedback, going from 5.18 to 7.02. Showing that signs in racing semantic field, such as the finish line or a flag, could be more representative of a process ending than the circle displayed with a thick border. It was clear for a good number of participants that the icon symbolized the end of the process, therefore reaching its communicative purpose. Intermediate Event, 24 suggestions, 24.1% of ideas were similar to traffic signs, particularly the stop sign. It decreased 1.87 in its average, but both symbols still scored lower than 5. So, neither element is effectively representative for participants.

Even though the number of suggestions for the Time Event were low, 9, it was our decision to test if the hourglass suggested by 44.4% would still affect the element's representativeness. Both signs using clock and an hourglass are iconic, since both share resemblance with the real object recalling their actual meaning (Table 2). It decreased 0.47, still reaching an average of 8.9. The Exclusive Gateway, another example of a symbol, 24 suggestions, approximately 33,3% drew arrows inside the gateway to symbolize possibilities. Most importantly, it was suggested to create different symbols to represent "*multiple entries*" and "*multiple exits*", therefore this element was transformed into Exclusive Gateway split and join (Table 2) for the second model. Separating the Exclusive Gateway into two different elements showed a positive response, in first phase the artifact scored 6.38 and in second phase, the split-gateway increased to 7.25 and the join-gateway to 7.2. The symbols of split and join complement each other's meanings, though the notation has as premise to minimize the number of artifacts to lessen the burden to learn the language, some symbols would benefit from a paired element to make meaning clearer for stakeholders.

Parallel Gateway, 24 suggestions, approximately 33,3% suggested parallel lines, the sign used in the second model (Table 2) is an attempt to merge some of these ideas. It is therefore, an attempt to transform a symbol into an icon, getting its abstract characteristic and implementing a more visual connection to its meaning. It is of the biggest decreases, dropping its score by 1.76 and reaching an average less than 5 marks. Which can show that even though arrows are more iconic, not always they will be ideal to represent certain meanings. Even if the arrows in the element created for the second model were placed in parallel with the intention to work as a sign for paths to be followed in parallel, participants could not reach that level of abstraction. Making the symbol of a plus sign in a diamond shape more representative, because its meaning had previously been internalized as such.

Table 2. Time Event, Gateways and Data Object.

	Time Event	Exclusive Gateway	Parallel Gateway	Inclusive Gateway	Data Object
BPMN					
First Phase					
	44.4%	33.3%	33.3%	25.6%	24.1%

Another item that tries to transform symbol into icon is the Inclusive Gateway (Table 2), confirming the tendency of participants to prefer gateways to indicate the number of directions they could follow. In total 20 suggestions, approximately 45%, made use of lines to symbolize more than one path, since this specific symbol appeared twice it was chosen to represent the Inclusive Gateway. Note that, BPMN already uses this element as the Complex Gateway to express splitting or merging of complicated process flow scenarios. Even though we knew about this case, the models presented in this research would not make use of Complex Gateways, so it was decided to use the participants' suggestions to understand if they would actually consist of better representation. The Inclusive Gateway did not change much in its score, only 0.51.

As for the symbolic Data Object, 13 suggestions, 23% suggested some type of notebook or notepad (Table 2). It, then, would still continue being a symbol since it would only represent the idea of keeping track of data, when writing in notebooks is only one of them. It represented the most drastic decrease, decreasing 2.24 marks, from 8.29 to 6.05. The blank paper brought by the notation has proven to be more representative than the sign of a notebook, at least for the participants of this re-search.

The same happens for the representation of Task, the notation conveyed and spread the idea that boxes with labels inside the Pools of a process mean a Task, as for the suggestions (12), 25% believed the most representative would be lists of activities/checklists (Table 3). However, they do not possess direct resemblance to a Task to be considered an icon. It decreased from 7.47 to 6.94.

Sequence Flow (Table 3) was discarded because out of 54 participants, there were only 5 drawing contributions. They presented striking similarity to the symbol used in BPMN (a continuum line with an arrow to the directed end). The only suggestions that could be effective in helping stakeholders make meaning out of the models were to implement the *"token"* idea, but since the models presented in this research were printed in papers researchers decided using a token would be more confusing than helpful at this point. So, it was pertinent maintaining this flow as suggested in the notation.

Table 3. Task, Flows, Association and Event-Based Gateway.

	Task	Sequence Flow	Message Flow	Association	Event-Based Gateway
BPMN	Task	⟶	⟩------⟩	............⟩	◎ ◇
First Phase		•⟶			{?} ◈
	44.4%	Not representative	Not representative	Not representative	Not representative

As for the `Message Flow` (Table 3), 13 contributions, keeping the essence striked lines and an arrow head at the end pointing the direction. Although one of the participants complemented the drawing by writing that his/her difficulty is to differentiate the connectors for exchanging `Messages` and `Data Objects`, the decision to keep both artifacts the same as BPMN was made because there weren't enough similarities between drawings to come up with a representative proposal.

`Association` (Table 3), was also kept the same from the notation when the second model was presented. Even though there were 10 suggestions they barely differed the graphic representations of what is currently in use. Finally, `Event-Based Gateway`, remained the same sign, despite 23 suggestions, most of them were similar to the one already used in BPMN. The different ones had no similarities between them, making it impossible to suggest a different graphic element.

4   Threats to Validity

Some threats to validity have been identified in relation to the *quasi*-experiment presented:

– Participants were free to refuse to answer the questions in the questionnaires, so there were few suggestions for drawings, especially in the first phase. Even though during analysis, this would not pose a difficulty, as only the suggested drawings were taken into account, it was a qualitative analysis, researchers still encouraged participants to reply the most they could.
– There were geographic and time constraints. Due to the need for the presence of a researcher during the application of questionnaires, the amount of data collected wasn't as big as intended. Ideally, connections with the community will allow for the research to be developed in different areas with a bigger sample.
– Also, due to difficulty of getting in touch with specialists in BPMN, it was difficult to find participants with more than 5 years of experience. This might affect quantitative results, but does not affect the discussion since the analysis was qualitative.

5   Related Works

In [16], the authors discuss different BPMLs, focusing on usability and quality of user experience. Whereby some criteria may influence cognitive effectiveness. In their analysis, they considered representational clarity, perceptual distinctiveness, perceptual mediocrity, visual expressiveness and graphic parsimony. They analyzed symbol sets from UML, YAWL, BPMN and EPC and discussed their weaknesses and strengths. They then proposed a preliminary assessment of the cognitive effective-ness of the modelling languages.

[13] discusses languages for requirements modelling, focusing on evaluating the impact of their concrete syntax on cognitive effectiveness. It also addresses understandability and the ability to review models, taking into account novice model users. The authors proposed and tested a method for assessing cognitive effectiveness by determining the ease, speed and accuracy of processing the information represented in the model. They analyzed two languages (KAOS and i*) and used an eye-tracker to evaluate syntactic aspects.

In both works there is a problem with nomenclature. Not as previously seen, not everything used in notations can be considered symbols, there are also icons. Icons contribute to quicker comprehension because users only have to look at them to relate that graphical representation to its real object. BPMN is based on the use of symbols, hence, it is necessary to learn the notation and the laws created for it to be able to understand the meaning of the model.

6   Conclusions

At this point it should be noted that it is not the aim of this paper to propose new graphic elements. Our aim was merely to understand, with the help of semiotic analysis, whether the elements used in BPMN are representative or not according to their semantics.

It can be concluded that the graphical elements of BPMN are symbolic signs, so training in notation is required to be able to recognize the intended meanings. Participants tend to prefer iconic signs, showing that they can remember the meaning of an object simply by looking at its representation. However, it is important to note that BPMN looks at the language as a whole, connecting the elements and visualizing the roles they play from start to finish. Participants did not have this knowledge because they assessed the elements individually and did not consider the syntax of the language, i.e., how the elements need to be connected in a system to create a meaningful diagram.

Nevertheless, it is important to focus on the meaning of the signals to increase the clarity of stakeholder communication. It is advisable to look in depth at the semiotics of the graphic elements to be used in new modelling languages, as this can help in the development of iconic models that facilitate understanding.

As future work, we would like to highlight the inclusion of a third phase to check how participants will understand the proposed signals (in the second phase) in the same process model with the most representative elements of BPMN (first phase). We also need to analyze the semantic transparency of all these graphical elements.

Acknowledgements. The authors would like to thank the NEPSI research group at UFPE for their support during this work, and CNPq (ref. 433419/2018-0) and FACEPE (ref. APQ-0867-6.02/22) for their financial support.

References

1. Kunze, M., Luebbe, A., Weidlich, M., Weske, M.: Towards understanding process modeling - the case of the bpm academic initiative. In: et al., Business Process Model and Notation, pp. 44–58. Springer, Heidelberg (2011). Doi:https://doi.org/10.1007/978-3-642-25160-3_4
2. Chinosi, M., Trombetta, A.: BPMN: an introduction to the standard. Comput. Stand. Interfaces **34**(1), 124–134 (2012)
3. Dumas, M., La Rosa, M., Mendling, J., Reijers, H.A.: Fundamentals of Business Process Management, 2nd edn.. Springer, Heidelberg (2018). Doi: https://doi.org/10.1007/978-3-662-56509-4
4. Mendling, J., et al.: Blockchains for business process management - challenges and opportunities. 9(1), Feb 2018
5. Evans, E.: Domain-Driven Design: Tackling Complexity in the Heart of Software. Addison-Wesley Professional, 1st edn. (2003)
6. Caire, P., Genon, N., Heymans, P., Moody, D.L.: Visual notation design 2.0: Towards user comprehensible requirements engineering notations. In: 2013 21st IEEE International Requirements Engineering Conference (RE), pp. 115–124 (2013)
7. OMG-BPMN. Business process model and notation (2.0.2). Technical report, Object Management Group (2014). https://www.omg.org/spec/BPMN
8. Harmon, P., Wolf, C.: Business process modeling survey, 2011. A BPTrends Report - Business Process Trends
9. Kossak, F., et al.: A rigorous semantics for BPMN 2.0 process diagrams, 1st edn. Springer (2014). Doi:https://doi.org/10.1007/978-3-540-79396-0_13
10. Mendling, J., Strembeck, M.: Influence factors of understanding business process models. In: Abramowicz, W., Fensel, D. (eds.) Business Information Systems, pp. 142–153. Springer, Heidelberg, (2008). Doi: https://doi.org/10.1007/978-3-540-79396-0_13
11. Santaella, L.: Semiótica Aplicada. Cengage Learning, 2nd edn. (2018)
12. Peirce, C.S.: Semiótica. Editora Perspectiva, 4th edn. (2017)
13. Santos, M., Gralha, C., Goulão, M., Araújo, J.: Increasing the semantic transparency of the KAOS goal model concrete syntax. In: et al., editor, Conceptual Modeling, pp. 424-439. Springer, Cham (2018). Doi:https://doi.org/10.1007/978-3-030-00847-5_30
14. Wohlin, C., Runeson, P., Host, M., Ohlsson, M.C., Regnell, B., Wesslen, A.: Experimentation in Software Engineering, 1st edn. Springer, Berlin, Heidelberg (2012)
15. Montgomery, D.C., Runger, G.C.: Applied Statistics and Probability for Engineers. John Wiley Sons, 6th edn. (2013)
16. Figl, K., Mendling, J., Strembeck, M.: Towards a usability assessment of process modeling languages. In: Proc. of the 8th Workshop Geschäftsprozessmanagement mit Ereignisgesteuerten Prozessketten (EPK 2009), pp. 118–138. CEUR Workshop Proceedings, Berlin, Germany (2009)

A Systematic Approach to Derive User Stories and Gherkin Scenarios from BPMN Models

Daniel Mateus[1]([✉]), Denis Silva da Silveira[2] [ID], and João Araújo[1] [ID]

[1] NOVA LINCS, NOVA School of Science and Technology, Caparica, Portugal
da.mateus@campus.fct.unl.pt
[2] Federal University of Pernambuco, Recife, PE, Brazil
dsilveira@ufpe.br

Abstract. Business process modelling is the key to structuring and eventually optimizing the organization's processes and provides the context to help produce quality information systems. To develop these systems, it is necessary to specify their requirements, which are obtained from documents, interviews, and from business process models. However, there is a lack of systematic approaches to bridge the gap between business processes and requirements elicitation and specification. This happens often due to failures in the communication between business analysts and developers, *e.g.*, when the information present in one of the process models is not consistent with the requirements extracted in the development of a system that aims to optimize this process. This implies rework of requirements and/or business processes. Considering the agile methodologies for developing these systems, user stories are the usual technique to specify requirements. Providing a systematic approach for extracting these user stories from business processes will ultimately assist stakeholders in the elaboration of system's functional requirements. To provide more detail to the extracted user stories and to handle exceptions in the business processes, the Gherkin scenarios can also be extracted from the models, which works as a complement to the user stories. The goal of this paper is to present transformation patterns for deriving user stories and scenarios from BPMN models to ensure traceability and consistency between business processes and requirements, and facilitating the communication between business analysts and developers.

Keywords: Business Process Models · BPMN · Requirements · User Story · Gherkin Scenarios

1 Introduction

Business process modeling helps organizations to understand and optimize their processes and also make profit through adequate processes management [1]. Considering the fact that modeling business process is receiving a great deal of attention in business administration and computer science communities, due to the increasingly important role of information systems in the realization of business processes, a common understanding of and productive interaction between these communities is essential [2].

B. Shishkov (Ed.): BMSD 2023, LNBIP 483, pp. 235–244, 2023.
https://doi.org/10.1007/978-3-031-36757-1_15

Thus, the goal of this work is to support the elicitation phase of functional requirements in an agile development context and to maintain communication between these two communities. Therefore, this paper presents a systematic approach to extract two different types of information from the business processes. Firstly, extracting from business processes a set of user stories (the main requirements artifacts in the agile development) that allows the specification of a system functionality from the user's perspective [3]. This promotes the elaboration of functional requirements and facilitates the analysis of these requirements by the development team. Secondly, to give some more detail and to be able to deal with the exceptions to the normal flow of a business process, Gherkin scenarios is extracted to describe scenarios using the "*Given-When-Then*" model, which aims to complement the user stories.

In summary, this paper presents an approach that facilitates the semi-automatic generation of user stories and Gherkins scenarios from process models, based on the use of transformation patterns. To accomplish this, we use the Business Process Modeling Notation (BPMN) [4] to represent business process models, and the transformation patterns are based on the partial metamodels of BPMN, user stories and Gherkin scenarios, and specified through templates.

This paper is structured as follows. Section 2 gives some background on BPMN and requirements, Sect. 3 describes the approach for extracting user stories and scenarios form business process models. Section 4 discusses the results, while Sect. 5 describes some related work. Section 6 draws some the conclusions and future work.

2   Background

In this section, we will give a brief introduction to the main topics of this work, *i.e.*, BPMN (including a partial metamodel), requirements engineering, and agile development (introducing user stories and Gherkin scenarios).

2.1   Business Process Modeling Notation

The purpose of BPMN [3] is to provide a notation understandable by different kinds of process modelers and users: (*i*) business analysts that sketch the initial documentation of the processes; (*ii*) technical developers which are responsible for actually implementing processes; (*iii*) businessmen which are accountable for processes' usage and monitoring [2].

BPMN is currently maintained by the Object Management Group (OMG) and inherits and combines elements from a number of previously proposed notations for business process modeling, including the XML Process Definition Language (XPDL) [5] and the Activity Diagrams component of the UML [6].

Process models in BPMN are defined by a metamodel built with the UML notation [6], which is a de facto standard for software engineering modeling. BPMN is structured in several layers, the most important being the Core layer which includes the most fundamental elements of BPMN, which are required for constructing BPMN diagrams [4]: Process, Choreography and Collaboration. In this work, the focus is on the process metamodel illustrated by a fragment in Fig. 1 [4]. Our transformation patterns will refer to this metamodel.

The partial BPMN metamodel in Fig. 1, show that the `metaclass` Process inherits from `FlowElementsContainer` which contains several `FlowNodes` (`Activity`, `Event`, `Gateway`) connected by `SequenceFlows`. A `SequenceFlow` shows the order in which activities are executed in a process and relates `Tasks`, `Gateways` and `Events` to each other.

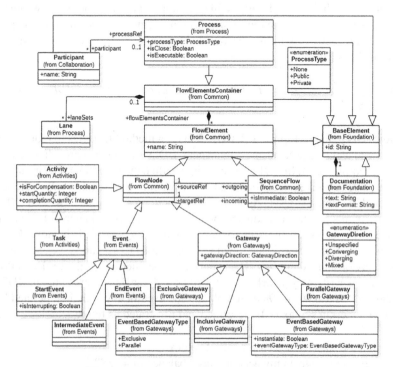

Fig. 1. Fragment of the BPMN metamodel [4].

2.2 Requirements Engineering and Agile Development

Sommerville [7] states that RE is the process of eliciting and specifying the requirements, i.e., the services that a customer requires from a system and the constraints under which it operates and is developed. One of the main objectives of requirements engineering is to detail and describe the proposed solution for the problem in question. To this end, Sommerville [7] proposes the spiral process model that represents the requirements process and highlights the phases of *Elicitation*, *Specification*, *Validation*, and *Management*. Our focus is on Requirements elicitation and specification, which must be tailored to the needs of the process, the project, the product, and the people doing the work. We are interested in the elicitation and specification phases applied during agile development, one of the most popular development approaches.

Agile software development presents an incremental vision in software development and has already proven that, nowadays, it returns many benefits to organizations and development teams ensuring an iterative process, adaptive to new risks, and *"people-oriented"* favoring the focus on people first and only then on technology [8]. Requirements in agile software development are elicited and specified using user stories and scenarios described in the Behavior-driven development (BDD) context described as follows.

User Stories. In the initial phase of agile development, user stories are written from the requirements elicited in the requirements engineering process, but from the point of view of the end user. We will use the well-known template for specifying user stories, shown as follows [9]:

– *As a* < type of user[1] >, *I want to* < desired goal[2] > *so that* < achieved value[3] >.

Behaviour-Driven Development (BDD). This is a method that tries to reduce the distance between technical and business managers. BDD is an agile approach for capturing and testing requirements. In BDD, behavior is specified through BDD scenarios with the participation of the stakeholders involved in the system's development. With the scenarios specified, acceptance tests are created. Enhancing testing practices. Thus, BDD is both requirements practice and, an acceptance tests construction approach. Also, BDD extends user stories to develop scenarios. A scenario is a possible behavior related to a user story. Each user story is instantiated with several BDD scenarios, i.e., scenarios for normal behavior and exceptions. The scenario is specified using the project's domain language and is written by stakeholders together with the development team. BDD scenarios have a *"Given-When-Then"* template to be used in any situation, defined by the well-known Gherkin syntax [10], described and illustrated as follows:

– Given: Describes the scenario's initial context.
     For example, "Given my account has a balance of 430€";

– When: Describes an event or action.
     For example, "When I send the money";

– Then: Describes the expected result.
     For example, "Then I should get the receipt".

Figure 2 shows a metamodel that specifies the model elements of user stories and Gherkin scenarios, and their relationships.

---

[1] Role or type of user;

[2] The need/functionality that the user intends to see fulfilled;

[3] Purpose of the functionality in question.

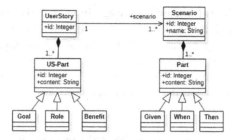

Fig. 2. User Story and Gherkins Scenario Metamodel.

3 Derivation of BPMN in Requirements

Business process models describe sequences of activities with the model elements being labeled following the business terminology in use in the application domain. In this context, business designers encode information such as activity, event, gateways, etc., in specific diagrams of the BPMN. Based on those diagrams a software engineer decodes the information modeled and develops the user stories. Thus, by doing this, the designer will ensure the consistency of the BPMN models with the requirements, *i.e.* user stories, in agile software development. Thus, some transformation patterns are presented as follows.

3.1 Transformation Patterns

The following patterns were extracted by analyzing various business models, resulting in a non-exhaustive list of patterns that are intended to be used for extracting user stories from various types of business models. This non-exhaustive list is presented below:

1. **Start event followed by an activity:** whenever a `SequenceFlow` is found with a `StartEvent` on the source (`+SourceRef`) and the target (`+TargetRef`) with an `Activity`, the correspondent user story has the following template:
    US_1: As «Lane» I receive a(n) «`StartEvent`» in order to «`Activity`»;

2. **Exclusive gateway join between two activities in the same lane:** when a `SequenceFlow` is found with an `Activity` in the source (`+SourceRef`) and in the target (`+TargetRef`) with an `Exclusive Gateway` Join and the `SenquenceFlow` of this `Gateway` Join has as target (`+TargetRef`) to another `Activity` in any `Lane` as the previous `Activity`, the corresponding user story will have the following form:
    US_2: As «Lane» I want to «$Activity_1$» in order to «$Activity_2$»;

3. **Exclusive gateway join between two activities in different lanes:** when a `SequenceFlow` is found with an `Activity` in the source (`+SourceRef`) and in the target (`+TargetRef`) with an `Exclusive Gateway` join and the `SenquenceFlow` of this `Exclusive Gateway` join has as target (`+TargetRef`) to another `Activity` in a different `Lane` from the previous one, the corresponding user story will have the following form:
    US_3: As «$Lane_1$» I want to «$Activity_1$» in order to «$Lane_2$» can «$Activity_2$»;

4. **Activity followed by a ("throw") message intermediate event:** when there is a
   SequenceFlow with the source (+SourceRef) in an Activity and the target
   (+targetRef) in a IntermediateEvent of the message ("throw") and that
   IntermediateEvent is the source (+SourceRef) of a MessageFlow, which
   has a Participant as target (+TargetRef) (actor external to the process), the
   corresponding user story has the following template:

   US_4: As «Lane» I want to «Activity» in order to send a(n)
   «IntermediateEvent» to «Participant»;

5. **Exclusive gateway join between a ("catch") message intermediate event and
   an activity:** when a SequenceFlow is found with an IntermediateEvent
   of a ("catch") message in the source (+SourceRef) in a Lane and the target
   (+TargetRef) with an Exclusive Gateway join and the SequenceFlow
   of this Exclusive Gateway join has target (+TargetRef) to Activity, the
   correspondent user story have the following template:

   US_5: As «Lane» I receive a(n) «IntermediateEvent» in order to
   «Activity»;

6. **Timer intermediate event followed by an activity:** when a SequenceFlow is
   found with a IntermediateEvent of the timer on source (+SourceRef) and
   the target (+TargetRef) with an Activity in a Lane, the corresponding user
   story has the following template:

   US_6: As «Lane» I want to wait for «IntermediateEvent» in order to
   «Activity»;

7. **Activity$_1$ followed by activity$_2$:** whenever a SequenceFlow is found with an
   Activity$_1$ in source (+SourceRef) and the target (+targetRef) with an
   Activity$_2$ in any Lane, the corresponding user story has the following format:

   US_7: As «Lane» I want to «Activity$_1$» in order to «Activity$_2$»;

8. **Message start event connected to a participant and a message end event:** whenever
   a MessageFlow is found with a Participant in source (+sourceRef) and
   target (+targetRef) with a StartEvent and an EndEvent of the message, the
   corresponding user story has the following template:

   US_8: As «Participant» I want to send «StartEvent» in order to get
   «EndEvent»;

9. **Activity followed by a message end event:** whenever a SequenceFlow is found
   with an Activity in source (+sourceRef) in a Lane and target (+targetRef)
   with an EndEvent and a MessageFlow is found with the same EndEvent in
   the source (+sourceRef) and target (+targetRef) with a Participant, the
   corresponding user story has the following template:

   US_9: As «Lane» I want to «Activity» in order to send «EndEvent» to
   «Participant».

3.2 Applying the Transformation Patterns

To analyze the applicability of the aforementioned Patterns, a BPMN model (Fig. 3), which specifies a property valuation request process, was used. Thus, applying the patterns to the model in Fig. 3, we extract the following US:

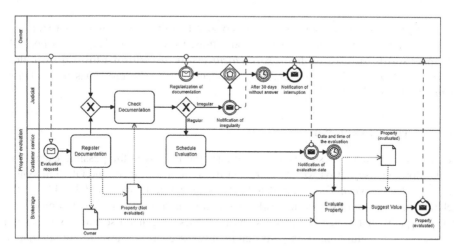

Fig. 3. BPMN Model.

- **Start event followed by an activity:**

  US: As *Customer Service* I receive an *Evaluation Request* in order to *Register Documentation*;
- **Exclusive gateway join between two activities in the same lane:**

  US: As *Customer Service* I want to *Register Documentation* in order to *Judicial* can *Check Documentation*;
- **Exclusive gateway join between two activities in different lanes:**

  US: As *Judicial* I want to *Check Documentation* in order to *Customer Service* can *Schedule Evaluation*;
- **Activity followed by a ("throw") message intermediate event:**

  US: As *Customer Service* I want to *Schedule Evaluation* in order to send a *Notification of Evaluation Date* to *Owner*;
- **Exclusive gateway join between a ("catch") message intermediate event and an activity:**

  US: As *Judicial* I receive a *Regularization of Documentation* in order to *Check Documentation*;
- **Timer intermediate event followed by an activity:**

  US: As *Brokerage* I want to wait for *Date and Time of the Evaluation* in order to *Evaluate Property*;
- **Activity₁ followed by activity₂:**

  US: As *Brokerage* I want to *Evaluate Property* in order to *Suggest Value*;

– **Message start event connected to a participant and a message end event:**
    US: As *Owner* I want to send *Evaluation Request* in order to get *Property (Evaluated)*;

– **Activity followed by message end event:**
    US: As *Brokerage* I want to *Suggest Value* in order to send *Property (Evaluated)* to *Owner*;

Analyzing the results obtained, it can be seen that the extraction of user stories is directed to the "*natural path*" of the model flow, which in turn leaves pen possible exceptions as is the case of the "*Check Documentation*" following the sequence flow to the path "*Irregular*" or after sending the "*irregularity notification*" passing "30 *days without response*".

3.3 Scenarios Integration

After extracting the user stories, it is now essential to look at the possible exceptions in the flow. The scenarios will be extracted from the model using the Gherkin syntax with the "*Given-When-Then*" template [11]. As shown in the metamodel in Fig. 2, the relationship between user stories and Gherkin's scenarios allows for detailing all the possible paths that a business process can take. First, a general scenario is presented to describe the feature under analysis and then two scenarios that represent alternative paths to the "*natural path*" of the flow will be detailed.

Feature: «Property Evaluation»

1. # Overall scenario.

Scenario: «Owner» «Evaluation Request»

When «Owner» sends «Evaluation Request»

Then «Owner» receive «*Property (Evaluated)* »

2. # Check documentation irregular path.

Scenario: «Judicial» «Check Documentation» leads to «Irregular»

Given «Judicial» made «Check Documentation»

When «Check Documentation» leads to «Irregular»

Then «Judicial» sends «Notification of irregularity»

3. # 30 days without answer.

Scenario: «Judicial» «Notification of irregularity» «After 30 days without answer»

Given «Judicial» send «Notification of irregularity»

When «After 30 days without answer»

Then «Judicial» sends «Notification of irregularity»

4 Discussion

It is important to mention that this position paper represents a work in progress in an academic context that, in turn, may and should undergo changes and improvements, such as the description of new patterns and the development of a prototype of transformations, that is being implemented and aims to demonstrate the potential of this approach.

This being so, the use of patterns to extract information from the business models, which typically present a gap when deriving requirements, allowed us to fill this gap, with a simple and effective approach as we quickly get to the user stories from a business process.

On the other hand, one of the challenges of this approach has been to find a way to embrace the exceptions present in the models, that are equally important. To do this, we used the scenarios with Gherkin syntax that allowed us to enhance this method by extracting a more complete set of requirements.

The next challenges of this work will involve: completing the transformations prototype; specifying a glossary of words that allows the natural flow path to be identified (allowing exceptions to be separated); continue the development of the conceptual model for the mentioned extraction process; identify and specify new patterns.

5 Related Work

In [12], we have a case study that analyzes the impact of using business process models to verify the consistency and traceability of requirements. It compares in the same scenario the requirements specification obtained through a conventional process and another requirements specification obtained from business process models. A comparison of the two methods is made, where the following points are analyzed: completeness, correctness, consistency, contextualization for the client and analyst, diversity in the set of requirements, and traceability.

In [13] considering that a use case is a set of actions that represent the behavior (interactions) between an actor and the system, to achieve a certain goal, this work proposes a new way of describing use cases using BPMN instead of text or the usual UML activity diagrams. Thus, this work is closer to ours since they also discuss an approach to derive requirements from BPMN models.

6 Conclusions

This paper presented a pattern-based approach to derive user stories and Gherkin scenarios from BPMN business process models. With this study, we were able to embrace a challenge to integrate business process modeling and requirements elicitation and specification. The result of the application of the transformation patterns on business process models reveals that it is possible to automate the extraction of user stories and scenarios from those models, thus improving the communication between business analysts and the development team.

For future work we will pursue the specification of new patterns, the implementation of the transformations, the application of the transformations to case studies, and the evaluation of the approach.

Acknowledgements. We thank FACEPE (ref. APQ-0867-6.02/22) and NOVA LINCS (UIDB/04516/2020) with the financial support of FCT.IP.

References

1. Dumas, M., La Rosa, M., Mendling, J., Reijers, H.A.: Fundamentals of Business Process Management, 2nd edn. Springer, Heidelberg (2018)
2. Weske, M.: Business Process Management - Concepts, Languages, Architectures, Springer, Heidelberg. ISBN 978–3–540–73521–2 (2012)
3. Cohn, M.: User Stories Applied: For Agile Software Development. Addison-Wesley Professional, 1st edn. (2004)
4. OMG-BPMN. Business process model and notation (2.0.2). Technical report, Object Management Group (2014). https://www.omg.org/spec/BPMN
5. Nathaniel Palmer. XML Process Definition Language, pages 3601–3601. Springer US, 2009
6. OMG-UML. Unified modeling language (2.5.1). Technical report, Object Management Group (2017). https://www.omg.org/spec/UML/About-UML/
7. Sommerville, I.: Software Engineering. Pearson, 10th edn. (2021)
8. Abrahamsson, P., Salo, O., Ronkainen, J., Warsta, J.: Agile software development methods: Review and analysis. arXiv preprint:1709.08439 (2017)
9. Pokharel, P., Vaidya, P.: A study of user story in practice. In and Industry: Way Towards a Sustainable Economy ICDABI, pp. 1–5. IEEE (2020)
10. Gherkin syntax. https://cucumber.io/docs/gherkin/
11. Moult, D., Krijnen, T.: Compliance checking on building models with the gherkin language and continuous integration. In: EG-ICE 2020 Workshop on Intelligent Computing in Engineering, Proceedings, pp. 294–303 (2020)
12. Cardoso, E., Almeida, J.P., Guizzardi, G.: Requirements engineering based on business process models: a case study. In: 2009 13th Enterprise Distributed Object Computing Conference Workshops, pp. 320–327. IEEE (2009)
13. Herden, A., Farias, P.P.M., Albuquerque, A.: An approach based on BPMN to detail use cases. In New Trends in Networking, Computing, Elearning, Systems Sciences, and Engineering, pp. 537–544. Springer, Cham (2015). Doi: https://doi.org/10.1007/978-3-319-06764-3_69

Composing an Initial Domain-Specific Modeling Language Notation by Reusing Icons

Ben Roelens[1,2(✉)] ⓘ, Rob Ebben[1], and Rogier van de Wetering[1] ⓘ

[1] Open Universiteit, Valkenburgerweg 177, 6419 AT, Heerlen, The Netherlands
{ben.roelens,rogier.vandewetering}@ou.nl, rob@ebben.nu
[2] Ghent University, Tweekerkenstraat 2, 9000 Ghent, Belgium

Abstract. Domain-Specific Modeling Languages (DSMLs) increasingly gain attention in the field of Conceptual Modeling as they target a particular problem in a delineated application domain by using concepts that are tailored to end-users. As such, DSMLs provide a flexible approach that can be used in different application domains. To realize their potential, the graphical notation of a DSML must be aligned with the users' knowledge and perceptions. In particular, an intuitively understandable DSML notation is important to facilitate communication with the end-users. Therefore, we propose a technique for composing an initial DSML notation by reusing icons. This technique is applied in the context of the Process-Goal Alignment (PGA) business modeling technique. Furthermore, we empirically evaluate the proposed technique by an experiment with 85 business users, in which we compare the intuitiveness of the newly developed and existing PGA notations. The results show that the semantic transparency of the newly developed notation is significantly higher than the existing PGA notations. More specifically, the composition technique based on the reuse of icons enables to derive the meaning of DSML concepts correctly.

Keywords: Domain-Specific Modeling Language · notation · icon · experimental evaluation

1 Introduction

DSMLs are increasingly developed to fulfill various application requirements in Conceptual Modeling domains such as Business Process Management, Enterprise Architecture Management and Software Engineering [8]. In contrast to General-Purpose Modeling Languages, a DSML realizes a better expressiveness and ease of use for a particular domain by using a visual modeling language, which is aligned with the knowledge and perceptions of end-users [7]. A DSML is composed of (i) an abstract syntax, which is defined using a meta-model that describes the fundamental concepts to create correct models, (ii) a concrete syntax, which is a notation that describes the graphical or textual representations of

B. Shishkov (Ed.): BMSD 2023, LNBIP 483, pp. 245–255, 2023.
https://doi.org/10.1007/978-3-031-36757-1_16

the elements in the meta-model, and (iii) semantics, which specifies the meaning associated with the elements in the abstract syntax [3]. An intuitive DSML notation is important for an efficient use and comprehension of the created models by users [1]. In this respect, intuitiveness refers to semantic transparency, which is a design principle that can be used to design visual notations optimized for communication and problem solving [11]. It is defined as "the extent to which a novice reader can infer the meaning of a symbol from its appearance alone" [11, p.765]. The Physics of Notations proposes using icons to realize semantic transparency as "symbols that perceptually resemble the concepts they represent" [11, p.765]. Icons are used in this research given their resembling or partly associated relationship with the concept they represent [9]. An icon is preferred to a symbol showing an arbitrary relationship with the represented concept.

Previous research proposed an iterative technique for evaluating and improving the semantic transparency of existing DSML notations [1]. The first phase evaluates the existing notation and the second phase aims at improving it. One of the major assumptions of this technique is that an initial notation can serve as input. However, the existence of such a notation might not always be realistic, e.g., in case of the design of a new DSML. As the Physics of Notations lacks explicit support for the design of new icons, the language designer might incorrectly apply the principle and the semantic transparency might decrease [6,9]. This raises the following research question: "How can the reuse of existing icons enable the development of an initial DSML notation?"

In this respect, we present a technique for composing an initial DSML notation by reusing icons from public databases. This technique is applied in the context of the PGA business modeling technique, a DSML that focuses on realizing strategic fit. Furthermore, we show the technique's effectiveness in an experimental evaluation by business users, in which we compare the semantic transparency of the newly developed and existing PGA notations. Although the composition technique is not bound to the PGA modeling technique, PGA allows to illustrate the application of the proposed technique and has two icon-based notations that provide a benchmark for the evaluation.

The paper is structured as follows. Section 2 reviews background literature about the PGA modeling technique and guidelines for icon design. While Sect. 3 describes the technique for composing an initial DSML notation, Sect. 4 describes the set-up of the experiment that was used for the empirical evaluation of this technique. Afterwards, we describe the results of applying the technique and the experimental evaluation in Sect. 5. This paper is concluded in Sect. 6.

2   Background Literature

2.1   PGA Modeling Technique

The PGA modeling technique is oriented toward achieving strategic fit, which is the alignment the company's strategic positioning with supporting activities [13]. PGA is introduced as a DSML that combines a conceptual modeling language with a system for setting and measuring performance goals through a heat map visualization. The design of PGA notation version 1.0 [13] (see left column in Table 2) was implemented by visual icons to adhere to the Semantic Transparency principle [11]. In follow-up research [1], PGA notation version 1.0 was evaluated by applying a technique that includes iterative evaluation and improvement tasks to steer the DSML notation toward semantic transparency. The notation revision had resulted in the redesign of four PGA entities (see Competence, Value Proposition, Internal Goal, and Customer Goal of version 2.0 in Table 2). Finally, the applied technique comprised a comparative experimental evaluation, which has shown that the semantic transparency of the notation in version 2.0 is higher than the original notation.

2.2 Icon Design Guidelines

Related research [4,12,15,16] describes guidelines for the design of visual icons, which are summarized in Table 1. The guidelines that were found can be categorized by physical and semantic characteristics. While physical characteristics of the real world appear frequently (e.g., vertical and horizontal orientations), semantic characteristics are regular occurrences in scenes and events (e.g., people encounter them when repeatedly performing the same actions in the same environment) [4]. By learning about semantic characteristics, people can recognize and remember events and objects in other scenes more easily [4]. Furthermore, each guideline is bound to a particular characteristic of the icon. The studied literature discusses the following characteristics: complexity, concreteness, aesthetics, familiarity, semantic distance, and representation strategy.

3 Technique for Composing an Initial DSML Notation

Designers need to apply the guidelines for developing an initial DSML notation [4]. However, knowledge and experience in designing icons is not common and searching for icons in databases can yield similar results [10]. We refined the procedure in [10] (see Fig. 1) to make it applicable to an initial DSML notation.

1. Determine the concepts to be represented by an icon. A DSML consists of entities, relations, and attributes [7]. First, one needs to choose which of these constituents should be represented by an icon based on the intended use of the DSML (e.g., elements that are crucial to understand the application domain). The resulting list of DSML concepts is input for step 2.
2. Search for icons in existing standards. In addition to icons that have been standardized in ISO-standards[1], existing notations of conceptual modeling languages can be reused or modified for the DSML purpose [10].
3. If no icon is found in step 2, databases are searched. As the naming of the DSML concepts might be too specific to directly search for suitable icons, a term association can be executed [1] by asking prospective end-users to make

---

[1] E.g., Unicode Block "Miscellaneous Symbols" [online], https://www.compart.com/en/unicode/block/U+2600, last accessed: 13.03.2023

Table 1. Icon Design Guidelines

Category	Icon characteristic	Guideline
Physical characteristics	Complexity: the degree of detail of an icon [12]	Use blurry, less detailed views for faster emotional reactions and sharp, more detailed views for slower conscious recognition [4]
		Use as few colors as possible [4]
	Concreteness: the extent to which the representation corresponds to an object from reality [12]	Only outlines of shapes should be shown, no outline of shadows or colors [4]
		Shadows must be omitted, or they must be darker than their surroundings [4]
		Use black lines on a white background and high contrast [4]
		Represent content in their canonical format [4]
		Use colors that resemble the representation of the real object or scene [4]
	Aesthetics: the degree of attractiveness of the icon [16]	The content should be regular and symmetrically designed [4]
		Contents should be represented from three-quarters viewpoints [4]
		If colors are used in a view, use a blue background [4]
		Avoid the colors red and green together [4]
Semantic characteristics	Familiarity: the extent to which people already encountered the icon [12]	Be aware of unintended meanings of forms and colors [4]
	Semantic distance: the degree to which the representation and meaning are separated [12]	Design icons for which the distance between the meaning and the representation is small [12,15]
	Representation strategy: basic rationale used to convert concepts into pictographs [12]	Classify which strategy (visual similarity, arbitrary convention or semantic association) has been followed in the design of the icon [12]

up to three textual associations with the meaning of a certain concept. After collecting data, the researcher lists the collected associations and identifies the most mentioned terms. This results in a list of search terms per DSML concept that is subsequently used to search for potentially suitable icons in the following databases: https://www.freeimages.com/icon?ref=findicons, https://www.iconfinder.com/icons, https://www.freepik.com/, https://stock.adobe.com/, https://icomoon.io/app/#/select, https://www.flaticon.com/.

4. Select icons from the results of step 2–3. First, variations of the same icon are unified to reduce the set of alternatives, while maintaining the spectrum of different designs [2]. Afterwards, relevant icons are selected based on the available knowledge about icon design.

5. Extend icon search to other languages. If the modeling language is used within an international context, also use search terms in other languages that are relevant for the use of the DSML [10].

6. Remove icons. From the symbols selected in step 4, those that were no longer found in the search in step 5, will be removed [10].

7. Rank icons on visual design guidelines. The resulting icons are scored according to the six characteristics in Table 1: complexity, concreteness, aesthetics, familiarity, semantic distance, and representation strategy. Each

characteristic is considered as a continuum (e.g., concreteness: from abstract (0) to concrete (100)) and assigned a score between 0 and 100, which results in final score between 0 and 600. Afterwards, all icons are ranked and the best scoring icon is selected. In case of a tie, the language designer chooses an icon based on knowledge about the end-users and the application domain.

8. Compile a coherent notation. A notation is compiled from the symbol candidates based on coherence between icons. More specifically, it must be checked whether the symbols are sufficiently different from each other (i.e., the principle of Perceptual Discriminability in [11]). Symbols for the concepts that are not in scope of the icon design (see step 1), should also be added to the notation [10]. However, the design of these symbols, which have an arbitrary relationship with the represented concept, is outside the scope of this paper.

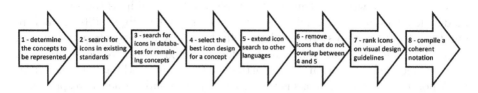

Fig. 1. Technique for composing an initial DSML notation.

4 Experimental Evaluation

The goal of the experimental evaluation is to assess the effectiveness of the proposed composition technique by comparing the semantic transparency of the newly developed with the existing PGA notations. As such, we analyze whether the new icons better resemble the concepts they should represent [11].

4.1 Variables and Measures

The semantic transparency is the dependent variable in this experiment. This variable can be measured by the 'hit rate' [5], which is the percentage of correctly associated meanings. This measure is implemented as a closed question, in which the icon of a notational element is shown and the respondent selects the corresponding meaning from the list of meta-model elements. The version of the PGA modeling technique to which the subject is confronted is the independent variable in the evaluation.

4.2 Hypotheses

This research proposes that a better adherence to the design guidelines (see step 7 in Sect. 3) results in a better understanding, recognition or interpretation of the resulting icons [4,12,15]. Since semantic transparency is the extent to which the graphical representation encodes the meaning of a modeling language concept [11], it can be assumed that a better recognition or interpretation also leads to better derivation of a meaning based on its appearance. Given the fact that semantic transparency can be measured by a hit rate variable, hypotheses $H_{1,v1.0}$ and $H_{1,v2.0}$ are put forward.

$H_{1,v1.0}$: The mean/median hit rate of the initial PGA notation based on the reuse of icons is higher than the PGA notation version 1.0.

$H_{1,v2.0}$: The mean/median hit rate of the initial PGA notation based on the reuse of icons is higher than the PGA notation version 2.0.

4.3 Procedure

There is an dependence between the use of hit rate questions and the respondents' familiarity with an icon. As the three notations address the same metamodel elements, a learning effect will occur if the same subject fills in hit rate questions for all versions. To avoid this effect, a between-subjects experimental design is applied [14], in which three independent groups of respondents work with one particular notation. More particular, the group working with the initial PGA notation by reusing icons is the experimental group, while the respondents confronted with PGA notation version 1.0 or 2.0 are part of two control groups.

The questionnaires are implemented in a survey tool that enables online distribution and objectively measures the time participants need to complete it. Before the survey is distributed, the three survey variants are run through by the researchers and one other person to correct errors in the text and structure. The first page of the questionnaire specifies how much time the experiment will likely take. Next, a consent page explains that participation is voluntary and that the respondent has the right to exit the experiment at any given point. Afterwards, three contextual questions are asked, including the subject's birth year, knowledge of or experience with conceptual modeling languages and involvement in realizing strategic fit in an organization. Next, the hit rate questions for the eight icons are shown on separate pages, which measures the time the respondents need to answer the hit rate question per icon. The questionnaire is concluded by thanking the subjects for their participation.

4.4 Participants

Business participants are approached from the LinkedIn network of the second author, which consists of 589 unique connections. These connections are divided into categories based on their professional business/IT function (i.e., administrator, IT support, architect, analyst, tester, and developer). In addition, an 'Other' category has been included for friends, commercial connections, etc. This category is not approached so that the final selection consists of 451 connections.

4.5   Data Analysis

The hit rate is measured as the percentage of correctly associated meanings. This is a ratio variable as the higher the percentage, the better the score on semantic transparency. As a between-subjects design is applied, an unpaired t-Test is required for a normal distribution and the Wilcoxon-Mann-Whitney test for a non-normal distribution of the dependent variable.

5   Results

5.1   PGA Modeling Language Notation

The questionnaire regarding the term associations (cfr., step 3 in Sect. 3) was sent by email to 20 participants, after which 11 questionnaires were returned, but three participants did not complete the questionnaire. Search terms were determined based on the eight questionnaires that were fully completed, after which the public databases were searched and three icons per search term have been selected. Afterwards, the researchers rated these icons against the design guidelines, after which the highest scoring icon per element was selected. The resulting icons of this procedure are shown in the right column of Table 2.

5.2   Experimental Evaluation

Responses and Demographic Data. The questionnaire has been sent to 451 participants, after which 88 complete questionnaires were returned (i.e., a response rate of 19.51%). Two completed questionnaires were removed because of missing consent and one because of repetitive answers. From the valid questionnaires, 32 relate to version 1.0, 23 to version 2.0 and 30 to the initial PGA notation based on the reuse of icons. The mean age of the respondents is 53 years, 49% of them have knowledge of or experience with conceptual modeling languages and 35% are involved in realizing strategic fit in their organization.

Descriptive Statistics. The descriptive statistics show the results of the different versions of the notation (see Table 3). The mean percentage of correctly associated meanings is higher in the group who has used the initial PGA notation based on the reuse of icons (i.e., 80.00%) compared to the groups working with the existing versions 1.0 (i.e., 59.38%) and 2.0 (i.e., 59.24%). It should be noted that the existing versions score below the ISO threshold for the hit rate of an effective notation, which should be at least 67% [5].

Table 2. Different versions of the PGA notation

PGA concept	Version 1.0 [13]	Version 2.0 [1]	Initial PGA notation by reusing Icons
Activity			
Process			
Competence			
Value Proposition			
Financial Structure			
Internal Goal			
Customer Goal			
Financial Goal			

Table 3. Descriptive statistics

PGA notation	n	Mean	Std. deviation
Version$_{1.0}$	32	59.38%	0.185
Version$_{2.0}$	23	59.24%	0.220
Version$_{InitialReusingIcons}$	30	80.00%	0.163

Normality Tests. The skewness (−0.308, Z-value = −1.180) and kurtosis (−0.597, Z-value = −1.097) of the hit rate variable indicate a slightly negatively skewed distribution. In combination with the Shapiro Wilk statistic [17] (p-value = 0.00092), the normal distribution (i.e., H_0) is rejected at the 0.05 level of significance. Consequently, we will employ non-parametric tests to analyze the hypotheses and post-tests.

Hypothesis Tests. As the hit rate variable is not normally distributed, the non-parametric independent-sample Wilcoxon-Mann-Whitney test is used to perform the hypothesis tests (see Table 4). The one-sided p-value for both hypothesis tests indicates that we can accept the alternative hypotheses at a level of significance below 0.001. In other words, the median hit rate of the initial PGA notation based on the reuse of icons is statistically higher than versions 1.0 and 2.0.

Table 4. Hypothesis tests

Hypothesis	Mean rank Initial reusing Icons	Mean rank v1.0/v2.0	Test Statistic	Sig. (one-sided)
$H_{0,v1.0}$	41.00	22.59	$Z = -4.112$	2.0×10^{-5}
$H_{0,v2.0}$	33.22	18.89	$Z = -3.410$	3.25×10^{-4}

Post-tests. Post-tests were performed to check whether demographic and time variables have any confounding effects on the hit rate variable. An independent-samples Kruskal-Wallis test was performed for the variables with more than two categories (i.e., knowledge of or experience with conceptual modeling languages and involvement in strategic fit). Finally, a Spearman's correlation analysis was employed to test whether there is a significant correlation (i.e., at 0.05 significance level) between the interval variables (i.e., birth year and answer time) and the hit rate. In Table 5, the post-test results show a significant correlation coefficient between the hit rate and both the birth year (i.e., 0.38, p-value = 3.4×10^{-4}) and answer time (i.e., -0.236, p-value = 0.0298). This indicates a moderate confounding effect of these variables on the hit rate.

Table 5. Results of the post-tests

Dependent variable	Independent variable	Test	Test Statistic	Sig.
Hit rate	Conceptual Modeling knowledge/experience	independent-samples Kruskal-Wallis test	6.019	0.198
Hit rate	Strategic fit involvement	independent-samples Mann-Whitney U test	1.722	0.787
Hit rate	Birth year	Spearman's correlation analysis	0.380	3.40×10^{-4}
Hit rate	Answer time	Spearman's correlation analysis	-0.236	0.023

6 Discussion and Conclusion

The study found that using existing icons instead of designing new ones from scratch results in a more semantically transparent notation. These findings confirm that it is indeed difficult to apply the semantic transparency principle when designing DSML notations [6]. Furthermore, comparable hit rate scores for the existing PGA notations were found, which differs from the experimental evaluation in [1] that showed a significant improvement in version 2.0. The differences with [1] include using hit rate questions in independent groups instead of comparing the two notations side by side and using respondents with IT-related profiles instead of students. As the respondents have a profile that corresponds with the prospective end-users of the PGA modeling technique and are not bound to a particular organization or sector, the external validity of the results is better preserved. However, it is prescribed that the scoring of the icons according to the icon design guidelines (see step 7 in Sect. 3) is only performed by the language designer. As this poses a threat to the reliability of the assessment, the involvement of at least two designers could improve this. Furthermore, the post-tests of the experimental evaluation show a confounding effect of both the birth year and answer time on the hit rate, which poses a threat to the internal validity of the results. However, the effect is only moderate and is evenly distributed between the experimental and control groups due to random assignment of respondents to both groups. As a result, the confounding effect is limited to a large extent.

In conclusion, this research addressed the issue of realizing an intuitively understandable DSML notation by the development of a technique for composing an initial notation based on the reuse of icons. The applicability of the technique is shown in the context of the PGA business modeling technique and evaluated by an experiment with 85 business users, in which we use hit rate questions to compare the semantic transparency of the different versions of the PGA notation. The results show that semantic transparency of the initial notation based on the reuse of icons is significantly higher than the PGA versions 1.0 and 2.0.

Future research should be performed as three roles are important for DSMLs: (i) the language designer, (ii) the modeler who develops model instantiations, and (iii) end-users of the model instantiations. As most design principles of icons are only oriented toward end-users, it is important for a language designer to also attune icons to the modeler. This requires further research as other experimental tasks are needed to mimic model creation instead of model use. Furthermore, Artificial Intelligence applications were recently developed that are able to design an image based on a textual description (e.g., DALL-E). These applications could be useful to replace the search for suitable symbols in step 2 and 3 of the proposed technique and to realize coherence between the different symbols (i.e., step 8).

References

1. Bork, D., Roelens, B.: A technique for evaluating and improving the semantic transparency of modeling language notations. Softw. Syst. Model. **20**(4), 939–963 (2021). https://doi.org/10.1007/s10270-021-00895-w
2. Bovea, M.D., et al.: Options for labelling circular products: icon design and consumer preferences. J. Clean. Prod. **202**, 1253–1263 (2018). https://doi.org/10.1016/j.jclepro.2018.08.180
3. Brambilla, M., Cabot, J., Cánovas Izquierdo, J.L., Mauri, A.: Better call the crowd: using crowdsourcing to shape the notation of domain-specific languages. In: 10th International Conference on Software Language Engineering, pp. 129–138. ACM, New York, NY, USA (2017). https://doi.org/10.1145/3136014.3136033

4. Bühler, D., Hemmert, F., Hurtienne, J.: Universal and intuitive? scientific guidelines for icon design. In: Proceedings of Mensch Und Computer 2020, pp. 91–103. MuC 2020, ACM, New York (2020). https://doi.org/10.1145/3404983.3405518

5. Caire, P., Genon, N., Heymans, P., Moody, D.L.: Visual notation design 2.0: towards user comprehensible requirements engineering notations. In: 21st IEEE International Requirements Engineering Conference (RE), pp. 115–124 (2013). https://doi.org/10.1109/RE.2013.6636711

6. El-Attar, M.: Empirically evaluating the effect of the physics of notations on model construction. IEEE Trans. Softw. **48**(7), 2455–2475 (2022). https://doi.org/10.1109/TSE.2021.3060344

7. Fill, H.G., Karagiannis, D.: On the conceptualisation of modelling methods using the adoxx meta modelling platform. EMISAJ **8**(1), 4–25 (2013). 10.18417/emisa.8.1.1

8. Karagiannis, D.: Conceptual modelling methods: the AMME agile engineering approach. In: Karagiannis, D., Lee, M., Hinkelmann, K., Utz, W. (eds.) Domain-Specific Conceptual Modeling: Concepts, Methods and ADOxx Tools, pp. 3–21. Springer International Publishing, Cham (2022). https://doi.org/10.1007/978-3-030-93547-4_1

9. Kuhar, S., Polančič, G.: Conceptualization, measurement, and application of semantic transparency in visual notations. Softw. Syst. Model. **20**(6), 2155–2197 (2021). https://doi.org/10.1007/s10270-021-00888-9

10. Laue, R.: Nutzung von bilddatenbanken zur erstellung von symbolen für graphische modellierungssprachen. In: Schaefer, I., Karagiannis, D., Vogelsang, A., Méndez, D., Seidl, C. (eds.) Modellierung 2018, pp. 87–102. Gesellschaft für Informatik e.V, Bonn (2018)

11. Moody, D.: The physics of notations: toward a scientific basis for constructing visual notations in software engineering. IEEE Trans. Softw. **35**(6), 756–779 (2009). https://doi.org/10.1109/TSE.2009.67

12. Nakamura, C., Zeng-Treitler, Q.: A taxonomy of representation strategies in iconic communication. Int. J. Hum. Comput. **70**(8), 535–551 (2012). https://doi.org/10.1016/j.ijhcs.2012.02.009

13. Roelens, B., Steenacker, W., Poels, G.: Realizing strategic fit within the business architecture: the design of a process-goal alignment modeling and analysis technique. Softw. Syst. Model. **18**(1), 631–662 (2017). https://doi.org/10.1007/s10270-016-0574-5

14. Saunders, M., Lewis, P., Thornhill, A.: Research Methods for Business Students. Pearson Education Limited, London, UK (2023)

15. Shen, Z., Xue, C., Wang, H.: Effects of users' familiarity with the objects depicted in icons on the cognitive performance of icon identification. i-Perception **9**(3), 946–953 (2018). https://doi.org/10.1177/2041669518780807

16. Sonderegger, A., Sauer, J.: The influence of design aesthetics in usability testing: effects on user performance and perceived usability. Appl. Ergon. **41**(3), 403–410 (2010). https://doi.org/10.1016/j.apergo.2009.09.002

17. Thode, H.: Testing for Normality. Taylor and Francis, Hoboken, NJ (2002)

Validating Trust in Human Decisions to Improve Expert Models Based on Small Data Sets

Johan Silvander[(✉)] and Shailesh Pratap Singh

Blekinge Institute of Technology, Karlskrona, Sweden
johan.silvander@bth.se

Abstract. When a model is built based on expert knowledge, a small data set will, in many cases, form the base for the model. It must be possible to validate the trustworthiness and model improvement potential of the provided information from humans or machines. In this study, we have investigated how to evaluate the information from humans to improve the model itself. We used evaluation research and collected the research data with the help of focus group interviews and questionnaires. The result of the study suggests a way to determine the trustworthiness of answers from humans and how to understand if these answers indicate a change to the underlying expert model. The introduction of divergence, and candidate areas, made it possible to evaluate the trustworthiness and changes to the expert model. These were deemed valuable by practitioners.

Keywords: Human Decisions · Trust Validation · Improving Expert Models

1 Introduction

In many areas, human experts are involved in creating decision support systems that are used in critical decision-making. Expert knowledge can be captured in different ways. Examples thereof are, the creation of rules [13], estimating probabilities [11], creating a model based on expert data and machine learning algorithms [1], or using heuristics in combination with data to create and validate a model [6].

In areas where human experts are involved in critical decision making the datasets might be "not-quite-big-enough" to use machine learning algorithms [1] to produce a valid model. These small data sets might be the results of; the same type of decision not being taken very often, the problem at hand is complex and it is not easy to compare the decisions between different problems, all decision points are not possible to record, some available information is not recorded, etc.

The data set used in this study is a small data set that contains expert decisions based on patient features. Due to the nature of the data set, we decided to use discrete bayesian networks [11] to build the expert model.

© The Author(s), under exclusive license to Springer Nature Switzerland AG 2023
B. Shishkov (Ed.): BMSD 2023, LNBIP 483, pp. 256–267, 2023.
https://doi.org/10.1007/978-3-031-36757-1_17

Since an expert model should be able to adapt to new knowledge, in a controlled and automated way, it is vital to understand which data points are eligible to incorporate into the next version of the model. When the model is based on small data sets it is crucial to evaluate the trustworthiness of new information before it is used to improve the model with this new knowledge. However, for the model to be able to adapt to new knowledge, not only information that conforms to the model should be used but information regarded as plausible to incorporate into the model should be evaluated as well.

In this study, we have evaluated how trustworthiness and knowledge adaption can be improved with the help of divergence areas and candidate areas. These areas are defined as probability areas for how new information conforms to the existing expert model. We have used bayesian statistics [5], probabilistic programming [2], and bayesian models derived from cognitive science, to implement our proposal. With the help of focus group interviews and questionnaires, we have validated our proposal with practitioners.

In Sect. 2 we present the background, the methodology is described Sect. 3, and the results are presented in Sect. 4. The analysis of the results, and a discussion are presented in Sect. 5, and finally, in Sect. 6, the conclusion and future research are presented.

2   Background

Together with Ericsson AB we are investigating and elaborating on the requirements needed to design an intent-driven system [12]. Intent-driven systems will be crucial for optimizing a telecom network and its support systems. Some of the models in an intent-driven system will be based on small data sets and heuristics and evolve based on inputs from humans and machines. To design an intent-driven system, the crucial ability is to evaluate if information from humans and machines can be used to improve the existing model.

One of our prior studies [13] presents a smart AAA (Authentication, Authorization, and Accounting) agent that employs an expert-system-based AI model comprised of knowledge fact bases and rule bases. These knowledge bases are further updated based on change scenarios and require updates to the model. Some of these knowledge bases are non-negotiable and thus mandatory, while others are just perception based. However, the new knowledge bases received based on the perceived knowledge of the humans or machine inputs are too small in number or population size for the system to learn. Besides, such perceptions need validation before incorporating a change to the complete existing model that has been working for existing scenarios. Thus arises the requirement for validating the human and machine inputs and decisions based on such a small data set. In this study, we form a base to improvements of the work done in [13].

When faced with a small data set, the focus shifts from model-centric AI to data-centric AI [4]. To be able to use machine learning algorithms [1], or deep learning [3], to produce a valid model, generation of synthetic data, based on the data set generated by experts, has been suggested [14]. Another possible way is to use tools like bayesian statistics [5], probabilistic programming [2], and bayesian networks [11] to support the data analysis and model creation. In this study, we will evaluate the latter approach.

3   Methodology

3.1   The Creation of the Expert Model

During our work with intent-driven systems, we were presented with a dataset based on human decisions. The dataset contains information about patients with stomach cancer, and a decision if an operation should be performed or not. The dataset was generated over several years and contains 55 records, which can be considered a small data set.

With the help of information from practitioners, we created a model in the form of a discrete Bayesian network, using the bnlearn package [10]. Before we created the Bayesian network, data points with missing data, and outliers detected by practitioners, were removed. The resulting model was validated against a causal model which was constructed based on the knowledge of the practitioners. When providing the model with values of its different features, the result is in the form of the probability of giving the patient treatment. This model is considered the expert model.

Since the expert model is based on a small data set we would like to use answers from practitioners to evaluate, and improve, the expert model itself. However, we aim to find a methodology that can validate the trustworthiness of the answers from practitioners and consider changes to the expert model based on the answers. This is done to prevent degeneration of the expert model based on feign or errors made by practitioners.

3.2   Study Design

To understand how to measure the trustworthiness of new data points, we used evaluation research [8]. The research data was collected in two different ways, during focus group interviews [8], and with the help of questionnaires. Two different focus groups were involved in the study.

For each focus group, the interviews were approximately two hours in length and were based on semi-structured focus group interviews [8]. After the questionnaires were answered, samples from the questionnaire were discussed among the practitioners. The validation and correction of the captured material were conducted with the members of a focus group on the same day as the interview was held.

The interview questions for the second focus group were adapted to the findings during the first focus group interviews. Only the second focus group was supported with pre-calculated values and pre-defined scales according to Table 2. The decision to add pre-calculated values and pre-defined scales to the questionnaire was taken after a retrospective with the first focus group.

The questionnaire data were analyzed with the help of R-Studio [9] for Mac (x86 64-bits). BUGS [5] was used during the decisions regarding if an answer could be used to evaluate, and improve, the expert model. The questionnaire instruments are described in Sect. 3.3.

3.3 The Questionnaire Data

We created three different data sets, each containing data from 12 unique fictive patients. The data sets were distributed equally to the practitioners in the groups. Our idea behind this was twofold; By using fictive patients, only documented factors should influence the decision, i.e., the decision is based on the data itself, and the homogeneity between decisions can be investigated, both within and between the focus groups.

The instruction for the decision is "The patient is scheduled for an operation, regarding stomach cancer, within 48 h. Do the information about age, CRP, current BMI, and the difference between BMI values[1], indicate a recommendation for an operation? (Yes/No)".

The questionnaires capture five independent features and one dependent feature. Table 1 describes the features.

Table 1. Questionnaire features

Name	Description
CRP	C-reactive protein is a measurement of the infection rate
Age	The age of the patient
BMInow	The Body Mass Index (BMI) value measured when the decision shall be taken
BMIbefore	The previous measured BMI value. This measurement should not be more than 12 months old
BMIdiff	The difference between BMInow and BMIbefore, in percentage
Treatment	Used by the practitioners to indicate if the patient should have a treatment or not

Three of the features have predefined ordinal scales. The predefined ordinal scale for $BMInow$, $BMIbefore$, and CRP are described in Table 2.

3.4 How the Expert Model is Used

The result of the expert model is in the form of the probability of an operation. To validate the trustworthiness of the answers and detect valid changes to the expert model, we divided the result into six different configurable areas with the

---

[1] Added as a pre-calculated value in the second version of the questionnaire.

Table 2. The feature grading

Feature	Value range	Grade	Description
BMI	0 – 18.5	−1	Underweight
	18.5 – 25.0	0	Normal
	25.0 – 30.0	1	Overweight
	30.0 –	2	Obese
CRP	0 – 10	0	Normal
	10 – 50	1	Infection
	50 –	2	High infection

help of four parameters α, β, γ, and δ, where $0 < \alpha < \beta < 0.5 < \gamma < \delta < 1$. The six areas are: 0 to α, α to β, β to 0.5, 0.5 to γ, γ to δ, and δ to 1.

When an answer from a practitioner is 1 ("Yes"), then: if the expert model gives a probability in the area of 0 to α the answer is in a divergence area and if in the area of β to 0.5, the answer is in a candidate area. When an answer from a practitioner is 0 ("No"), then: if the expert model gives a probability in the area of δ to 1, the answer is in a divergence area, and if in the area of 0.5 to γ, the answer is in a candidate area.

The naming of these areas is in the context of answers contradicting the expert model, meaning contradicting answer in a divergence area indicates low trustworthiness, and in a candidate area, possible valid changes to the expert model.

3.5 The Data Validation Methods

We investigate methods to validate the trustworthiness of a specific decision when it contradicts an expert model. To find answers considered as divergent or candidates, we utilize the fact that the expert model express answers in the form of a probability.

When we use an expert model in an open environment, it might not be possible to identify the person behind the decision. However, this problem might arise in a closed environment due to the information retrieval process or legal reasons. Another reason might be that only one decision exists from a specific identity. When analyzing decisions taken in this environment, it might be necessary to group the decisions by a meta-data context, for example, time or geography. We call these types of decisions "Decisions grouped by meta-data context". With this kind of grouping, the homogeneity of the answers in the group can be analyzed.

When it is possible to connect answers to a specific individual identifier or a group identifier, it is possible to validate the answer based on how these known entities have responded. We call these types of decisions "Decisions grouped by identity context". With this kind of grouping, the homogeneity of the answers in the group, the performance of an identity compared to the expert model, and the performance of an identity compared to the other identities in the group, can be analyzed. Section 3.6 describes the models used for the analysis.

3.6 Models Used for Analysis

Youden's J Analyze. Youden's J [15] calculates a measure using true positives and negatives, together with false positives and negatives. A probability above 0.5 indicates acceptable performance.

We use a set of rules to adjust for divergence and candidates. The "raw" result is the number of correct and incorrect answers based to the expert model. We add two to the sum of incorrect answers when an incorrect answer is in the divergence area. To understand if there is a preference towards "Yes", the number of correct and incorrect answers in the candidate area for a "No" answers are swapped. To understand if there is a preference towards "No", the number of correct and incorrect answers in the candidate area for a "Yes" answer are swapped. Only when the divergence-adjusted figure is smaller than a preference value the preference value indicates a drift toward its measured preference.

We calculate the J value with the help of three latent variables, α (model says "Yes"), β (both model and practitioner say "Yes"), and γ (both model and practitioner say "No").

$$J = \frac{TP}{TP + FP} + \frac{TN}{TN + FN} - 1 \tag{1}$$

$$TP = \alpha * \beta \tag{2}$$

$$FP = \alpha * (1 - \beta) \tag{3}$$

$$FN = (1 - \alpha) * (1 - \gamma) \tag{4}$$

$$TN = (1 - \alpha) * \gamma \tag{5}$$

$$\alpha, \beta, \gamma \sim Beta(1, 1) \tag{6}$$

Score Analyze. The score analysis is used to understand how well a certain identity is aligned with the expert model. We try to find two different latent groups, those who guess and those who have some knowledge about the area. The output is in the form of probability of alignment with the expert model. A probability below 0.5 indicates guessing. The same rules as in Sect. 3.6 are used for candidates but the rules to adjust for divergence differ. When an answer is incorrect and is in the divergence area, a correct answer is subtracted from the sum of correct answers.

Depending on the number of correct answers, an identity (i) will have a success rate and a latent group membership as a guesser or informed.

$$success\_rate_i = \text{if } membership_i == 1 \text{ then } informed \text{ else } guesser \tag{7}$$

$$membership_i \sim Binomial(1, 0.5) \tag{8}$$

$$correct\_answers_i \sim Binomial(questions, success\_rate_i) \tag{9}$$

$$informed \sim Uniform(0.5, 1) \tag{10}$$

$$guesser = 0.5 \tag{11}$$

Feign Analyze. The feign analysis is used to understand how well a certain identity performs related to the other identities. We try to find two different latent groups, those who underperform and those who have a performance in-line with the other identities. The output is in the form of the probability of feigning. A probability below 0.5 indicates acceptable performance. The same rules as in Sect. 3.6 are used to adjust for divergence and candidates.

Depending on the number of correct answers to the other identities, an identity (i) will be given a probability of belonging to one of the two latent groups honest or feign.

$$group\_rate_i = if \ membership_i == 1 \ then \ feign_i \ else \ honest_i \tag{12}$$

$$correct\_answers_i \sim Binomial(questions, group\_rate_i) \tag{13}$$

$$membership_i \sim Binomial(1, 0.5) \tag{14}$$

$$honest_i \sim Normal(\mu, \lambda) \tag{15}$$

$$feign_i \sim Uniform(0, honest_i \tag{16}$$

$$\mu \sim Beta(1, 1) \tag{17}$$

$$\lambda \sim Gamma(0.001, 0.001) \tag{18}$$

4   Result

4.1   Information from the Practitioners

We started with a questionnaire that only contained measured values for the following features; CRP, Age, $BMInow$, $BMIbefore$, and the dependent variable $Treatment$. During the first data gathering, updates to the questionnaire were discussed with the practitioners. The following updates to the questionnaire were performed; One feature with derived measured value was added, $BMIdiff$. $BMIdiff$ is the difference between $BMInow$, and $BMIbefore$, in percentage. Three of the measured values were translated into the predefined ordinal scales, described in Table 2, and provided in the questionnaire, as a support to the practitioners.

Several of the practitioners expressed frustration when confronted with the questionnaire data. The practitioners are used to interacting with the patients, which will help them to take their decisions. Another vital remark was that the data alone might not be enough, but need to be combined with visual information, an example is the BMI information. The shape of the body can indicate if obesity shall be considered a risk or not.

4.2   Decisions Grouped by Meta-data Context

Table 3 shows the results when we use Youden's J to analyze decisions that are grouped by a meta-data context. We analyze three different groupings of the data, the total number of answers from both the survey groups and the answers from each survey group. In Table 3 we can see a weak alignment between the total number of answers and the expert model when we consider the "raw" answers. No alignment exists when we adjust for divergence and consider preference towards "Yes" or "No". Regarding the answers from survey group 1, no alignment with the expert model exists. The answers from survey group 2 show an alignment with the expert model as is.

Table 3. Youden's J analysis of decisions grouped by meta-data context

Contex	Raw	Divergence adjusted	Prefer Yes	Prefer No
Total	*0.583*	0.440	0.440	0.274
Group 1	0.389	0.237	0.237	0.237
Group 2	*0.738*	*0.648*	0.648	0.340

4.3   Decisions Grouped by Identity Context

In Tables 4, 5 and 6, the identities P1–P6 belong to practitioners in survey group one, and the identities P7–P12 belong to practitioners in survey group two.

Youden's J Analyze. Table 4 shows the results when we use Youden's J to analyze decisions that are grouped by an identity context. In Table 4 we can see an alignment to the expert model of divergence-adjusted values for Practitioner P4, P7, P9, P11, and P12. The preference towards "Yes" is supported by Practitioner P8 while Practitioners P9, P11, and P12 are indifferent. Only Practitioners P3 and P4 show an alignment to a preference towards "No". If we consider strict trustworthiness, only P4, P9, and P11, show alignment with the expert model.

Table 4. Youden's J analysis of decisions grouped by identity context

Identity	Raw	Divergence adjusted	Prefer Yes	Prefer No
P1	0.104	0.056	0.195	−0.134
P2	−0.122	−0.258	−0.075	−0.488
P3	0.419	0.356	0.356	*0.555*
P4	*0.530*	*0.530*	0.319	*0.709*
P5	0.494	0.494	0.241	0.494
P6	0.345	0.231	0.231	0.231
P7	*0.619*	*0.547*	0.346	0.375
P8	*0.510*	0.413	*0.551*	−0.153
P9	*0.751*	*0.751*	0.751	0.525
P10	*0.537*	0.413	0.221	0.262
P11	*0.633*	*0.633*	0.633	0.120
P12	*0.632*	*0.558*	0.558	0.350

Score Analyze. Table 5 shows the results when we use score analysis to analyze decisions that are grouped by an identity context. In Table 5 we can see an alignment to the expert model of divergence-adjusted values for Practitioner P4, P5, P7, P9, P11, and P12. The preference towards "Yes" is supported by Practitioners P8 and P12, while Practitioners P9 and P11 are indifferent. Practitioners P3, P4, and P5 show an alignment to a preference toward "No".

Table 5. Score analysis of decisions grouped by identity context

Identity	Raw	Divergence adjusted	Prefer Yes	Prefer No
P1	0.748	0.183	0.513	0.046
P2	0.005	0.000	0.005	0.001
P3	0.764	0.412	0.513	*0.938*
P4	*0.950*	*0.934*	0.819	*0.997*
P5	*0.955*	*0.939*	0.527	*0.946*
P6	0.752	0.181	0.224	0.276
P7	*0.983*	*0.938*	0.806	0.526
P8	0.742	0.429	*0.937*	0.526
P9	*0.998*	*0.997*	*0.998*	*0.935*
P10	*0.936*	0.418	0.224	0.108
P11	*0.986*	*0.987*	*0.982*	0.255
P12	*0.988*	*0.930*	*0.940*	0.518

Feign Analyze. Table 6 shows the results when we use feign analysis to analyze decisions that are grouped by an identity. In Table 6 we can see the difference between the survey groups on an identity level. All of the six identities in survey group two can be regarded as trustworthy regarding divergence-adjusted values, but only three in survey group one.

Table 6. Feign analysis of decisions grouped by identity context

Identity	Raw	Divergence adjusted	Prefer Yes	Prefer No
P1	0.368	*0.621*	0.400	*0.754*
P2	*0.941*	*0.990*	*0.950*	*0.967*
P3	0.359	0.441	0.412	0.169
P4	0.209	0.202	0.262	0.068
P5	0.224	0.181	0.393	0.180
P6	0.341	*0.601*	*0.563*	0.480
P7	0.131	0.196	0.272	0.358
P8	0.357	0.301	0.179	0.359
P9	0.065	0.073	0.076	0.178
P10	0.222	0.431	*0.575*	*0.620*
P11	0.133	0.129	0.131	0.485
P12	0.136	0.193	0.190	0.377

5   Analysis and Discussion

The main indicators for a change in the expert model are the values of preference towards "Yes" and preference towards "No". However, these values must be seen in relation to the divergence-adjusted value. The values in Table 3 shows that the answers from the practitioners do not indicate any changes to the expert model (Sect. 3.4). The significant difference between the groups can be explained with the improved questionnaire used by Group 2, see Sect. 4.1. In Table 4 we can see that only two practitioners from each group do not have a difference between the raw value and the divergence adjusted value, which means they did not give any answer which is deemed as unrealistic by the expert model. An explanation for the results might be the lack of visual information, which practitioners expressed as frustrating since they felt they could not do good judgments. Another explanation might be the number of judgments during a limited time. During our discussions, some practitioners found errors while glancing through their answers. We decided to not correct the results.

When looking at the values in Table 5 the number of reliable scores between the groups are three and five. The number of under-performers are three and zero, according to Table 6. This information indicates that Group 2 performed according to what can be expected.

Implementing the expert model as a discrete Bayesian network gives us several possibilities to decide how an answer can affect the expert model. Since we base our expert model on a small data set, not all of the feature combinations have a decision. These areas will have an initial probability of 0.5 and will benefit from practitioner information to give better guidance. The stiffness of the model can be controlled at design time. For example, if an area has its probability based on four answers, a new answer included in the model might introduce a big change. Multiplying the initial answers with a factor will give each new included answer less impact and make the expert model change more smoothly.

The use of score analysis for "raw" indicates how the answers would have been analyzed when only looking at how well a practitioner is aligned with an expert model. The feign analysis focuses on how aligned a group of practitioners is, which can indicate a desired change to the expert model even if the scores themselves are worse than guessing. Both of these methods require several answers to belong to the same identity and the performance of the identities is analyzed. Another restriction is the number of answered questions which must be the same between the identities. The use of Youden's J removes these constraints. We decided to use Youden's J instead of Choen's kappa since Youden's J is preferred in the area of machine learning and Cohen's kappa is related to some known problems [7].

The introduction of the divergence areas made it possible for practitioners to evaluate not only the score as such but the trustworthiness of the answers. The introduction of the candidate areas made it possible to understand the strength of the facts to change the expert model. A group of answers in which only half of them are correct can indicate a strong change toward a specific answer, for example, can Youden's J be zero for the "raw" data, but one for a preferred answer.

The decision about the values of the parameters α, β, γ, and δ, for defining divergence areas and candidate areas will be left to the practitioners to decide. The same is true for the decision of how much divergence is tolerated and the strength of an indicated change when using answers to change the expert model.

However, we will further investigate how to support practitioners with information about when old data should no longer be part of the model or when new data should be added to the expert model, based on the practitioner decisions discussed in the former paragraph.

6   Conclusion and Future Work

In this study, we have investigated and suggested a way to determine the trustworthiness of human decisions and how to understand if these decisions indicate a change to the underlying expert model. Since we use a small data set as our base for the expert model, the number of answers made by humans might be limited, which makes it vital to understand if these answers are trustworthy and can be used to improve the model. We have introduced the possibilities for practitioners to define divergence, and candidate areas, based on Bayesian methods. With the help of Bayesian implementations of Youdan's J, score, and feign analysis. It is possible to determine if answers are trustworthy or candidates for improving the expert model.

To apply the results in an intent-driven system, we need to find a framework supporting the realization of the processes. This framework will include a causal analysis of the underlying causal model and functionality. Further, it will support decision-making regarding updates of an expert model.

References

1. Burkov, A.: The Hundred-Page Machine Learning Book. Andriy Burkov (2019)
2. Davidson-Pilon, C.: Bayesian Methods for Hackers. 1st edn. Addison Wesley Data & Analytics Series (2016)
3. Goodfellow, I., Bengio, Y., Courville, A.: Deep Learning. MIT Press (2016)
4. Jarrahi, M.H., Memariani, A., Guha, S.: The Principles of Data-Centric AI (DCAI). arXiv preprint arXiv:2211.14611 (2022)
5. Lunn, D., Jackson, C., Best, N., Thomas, A., Spiegelhalter, D.: The BUGS Book. CRC Press (2013)
6. Pearl, J., Glymour, M., Jewell, N.P.: Causal Inference in Statistics. First edn. John Wiley and Sons Inc. (2016)
7. Powers, D.M.W.: The problem with kappa. In: Proceedings of the 13th Conference of the European Chapter of the Association for Computational Linguistics, pp. 345–355 (2012)
8. Robson, C.: Real World Research: A Resource for Users of Social Research Methods in Applied Settings, 3rd edn. Wiley, Chichester (2011)
9. RStudio: RStudio. https://rstudio.com/. Accessed 12 Sept 2019
10. Scutari, M., Silander, T., Ness, R.: bnlearn. https://cran.r-project.org/web/packages/bnlearn/index.html. Accessed 10 Oct 2022
11. Scutari, M., Denis, J.B.: Bayesian Networks. CRC Press (2015)
12. Silvander, J.: Towards intent-driven systems based on context frames. Doctoral dissertation, Blekinge Institute of Technology (2021)
13. Singh, S., Ali, N., Lundberg, L.: Smart and adaptive architecture for a dedicated Internet of Things network comprised of diverse entities: a proposal and evaluation. Sensors 22(8), 3017 (2022)
14. Strickland, E.: Andrew Ng: Unbiggen AI. https://spectrum.ieee.org/andrew-ng-data-centric-ai. Accessed 05 Dec 2022
15. Youden, W.J.: Index for rating diagnostic tests. Cancer 3(1), 32–35 (1950)

How is Affect Social Justice Tensions: A Case Study of Asylum Management

Tamara Roth[1,2]([envelope]) [iD], Alexander Rieger[1] [iD], Gilbert Fridgen[1] [iD], and Amber Young[2] [iD]

[1] Interdisciplinary Centre for Security, Reliability, and Trust at the University of Luxembourg, Kirchberg, Luxembourg
{tamara.roth,alexander.rieger,gilbert.fridgen}@uni.lu,
tr036@uark.edu
[2] Sam M. Walton College of Business at the University of Arkansas, Fayetteville, USA
ayoung@walton.uark.edu

Abstract. Asylum management is rife with questions surrounding social justice. The use of information systems in this context is often complex and fosters social injustices instead of promoting social justice. The reason for this complexity may be the result of conflicting conceptualizations of social justice. By conducting an inductive and embedded single-case study of one blockchain systems for asylum management, we find that such conflicts can occur across and within the individual, group, and supra-group levels, and result in tensions. These tensions can be addressed through the implementation of information systems in four ways: reinforcement, stabilization, mediation, and resolution. This dynamic negotiation through information systems may prevent the materialization of one specific social justice conceptualization and distributes the quest for social justice across multiple levels.

1 Introduction

In 2015, refugees fleeing war and terrorism in their home countries poured into Germany and surrounding countries [1, 2]. As more than a million new asylum applications came in, Germany struggled to coordinate the asylum procedure in a socially just but efficient manner. Paperwork was lost, processes were delayed, and life-altering mistakes were made as Excel spreadsheets were passed back and forth across and within government agencies inside of and beyond state borders [2]. In addition to the coordination challenges, competing interests and conflicting conceptualizations of justice across stakeholders and levels of organizing proved difficult to manage. Government representatives were interested balancing the rights of refugees and concerns of German citizens [3]. German states were interested in distributing the responsibility such that each state contributed equitably [4]. Refugees were interested in transparency and equal opportunities [5]. The European Union aimed to redistribute responsibilities to not overburden single nations and improve opportunities for asylum seekers [3].

Difficulties in aligning these various goals, in addition to the large number of incoming asylum seekers, created a strong need for more efficient, secure, and just handling of asylum procedures. This need extended to how the involved authorities managed

B. Shishkov (Ed.): BMSD 2023, LNBIP 483, pp. 268–277, 2023.
https://doi.org/10.1007/978-3-031-36757-1_18

their internal processes and how they coordinated work across organizational boundaries [2]. In a first step, Germany's Federal Government modernized and expanded its
IT infrastructure to allow for full digitalization of its processes and effective handling
and coordination of an increasing number of applications [18, 19]. These investments
increased information availability and helped the Federal Government develop its internal processes. Yet, coordinating with state authorities proved more difficult to digitalize.
In particular, the creation of a joint IT system for cross-organizational process coordination was complicated by the federal separation of competencies. To mediate these
challenges, the federal and state governments began to investigate a blockchain system
that could reflect the organizing principles of federal procedures [19]. In late 2021, the
rollout of the national FLORA system across Germany began.

While any blockchain system in a federally structured environment provides opportunity to observe the struggle for a dominant social justice conceptualization [6], asylum
management, which is replete with cross-organizational procedures, provides opportunity for particularly rich insights. Procedures in asylum management often reach across
national borders [5] challenging traditional conceptualizations of distributive social justice. These are typically bounded within a society, i.e., nation-states that share a cultural
identity and political ideology, and possess the relevant structures to enforce social
justice rules [7, 8]. To understand social justice in an asylum management context, a
broader perspective is needed, one that includes more universal conceptualizations of
social justice, such as egalitarian social justice or – to redress injustices – elements of
commutative social justice. Employing a theory-building approach, we investigate the
following research questions:

*How does strategic use of information systems to negotiate concurrent but
divergent conceptualizations of social justice shape social justice outcomes?*

To build our theory, we conduct a single-case study [9] of the FLORA system and
the subprojects that surrounded its development. Our investigation reveals how tensions
emerge from different social justice conceptualizations at the individual, group, and
supra-group levels of organizing. Information systems can be implemented strategically
to influence these tensions in four different ways: they can exacerbate (reinforcement
strategy), maintain (stabilization strategy), reduce (mediation strategy), and eliminate
(resolution strategy) tensions. When tensions occur at levels of organizing with asym-
metric resources, resources can be leveraged to increase the chances of success and,
ultimately, which social justice conceptualization will dominate.

The rest of the paper is organized as follows. The next section provides an overview
of the research on social justice and IT. Next, we present details of our case study
design, data collection, and data analysis. We then present the theoretical framework
that emerged from our analysis of the case. The paper concludes with a summary of key
insights from our analysis and an outlook on future research.

2 Theoretical Background

The search for a uniform conceptualization of justice has a longstanding tradition. First approaches date back to Aristotle and Plato, and even old religious texts, such as the Talmud and the Bible, elaborate on problems of just distribution of resources [7, 8]. This most fundamental type of justice, termed distributive justice, attempts to find answers to the question of "how a society or group should allocate its scarce resources or products among individuals with competing needs or claims" [10]. While this question is still a key issue in contemporary theories of justice, the specific term "social justice" entered political discourse only after the advent of socialist movements and the industrial revolution, which brought about substantial socioeconomic changes [7, 8]. As a rather young concept tied to socioeconomic development, social justice received particular attention in the early years of the 20th century. Principles resulting from these modern debates—such as need, merit, and equality—are still central to theorizing about social justice today [8].

An exemplary context for the visibility of social justice challenges at different levels of social organizing is asylum. While the reasons for asylum typically extend beyond national borders, the social justice negotiations that surround it occur within the boundaries of host nations [11]. To understand social justice in an asylum management context, a broader perspective is needed, beyond distributive social justice, such as egalitarian social justice or – to redress injustices – elements of commutative social justice [7]. In line with distributive social justice conceptualizations [7], nations first aim to ensure the well-being and safety of their own citizens [12]. This becomes particularly visible in the various containment and immigration policies, which distinguish legal from illegal or unwanted migration. Such distinction puts most asylum seekers outside of the national community of their host country and promotes a citizen–noncitizen relationship [11]. A lack of ties to the national community and being regarded as an outsider may not only affect asylum seekers' well-being, but also raises social justice concerns. Despite a potential outsider perspective, a basic level of justice is ensured by mandates of procedural social justice, i.e., due process and transparent as well as verifiable and lawful processes [8].

A yet-understudied possibility to foster and improve on social justice at different levels of social organizing is the use of information systems. More specifically, many new technologies have emerged in recent years that may possess characteristics that can help improve social justice. One such development, which has been hyped by libertarians for its high degree of decentralization and redistribution of digital power to the individual, is blockchain technology. Blockchains are databases that store transactions in a distributed network [13, 14]. Consisting of a chronologically ordered chain of blocks, blockchains provide a high degree of tamper resistance and transparency. More specifically, each new block references information from its predecessor, making retrospective changes to the order of blocks easy to detect. The comparatively quick detection of fraudulent behavior and the high degree of transparency is often perceived to contribute to an equal distribution of power and information among involved actors. This perceived democratization of information and power—although blockchains may also be designed in a way that they allow for a certain degree of inequality, for instance, regarding the availability of sensitive information [15, 19] – may add to social justice at all levels.

While social justice plays a major role at the individual level, where individuals measure the degree of equity by comparing themselves with a referent, equality perceptions may also play an important role at the group and supra-group levels [12].

3 Research Method

As theorizing on the effects of information systems on social justice negotiations is limited, we chose a theory-building case study approach. Case studies allow for an "in-depth" investigation of a socially embedded phenomenon and can support the emergence of new theory [9, 17]. Case study research is particularly fruitful for investigating an under-explored phenomenon or an "under-represented perspective in a well-researched literature" [16]. As social justice negotiations are often multifaceted and highly context-specific [7, 8, 12], we opted against a multiple-case design. Instead, we built our investigation around a comprehensive case that would foster depth and richness [3, 9]. This reasoning led us to select the FLORA project, a revelatory and longitudinal case that balances depth and breadth and allows for cross-synthesis [9].

3.1 Case Description

We study the FLORA project, which is developing a blockchain-based system for the exchange of process information between German authorities involved in German and European asylum procedures. To address the coordination and justice challenges introduced by the wave of refugees in 2015, the federal and some state governments began to invest heavily into new IT systems. However, these efforts were often limited by the bureaucratic structure of Germany's asylum procedure. The procedure's completion requires close collaboration and information exchange between various authorities at the local, state, and federal levels.

The federal government has thus explored 'decentralized' technical alternatives that can accommodate the bureaucratic nature of the asylum procedure and are compatible with government IT systems. As part of this exploration, the federal government developed a blockchain enabled system for the exchange of important process information between federal and cooperating state governments. The government also partnered with academe and contracted, among others, the second and fourth author of this study to ensure the design of the system was appropriate and promoted justice for stakeholders at multiple levels of organizing. The system started as a proof-of-concept (PoC) in January 2018, was subsequently piloted in the German state of Saxony, and has been rolled out across other German states in a step-by-step manner since the end of 2021. In 2020, it also motivated the European Blockchain Partnership (EBP) to establish a working group headed by Germany and France that will extend the European Blockchain Service Infrastructure (EBSI) to support the transfer of refugees between European member states.

3.2 Data Collection

Our inductive analysis draws on 45 semi-structured interviews with partners directly and indirectly involved with the FLORA project as well as 20 semi-structured interviews with asylum applicants and support organizations. These were conducted using an interview guide which helped to ensure comprehensive coverage of the subject area [3, 9]. The protocol of our semi-structured interviews involved a brief introduction followed by questions on interviewees' perceptions of social justice tensions, and on the opportunities, challenges, and success factors for the blockchain project. During the interviews, we adapted the questions to shift the focus depending on the respective interviewee's knowledge and interactions with the system [3, 9]. We mirrored the interviewees' verbal posture and vocabulary and allowed the interviewees to go in directions that they found interesting [9]. In selecting our interviewees, we focused on incorporating a broad variety of perspectives. That is, we selected interviewees with technical expertise and in-depth knowledge of the asylum procedure. Likewise, we included the perspectives of governmental employees, external consultants and IT service providers, refugees, and refugee support organizations. Our interviews lasted between 30 and 60 min, were audio-recorded and, afterward, fully transcribed. To increase construct validity, we also obtained interviewees' feedback on the draft case study reports.

We also draw from a comprehensive database of historical project information to triangulate our findings. We analyzed over 400 pages of documentation on the collaboration software Confluence and over 200 pages of technical concepts and functional specifications. Moreover, we gathered field observations from bi-weekly sprint reviews and management meetings, as well as over 50 project workshops with different departments, authorities, and organizations.

We used qualitative analysis techniques and the analysis software MAXQDA to analyze our data. We undertook three stages of data analysis: open, axial, and selective coding [16]. The codes were either based on our theoretical lens (deductive coding) or emerged during data collection (inductive coding) [17].

4   Preliminary Findings

Reinforcement occurred where the FLORA systems were strategically used to impose higher-level conceptualizations of social justice at the expense of lower-level ones. In these instances, the systems contributed to the amplification of social justice tensions. The reinforcement effect was prominent between the group and the individual levels. In the national procedure, Germany's asylum laws emphasize equitable distribution of refugees across German states in line with federal and state quota systems. These quota systems are based on tax revenue and population numbers, and typically support supra-group- and group-level conceptualizations of social justice. Consequently, many refugees fear that the strategic use of the FLORA system to enforce quotas disadvantages them. For instance, some believe that rural areas offer fewer opportunities to demonstrate their readiness to integrate, such as internships and vocational trainings. One refugee explains this "fair-procedure" tension between the group and individual levels:

> "*The law says that you cannot work somewhere else from where you live. The law also says that you cannot move to another municipality. At the same time, they require you to get [...] an internship to show your willingness to integrate. [...] This puts me in a position where I cannot move forward and show my willingness to integrate.*"

The national FLORA system exacerbates this 'fair procedure' tension by enforcing a federal and state conceptualization of quotas as a means to social justice. Federal and state representatives strategically implemented FLORA to better manage "hand-overs" in case the quota systems demand relocation. FLORA also helps federal and state representatives identify refugees who have gone missing during hand-overs.

Stabilization was possible where the two FLORA systems facilitated a compromise. These compromises helped stabilize existing tensions and prevented their further exacerbation. A particular prominent stabilization example is information access. The General Data Protection Regulation and other pertinent laws grant refugees the right to know how their personal information is processed. Yet, refugees or their lawyers must direct a formal request to the competent authorities before such information is disclosed. Authorities are cautious about these requests, as some refugees use this information to anticipate repatriation or transfer actions and "disappear." A quote by one refugee assistant illustrates this 'information access' tension:

> *"Quicker and less error-prone processes would, of course, also lead to quicker repatriations. It would only increase the value for asylum seekers who are rightfully in this country. You cannot have a solution that benefits everyone. [...] But it could well be that asylum seekers who learn in advance of a pending repatriation simply go underground for a while."*

FLORA has an ambiguous effect in this regard. On one hand, it increases the level of detail of the available information that refugees can request. Moreover, refugees can petition more authorities for information because the systems ensure consistent sharing of process information between all authorities involved in a refugee's asylum procedure. Yet, FLORA does not change the status quo in that this information is shared with refugees only reactively, and refugees still need to petition involved authorities for disclosure of the processed information. A quote by one of the government officials working with FLORA illustrates:

> *I don't think that FLORA makes much of a difference regarding our work with asylum seekers. [...] Status updates and appointments are still issued over the provincial headquarters [...] and refugee asylum seekers have to ask for this information, [...] especially their status. [It's more] the internal way of dealing with their applications instead of or rather in addition of the lists."*

In some instances, the FLORA systems could be strategically implemented in ways that aligned social-justice conceptualizations and reduced tensions. *Mediation* effects were especially apparent for FLORA at the group and individual levels. One prominent example for mediation between the group and individual levels was faster, more secure procedures. Before the introduction of the national FLORA system, process information was often exchanged using e-mails and Excel files, and sometimes fax messages and phone calls. These communication channels were slow and prone to errors, as they involved many manual steps, such as copying data from and into the Excel files. Slow and faulty procedures not only place undue mental strain on refugees and workers, but also could lead to grave errors, such as unlawful repatriations. One of our FLORA project managers explains this "lawfulness of the procedure" tension:

"Above all, asylum applications should not only be processed efficiently, but efficiently and correctly. At that time, there was the scandal in Bremen—let's call it 'scandal' because it was one—where wrongful asylum decisions were made and people [were] deported who should have been allowed to stay. At that point, there was agreement that we need a more transparent solution, to avoid similar mistakes in the future."

The introduction of the national FLORA system perceptibly improved the exchange of process information. Waiting times between process steps were reduced by almost half and Excel files were retired. Moreover, the system decreased the risk of procedural errors and unlawful actions. These changes were positively received by the involved authorities, as well as many refugee assistants and refugees.

Finally, the FLORA systems were strategically implemented to settle social-justice tensions. We found evidence for these **resolution** effects across the supra-group and group levels, as well as between different conceptualizations at the group level. A prominent resolution effect occurred in relation to the federal nature of Germany's asylum procedure. This nature means that the overall procedure is standardized, but that many authorities with regional differences are involved. Federal organizing principles empower regional branches of the federal government and their partner authorities at the state and municipal levels to foster social justice locally. Yet, they also complicate standardization efforts at the federal level, as well as the introduction of shared IT systems that would make the procedure more just globally. One of FLORAs project managers explains this "separation of competencies" tension between the supra-group and group levels:

"We have tasks at the federal level. We have tasks at the state level, the municipal level, and all kinds of areas where not everyone is always allowed to see everything. That's why many processes are not so well connected. Everyone has their own responsibilities."

The national FLORA system was strategically implemented to successfully resolve this tension. It standardizes the exchange of process information and encourages the use of a single IT system. At the same time, it permits regional branches and their partner authorities to maintain their regional subprocesses. This perception that the FLORA system could be used as an enabler of federalism is an essential motivator for state governments to adopt the system.

"Blockchain offers the possibility to map regional differences, leaves enough room for flexibility, and still allows for standardization. Thus, the technology strengthens local autonomy, preserves federal structures, and even strengthens the latter. People retain their responsibility and, using [the FLORA system], also take on joint responsibility for the task."

Resources played an important role in determining how the FLORA systems were strategically implemented to address social justice tensions. We found that the systems tended to be implemented in ways that strategically advantaged those with greater resources. This pattern was observed across levels. Because the EU, federal, and state authorities control the FLORA systems, they were often implemented in a way that privileged higher-level conceptualizations of social justice. Yet, strategic use of the FLORA systems for mediation was more common when procedural errors and resulting injustices at the individual-level warranted action, and when states and municipalities with diverging resources quarreled about just distribution.

5 Discussion

We contribute to the literature on social justice by unpacking how social justice negotiations can be complicated by conceptual differences. These negotiations typically occur at three conceptual levels: individual, group, and supra-group. At the individual level it is about being materially right in finding a just solution for the individual cases. For the group level, solutions that collectively do justice to the social groups involved ensure being materially right on the aggregate level. The supra-group level mandates the upholding of rules to be formally right. While the literature on social justice already indirectly distinguishes between these levels [7, 8] our case study allows us to directly observe their distinctness and arising tensions. As observed tensions between the levels show, social justice negotiations cannot be simplified by providing a common definition; it is paramount to account for their messiness by allowing for their coexistence, even if the hierarchical model complicates negotiations that span cultural and group boundaries. More specifically, the negotiation of different social justice conceptualizations may deliver more socially just outcomes than the enforcement of one universal definition (Fig. 1).

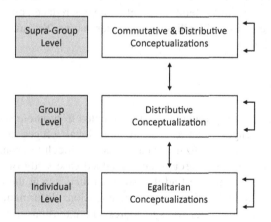

Fig. 1. Emergence of social justice tensions from different conceptualizations

This research contributes also to the IS literature by describing four ways information systems can be implemented to shape negotiations of meaning around social justice (Fig. 2). We term the first strategy reinforcement. When an information system is implemented to impose a particular conceptualization, the effect is amplified tensions. The second strategy, which we call stabilization, facilitates compromise and maintenance of the status quo and helps to avoid exacerbation of existing tensions. The third strategy, mediation, aligns different social justice conceptualizations and aims to reduce tensions. Finally, information systems can be strategically implemented toward resolution, or to settle social justice tensions.

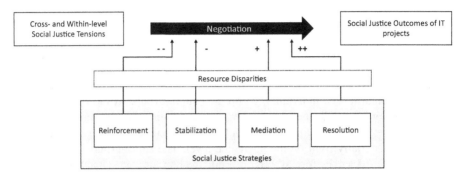

Fig. 2. Social Justice Strategies for IT projects

Information systems can be powerful tools for the negotiation of social justice. When they are used judiciously, they do not limit the complexity of these negotiations. Instead, they support navigation through the plethora of tensions that define social justice negotiations. Some of these tensions can be resolved, others mediated or stabilized. At still other times, a reinforcement strategy may be adopted to promote a higher-level social justice objective. In such cases, the risk of unjustly favoring dominant conceptualizations of social justice is high. Reinforcement strategies reduce complexity, which can lead to performance gains and facilitate a straighter course. Yet, such an approach may oversimplify social justice in an unjust manner.

6 Conclusion

Information systems can be strategically implemented to promote social justice in the face of societal challenges, such as the ongoing global refugee crisis [1]. Yet, conflicting social justice conceptualizations can make it difficult to promote social justice through information systems. Through an embedded case study of a blockchain system for asylum management, we find that such conflicts can at the individual, group, and supra-group levels, and lead to social justice tensions. Information systems can be strategically implemented in four ways to address these tensions: reinforcement, stabilization, mediation, and resolution. The effectiveness of each of these strategies depends on the extent to which negotiating parties leverage financial and technical resources to champion their conceptualization of social justice.

Acknowledgements. This research was funded in part by: the Luxembourg National Research Fund (FNR) grant reference 14783405; FNR and PayPal, PEARL grant reference 13342933/Gilbert Fridgen; and the European Union (EU) within its Horizon 2020 programme, project MDOT (Medical Device Obligations Taskforce) grant agreement 814654. For the purpose

References

1. AbuJarour, S., et al.: ICT-enabled refugee integration: A research agenda. Commun. AIS, **44**(1), 874–891 (2019). https://doi.org/10.17705/1CAIS.04440
2. Dittmer, C., Lorenz, D.F.: Disaster situation and humanitarian emergency – in-between responses to the refugee crisis in Germany. Int. Migr. **59**(3), 96–112 (2021). https://doi.org/10.1111/imig.12679
3. Aligica, P.D., Savidge, T.: The European Migrant Crisis: a case study in failure of governmental and supra-governmental responses. In: Haeffele, S., Storr, V.H. (eds.) Government Responses to Crisis. Mercatus Studies in Political and Social Economy, pp. 129–141. Springer, Cham (2020). https://doi.org/10.1007/978-3-030-39309-0_8
4. Ericson, R.E., Zeager, L.A.: Coordination and fair division in refugee responsibility sharing. J. Conflict Resolution **66**, 00220027221080985 (2019). https://doi.org/10.1177/00220027221080985
5. Andrade, A.D., Doolin, B.: Information and communication technology and the social inclusion of refugees. MIS Q. **40**(2), 405–416 (2016)
6. Moreau, M.-A.: Labour relations and the concept of Social Justice in the European Union. In: Micklitz, H.-W. (ed.) The Many Concepts of Social Justice in European Private Law. Edward Elgar Publishing (2011). https://doi.org/10.4337/9780857935892.00024
7. Jackson, B.: The conceptual history of social justice. Political Stud. Rev. **3**(3), 356–373 (2005). https://doi.org/10.1111/j.1478-9299.2005.00028.x
8. Miller, D.: Principles of social justice. Harvard University Press (1999)
9. Yin, R.K.: Case study research: design and methods (6th ed.) SAGE Publications, Inc. (2017)
10. Roemer, J.E.: Theories of distributive justice. Harvard University Press (1996)
11. Pisani, M.: 'Illegal bodies' on the move: a critical look at forced migration towards social justice for young asylum seekers. In: Council of Europe (ed.), Healthy Europe: Confidence and uncertainty for young people in contemporary Europe, pp. 83–98 (2016)
12. Pogge, T.W.: An egalitarian law of peoples. Philos. Public Aff. **23**(3), 195–224 (1994). https://doi.org/10.1111/j.1088-4963.1994.tb00011.x
13. Beck, R., Müller-Bloch, C., King, J.L.: Governance in the blockchain economy: a framework and research agenda. J. Assoc. Inf. Syst. **19**(10), 1 (2018). https://aisel.aisnet.org/jais/vol19/iss10/1
14. Chanson, M., Bogner, A., Bilgeri, D., Fleisch, E., Wortmann, F.: Blockchain for the IoT: privacy-preserving protection of sensor data. J. Assoc. Inf. Syst. **20**(9), 1274–1309 (2019). https://doi.org/10.17705/1jais.00567
15. Lumineau, F., Wang, W., Schilke, O.: Blockchain governance—a new way of organizing collaborations? Organ. Sci. **32**(2), 500–521 (2021). https://doi.org/10.1287/orsc.2020.1379
16. Eisenhardt, K.M.: What is the Eisenhardt Method, really? Strateg. Organ. **19**(1), 147–160 (2021). https://doi.org/10.1177/1476127020982866
17. Corbin, J.M., Strauss, A.: Grounded theory research: Procedures, canons, and evaluative criteria. Qualitat. Sociol. **13**(1), 3–21 (1990). https://doi.org/10.1007/BF00988593

Applying Augmented Reality in Tourism: Analyzing Relevance as It Concerns Consumer Satisfaction and Purchase Intention

Faisal Aburub$^{(\boxtimes)}$

University of Petra, Amman, Jordan
faburub@uop.edu.jo

Abstract. Augmented Reality (AR) has become increasingly popular in recent years and is being used in a variety of fields, including education, entertainment, marketing, healthcare, and tourism. AR has appeared as a vital marketing technique, making the hotels improve the way the guests perceive the environment they in. AR can be a powerful tool for hotels looking to improve the guest experience, increase revenue, and differentiate themselves from competitors. By leveraging AR technology, hotels can create memorable and engaging experiences that leave a lasting impression on guests. The present research expands on the "Uses and Gratifications" framework, which was previously applied to web contexts, and now extends its application to a new context, namely augmented reality. It seeks to investigate the effect of the key benefits generated from interacting with AR on consumer satisfaction and purchase intentions within Hotel sector. Consequently, the research will integrate the Uses and Gratifications model with Technology Acceptance Model to investigate the effect of augmented reality on consumer satisfaction and purchase intentions. An empirical investigation was conducted in hotel sector in Jordan. Hypotheses were tested and the results showed that AR has significant impact on consumer significant and purchase intention.

Keywords: Business Modeling · Augmented Reality · Consumer Satisfaction · Purchase Intention

1 Introduction

Nowadays, hotels aim to attract many guests, retain and give them great experience. Hotels are willing to use many methods and techniques to do that. One of these techniques is Augmented Reality (AR). In recent years, AR has an appeared as a vital marketing technique, making the hotels improve the way the guests perceive the environment they in Whang et al. [1]. AR can be considered as valuable technology to hotels as they provide physical environment to the consumers, which can be extremely improved through AR. Moreover, AR enhance consumers' experience of exploring hotels and its nearby area. Moreover, AR can be used to create personalized and interactive experiences for customers in retail and hospitality industries. For example, customers can use AR to try on clothes or visualize products in their own space before making a purchase.

B. Shishkov (Ed.): BMSD 2023, LNBIP 483, pp. 278–288, 2023.
https://doi.org/10.1007/978-3-031-36757-1_19

According to Yavuz et al. [2], AR is a quickly developing technology, and the number of users of this type of technology is growing day by day. Many large organizations have started using AR in different businesses. In 2019, the global market of AR was around $10.7 billion. In 2024, this expected to reach $72.7 billion [3]. The popularity and growing of AR drive many industries to integrate AR technologies into their business models. Furthermore, AR has become ubiquitous as the huge spread use of tablets and smartphones. According to Hackl & Wolfe [4], AR technologies improve users experience by using computer vison and object recognition to impose electronic contents like audio, videos and graphics onto users' physical environment.

Moreover, the widespread use of smartphones devices has led to development mobile augmented reality (MAR), with emergence of MAR technologies, travelers can access to many tourists' sites related to their travel choices directly from their devices. According to Do et al. [5], MAR technologies enhance tourisms experience and this may lead to significant potential for building the tourism industry and increasing opportunities for promoting tourisms related retail.

Therefore, AR has received big attention from both practitioners and academics. Many researches have conducted to review impact of AR on different industries such as healthcare, manufacturing, hospitability and education [6, 7]. According to McLean & Wilson [8], some organizations like Amazon and Target have offered to search using images taken by mobile AR, this makes users to take a photo of a product using their smart devices and use that photo to search for the product within the mobile apps.

Accordingly, researchers have investigated many approaches such as the Technology Acceptance Model, and the Stimulus-Organism-Response (SOR) framework [5, 9], to help practitioners to understand why and how organizations adopt AR. Although, the previous studies were important and explained set of aspects of why adopting the AR. Most of these aspects focused on the AR itself or the operator of the AR or sociological aspects of users. For example, security and trust. Value of experiential consumers' engagement needs more research and investigation. Accordingly, the "Use and Gratification" (U&G) approach which was proposed by Katz [10], showed that consumers' engagement experiences with the surrounding media can be a source of a number of benefits, and this could be a foundation for motivation to use AR [11]. Empirical research is required to investigate more for these benefits and to know what are the changes that faces operators of AR to attract and retain more costumers.

The present research expands on the "Uses and Gratifications" framework, which was previously applied to web contexts, and now extends its application to a new context, namely augmented reality. It seeks to investigate the effect of the key benefits generated from interacting with AR on consumer satisfaction and purchase intentions within Hotel sector. However, few studies examine the effect of augmented reality on consumer satisfaction and purchase intentions, particularly in the hotels sector. As a result, the current research aims to maximize the marketing potential of AR through three primary objectives: 1- Expanding the U&G approach to AR context to explore the advantages that consumers obtain from interacting with AR applications. 2- Examining the impact of these benefits on consumer satisfaction and purchase intentions. 3- Validating the correlation between consumer satisfaction and purchase intentions within AR context.

4- Integrating the Uses and Gratifications model with Technology Acceptance Model to investigate the effect of AR on consumer satisfaction and purchase intentions.

Consequently, 13 hypotheses were proposed. And tested using questionnaire-based approach. The remainder of the paper is structured as follows: In Sect. 2, background is presented. In Sect. 3, Hypotheses were formulated. Research approach was presented in Sect. 4 followed by conclusion in Sect. 5.

2 Background

2.1 Augmented Reality

AR can be defined as a "technology that allows virtual images generated by a computer to be embedded in the real environment" [12]. AR can combine real and virtual objects, interact in real-time, and registered in real world. As fast development of AR, currently there are many forms AR. AR can be applied not only on computer devices but also on smartphones, tablets, wearable glasses, helmet …..etc.

AR can be considered as ac communication tool that enhance product presentation by adding virtual object in the real environment, improve consumer information processing, and enrich consumer experience [13].

According to Sung [14], mobile augment reality can increase engagement of consumers' senses and effects their behavior, perception, and judgment. This can be performed through the sensory interfaces such as augmented 3D visual effects and sounds and touchscreen items. This can also contribute in building brand awareness, and leading to profits.

2.2 Relevant Models and Approaches

TAM model which was proposed by Davis [15] provides a mean to explore the adoption and communication of new ideas and innovations. TAM uses two measures to predict the users' decision for accepting or rejecting new technologies. These measures are Perceived Usefulness and Perceived Ease of Use. TAM model is widely used in many research areas particularly information technology to investigate the users' responses. Consequently, few studies have been conducted to investigate the acceptance of AR I hotel sector [5]. This research integrates TAM and U&G models to develop a new research model for investigating the impact of AR on consumer satisfaction and intention to purchase within hotels sector.

U&G approach clarifies the audience's role in selecting a specific type of information technologies and proposes technology users to be driven by personal needs and gratification-seeking motives [11]. Based on U&G approach, four types of benefits can audience derive from using sort type of technology or media as follows: hedonic benefits, cognitive benefits, personal integrative benefits, and social integrative benefits.

Hedonic benefits may include enhancing pleasure experience, escaping from problems, gaining enjoyment and having fun [16]. In terms of augment reality context, it indicates the ability of AR to Make consumers feel relaxed, have fun while engaged, obtain enjoyment, and make them not want to stop using AR.

Cognitive benefits may include gaining information to increase the understanding of the situation, self-education and learning, knowing about related events in surrounding, society and the world, acquiring a sense of security through information, obtaining advice and decision choices [16]. In terms of augment reality context, cognitive benefits can be the ability of AR to precisely describe and visualize the product, help consumers to collect required information to learn more about product, and stimulate the consumers to think about the products or services in different way.

Personal integrative benefits may include enhancing credibility and confidence of persons and finding reinforcement for personal values [16]. In terms of augment reality context, it indicates the ability of AR to enhance confidence, status and credibility of consumers.

Social integrative benefits may include obtaining sense of belonging, making persons connecting with friends, society and families, finding common ground with others for discussion [16]. In terms of augment reality context, to what extent AR promotes values that are similar to their consumers and make them feel a part of their society.

3 Hypotheses

3.1 Relationship between U&G, Consumer Satisfaction and Purchase Intention

According to Do et al. [5], augmented reality offers many more chances for interaction than conventional websites, including more individualized and personalized features. Website interactivity significantly influences consumer satisfaction and purchase intention. Moreover, highly tailored messages lead to better perceptions of interaction, which further increases user satisfaction and purchase intention. Many researches indicated that a favorable correlation between e-quality characteristics and satisfaction. Lin & Sun [17] investigated the relationship between technology acceptance factors and consumer e-satisfaction and e-loyalty. Accordingly, the following hypotheses are proposed:

H1: Perceived usefulness has a positive impact on consumer satisfaction of using AR.

H2: Perceived ease of use has a positive impact on consumer satisfaction of using AR.

H3: Perceived usefulness has a positive impact on purchase intention of using AR.

H4: Perceived ease of use has a positive impact on purchase intention of using AR.

Augmented reality, which provide consumers with enjoyable, fun and emotional experiences, and allow them to escape from stress and daily demands, are seen as entertaining and engaging. As a result, many companies have started to include hedonic design elements in their mobile apps, such as in-app games and infotainment, which go beyond the primary utilitarian purpose [11]. Studies have shown that consumers repeatedly appreciate the added pleasure when using grocery shopping apps and describe a gamification effect from app usage that brings emotional and psychological gratification. This means that AR may provide an intrinsic reward that leads to a pleasurable experience, which is expected to increase consumer satisfaction and encourage them to buy through AR. The enjoyment factor is seen as a significant influence on consumers' attitudes towards the adoption of a system or new technology. Accordingly, the following is hypothesized:

H5: Hedonic benefits offered by using AR has a positive impact on consumer satisfaction.

H6: Hedonic benefits offered by using AR has a positive impact on purchase intention.

AR is considered to be valuable tool that can provide both factual and practical information about brands. The experience of using AR and the belief that it can offer benefits to consumers' understanding of products can enable consumers to use products more effectively. Additionally, AR can offer features like searchable product catalogs, sales, and virtual stores that can enhance the experiential knowledge obtained from using them. AR can also provide in-store assistance by displaying virtual assistants, videos, coupons, or other relevant information when consumers approach a new display, as well as helping them navigate the store with turn-by-turn directions to find what they are looking for [18]. Based on this, the following hypotheses have been proposed.

H7: Cognitive benefits offered by using AR has a positive impact on consumer satisfaction.

H8: Cognitive benefits offered by using AR has a positive impact on purchase intention.

AR has advanced features such as real-time integration, contextual information, enhanced visualization, interactivity and location-based service that allow users to communicate with the sponsors while browsing. This type of one-on-one communication, which focuses on product-related content, is expected to increase the chances for consumers to establish or enhance their reputation among peers and achieve a sense of self-efficacy by influencing other consumers [19]. Accordingly, the following hypotheses are formulated:

H9: Personal integrative benefits offered by using AR has a positive impact on consumer satisfaction.

H10: Personal integrative benefits offered by using AR has a positive impact on purchase intention.

Interactions among users through AR applications can take various forms, such as following/unfollowing people, direct conversations, and inviting contacts from existing social networks and can result in building a community for socializing. Furthermore, when interactions among users are extensive, it increases the chances of understanding each other's product-related issues and problems, which in turn allows for consumers to establish more connections with other consumers, thus enhancing their beliefs about the product [11]. These ideas form the basis for the proposed hypotheses:

H11: Social integrative benefits offered by using AR has a positive impact on consumer satisfaction.

H12: Social integrative benefits offered by using AR has a positive impact on purchase intention.

3.2 Relationship between Satisfaction and Purchase Intention

Many studies indicated that there is a relationship between online consumer satisfaction and online consumer purchase intention [20]. Moreover, the level of satisfaction of consumers when shopping online is seen as a significant factor that influences their intention to make a purchase. As a result, the following hypothesis is proposed:

H13: Consumer satisfaction has a positive impact on purchase intention of using AR.

Figure 1 shows research model.

4   Approach

4.1   Items Generation

This research used and adapted items from studies Koufaris [21], Calder et al. [16], Khalifa & Liu [22], Spears & Singh [23], and Nambisan and Baron [24] to measure the 8 constructs namely: Hedonic benefits, cognitive benefits, personal integrative benefits, social integrative benefits, consumer intention, and purchase intention. In the current research, some of the items were carefully rephrased to ensure their suitability. A five-point Likert scale was utilized to measure all the scales.

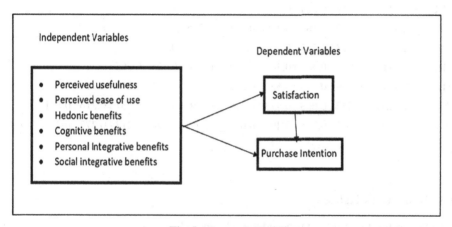

Fig. 1. Research Model

4.2   Data Collection

Data were collected using questionnaire. A purposive sample was used. Only respondents who had experience in using AR were selected.

The questionnaires have been distributed to 370 respondents. Thirty-six questionnaires were excluded due to their incompleteness. Furthermore, 334 questions were usable questionnaires. 58.4% of participants were male and 41.6% were females.

4.3   Measurement Validation

Factorial analysis results indicate that 9 items have been deleted due to low factorability (<0.50) and/or cross loading (>0.30). Confirmatory analysis has been performed using AMOS. The results show the following: indicators reliability was significant for all constructs at 0.001, composite reliability (CR) is higher than threshold for all constructs ranging from 0.813 to 0.911. Convergent validity was conducted using average variance extracted (AVE). All the scales exceeded the minimum threshold value of 0.50, ranging from 0.579 to 0.798. Discriminant validity was evaluated using the criterion of Fornell and Larcker [25], which indicates that the AVE exceeded the squared correlations between all pairs of variables (Table 1). Our proposed model was tested as eight first-order factors correlated with each other. This conceptualization provided a good fit: CMIN/DF (1.512), RMSEA (0.054), GFI (0.881), IFI (0.911), TLI (0.899) and CFI (0.941).

Table 1. Measurement Validation

	Reliability	CR	AVE	PU	PEU	HB	CB	PIB	SIB	Sat	PI
PU	0.76–0.83	0.882	0.641	0.798							
PEU	0.71–0.81	0.841	0.624	0.358	0.711						
HB	0.69–0.79	0.852	0.582	0.310	0.221	0.725					
CB	0.72–0.85	0.823	0.597	0.462	0.151	0.325	0.781				
PIB	0.73–0.80	0.813	0.609	0.301	0.314	0.314	0.325	0.765			
SIB	0.75–0.84	0.879	0.579	0.554	0.358	0.284	0.251	0.211	0.774		
Sat	0.78–0.87	0.842	0.668	0.473	0.214	0.236	0.283	0.267	0.216	0.821	
PI	0.81–0.88	0.911	0.798	0.498	0.0365	0.264	0.274	0.217	0.279	0.472	0.931

4.4 Hypotheses Testing

AMOS was used to test the proposed hypotheses as follows:

The results support H1 ($\gamma = 0.325$, $P \leq 0.05$, R2 = 0.54), H2 ($\gamma = 0.291$, $P \leq 0.05$, R2 = 0.48), H4 ($\gamma = 0.335$, $P \leq 0.05$, R2 = 0.55) and H5 ($\gamma = 0.298$, $P \leq 0.05$, R2 = 0.49) confirming positive association between perceived usefulness and perceived ease of use with consumer satisfaction and purchase intention using AR in the Jordanian hotel sector. The results also support H5 ($\gamma = 0.331$, $P \leq 0.05$, R2 = 0.49), H6 ($\gamma = 0.328$, $P \leq 0.05$, R2 = 0.51), H7 ($\gamma = 0.289$, $P \leq 0.05$, R2 = 0.51) and H8 ($\gamma = 0.288$, $P \leq 0.05$, R2 = 0.52) confirming positive association between hedonic benefits and cognitive benefits with consumer satisfaction and purchase intention using AR in the Jordanian hotel sector.

Moreover, the results did not support H9 ($\gamma = 0.05$, $P \geq 0.05$), H10 ($\gamma = 0.04$, $P \geq 0.05$), H11 ($\gamma = 0.06$, $P \geq 0.05$) and H12 ($\gamma = 0.05$, $P \geq 0.05$). Therefore, the relationship between personal and social integrative benefits with consumer satisfaction and purchase intention using AR in the Jordanian hotel sector is not significant.

The results also support H13 ($\gamma = 0.345$, $P \leq 0.05$, R2 = 0.53), confirming positive association between consumer satisfaction and purchase intention using AR in the Jordanian Hotel Sector.

Based on that, AR application can provide value to consumers through their interactions with it, influencing their satisfaction and likelihood to make future purchases. These applications can do this by providing information on topics the consumer cares about, encouraging new perspectives, improving mood, and increasing the consumer's reputation among peers and the application's sponsor. Additionally, if the application aligns with the consumer's values and makes them feel more connected to their community, it can improve their decision-making and overall satisfaction.

The current research explores the benefits of interacting with branded AR applications through an experiential approach and using the U&G approach and TAM model as a theoretical foundation. It finds that these benefits, which have previously been discussed in offline contexts, can also be applied to AR applications and can serve as a competitive advantage for businesses. Six specific benefits were identified in the context of AR applications: learning benefits, personal integrative benefits, social integrative benefits, hedonic benefits, perceived ease of use and perceived usefulness. This research also expands on previous research in online settings such as virtual consumer environments, demonstrating that these benefits are valid, reliable, and have predictive validity in the context of AR applications.

Table 2 summarizes the findings of research hypothesizes.

Table 2. Hypotheses testing

Hypotheses	γ	Sig. Level	R2
H1: Usefulness ➜ Satisfaction	0.325	0.05	0.54
H2: Ease of Use ➜ Satisfaction	0. 291	0.05	0.48
H3: Usefulness ➜ Purchase intention	0.335	0.05	0.55
H4: Ease of Use ➜ Purchase intention	0.298	0.05	0.49
H5: Hedonic benefits ➜ Satisfaction	0.331	0.05	0.49
H6: Hedonic benefits ➜ Purchase intention	0.328	0.05	0.51
H7: Cognitive benefits ➜ Satisfaction	0.289	0.05	0.51
H8: Cognitive benefits ➜ Purchase intention	0.288	0.05	0.52
H9: Personal integrative benefits ➜ Satisfaction	0.060	Insignificant	-
H10: Personal integrative benefits ➜ Purchase intention	0.040	Insignificant	-
H11: Social integrative benefits ➜ Satisfaction	0.050	Insignificant	-
H12: Social integrative benefits ➜ Purchase intention	0.050	Insignificant	-
H13: Satisfaction ➜ Purchase intention	0.345	0.05	0.53

5   Conclusion

AR technology is highly important as it provides a rich and interactive user experience that enhances the way people perceive and interact with the world around them. In the context of hotel accommodation, AR has the potential to revolutionize the way guests interact with the property and amenities. By using AR, hotels can provide guests with immersive and personalized experiences that enhance their stay and create a lasting impression.

New research model has been developed using TAM model and U&G approach, to investigate the impact of AR on consumer satisfaction and purchase intention within Jordanian hotel sector. The results show that perceived usefulness, perceived ease of use, hedonic benefits, and cognitive benefits have positive relationship with consumer satisfaction and purchase intention. While, personal and social integrative benefits do not have significant relationship with satisfaction and purchase intention. Based on that, design of AR must contain both hedonistic aspects, which aim to provide self-fulfilling value to the consumer and cognitive elements, which aim to provide instrumental value to the consumer.

This research also investigated aspects related to consumers actual interactions with AR not properties of AR or sponsor of it.

This research built upon the "Uses and Gratifications" framework that had previously been applied to web contexts, and extended its application to a new context: augmented reality. The research explored how the key benefits of interacting with AR impact consumer satisfaction and purchase intentions within the hotel sector.

Future research can investigate the following areas. First, as the current study was conducted in a Middle Eastern culture, it is recommended that future research is conducted in another context, such as a Western culture, to verify the findings. This would provide additional evidence on the nature of these benefits and their impact on user satisfaction and purchase intention. Second, the examination of how relevant product and consumer characteristics (such as product type, price, and gender) moderate the relationship between interaction-based benefits of AR and user satisfaction and purchase intention.

Acknowledgments. This work was supported by University of Petra – Deanship of Scientific Research [4/2/2022].

References

1. Whang, J.B., Song, J.H., Choi, B., Lee, J.H.: The effect of augmented reality on purchase intention of beauty products: the roles of consumers' control. J. Bus. Res. **133**, 275–284 (2021)
2. Yavuz, M., Çorbacıoğlu, E., Başoğlu, A.N., Daim, T.U., Shaygan, A.: Augmented reality technology adoption: case of a mobile application in Turkey. Technol. Soc. **66**, 101598 (2021)
3. Qin, H., Osatuyi, B., Xu, L.: How mobile augmented reality applications affect continuous use and purchase intentions: a cognition-affect-conation perspective. J. Retail. Consum. Serv. **63**, 102680 (2021)
4. Hackl, C., Wolfe, S.G.: Marketing new realities: An introduction to virtual reality & augmented reality marketing, branding, & communications (2017)
5. Do, H.N., Shih, W., Ha, Q.A.: Effects of mobile augmented reality apps on impulse buying behavior: an investigation in the tourism field. Heliyon **6**(8), 4667 (2020)
6. de Souza Cardoso, L., Mariano, Q., Zorzal, R.: A survey of industrial augmented reality. Comput. Ind. Eng. **139**, 106159 (2020)

7. Ng, Y.L., Ma, F., Ho, F.K., Ip, P., Fu, K.W.: Effectiveness of virtual and augmented reality-enhanced exercise on physical activity, psychological outcomes, and physical performance: a systematic review and meta-analysis of randomized controlled trials. Comput. Hum. Behav. **99**, 278–291 (2019)

8. McLean, G., Wilson, A.: Shopping in the digital world: examining consumer engagement through augmented reality mobile applications. Comput. Hum. Behav. **101**, 210–224 (2019)

9. Yang, C.: Bon appétit for apps: young American consumers' acceptance of mobile applications. J. Comput. Inf. Syst. **53**(3), 85–96 (2013)

10. Katz, E., Blumler, J., Gurevitch, M.: Utilization of mass communication by the individual. In: Blumler, J.G., Katz, E. (eds.) The Uses of Mass Communications: Current Perspectives on Gratifications Research, pp. 19–32. Sage, Beverly Hills (1974)

11. Alnawas, I., Aburub, F.: The effect of benefits generated from interacting with branded mobile apps on consumer satisfaction and purchase intentions. J. Retail. Consum. Serv. **31**, 313–322 (2016)

12. Muff, F., Fill, H.G.: Use cases for augmented reality applications in enterprise modeling: a morphological analysis. In: Shishkov, B. (eds.) Business Modeling and Software Design. BMSD 2022. Lecture Notes in Business Information Processing, vol. 453, pp. 230–239. Springer, Cham (2022). https://doi.org/10.1007/978-3-031-11510-3_14

13. Fan, X., Chai, Z., Deng, N., Dong, X.: Adoption of augmented reality in online retailing and consumers' product attitude: a cognitive perspective. J. Retail. Consum. Serv. **53**, 101986 (2020)

14. Sung, E.C.: The effects of augmented reality mobile app advertising: viral marketing via shared social experience. J. Bus. Res. **122**, 75–87 (2021)

15. Davis, D.: Perceived usefulness, perceived ease of use, and user acceptance of information technology. MIS Q. **13**(3), 319–340 (1989)

16. Calder, B.J., Malthouse, E.C., Schaedel, U.: An experimental research of the relationship between online engagement and advertising effectiveness. J. Interact. Mark. **23**(4), 321–331 (2009)

17. Lin, T., Sun, C.: Factors influencing satisfaction and loyalty in online shopping: an integrated model. Online Inf. Rev. **3**(3), 458–475 (2009)

18. Ronaghi, M., Ronaghi, H.: Investigating the impact of economic, political, and social factors on augmented reality technology acceptance in agriculture (livestock farming) sector in a developing country. Technol. Soc. **67**, 101739 (2021)

19. Sun, C., Fang, Y., Kong, M., Chen, X., Liu, Y.: Influence of augmented reality product display on consumers' product attitudes: A product uncertainty reduction perspective. J. Retail. Consum. Serv. **64**, 102828 (2022)

20. Wu, L., Kang, M., Yang, B.: What makes users buy paid smartphone applications? Examining app, personal, and social influences. J. Internet Bank. Commer. **20**(1), 1–22 (1970)

21. Koufaris, M.: Applying the technology acceptance model and flow theory to online consumer behavior. Inf. Syst. Res. **13**(2), 205–223 (2002)

22. Khalifa, M., Liu, V.: Online consumer retention: contingent effects of online shopping habit and online shopping experience. Eur. J. Inf. Syst. **16**(6), 780–792 (2007)

23. Spears, N., Singh, N.: Measuring attitude toward the brand and purchase intentions. J. curr. issues res. advertising **26**(2), 53–66 (2004)

24. Nambisan, S., Baron, A.: Interactions in virtual consumer environments: implications for product support and consumer relationship management. J. Interact. Mark. **21**(2), 42–62 (2007)

25. Fornell, C., Larcker, F.: Structural equation models with unobservable variables and measurement error: algebra and statistics. J. Mark. Res. **18**, 382–388 (1981)

26. Gerlich, N., Drumheller, K., Babb, J., De'Armond, A.: App consumption: an exploratory analysis of the uses & gratifications of mobile apps. Acad. Mark. Stud. J. **19**(1), 69–79 (2015)

27. Lin, Y.-H., Fang, C.-H., Hsu, C.-L.: Determining uses and gratifications for mobile phone apps. In: Park, J.J., Pan, Y., Kim, C.-S., Yang, Y. (eds.) Future Information Technology. LNEE, vol. 309, pp. 661–668. Springer, Heidelberg (2014). https://doi.org/10.1007/978-3-642-55038-6_103

28. Kleijnen, M., De Ruyter, K., Wetzels, M.: An assessment of value creation in mobile service delivery and the moderating role of time consciousness. J. Retail. **83**(1), 33–46 (2007)

29. Park, J., Yang, S.: The moderating role of consumer trust and experiences: Value driven usage of mobile technology. Int. J. Mob. Mark. **1**(2), 24–32 (2006)

30. Van der Heijden, H.: Factors influencing the usage of websites: the case of a generic portal in the Netherlands. Inf. Manag. **40**(6), 541–549 (2003)

Comparing Sensor-Based Computing and Predictive Data Analytics for Usage in Context-Aware Applications

Boris Shishkov[1,2,3]([✉]), Georgi Yosifov[4], and Boyan Bontchev[4]

[1] Institute of Mathematics and Informatics, Bulgarian Academy of Sciences, Sofia, Bulgaria
b.b.shishkov@iicrest.org
[2] Faculty of Information Sciences, University of Library Studies and Information Technologies, Sofia, Bulgaria
[3] Institute IICREST, Sofia, Bulgaria
[4] Faculty of Mathematics and Informatics, Sofia University St. Kliment Ohridski, Sofia, Bulgaria
mail@gyosifov.com, bbontchev@fmi.uni-sofia.bg

Abstract. Context-aware information systems count on sensors for establishing the user situation and adjusting their behavior accordingly. Nevertheless, there are quite some situations where sensors would be insufficiently effective: (a) Sometimes it is physically challenging to mount sensors at the optimal position, resulting in lower quality of the gathered data; (b) Mental aspects, such as user intentions, emotions, arousal, motivation, and engagement, are not easy to capture by means of sensors; (c) Data fusion concerning data from different sensors could result in wrong inferences. We propose combining / augmenting sensor-based approaches with data analytics that can make predictions about larger groups of users. When the focal user is a member of that larger group and when there are more users with a similar profile, predictions about the focal user can be made. We combine context awareness conceptualizations and relevant data analysis techniques, and we reflect on these choices in a discussion concerning the usefulness of applying data analytics in facilitating context-aware computing. The paper illustrates the concepts with an example from the transport domain.

Keywords: Context awareness · Sensor-based computing · Predictive data analytics

1 Introduction

The views of Mark Weiser from the early 1990s (when the use of a (personal) computer would not assume dynamics related to user needs), featuring ubiquity of connected hardware/software elements [1] have inspired the development of *context-aware computing* [2]. Relevant enabling technologies, featuring *device miniaturization*, *high-bandwidth wireless communication*, and *sensor networks*, have helped in this regard [3, 4], allowing developers to consider *user needs* as *highly dynamic* and potentially *evolving over time* [5]. Hence, *context awareness* improves IT-services, facilitating the development of *systems that adapt their servicing to the situation and/or needs of the user* [6–10].

© The Author(s), under exclusive license to Springer Nature Switzerland AG 2023
B. Shishkov (Ed.): BMSD 2023, LNBIP 483, pp. 289–298, 2023.
https://doi.org/10.1007/978-3-031-36757-1_20

Considering *context awareness* projects, such as CyberDesk [11], AWARENESS [3, 12], and SECAS [13], we observe that *context-aware systems* using the Internet-of-Things [4] mostly count on sensors for ESTABLISHING THE (USER) SITUATION, by capturing physical world dimensions or phenomena. Besides this *physical environment context*, context awareness may be based on either *person/human individual or group context* including preferences, prior knowledge, emotions, and so on. And we may consider as well *virtual environment context* represented by services in distributed systems [15].

We argue nevertheless that there are quite some situations where *sensors* would just be insufficiently effective: (a) Sometimes it is physically challenging to mount sensors at the optimal position, resulting in lower quality of the gathered data; (b) Mental aspects, such as user intentions, emotions, arousal, motivation, and engagement, are not easy to capture by means of sensors; (c) Data fusion concerning data from different sensors could result in wrong inferences.

Inspired by relevant current possibilities concerning *Artificial Intelligence (AI)*, we are addressing various *AI*-related techniques, such as: *Decision Trees, Covering Algorithm, Naïve Bayesian Classification*, and so on [14], analyzing their strengths as it concerns the challenge of PREDICTING the "upcoming" user situation, fueled by relevant *training data*. Hence, we propose combining / augmenting sensor-based approaches with data analytics that can make predictions about larger groups of users. When the focal user is a member of that larger group, and when there are more users with a similar profile, predictions about the focal user can be made. Various scenarios could be addressed in this regard, such as:

- Capturing the "upcoming" user situation, by positioning the user in one of several user-situation classes, based on considering corresponding *attribute values* featuring *history data* from other users that has been used as "training data";
- Effectively profiling the "upcoming" user, based on his/her *past activities*, such that the system is facilitated in its capturing relevant *user needs*, *preferences*, and *expectations*.

Further, we may consider applying user profiling for the sake of: (a) adapting system behavior accordingly, e.g. dynamic difficulty adjustment in computer video games [19], context-sensitive decision making [20], or context-aware access control mechanisms [16]; (b) personalizing user-oriented content and/or its representation [21]; (c) tailoring specific system qualities, such as data interoperability, security, performance, or learnability [22].

For this, we combine *context awareness* conceptualizations and relevant *data analysis techniques*, and we reflect on these choices in a discussion concerning the **usefulness of applying data analytics in facilitating context-aware computing**. The paper illustrates the concepts with an example from the transport domain.

Finally, the current paper is descriptive only. Validation is left for follow-up research.

The remainder of the paper is structured as follows: Sect. 2 firstly presents a conceptual model of context awareness (particularly focusing on the user situation determination), applying a functional perspective and taking into consideration related work, and then briefly outlines several relevant data-analytics-related algorithms. In Sect. 3 we outline important issues concerning sensors-driven and predictions-driven (user-centric) context awareness, making accordingly observations, claims, and solution-directions-related proposals. In Sect. 4 we present: (i) a fictional example that illustrates our views on dealing with context awareness by applying data analytics; (ii) a discussion featuring corresponding benefits and limitations. We conclude the paper in Sect. 5.

2   User-Centric Context Awareness

As mentioned in [17], *context-aware systems* are expected to be providing **context-specific services to users in accordance with their context-dependent needs**. This relates to the vision of scientists, such as Mark Weiser (see Sect. 1) and particular technical developments, such as *wireless networking, device miniaturization* and *sensor technologies*. This allows for considering *evolving* (as opposed to constant) *user needs*, assuming that in consuming services, the user is in his/her context and hence adequate service delivery should be adapted accordingly. We consider two key processes in this regard, that often go one after another, namely **situation determination** and **behavior adaptation**: The service provider is to be AWARE of the "current" situation (i.e. situational context) of the user, which means that *situation determination* should go first. Further, *behavior adaptation* is needed such that *service delivery* is *aligned* with the *context situation* and corresponding (*user*) *needs*. This has effect on what the system is "doing", materialized by *actuators*. Finally, *context management* is needed to <u>align incoming (sensor) data and the corresponding system behavior adaptation</u>. This all concerns the following: (i) When a situation is determined, it should be established to which corresponding (user) needs it points; (ii) When the actual (user) needs are established, the "context manager" would "ask" the system to adapt its servicing accordingly; (iii) Finally, the system has to validate the level of effectiveness of its behavior adaptation towards the current user situation, i.e. to make a quantity assessment of how the system behavior adaptation has matched (satisfied) the current situation of the user. Hence, the above issues present <u>user-centric context awareness</u>, taking a functional perspective and assuming that servicing is to be adapted based on the situation of the *user*. For the sake of exhaustiveness, it is to be noted that it is possible that servicing is adapted based on the functioning of the system itself, based on a necessity to stick to relevant public values, and so on – those are left beyond the scope of the current paper. For more information on those issues, interested readers are referred to [18].

In this paper, we particularly focus on the USER SITUATION DETERMINATION, acknowledging that currently most context-awareness-related projects (see above) consider sensors as the enabler as it concerns situation determination. In the previous section, we have presented some limitations in this regard and justified a consideration of *data-analytics-driven predictions*. We go back to this discussion – see Fig. 1.

As the figure suggests, <u>when counting on sensors</u>: [SENSOR DATA GATHERING] Low-level sensor data is to be gathered – imagine that sensors are physically attached to the body of a person or a surface $=$ $>$ This is in a way "data sampling" that represents our source of information concerning the context-aware servicing. [DATA PRE-PROCESSING] Often gathered data is of limited use because of low quality-of-data levels – imagine that a sensor is not well attached for some time, or connectivity is poor to transmit data, or some batteries are low that affects sensors and/or communication,

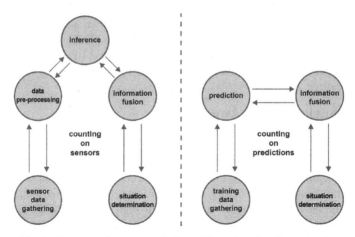

Fig. 1. Sensors-driven vs predictions-driven situation determination

and so on = > Data pre-processing may be needed, in order to make sure that what we gather as data is adequate – this may include using a larger number of data samples, trimming values, making approximations, and so on. [INFERENCE] When we have low-level sensor data of good quality, we would need to "translate" it to higher-level "meaningful" information that would be usable by the system to "understand" the situation of the user. Said otherwise, inference is needed that can be realized by means of reasoning techniques/algorithms – imagine that a person (user) is "wearing" optical sensors (e.g., a photo-plethysmograph) to measure user blood pressure. The low-level optical readings have no meaning in terms of semantics and need to be translated to meaningful statements, such as "blood pressure is normal" or "blood pressure is high", or "blood pressure is low", for example. [INFORMATION FUSION] Often one data source is not enough for determining the situation of the user and we may need to adequately combine (with possibly applying weights) a number of data sources, referred to as "information fusion" – imagine that knowing the blood pressure of somebody is not enough alone for determining his/her condition and more information is needed such as data of galvanic skin response. Therefore, it is important to have clarity about which are the information items of interest and what are their corresponding weights as it concerns the "big picture". [SITUATION DETERMINATION] Finally, we are capable of determining the current situation of the user (and if it differs from the "previous" one, then system behavior adaptation would be needed) – imagine that we conclude that the situation of the monitored person is normal and we only need to keep on monitoring him/her. All this is visualized at the left side of the abovementioned figure, representing what is currently covered by existing technology and best practices. This fuels our comparative analysis concerning also the vision of determining situations driven by predictions – as also visualized in Fig. 1.

As suggested by the right side of the figure, when counting on predictions, we need TRAINING DATA first. That is because we are PREDICTING (as opposed to CAPTURING) information. Said otherwise, instead of establishing the situation of the user, we make a conclusion what most likely this situation is (or will be), assuming of course some confidence intervals accordingly. This means that we have an ITEM TO BE CLAS-SIFIED, using existing relevant data concerning OTHER ITEMS. Each item is described considering a number of attributes and it is assumed that we know all attribute values concerning all items. Further, we know the class of the "other" items. Finally, we do not know the class of the item that is to be classified. Hence, by classifying this item, we de facto realize a prediction along the lines of the above. Imagine that a booking system would "treat" somebody in one way, if it is known that (s)he is more likely to make a booking (Context Situation A), and this same system would "treat" him/her in another way if it is known that more likely (s)he is just browsing (Context Situation B). Imagine also that we have training data featuring 100 persons and we know all corresponding attribute values as well as whether or not each of them did booking or was just browsing. Hence, we are capable of classifying accordingly the "new" person, advising the system what should be expected. This points to: [TRAINING DATA GATHERING] - the gathering of relevant training data and [PREDICTION] - the prediction itself. This is at the "level" of "inference" from the "sensor side"; thus, this is the point when we have semantically rich information. Then we have [INFORMATION FUSION] – the corresponding fusion of information and [SITUATION DETERMINATION] – the determination of the situation, that are quite similar to what we have at the left-hand side of the figure.

As it concerns what the right-hand side of the figure suggests, some information is still needed on the user or of the user situation to be able to make a situation determination. Otherwise, the prediction would be purely a probabilistic one. In contrast, we need a prediction for a particular user in a particular situation – for this reason, we would possibly need to combine user data with the fused information for the sake of aligning the user (situation) with the data. Actually, some user data might also be useful as it concerns what the left-hand side of the figure suggests, but given the fact that the sensors measure the current situation or context of the user directly, the extra data would not necessarily be needed. Hence, this emphasizes further the difference between the sensor-based and the prediction-based approaches.

And in the end, to briefly outline several relevant data-analytics-related algorithms (as promised – see above), we refer to the ones already mentioned in the Introduction, namely: *Decision Trees*, *Covering Algorithm*, and *Naïve Bayesian Classification*. For the sake of brevity, we are not going to discuss them – interested readers are referred to [14]; what we do nevertheless is to position those algorithms with regard to underlying scientific disciplines, such that their corresponding benefits are explicitly seen:

- Decision Trees and Covering Algorithm are mostly rooted in **Computer Science** and concern current **Machine-Learning**-related developments, mainly pointing to *supervised machine learning*, where **labelled data** is used to train the system and achieve the generation of **RULES** that in the end help *classifying an item*.
- In contrast, the Naïve Bayesian Classification approach is rooted in **Statistics** (in general) and particularly – in **Probability Theory**; this means that we apply *probabilities* (studying existing *training data*) for the sake of *classifying a new item*.

The analysis presented in the current section is considered useful in our proposing (in Sect. 3) solution directions featuring a "*sensors-predictions-synergy*" for the benefit of *context-aware information systems*, with a particular focus on the *determination of the situation of the user*.

3 Issues with Sensors-Driven and Predictions-Driven Situation Determination

In this section, we outline some important issues regarding the two types of user-centric context awareness – driven by sensors and by predictions. Further, these issues are going to be elaborated accordingly in Sub-Sect. 4.1, while discussing an illustrative example. We make claims/observations as follows:

- Predictions have wider "coverage" compared to sensors because applying predictions would not assume physical restrictions as in the case of using sensors.
- Reliability is a challenge with regard to both (sensors and predictions) because sensors can give wrong data because of physical issues while predictions may be insufficiently reliable because of probabilistic issues.
- Neither sensors nor predictions are "green-field" usable – sensors require calibration while predictions require training data.

We would therefore not consider sensors and predictions as "competitive" alternatives only but also as items of SYNERGY. In this, we claim that a key strength of sensors is (low-level) data capturing while a key strength of predictions concerns the data-driven classification. In addition, we would not consider computer-science-rooted algorithms as "competitive" to statistics-rooted ones because BOTH end up with some kind of classification based on data featuring some history information, referred to as "training data" (see above). Also, we emphasize the importance of TRAINING DATA; considering it via relevant ATTRIBUTES (whose corresponding VALUES are captured) is often adequately doable by means of SENSORS. Said otherwise, sensors can be used for capturing training data that may be used in turn for predictions-driven situation determination.

Finally, it is important what the target CLASSIFICATION SCHEME is – an issue concerning the SYSTEM DESIGN. We therefore consider ITEM CLASSIFICATION as crucial, to be based on a case-relevant algorithm.

We consider the issues outlined in this section as inspirational with regard to possibly combining *sensor-based computing* and *predictive data analytics* for usage in *context-aware applications*. These points are subject of the elaborations that follow in Sect. 4.

4 Evaluation

The current section presents a fictional example that illustrates our views on dealing with context awareness by applying data analytics; this is followed by a discussion of corresponding benefits and limitations.

4.1 Illustrative Example

To date, city transportation optimization is considered a multifaceted task concerning important aspects, such as time, air pollution, price, fuel consumption, public transport hops, scheduling, and so on [23]. In the current example, we consider a *vehicle* traveling from *Point A* to *Point B*, in a *city*, assuming that we know the *departure time*. What would the FASTEST ROUTE be?

Let's firstly consider *static user needs* (with regard to what a *system* is offering in terms of *services*), regardless of the surrounding situation. Then our task would be as simple as using an algorithm for finding the shortest path in a graph. Further, let's refer to Sect. 2 and assume *context awareness* featuring context-dependent user needs in the sense that different needs correspond to different context situations. We argue that this corresponds to most real-life situations and is hence worthwhile investigating.

Assuming a *user-centric* approach, we consider *three context awareness perspectives* where service delivery is adapted with regard to details concerning: (i) the user character – e.g., a more experienced driver would reach Point B faster than a less experienced one, a more accurate driver would be slower in reaching Point B, and so on; (ii) the user environment – for example, it would take more time for somebody to reach Point B when it is raining, compared to sunny days; (iii) relevant public values, such as privacy, transparency, accountability, local city regulations, and so on [18] – imagine that it would take more time for the same driver to reach Point B when driving is restricted in some areas for a short time period, e.g. the siesta in Spain.

For those three TYPES of *context*, we use labels as follows: *UC – User-related Context* such as age, gender, violations history, skills, and so on, *SC – Surrounding* (with regard to the *User*) *Context* like weather conditions, surrounding traffic, etc., and *VC – public-Values-related Context* such as privacy, transparency, and so on. This is illustrated in Fig. 2, featuring a *generalization hierarchy* of these context awareness perspectives. Note that the middle part of the figure is highlighted in grey, to indicate that in the remainder of the current section, for the sake of brevity, we would only consider *surrounding (i.e., environmental) context*, and in particular, the *instances* WEATHER and (surrounding) TRAFFIC. Counting on *sensors*, one could get accurate weather-related data in real-time (there are wind sensors, humidity sensors, temperature sensors, air-pressure sensors, and so on) while cell-phone/GPS data and surveillance footages could help us get actual traffic information [25].

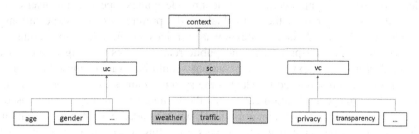

Fig. 2. Context-awareness perspectives

As suggested in previous sections, we use such initial information as a basis for PREDICTING an "outcome" and we consider relevant history information as TRAIN-ING DATA. Imagine that we have observed a number of persons driving between Point A and Point B in EQUAL "other" conditions, and we have used the abovementioned instances (namely: *weather* and *traffic*) as DESCRIPTOR ATTRIBUTES. Further, we can categorize corresponding ordinal values as follows: (a) Weather – "clear", "rain", "fog", "snow", and "storm", putting combinations beyond the scope of the current investigation; (b) Traffic – "no traffic", "mild traffic", and "high traffic". Finally, we have a CLASSIFICATION for the "outcome" featuring three timing-related categories as follows: "normal", "slow", and "fast"; we assume that for each training data entity, we KNOW the outcome.

Fig. 3. Towards context-driven predictions

Hence, when we would have to predict timing concerning a "new" entity, we USE sensor, GPS and other data (see above) to get the corresponding VALUES featuring the abovementioned TWO attributes (*weather* and *traffic*); next to that, some TESTING may be carried out for the sake of avoiding possible overfitting (see Fig. 3). As the figure suggests and assuming availability of *training data*:

- It is firstly necessary to **derive attribute values** (in our case, those are values concerning the attributes weather and traffic) and this we do by means of SENSING (counting on sensors – see above).
- It is then necessary to **classify the current output** (in our case, this concerns the "current" person's reaching Point B in his or her vehicle) and this we do by means of PREDICTING (counting on data-analytics-related algorithms – see Sect. 2).
- Finally, it is necessary to **store** the new data in our base of *training data*, for future use.

4.2 Discussion

Modern context-aware applications should provide context-specific and user-centric services that are tailored to the individual needs, preferences, and expectations of users. On the other hand, such context-aware services should take into account specific environment-related properties and public-related issues existing at the current moment. Therefore, context-aware applications should be aware of these three groups of properties and are supposed to adapt some system features to some or all of them. For example, a music application can adjust the volume and playback speed based on the user's location and the ambient noise level, while an adaptive video game can tailor game difficulty or behavior of virtual players according to the emotional state of the player [24].

Other types of context-aware applications are oriented to the provision of personalized recommendations to users based on their previous activity, preferences, and behavior patterns. Such systems often use collaborative filtering to provide personalized recommendations to users based on the behavior and preferences of other users with similar profiles. For example, social media platforms recommend friends or groups to users based on their interests and connections; e-commerce websites recommend products based on a user's past purchases, search and browsing history, wish list, and reviews; an educational game can present personalized didactic content based on the student age, learning style, previous outcomes, etc. [21]. On the other hand, context-aware systems may provide location-based services to users based on their current location. For example, a navigation application can provide directions to nearby restaurants or tourist attractions, while weather applications alert users about upcoming storms or bad weather conditions based on their location. Hence, modern software systems are supposed to use predictive analytics to anticipate the user's needs by analyzing user data and behavior patterns and, thus, to provide services tailored to individual user's needs and preferences, together with proactive recommendations.

5 Conclusions

Furthering previous work that concerns context-aware information systems, we have addressed the challenge of situation determination, particularly referring to user-centric context-aware systems.

Acknowledging the key role of sensor technology in this regard, we have emphasized particular limitations of this technology when it comes to establishing the user situation; this justifies the research-in-progress reported in the current paper, aiming improvements concerning the determination (in an effective and efficient way) of the (user) situation. We have considered predictive data analytics from this perspective, identifying relevant strengths and potentials featuring a "*sensors-predictions-synergy*", and proposing solution directions accordingly. They assume the application of: (i) sensors-driven data capturing and (ii) predictions-driven algorithmic classification of items, such that (i) and (ii) may be complementing to each other. This solution directions proposal stems from a comparison concerning sensor-based computing and predictive data analytics, for usage in context-aware applications.

We have illustrated our views by considering a fictional example concerning the transport domain.

What is left for follow-up research is two-fold: (a) Maturing the proposed high-level solution directions, by means of conceptual and technical reinforcements; (b) Using the considered example as inspiration for carrying out an exploratory case study, for the sake of validation (proof-of-concept).

Acknowledgement. This work is partially supported by the Institute of Mathematics and Informatics – Bulgarian Academy of Sciences and the Faculty of Mathematics and Informatics, Sofia University "St. Kl. Ohridski", Bulgaria. Further, we express gratitude to Alexander Verbraeck for his inspiring feedback.

References

1. Weiser, M.: The computer for the 21st century. SIGMOBILE Mob. Comput. Commun. Rev. **3**(3), 3–11 (1999). ACM, New York, NY, USA (1999)
2. Dey, A.: Context-aware computing. In: Krumm J. (eds.) Ubiquitous Computing Fundamentals, Chap. 8. Taylor and Francis Group, LLC (2009)
3. Wegdam, M.: AWARENESS: A project on context AWARE Mobile NEtworks and ServiceS. In: Proceedings: 14th Mobile & Wireless Communications Summit. EURASIP (2005)

4. Shishkov, B.: Designing Enterprise Information Systems: Merging Enterprise Modeling and Software Specification. Springer, Cham (2020). https://doi.org/10.1007/978-3-030-22441-7
5. Dey, A., Abowd G., Salber D.: A conceptual framework and a toolkit for supporting the rapid prototyping of context-aware applications. Hum. Comput. Interact. **16**, 2 (2001)
6. Dey, A.K., Newberger, A.: Support for context-aware intelligibility and control. In: Proceedings of SIGCHI Conference on Human Factors in Computing Systems. ACM, USA (2009)
7. Bosems, S., van Sinderen, M.: Models in the design of context-aware well-being applications. In: Meersman, R., et al. (eds.) On the Move to Meaningful Internet Systems: OTM 2014 Workshops. LNCS, vol. 8842, pp. 37–42. Springer, Heidelberg (2014). https://doi.org/10.1007/978-3-662-45550-0_6
8. Alegre, U., Augusto, J.C., Clark, T.: Engineering context-aware systems and applications. J. Syst. Softw. **117**, 55–83 (2016)
9. Alférez, G.H., Pelechano, V.: Context-aware autonomous web services in software product lines. In: Proceedings of 15th International SPLC Conference. IEEE, CA, USA (2011)
10. Abeywickrama, D.B., Ramakrishnan, S.: Context-aware services engineering: models, transformations, and verification. ACM Trans. Internet Technol. J. **11**(3), 10 (2012). ACM (2012)
11. Dey, A.K.: Context-aware computing: the CyberDesk Project. In: AAAI Spring Symposium on Intelligent Environments, AAAI Technical Report SS-88-02, pp. 51–54 (1998)
12. van Sinderen, M., van Halteren, A., Wegdam, M., et al.: Supporting context-aware mobile applications: an infrastructure approach. IEEE Commun. Mag. **44**(9), 96–104 (2006)
13. Chaari, T., Laforest, F., Celentano, A.: Adaptation in context-aware pervasive information systems: the SECAS project. Int. J. Perv. Comput. Commun. **3**(4), 400–425 (2007)
14. Han, J., Kamber, M., Pei, J.: Data Mining: Concepts and Techniques, 3rd edn. Morgan Kaufmann Publ. Inc., San Francisco (2011)
15. Poslad, S.: Ubiquitous Computing, Smart Devices. Environments and Interactions. Wiley, West Sussex (2009)
16. Kayes, A.S.M., et al.: Survey of context-aware access control mechanisms for cloud and fog networks: taxonomy and open research issues. Sensors **20**, 2464 (2020)
17. Shishkov, B., Fill, H.G., Ivanova, K., van Sinderen, M., Verbraeck, A.: Incorporating trust into context-aware services. In: Shishkov, B. (ed.) BMSD 2023. LNBIP, vol. 483, pp. xx–yy. Springer, Cham (2023)
18. Shishkov, B., Larsen, J.B., Warnier, M., Janssen, M.: Three categories of Context-Aware Systems. In: Shishkov, B. (eds.) Business Modeling and Software Design. BMSD 2017. LNBIP, vol. 309. Springer, Cham (2018). https://doi.org/10.1007/978-3-319-94214-8_12
19. Liu, C., Agrawal, P., Sarkar, N., Chen, S.: Dynamic difficulty adjustment in computer games through real-time anxiety-based affective feedback. Int. J. Hum. Comput. Interact. **25**, 506–529 (2009). https://doi.org/10.1080/10447310902963944
20. Vieira, V., Tedesco, P., Salgado, A.C.: Designing context-sensitive systems: an integrated approach. Expert Syst. Appl. **38**(2), 1119–1138 (2011)
21. Terzieva, V.: Personalisation in educational games–a case study. In: Proceedings of EDULEARN19, IATED, pp. 7080–7090 (2019)
22. Dong, Z.Y., Zhang, Y., Yip, C., Swift, S., Beswick, K.: Smart campus: definition, framework, technologies, and services. IET Smart Cities **2**(1), 43–54 (2020)
23. Kang, L., Chen, S., Meng, Q.: Bus and driver scheduling with mealtime windows for a single public bus route. Transp. Res. Part C: Emerg. Technol. **101**, 145–160 (2019). https://doi.org/10.1016/j.trc.2019.02.005
24. Naydenov, I., Adamov, I.: Clustering of non-annotated data. In: Big Data, Knowledge and Control Systems Engineering (BdKCSE'2021), pp. 1–6. IEEE (2021)
25. Pramanik, A., Sarkar, S., Maiti, J.: A real-time video surveillance system for traffic pre-events detection. Accid. Anal. Prev. **154**, 106019 (2021). https://doi.org/10.1016/j.aap.2021.106019

A Model of a Multi-sensor System for Detection and Tracking of Vehicles and Drones

Ivan Garvanov[1(✉)], Magdalena Garvanova[1], Daniela Borissova[1,2], and Gabriela Garvanova[2]

[1] University of Library Studies and Information Technologies, Sofia, Bulgaria
{i.garvanov,m.garvanova}@unibit.bg, dborissova@iit.bas.bg
[2] Institute of Information and Communication Technologies, Bulgarian Academy of Sciences, Sofia, Bulgaria
gabigarvanova@abv.bg

Abstract. This paper proposes a model of a multi-sensor system for detection and tracking of road vehicles and drones, based on developed original methods and algorithms for signal and data processing, which is a fundamental scientific task. The proposed model uses the polar Hough transform to combine the heterogeneous data in a multi-sensor system.

Keywords: Smart cities · Air traffic management · Computer model

1 Introduction

Road traffic management in modern cities is monitored with numerous sensors and regulated using traffic lights, GPS navigation systems and others. Solving the problem of land transport management is a fundamental scientific task, for the solution of which management systems are constantly being improved [1]. Road traffic and traffic safety is constantly improving with the introduction of more and more diverse smart systems in cars [2]. Modern cars have parking systems, inter-vehicle communication systems, navigation systems, road monitoring systems and others, all of which are controlled by on-board computers [3]. Systems are being created to predict events and prevent catastrophes. Road traffic management systems are extremely important, but the emergence of new vehicles requires offering new technological solutions and systems.

Aircraft management is also very well-regulated [4]. Communication systems exist between aircraft transponders and ground-based radars, and in the absence of communication, primary radars can detect and track the aircraft object. Aircraft detection and tracking systems is also a fundamental scientific problem, the solution of which has been worked on for decades [5].

We build upon work concerning the detection and tracking of unmanned, land, sea, and air vehicles. This scientific task is fundamental and requires the application of various methods and algorithms for processing multi-sensor data consisting of various types of signals and images.

B. Shishkov (Ed.): BMSD 2023, LNBIP 483, pp. 299–307, 2023.
https://doi.org/10.1007/978-3-031-36757-1_21

Some modern road vehicles and/or drones are quite diverse, which makes it difficult to detect them and track them [15, 16]: they range in size from a matchbox to the size of an airplane; they can be powered with or without motors, the motors can be electric or fuel; the materials from which they are constructed are numerous, the majority of which are radio transparent and extremely difficult to detect by radar.

We have witnessed many incidents of drones flying undisturbed over Europe and passing various detection and early warning systems from unidentified aircraft without a problem [17]. Modern air traffic surveillance systems are ineffective in detecting this type of aircraft.

In the literature, various technical solutions are proposed for the detection of new types of vehicles and drones, which are based on video surveillance, radio interception, radar systems, sound signal processing, thermal image processing and others, effective in certain conditions and ineffective in others [6, 7]. The variety of existing drones, considering their geometric dimensions, materials for their manufacture, the type of their propulsion, maneuverability and speed of movement, the type of their control (radio-controlled or not), the type of communication with them, their purpose, etc., makes drones practically undetectable with a single system [8]. This is also the main reason for the paper to seek a solution with the use of a multi-sensor system based on the available sensors in modern cities. The paper envisages making theoretical calculations and conducting real experiments to test the developed original algorithms and programs for the detection of moving objects and to propose a model for unifying heterogeneous data received from sensors in a smart city for joint detection and escorting various vehicles and drones.

To improve the speed and quality of operation of modern systems for detection and tracking of moving objects, the use of several sensors working in the network is offered [9]. To implement a multi-sensor mode, information obtained from the sensors, automated to unite into a single information system, is required. In the unification of information, technical difficulties that come from the various technical characteristics of the sensors are obtained [9, 10]. In most cases, each sensor has its own technical characteristics such as: frequency range of operation; signal radiation power; sensor rotation speed; error of distance measurement and azimuth to the target, etc. The unification of information from several sensors requires complex processing of signals and data to synchronize them.

In this paper, a model of a system for combining data from many sensors, based on polar Hough transform, is offered. The advantage of this transform is that it can be used as a tool for combining data obtained from sensors with different technical parameters. Using the polar Hough transform, all sensor data are combined into a common Hough space [11].

The remainder of the current paper is organized as follows: Sect. 2 focuses on the problem of data fusion into a multi-sensor system, while Sect. 3 describes the polar Hough transform and Sect. 4 one channel polar Hough detector of target and trajectories. Section 5 provides a model for combining data into a multi-channel sensor network, using polar Hough transform. In Sect. 6, an example of testing the proposed model for combining data into the multi-sensor system is applied. Finally, we conclude our research in Sect. 7.

2 Data Fusion in a Multi-sensor System

In practice, information acquired from various sensors is used to solve various applied tasks. Data fusion in multi-sensor systems is a complex process requiring complete synchronization of sensor parameters. The merging of information in most cases can be realized at different stages of the system's signal or data processing. For example, when solving a task of moving object detection and subsequently detecting its trajectory, it is possible to combine the information arrays from the different channels at the signal level, at the surface level (detected target) and at the trajectory level. Depending on where the data is aggregated in a multi-channel sensor system, different advantages and disadvantages will result.

Combining the information in a multi-channel sensor system at the signal level is theoretically the most effective – it should minimize the loss of energy and information from the various sensors. At the same time, this merging of information is very difficult and resource intensive. To achieve this level of information fusion, very fast and complete synchronization of large signal streams from the various sensors is required. The implementation of such a multi-channel system will require large computing resources [12].

Data fusion at the plot level in the so-called "range-azimuth" space consists in unifying the coordinates of all targets detected by the sensors of the system (plots), that is, combining all the data from the plot extractors. The combination of plots in a multi-channel sensor system is obtained after synchronization of each of the channels [13].

When combining the data at the trajectory level, a decision is made about the presence of a target after applying a binary decision rule to the output of all sensor channels. After the detection of the trajectory in each of the channels of the system, the data is merged at the trajectory level in the center for making a decision on the presence or absence of a trajectory. This multi-sensor information fusion structure is the easiest to implement. It does not require any synchronization of the sensors, as each one of them works independently. The final decision about the presence or absence of a target is made based on the results of all sensors, but the probability of detection in this system and the overall quality of its work is unsatisfactory.

In the presence of more moving targets and/or impulse disturbances, it becomes difficult to detect the objects and the trajectory, and it is necessary to use non-traditional detection methods. One such method is the trajectory detection method before target detection. This method can be implemented using the Hough transform.

To improve the performance of a multi-sensor system for target and trajectory detection, this paper proposes a data fusion model, using polar Hough transform.

3 Polar Hough Transform

The polar Hough transform (PHT) was proposed by Garvanov in [10] and is a variant of the Hough transform, proposed by Paul Hough [14]. The polar Hough transform is designed to detect straight lines whose points are defined by polar coordinates. For this purpose, a transition from the two-dimensional polar space to the Hough parametric space is performed. The PHT transforms any point in space into a set of points in Hough space. The task of detecting the straight line is reduced to detecting accumulated peak values in Hough space. The polar Hough transform is performed, using the expression:

$$\rho = r \cos(a - \theta), \ 0 < (a - \theta) \leq \pi \qquad (1)$$

where r and a are the polar coordinates of the points of the straight line (distance and azimuth), θ is the angle between the perpendicular to the straight line and the abscissa axis, and ρ is the smallest distance to the trajectory from the origin of the coordinate system. The main idea of the polar Hough transform is to determine the key characteristics of the straight line (ρ and θ). Using Eq. (1), any point in polar space (Fig. 1a) with coordinates (r, a) can be transformed into a sinusoid in (ρ, θ) parametric space (Fig. 1b).

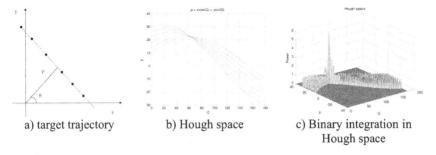

| a) target trajectory | b) Hough space | c) Binary integration in Hough space |

Fig. 1. Hough transform

By assigning values to the parameter θ, values for ρ are obtained. Thus, any straight line defined in polar coordinates can be represented as a set of sinusoids in parametric space. The intersection of the sinusoids in this space has coordinates (ρ, θ) that characterize the straight line.

For the automatic detection of the intersection of the sinusoids, an accumulation (summation) of the sinusoids (binary or incoherent) is performed. This accumulation gives the other name of the Hough parametric space, namely – accumulation space (Fig. 1c).

This accumulation results in a peak at the intersection of the sinusoids that must be detected. Various algorithms for its detection are found in the literature, but most often it is an algorithm comparing all cells of the space with a constant threshold. If the threshold is exceeded, there is a straight line in the image characterized by the parameters ρ and θ. By performing an inverse Hough transformation, the straight line in the Cartesian coordinate system is obtained.

4 Track Before Target Detection, Using Polar Hough Transform

PHT is suitable for use in radar systems to detect trajectories of moving objects in a straight line. The operation of radars in the detection of moving objects can be difficult in the presence of strong impulse interference. In such cases, it is recommended to take several radar scans and find the target trajectory first. These algorithms are called *track before detect algorithms*.

In the radar systems and in the most sensor systems, object coordinates are obtained in polar coordinates (range – r and azimuth – a) or the input parameters of the transformation match the output parameters of space observation radars. Another important advantage of the polar Hough transform is that it can also be used with targets changing their speed and passing through different radar azimuths. The structure of a single-channel detector with a polar Hough transform, using binary accumulation of the data in the Hough parameter space, is shown in Fig. 2.

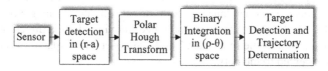

Fig. 2. Block diagram of a single-channel Hough detection

From the consideration of the polar Hough transform, we can conclude that it can be used both in single-channel sensor systems and in multi-sensor systems for detecting straight trajectories and targets. The interest of the present research is the Hough detection of targets and trajectories with the data fusion in the Hough parametric space.

5   Models of Multi-sensor Systems for Detection and Tracking of Moving Targets

The structure of a multi-channel Hough detector with data fusion in the Hough space is shown in Fig. 3.

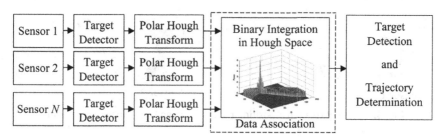

Fig. 3. Multi-channel detector (fusion in the Hough space – Hough association, "HA")

As it was said above, the radars have different technical characteristics, as a result of which different information matrices are obtained with information about the local observation spaces of each of the radars. To combine this information into a single information matrix with uniform characteristics, in the present case, the polar Hough transform is used. The only condition that the system must meet is that the parameters of the Hough space for the different channels have the same values [13].

Applying the polar Hough transform to each of the channels, regardless of the value of the parameters: the distance and azimuth resolution; antenna rotation speed and space scan time, sinusoids are obtained in the Hough parametric space, discretized with the same step for all channels. Since the Hough space is the same for all channels, it is where the information from all radar sensors is combined.

6   Results

The effectiveness of the proposed multi-channel detector with data fusion in the Hough space is tested by means of modeling in the MATLAB environment. The model consists of three radars located in one plane and forming an equilateral triangle between them, as shown in Fig. 4. A moving target is modelled, moving along a direction coinciding with the 45th azimuth of the first radar. The local observation spaces of the sensors in the model are oriented to the north.

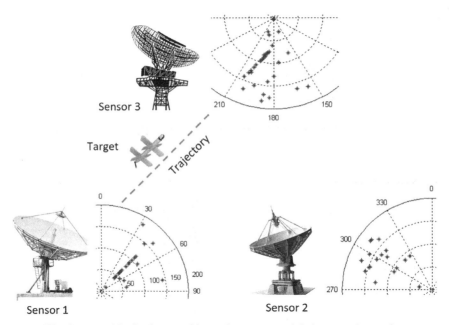

Fig. 4. A model of a three-position radar system and their space observation

The target model is a drone moving in a straight line. The environment in which the target moves consists of white Gaussian noise and randomly occurring impulse disturbances characterized by an occurrence probability of 0.1 and an average power of 10dB. After processing with an averaging Constant False Alarm Rate (CFAR) detector of the three information matrices thus modeled, only the surfaces of the target and possible false targets are obtained.

After 10 scans of the radars, three information arrays of plots are obtained, which are visualized in Fig. 5. The trajectory of the target was formed in the information matrix of the first and third radars. In the first radar scans, the target was detected by the first radar with high probability due to its close position to it and correspondingly high signal-to-noise ratio (SNR). As the target moves away from the first radar, the SNR decreases and the probability of correct detection also decreases. With the third radar from the scheme, the situation is exactly the opposite – as the target approaches it, the SNR grows and the probability of correct detection also increases. This effect can be seen in Fig. 4. The third radar appears far away from the target and its detection is very unlikely.

For this reason, in his space, the trajectory of the target is not noticeable. If we apply a polar Hough transform to these three information matrices, the results of Fig. 4 will be obtained. As shown in this figure, for the first and third radars, distinct peaks corresponding to the target trajectory have formed. In the Hough space, the third target space does not have a well-defined peak to indicate that a rectilinear trajectory from a moving target exists in observation space. If there are more false targets or if the SNR is lower, a situation may arise where the trajectory will not be detected by any of the radars.

For the considered example of a three-position radar system, we apply a polar Hough transform to all detected targets from the three radars and we accumulate binary the resulting sinusoids into a global Hough space. The result of this processing is shown in Fig. 5, where a distinct peak has formed and corresponded to the trajectory of the target. Merging the information from the three radars in the Hough space increases the probability of correct trajectory detection.

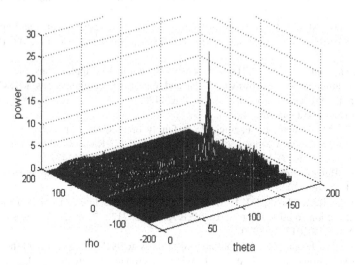

Fig. 5. A global binary Hough parameter space for the three radars

In the considered example, it is assumed that all three radars measure the parameters of the target without error. In the presence of such an error, the peak obtained in Fig. 5 would be of much lower power and detection would be difficult.

7 Conclusions

The proposed model of a multi-channel detector with unification of information in the Hough parametric space does not require additional synchronization of the channels and it is convenient for use in multi-channel systems with different technical characteristics. Increasing the number of sensors should improve the probability of detecting targets and their trajectories.

The use of the Hough transform leads to an increase in the probability of correct detection and a decrease in the probability of a false alarm. Our future research will be aimed at investigating the proposed model in a real-world environment.

Acknowledgement. This work is supported by the Bulgarian National Science Fund, project title "Synthesis of a dynamic model for assessing the psychological and physical impacts of excessive use of smart technologies", KP-06-N 32/4/07.12.2019.

References

1. Dorofeev, A., Altukhova, N., Filippova, N., Pashkova, T., Ponomarev, M.: Development of transportation management system with the use of ontological and architectural approaches to ensure trucking reliability. Sustainability **12**, 8504 (2020). https://doi.org/10.3390/su12208504

2. Rohling, H., Moller, C.: Radar waveform for automotive radar systems and applications. In: 2008 IEEE Radar Conference, pp. 1–4 (2008). https://doi.org/10.1109/RADAR.2008.4721121

3. Klotz, M., Rohling, H.: 24 GHz radar sensors for automotive applications. In: 13th International Conference on Microwaves, Radar and Wireless Communications. MIKON - 2000. Conference Proceedings, IEEE Cat. No. 00EX428, pp. 359–362, vol. 1 (2000). https://doi.org/10.1109/MIKON.2000.913944

4. Angelilli, M., Infante, L., Pacifici, P.: A family of secondary surveillance radars based on conformal antenna array geometries. In: 2017 IEEE Radar Conference (RadarConf), pp. 1681–1684 (2017). https://doi.org/10.1109/RADAR.2017.7944477

5. Gini, F., Rangaswamy, M.: Knowledge based radar detection, tracking and classification. Wiley, Hoboken (2008)

6. Sturdivant, R.L., Chong, E.K.P.: Systems engineering baseline concept of a multispectral drone detection solution for airports. IEEE Access **5**, 7123–7138 (2017). https://doi.org/10.1109/ACCESS.2017.2697979

7. Ramesh, P.S., Jeyan, M.L.: Mini unmanned aerial systems (UAV): a review of the parameters for classification of a mini UAV. Int. J. Aviation Aeronautics Aerospace **7**(3) (2020). https://doi.org/10.15394/ijaaa.2020.1503

8. Raja Abdullah, R.S.A., Abdul Aziz, N.H., Abdul Rashid, N.E., Ahmad Salah, A., Hashim, F.: Analysis on target detection and classification in LTE based Passive Forward Scattering Radar. Sensors **16**, 1607 (2016). https://doi.org/10.3390/s16101607

9. Chernyak, V.: Effective simplified decentralized target detection in multisensor system. In: Fusion 2000. Proceedings of the Third International Conference on Information Fusion, vol. 2, pp. 10–13, July 2000 (2000)

10. Ecabert, O., Thiran, J.: Adaptive Hough transform for the detection on natural shapes under weak affine transformations. Pattern Recogn. Lett. **25**, 1411–1419 (2004)

11. Garvanov, I., Kabakchiev, C.: Radar detection and track determination with a transform analogous to the Hough transform. In: Proceedings of International Radar Symposium – IRS 2006, IEEE Catalog Number: 06EX1284, Krakow, Poland, 24–26 May 2006, pp. 121–124 (2006)

12. Kabakchiev, C., Garvanov, I., Rohling, H.: Netted radar Hough detector in randomly arriving impulse interference. In: Proceedings of the IET International Conference on Radar Systems, RADAR 2007, UK, CD ROM 7a.1, p. 5 (2007)

13. Kabakchiev, C., Garvanov, I., Doukovska, L., Kyovtorov, V., Rohling, H.: Data association algorithm in multiradar system. In: Proceedings of the 2008 IEEE Radar Conference, IEEE Catalog N-08CH37940C, Rome, Italy, pp. 1771–1774 (2008)

14. Hough, P.: Method and means for recognizing complex patterns. US Patent - 3,069,654, 18.XI.1962 (1962)

15. Shishkov, B., Ivanova, K., Verbraeck, A., van Sinderen, M.: Combining context-awareness and data analytics in support of drone technology. In: Shishkov, B., Lazarov, A. (eds) Telecommunications and Remote Sensing. ICTRS 2022. CCIS, vol. 1730, pp. 51–60. Springer, Cham (2022). Doi: https://doi.org/10.1007/978-3-031-23226-8_4

16. Shishkov, B., Branzov, T., Ivanova, K., Verbraeck, A.: Using drones for resilience: a system of systems perspective. In: 10th International Conference on Telecommunications and Remote Sensing (ICTRS 2021). Association for Computing Machinery, New York, NY, USA (2021)

17. Shishkov, B., Hristozov, S., Janssen, M., van den Hoven, J.: Drones in land border missions: benefits and accountability concerns. In: Proceedings of the 6th International Conference on Telecommunications and Remote Sensing (ICTRS 2017). Association for Computing Machinery, New York, NY, USA (2017)

A Web-Based Approach for Traceability in Rule-Based Business Information Systems

Lloyd Rutledge[(✉)], Brent Berghuis, Kelvin Lim, and Mark Soerokromo

Open University of the Netherlands, Heerlen, The Netherlands
`Lloyd.Rutledge@ou.nl`

Abstract. We present how Web standards and technologies can implement traceability in business rules. This enhances transparency of business systems with facilitated integration of system components and data. Such traceability provides end-users access to source documents describing rules and facts that apply to users. This helps both users and developers ensure that how systems work aligns with documentation they derive from. Important features of Web standards include, links to document fragments, and links from not just concepts but assertions about them. In addition, a shared identifier infrastructure enables the integration of these functions of the document and Semantic Webs. We investigate how and to what degree conforming tools for existing standards can implement this communication between these layers. Analysis of how these standards and their applied components work here provides insight into what traceable business rule implementation requires in general. Our approach is to implement an illustrative scenario with standards to demonstrate their utility and provide insights into the issues involved. This scenario comes from the General Data Protection Regulation (GDPR), which related work often uses in examples of business rule implementation.

Keywords: Business rules · Traceability Semantic Web · Web standards

1 Introduction

Transparency in business systems is important for maintaining user trust, and for ensuring that the system functions as intended. Traceability is a fundamental function for supporting transparency. This traceability provides users access to the original documents behind a law or regulation that the system applies to the user, and to online sources for facts that trigger that rule. Traceability is thus important for understanding how a system works, and for gaining the user's trust in both the automated and human components of the system.

However, some business systems cannot provide traceability because they lack either the feature itself or the information it requires. Source documents

© The Author(s), under exclusive license to Springer Nature Switzerland AG 2023
B. Shishkov (Ed.): BMSD 2023, LNBIP 483, pp. 308–318, 2023.
https://doi.org/10.1007/978-3-031-36757-1_22

often provide developers with the requirements from which to program a system. However, developers do not always maintain information about these documents in the resulting systems. It usually requires extra effort by the programmers, and often additional technology, to maintain this source information. There can be several layers to system development, and source document information must be maintained through all of these layers. Finally, not all systems can associate document sources for rules with system components that implement them.

One such layer is analyzing source documents to express their rules in Controlled Natural Languages (CNLs). Using a CNL can help make requirements both understandable by non-technicians and unambiguously programmable. However, in order to maintain traceability when CNL's are involved in system development, document source information needs to be linked to portions of CNL code that define it. Furthermore, this source document information needs to be passed from the CNL encoding into the system itself when the system is created using the CNL. Traceability will not work unless source document information can be passed through CNL code. In this work, we apply Semantics of Business Vocabulary and Business Rules (SBVR) as a CNL for business rules [12]. The standards organization the Object Management Group (OMG) developed SBVR, and much related research applies it.

In related work, research on value-sensitive design emphasizes transparency as a public value, with ethical importance in AI and logic-based systems [5]. On the technical side, requirements traceability is important in software development for linking requirement sources to aspects of their application during development. Murtazina made a Semantic Web ontology to support requirements traceability during development [9]. In our research, we see laws and rule descriptions as these requirement sources, and the links as for end-users instead of developers. Having CNLs be executable helps ensure their correctness, in part by providing automated prototype system generation [3]. The s2o (SBVR to OWL) server converts SBVR into OWL (Web Ontology Language), which makes SBVR executable on Semantic Web software [7].

In earlier work, we presented a reference architecture for traceability (RA4T) as a basis for developing prototypes for business systems [16]. There, we applied Semantic Web technologies to implement the data processing and logical reasoning within these prototypes. These prototypes implemented the basics of business systems, but still without some components required for traceability according to the RA4T. In particular, links from components of implementation back to their encoded in CNL and to their source documentation remained unimplemented. We now show how Semantic Web technologies can implement these necessary components of traceability as well. In particular, we use Semantic Web annotation properties to link from the Semantic Web to the document web. These annotation properties apply text fragment identifiers to enable links to specific portions of these documents without editing the documents themselves. In addition, Semantic Web reification applies here to make not only concepts traceable but also assertions about them. We also show how the Semantic Web presentation interface language Fresnel [14] can present links from this reified logic to its source text.

We use a portion of the EU's legal definition for the GDPR (General Data Protection Regulation) to make an illustrative scenario for how standards can implement traceability. The GDPR's Article 6 about "Lawfulness of processing" applies here in particular [6]. One portion of this article states that processing data is lawful only under certain circumstances, including that the data subject, the person the data is about, gives consent to that processing. Consent is important because it allows organizations to process personal data of an individual, and to ensure the privacy of that person. In this scenario, the user sees that processing of the data object "Joe's likes" is lawful. They click for an explanation, and see the underlying facts that it is Joe's data and that Joe gives consent, and the rule applied: that consented data is lawfully processed. The user can click on a link from that rule to its definition in CNL, and to its original description in the online legal document.

The sections ahead each describe the standards that can implement certain components required for business rule traceability. Applying SBVR and HTML for implementing and integrating SBVR in the broader system is described in Sect. 2. Section 3 shows how to link the Semantic Web's implementation of logic with the World Wide Web implementations for source documents. Section 4 describes the use of reification to identify logical components, along with the use of Fresnel to present the end user with links from these reified logical components to their source documentation. In Sect. 5, we conclude the paper.

2   Hyperlinked SBVR with HTML

Many documents, such as laws, that can act as sources for rule implementation, are online. This makes such documents accessible to systems developed from them. However, usually only small portions of these original documents apply to individual rules. In addition, these document are typically uneditable, making internally defined link destinations for these relevant portions impossible. Here, we apply text fragments [20] as a standards-oriented implementation for non-invasive links. In its simplest form, one implements a text fragment by adding to the end of a source document's URL the characters :~:`text=` followed by the text of the phrase in the source document to link to, or by the starting text and ending text of the phrase separated by a comma. The most commonly used web browsers when given this URL will open the source document and scroll to the location of that text, and highlight that text. Advantages of text fragments for this purpose are their simplicity and widespread implementation.

The text fragment from article 6 of the GDBR that we apply in our scenario reads "lawful only if and to the extent that at least one of the following applies: a. the data subject has given consent". The text fragment URL that locates it is:

```
https://gdpr.eu/article-6-how-to-process-personal-data-legally#:~:
text=lawful,consent
```

This is a rather rudimentary solution that relies on the identifying text being unique in the document. The standard XLink provides much more functionality for non-invasive unique identification of text fragments of documents [4]. However, no current software supports XLink in general-purpose XML. Another challenge for legal text fragment identification is versions of laws that change over time. Ideally, rule traceability links go to the relevant text of the current version of the legal document, even if the system was developed during an earlier version of that law. The solution here lies mostly in the forming of versioned laws and legal documents, which we handle as outside the scope of this work.

While several CNLs for business rules exist and are used in practice, Semantics of Business Vocabulary and Business Rules (SBVR) [12] is the most formally standardized, and is widely applied in research, so we adopt it here. There is an XML Schema for SBVR [11]. Applying this XML Schema here would provide more standardized, enforced structure to the SBVR file, to help ensure its validity. CSS could make this XML appear as its equivalent in HTML (Hyper-Text Markup Language) on a Web browser. However, CSS cannot enable user-navigable hyperlinks in non-HTML XML documents.

The Web Annotation Data Model (WADM) encodes annotations to source Web documents are non-invasive [21]. WADM is an export format for the legal text annotation software iKnow Cognitation [2], which then facilitates editing these annotations further into a CNL similar to SBVR. This standard uses URLs to link "targets" of the annotations with annotations themselves, which WADM can also link to with URLs. If applied here, the targets would be passages of legal text, or other document sources for business rules, and the annotations could be links to fragments of SBVR.

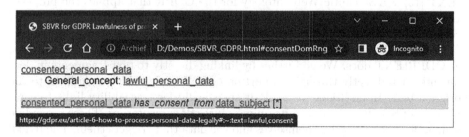

Fig. 1. A web browser display of the SBVR for the consent scenario, with mouse over on the traceability link showing its source document web address.

We apply here a simpler approach than XML or WADM: the use of HTML for presenting the SBVR code. This HTML displays SBVR code in web browsers and enables both the ingoing links from the system interface and outgoing links to the source documentation. When traversing such a link, it helps if the user can see the text fragments on both sides: the selected CNL portion, and the phrase in the source document that it defines. This clarifies to the end user which text in the source document is relevant for the rule that was just applied in their session with the system. Figure 1 shows a browser display for the SBVR for the GDPR scenario, with a traceability link going back to the source document's text fragment. This SBVR code states that the SBVR concept, or class or set, of lawful_personal_data generalizes the concept of consented_personal_data. This means that if data is consented, then it is also lawful. The code also states that the SBVR verb, or relation, called has_consent_from, goes from a consented_personal_data to a data_subject. Therefore, if something starts a has_consent_from relation, then it must be consented_personal_data.

Software exists for directly converting SBVR and other CNLs into executable business system code. For example, s2o (SBVR to OWL) converts SBVR into Semantic Web code [7]. In our approach, the text displayed in a browser for this HTML code can be feed into current converters such as s2o. However, this approach requires new software that passes the SBVR and document source links onward into the implementation. The next section shows how a Semantic Web implementation can encode these links, and thus what the output of such a conversion would be.

3   Linking the Semantic and Document Webs with rdfs:isDefinedBy Subproperties

To link from resources on the Semantic Web to HTML document content, rdfs:isDefinedBy [19] is an obvious choice. This RDFS property links a resource on the Semantic Web to a web resource that defines its meaning. The RDFS specification suggests that it links to Semantic Web code for defining a resource, but then explicitly allows for displayable content as well. GDPR-tEXT [13] is a Semantic Web ontology for the GDPR that applies the property rdfs:isDefinedBy. It assigns an online textual legal document to its ontological components with rdfs:isDefinedBy.

Here, we propose applying rdfs:isDefinedBy to link to document sources, as GDPRtEXT does. We go further by linking directly to text fragments in documents, or indirectly through its portion of CNL code, which then links to the original text. In addition, we apply it specifically for traceability links to components of SBVR code and to its online source documentation. These are online sources for both the rules themselves and the data that triggers them. The RA4T proposes two types of traceability link endpoints: one goes to CNL code, and the other goes all the way back to source documentations. Because these are two types of links for traceability in the RA4T, we propose adding two subproperties of rdfs:isDefinedBy for them: ra4t:sourceCNL and ra4t:sourceText.

Here, we convert SBVR to OWL with the s2o converter [7]. This scenario's SBVR code applying concept generalization is converted to OWL as consented_personal_data being a subclass of lawful_personal_data. In addition, s2o creates the property has_consent_from__data_subject with an RDFS domain of consented_personal_data and a range of data_subject.

This work uses the Semantic Web ontology editor software Protégé [10] to make displays that demonstrate the execution of Semantic Web logic in our scenario. Figure 2 shows a portion of an RDF file that generates Protégé displays for our illustrative scenario from the GDPR. It includes RDFS and OWL code for defining `ra4t:sourceCNL` and `ra4t:sourceText` as subproperties of `rdfs:isDefinedBy`. This RDF file also imports the OWL file that s2o generates from the SBVR code in Fig. 1. Test data also appears in this RDF: a data subject Joe, and his data about what he likes on social media, and that he gives consent for processing that data. This file also applies `rdfs:isDefinedBy` to assign the URL in Fig. 1 as the source for the property `has_consent_from__data_subject`.

```
ra4t:sourceCNL  rdfs:subPropertyOf rdfs:isDefinedBy .
ra4t:sourceText rdfs:subPropertyOf rdfs:isDefinedBy .
<ns:s2o#has_consent_from__data_subject>
  ra4t:sourceCNL  "file:///D:/Demos/SBVR_GDPR.html#consentDomRng" ;
  ra4t:sourceText "https://gdpr.eu/article-6-how-to-process-personal-data-
  legally#:~:text=lawful,consent" .
:Joe rdf:type <ns:s2o#data_subject> .
:JoesLikes <ns:s2o#has_consent_from__data_subject> :Joe .
```

Fig. 2. RDF code for the GDPR consent scenario.

Figure 3 shows a Protégé explanation box for the GDPR scenario. It shows the data and logic behind this conclusion. It has a link to another Protégé interface component with data about that rule. Opening this URL in a browser displays the corresponding component in the SBVR HTML file.

Here, a DL query for members of the class `lawful_personal_data` shows `JoesLikes` as an inferred member. Clicking on the question mark icon next to the listing of `JoesLikes` triggers the pop up of the explanation box for that inference. What the given triples mean is that Joe has given consent for the likes. This explanation box shows the logical, ontological components that apply here, which includes those that s2o generates from this scenario's SBVR code. The class `consented_personal_data` is a subclass of `lawful_personal_data`. The semantics behind this are that consent is one way to make data lawful to use. This is similar to how GDPRtEXT's `GivenConsent` class is a subclass of `LawfulBasisForProcessing`. The corresponding port of the data model in Privacy as a Service (PraaS), on the other hand, assigns consent status as a property of an information unit instead of as a subclass [15]. Our scenario's property `has_consent_from__data_subject` has `consented_personal_data` as its domain. This causes any assignment of the property to data to infer that that data has consent, which the subclass relation above then infers that it is lawful. Therefore, it is lawful to process Joe's likes.

4   Fresnel for Presenting Traceability Links for Assertions

The previous section shows how current Semantic Web software such a Protégé can support traceability links for subjects, or resources. Our example assigns

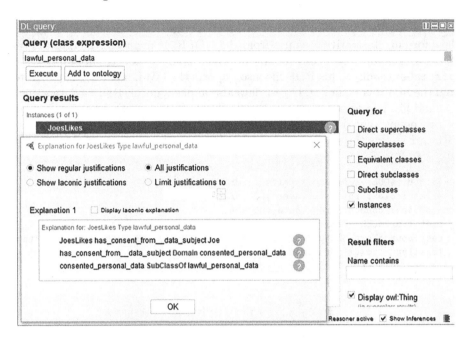

Fig. 3. A Protégé explanation display for the GPDR scenario.

traceability links to a property, which this code treats as a single resource on the Semantic Web. Here, the `ra4t:sourceCNL` annotates the property `has_consent_from__data_subject`, as the code in Fig. 2 shows. This approach can also provide origins for other properties, as well as classes. However, triples also define ontological components on the Semantic Web. A relevant triple in our example is the domain assignment, which is a more specific implementation of the course CNL and text. Reification on the Semantic Web is the annotation of entire triples, and can thus assign traceability properties to this domain triple. We propose here that one can apply the RA4T subproperties of `rdfs:isDefinedBy` to not just resources but also to triples by using reification. However, reification has relatively little targetting implentation in current software.

Fresnel defines the conversion of Semantic Web information from a given ontology to HTML displays for interaction with a user, in the form of a semantic browser [14]. As such, it provides a general model for presenting Semantic Web data to end users. Fresnel focuses on the presentation of data regarding single resources. This presentation is typically in the form of a two-column table showing the predicates and objects of those triples, similar to infoboxes on Wikipedia.

Transparent Fresnel is a proposed extension to Fresnel to support reification [17]. It does so by adding to Fresnel's box-based presentation model a "reify" box for information about a whole triple, after the boxes for the property and then objects of the triple. That previous work then applies it to emulate the links that lead to Protégé's explanation boxes, such as in Fig. 3. There, a Fresnel-defined stylesheet put the text "(?)" in the reify box next to each inferred triple's display and gives it a link to that triple's explanation display. In this work, we propose adapting this technique for traceability links.

Figure 4 has RDF code with reification that assigns the CNL source to the triple instead of just the property for our GDPR illustrative scenario. It uses the standard RDF properties for making a reified statement with its triple components, along with metadata triples about it. For brevity, we assign it as a blank node, without its own identifier. This is the standards-based representation of the assignment of the CNL link to this ontological triple. The next step is a standards-based presentation of this link.

```
[ rdf:type rdf:Statement ;
  rdf:subject    ns:s2o#consented_personal_data ;
  rdf:predicate ns:s2o#has_consent_from__data_subject ;
  rdf:object    ns:s2o#data_subject ;
  ra4t:sourceText "https://gdpr.eu/article-6-how-to-process-personal-data-
  legally#:~:text=lawful,consent" ]
```

Fig. 4. RDF code for GDPR consent scenario, which assigns a traceability link to a whole triple with reification.

Figure 5 shows our Transparent Fresnel code that provides a link from a triple to its document source. It defines a Fresnel format, which describes how to format, or present, the link. The SPARQL query of its `transfr:reifyFormatDomain` property looks for assignments of `ra4t:sourceText` to the reified triple. If it finds one, this format places the text "[#]" next to the triple's display, with a link from it to the URL in `ra4t:sourceText`. Clicking that link presents the equivalent of what Fig. 1 shows. Here we see the need for reification to assign the proper traceability provenance to the ontological triple. We also see how Fresnel with reification enables presentation of this traceability link to the user. Minor adaptations to the code in Fig. 5 could link to the source CNL code instead.

```
:traceLinkFormat rdf:type fresnel:Format ;
  transfr:reifyFormatDomain """ SELECT ?traceLink WHERE {
    ?reification a rdf:statement ; ra4t:sourceText  ?traceLink ;
    rdf:subject    $thisSubject   ; rdf:predicate $thisPredicate ;
    rdf:object    $thisObject   . }"""^^fresnel:sparqlSelector ;
  transfr:reifyLabel "[#]"^^xsd:string .
```

Fig. 5. Fresnel code linking to the CNL code from the reified triple that encodes it.

5   Conclusion

We presented how to make business rules traceable in Web-based information systems. This implementation involves text fragment IDs for linking to online document components, reification for linking from assertions of facts and logic, and the shared hyperlink infrastructure joining the document and Semantic Webs. HTML applies to giving CNL code for business rules outgoing links to source documents as well as incoming links for its implementation in an information system. New Semantic Web annotation properties link data and logic in the system to both their human-readable CNL and their original document sources. Finally, we showed how Fresnel can model the presentation of access to document sources for entire assertions about facts and logic to end users. Altogether, this work described how standards can implement the full circle of identifying and communicating the components involved in business rule traceability.

We presented these techniques with a single, simple scenario. Future work could evaluate these techniques more extensively with more, and more elaborate, scenarios that involve a wider variety of SBVR and Semantic Web constructs. SBVR conversion software could process the HTML encoding of SBVR to output the traceability links along within the converted Semantic Web code. The existing, limited implementations of Fresnel such as RuleStyle [17] could be extended to support the traceability example code presented here. Such converter and Fresnel software would test the programming feasibility of this approach, and enable faster and more extensive evaluations of the general approach.

Acknowledgments. This work comes from the Master's Theses in the Traceable Rules Thesis Circle in the BPMIT (Business Process Management and Information Technology) Master's program at the Open University of the Netherlands [1,8,18,22]. Ella Roubtsova was the co-supervisor for the group and provided important feedback on their research.

References

1. Berghuis, B.: Enabling business rule traceability as guidance to regulation origination in finance. Master's thesis, Open University of the Netherlands, Heerlen, The Netherlands (2022)
2. Bulles, J., Cartigny, B., Bollen, P.: Analyzing the new 2019 Dutch environment and planning act. In: Debruyne, C., et al. (eds.) OTM 2017. LNCS, vol. 10697, pp. 163–172. Springer, Cham (2018). https://doi.org/10.1007/978-3-319-73805-5_17
3. Colombo, C., Grech, J.P., Pace, G.J.: A controlled natural language for business intelligence monitoring. In: Biemann, C., Handschuh, S., Freitas, A., Meziane, F., Métais, E. (eds.) Natural Language Processing and Information Systems, pp. 300–306. Springer International Publishing, Cham (2015). https://doi.org/10.1007/978-3-319-19581-0_27
4. DeRose, S.J., Maler, E., Orchard, D., Walsh, N.: XML Linking Language (XLink) Version 1.1. Tech. Rep. (3 2010)

5. Dexe, J., Franke, U., Nöu, A.A., Rad, A.: Towards increased transparency with value sensitive design. In: Degen, H., Reinerman-Jones, L. (eds.) Artificial Intelligence in HCI, pp. 3–15. Springer International Publishing, Cham (2020). https://doi.org/10.1007/978-3-030-50334-5_1
6. European Union: general data protection regulation (GDPR) art. 6 GDPR lawfulness of processing (2018). https://gdpr.eu/article-6-how-to-process-personal-data-legally
7. Karpovič, J., Kriščiūnienė, G., Ablonskis, L., Nemuraitė, L.: The comprehensive mapping of semantics of business vocabulary and business rules (SBVR) to OWL 2 ontologies. Inf. Technol. Control **43**(4) (2014)
8. Lim, K.C.: Providing traceability of the exception in business rules for the privacy domain. Master's thesis, Open University of the Netherlands, Heerlen, The Netherlands (2023)
9. Murtazina, M., Avdeenko, T.: An ontology-based approach to support for requirements traceability in agile development. Procedia Comput. Sci. **150**, 628–635 (2019). In: Proceedings of the 13th International Symposium "Intelligent Systems 2018" (INTELS'18), 22–24 October, 2018, St. Petersburg, Russia
10. Musen, M.A., Protégé, T.: The Protégé Project: a look back and a look forward. AI Matters **1**(4), 4–12 (2015)
11. Object Management Group: SBVR XML Schema in terms of XMI (2016)
12. Object Management Group: semantics of business vocabulary and business rules (SBVR) (2016)
13. Pandit, H.J., Fatema, K., O'Sullivan, D., Lewis, D.: GDPRtEXT GDPR as a linked data resource. In: Gangemi, A., et al. (eds.) The Semantic Web, pp. 481–495. Springer International Publishing, Cham (2018). https://doi.org/10.1007/978-3-319-93417-4_31
14. Pietriga, E., Bizer, C., Karger, D., Lee, R.: Fresnel: a browser-independent presentation vocabulary for RDF. In: Cruz, I., et al. (eds.) ISWC 2006. LNCS, vol. 4273, pp. 158–171. Springer, Heidelberg (2006). https://doi.org/10.1007/11926078_12
15. Roubtsova, E., Bosua, R.: Privacy as a Service (PraaS): a conceptual model of GDPR to construct privacy services. In: Shishkov, B. (ed.) BMSD 2021. LNBIP, vol. 422, pp. 170–189. Springer, Cham (2021). https://doi.org/10.1007/978-3-030-79976-2_10
16. Rutledge, L., Corbijn, J., Cuijpers, B., Wondal, L.: Rapid prototyping of business rule-based systems with controlled natural language and semantic web software. In: Shishkov, B. (ed.) 12th International Symposium on Business Modeling and Software Design (BMSD2022). Lecture Notes in Business Information Processing, vol. 453, pp. 3–20. Springer International Publishing AG (Jul 2022). https://doi.org/10.1007/978-3-031-11510-3_1
17. Rutledge, L., Mellema, P., Pietersma, T., Joosten, S.: Displaying triple provenance with extensions to the Fresnel vocabulary for semantic browsers. In: Proceedings of the Sixth International Workshop on the Visualization and Interaction for Ontologies and Linked Data. CEUR Workshop Proceedings, vol. 3023, pp. 103–114. CEUR-WS.org (Oct 2021)
18. Soerokromo, M.: Business Rule Traceability als hulpmiddel bij softwareontwikkeling in de justitiële context. Master's thesis, Open University of the Netherlands, Heerlen, The Netherlands (2022)
19. The World Wide Web Consortium (W3C): RDF Schema 1.1 W3C recommendation 25 February (2014). https://www.w3.org/TR/rdf-schema/
20. The World Wide Web Consortium (W3C): text fragments. https://wicg.github.io/scroll-to-text-fragment/

21. The World Wide Web Consortium (W3C): web annotation data model. https:// www.w3.org/TR/annotation-model/
22. de Warle, A.H.: Providing traceability in business rules to customers of a commercial organisation. Master's thesis, Open University of the Netherlands, Heerlen, The Netherlands (2023)

A Conceptual Model for the Selection of Methods for Software Engineering Process Improvement

Tiago Amorim$^{(\boxtimes)}$ and Andreas Vogelsang

University of Cologne, Cologne, Germany
amorim@cs.uni-koeln.de

Abstract. One way of improving the efficiency of system development is through the adoption of new methods. These, upon adoption, can provide the development team with the capabilities to address the current challenges. Once a team decides to follow this path, selecting which methods to adopt is a task ahead. The state-of-the-art provides a plethora of options. The criteria should be choosing methods yielding the highest net benefit towards the adoption goal. Many criteria influence the assessment of methods' value. Knowing which ones are relevant and how they are related is essential to complete this task with excellence. In this paper, we propose a conceptual model describing elements of the decision-making process when selecting software engineering methods to be adopted by development teams. We aim to make explicit much of the knowledge involved in this process, i.e., mechanisms and influencing factors, to foster proper value assessment of methods. For researchers, our work can serve as guidelines to describe methods, for the industry, the model allows the comparison of assessment methods and better-motivated business plans.

Keywords: Process improvement · Decision-making · Conceptual model

1 Introduction

As technology evolves, development teams face problems with the increasing complexity of software-intensive systems. New functionalities are replicated by market competitors, which soon become a commodity, pushing teams to deliver in less time to gain competitive advantage, and nevertheless with top quality. All this must be addressed at a global-dictated market-compatible cost that shrinks at every new development cycle.

One solution to the aforementioned problems is the replacement of development methods with more appropriate ones. The software engineering community has produced many methods to address most current challenges [9]. Thus, teams must select methods yielding the most significant returns toward alleviating their problems.

However, the constructs and their relations relevant to this type of analysis are not explicit. Usually, teams must infer method suitability in an ad-hoc manner (e.g., comparing the contextual characteristics of their teams and needs to

© The Author(s), under exclusive license to Springer Nature Switzerland AG 2023
B. Shishkov (Ed.): BMSD 2023, LNBIP 483, pp. 319–329, 2023.
https://doi.org/10.1007/978-3-031-36757-1_23

eventual case studies provided). Missing proper appraisal can cloud the decision-making process. Consequences range from the inability to replicate the rationale to selecting inappropriate methods. The importance of alignment with the team's adoption goal is emphasized in a report released by the Project Management Institute (PMI) [1]. Projects and programs aligned with a team's strategy are completed successfully more often than misaligned projects (77% vs. 56%). At the same time, only 60% of strategic initiatives meet their original goals and business intent. The report states that most executives admit a disconnection between strategy formulation and implementation [19].

In previous work, we have studied change management in software engineering process adoption and improvement. First, we investigated the forces felt by stakeholders that play a role in the decision to undergo a process improvement endeavor [25]. Later we studied strategies and best practices that increase the success of the endeavor [5]. And finally, we devised an approach to prioritize candidates according to the adoption goal and the development team's context [4]. In this work, we expand the operationalization of strategic goals with a conceptual model bearing relations and properties (e.g., associated sacrifices, environment's context) not addressed by our previous studies while keeping semantic similarity.

The contribution of this paper is a conceptual model for selecting methods to be adopted by software development teams. Conceptual models are schematic descriptions of a phenomenon. They explicitly represent constructs, activities, properties, and relations within a specific problem domain in a reasonably complete manner [23]. We find two issues specially relevant: proper association of process improvement goals with the candidate methods and their contextual suitability towards achieving the defined goal. Additionally, related sacrifices must be considered to find methods bringing the best net benefit (i.e., benefits minus sacrifices). The model can improve the interoperability of methods that function at different granularity levels (i.e., vertically related), or the same level (i.e., horizontally related) through semantic interpretation of the languages' constructs [21]. Moreover, it can serve as a reference model to assess modeling approaches regarding the selection of methods based on value.

The remainder of the current paper is structured as follows: Sect. 2 describes the relevant theories backing up the development of the conceptual model. Section 3 presents the approach. Section 4 provides a small example to illustrate the model elements. In Sect. 5, we discuss the model and its implication for industry and research, and Sect. 6 brings the concluding remarks.

2   Background

2.1   Relevant Theories

The perception of value results from a conceptualization of the object being assessed in terms of a desired end, i.e., whether the object's qualities allows the agent assessing its value to fulfill an end [20]. Thus, different agents will assess different values to the same object according to their goals, i.e., value is a relational and emergent characteristic. Additionally, the definition of the goal and the benefit harvested from the qualities is context-dependent [6]. Value is composed not only of benefits but the relation of benefits and the associated sacrifices involved in acquiring and using the object, i.e., the net benefit. This value theory underpins the model proposed in this paper.

Process improvement initiatives aim at selecting and implementing new methods. These initiatives are guided by goals that are strongly related to context [3], either because there is a need to change the status quo (e.g., become market leader, improve code quality) or to keep it as it is (e.g., maintain the market share). Thus, properly assessing the value of candidate methods allows for a higher goal achievement rate.

2.2   Related Work

The Business Motivation Model (BMM) [17] aims to model why an enterprise chooses a particular approach for its business activities. The model achieves this through two elements, namely "ends" and "means." The former is a placeholder for the goal or objective an enterprise wishes to achieve. The latter describes ways of attaining those ends (e.g., tactics, strategies), and directives from the organization or the business. Since the model focuses on the enterprise, it has elements to define the organization's Vision and Mission. Our model focuses on the method adoption goals of a smaller organization unit, namely the development team. The granularity level that this model is represented is the same as our approach.

Papatheocharous et al. created a taxonomy to document architectural decisions, the GRADE taxonomy [18]. Five dimensions for architecture decision-making were defined: goal, roles, assets, decision methods and criteria, and environment. The authors claim that the knowledge they provide is important for replicating successful architectural decisions or avoiding inefficient ones. Since their contribution is limited to a taxonomy, the relations between elements are out of scope. Additionally, they only consider the environment context.

Andersson et al. [6] propose an ontology of value ascription for enterprise modeling focusing on economic resources. Sales et al. [22] extended the previous approach to value proposition (i.e., defines what a company delivers to its customers). In a further work [21], they analyzed the risk and its relation to use value. We extended these works by adapting them to the selection of methods for software engineering process improvement.

On describing attributes to support method selection, Ågerfalk and Wistrand [2] propose including the rationality dimension in describing methods to store the author's values and assumptions about the problem domain upon method creation. It is divided into two kinds of sub-rationale: method prescriptions anchored in goals, referred to as goal rationale, and goals anchored in values, namely value rationale. The author must define a method's value and connection to goals in this approach. A similar reasoning is used in our model, i.e., a method helps to achieve goals. However, the relevant criteria (e.g., contextual characteristics) are only implicitly considered, which requires the method creator to deliver information ad-hoc.

In Gonzalez-Perez et al. [12], the authors propose a goal-based approach to select so-called method fragments. Their approach proposes to model the adoption goal based on prioritizing specific attributes. The authors propose ten attributes grouped into three areas: Product, Project, and Organization. The method fragments are evaluated towards enhancing or deteriorating each attribute using a five-level scale: strongly enhances, enhances, neutral, deteriorates, and strongly deteriorates. Finally, Goal analysis is used to select the set of method fragments that most enhance the prioritized attributes. This approach includes benefits and sacrifices through a scale ranging from negative to positive influence. They use pre-defined attributes to link goals and the method fragments. The relation between elements, although sometimes implicit, is similar to the one described in our model.

Many goal-oriented requirements engineering (GORE) methods have been proposed [14] (e.g., KAOS, i*, Troppos). These focus on goals, sub-goal refinement, soft goals, and requirements generation. Some also provide reasoning techniques to decide between alternatives for goals' refinement. In these approaches, sacrifices, benefits, and context might appear in the refinement. However, these elements are not explicit, thus being considered ad-hoc. Our model promotes these elements to first-class citizens, giving them more importance.

Current approaches from the literature recognize the need to link high-level goals and context with the implementation. However, these relations and relevant elements are sometimes implicit or incomplete, thus, requiring an ad-hoc effort. Once addressed, these shortcomings can foster more successful projects, which we would like to achieve with our model.

3   Proposal

This section describes the conceptual model for selecting methods for software engineering process improvement (CMSM). The selection criteria are based on the net benefits of adopting these methods. The benefits help the team achieve an envisioned future state described by the adoption goal and are composed by the tuple {Adoption goal, Candidate method qualities, Context}. The Candidate method qualities are intrinsic to the method and generate benefits. The Context influences the adoption goal and describes the characteristics of the team, environment (e.g., new regulations need to be followed), project, and product. The Context also influences how the method qualities can contribute to the adoption goal. The team should also consider possible sacrifices for the new method (e.g., running costs). The net benefit of a method is the benefit minus sacrifices, which is the result of the method value assessment. The outcome of the value assessment can be used to compare methods and decide on the ones that better achieve the goal.

We use the Unified Modeling Language (UML) [8] notation to describe the model, which is depicted in Fig. 1. Three labels are used in the model's associations, namely *q dep*, *+q dep*, and *-q dep*. The first characterizes relationships with a qualitative influence on other elements, which can be positive or negative. The second label represents positive qualitative influence. The third label

represents negative influence relationships. For instance, `Sacrifices` has a -*q*
dep relation to the `Assessment relationship` while `Benefits` has a +*q*
dep relationship. `Context` has a *q dep* relationship to *Sacrifices*, meaning it can
have either positive or negative influence.

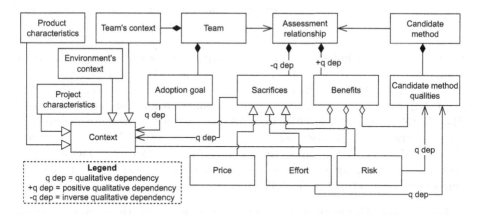

Fig. 1. Conceptual model for the selection of methods (CMSM).

In the following, we describe the model constructs. They are written in ordinary text using `Courier` font. We provide a simple example to illustrate the
concepts in Sect. 4. The goal of the example is to instantiate each of the constructs. Since this is a conceptual model, we do not provide a decision on the
example.

Adoption Goal. describes why a software development team (i.e., `Team`) is undergoing process change based on a future state it wants to achieve. This element is influenced by the `Context` through a qualitative dependency relation.
For instance, the `Team's context` describes capabilities and characteristics
that need to be improved or are lacking in the `Team`, or the `Environment's`
`context` drives the `Team` to reach out to new regulations or develop capabilities
to better compete with other market players.

Team. is the software development team undergoing process change and performing the value assessment in the `Candidate` methods, which is related
through the `Assessment relationship` element. The `Adoption goal`
and the `Team's Context` have a composite relation to the team.

Candidate Method. is the method appraised by the `Team` that might be implemented in the process change endeavor. The term method includes tasks, activities, processes, methodologies, method fragments, and related. The `Candidate`
`method` has a connection to two other elements; it shares a composition relationship with the `Candidate method qualities` and an association with
the `Assessment relationship`.

Candidate Method Qualities. are intrinsic properties of the `Candidate` method that upon adoption help the `Team` to achieve the `Adoption goal`, thus, directly influencing the perception of `Benefits`. Qualities may refer to the kind of products that the method can help build, the project type used to tackle such activities, and the team's characteristics where these projects may take place. They influence `Effort` (i.e., adoption and execution efforts), and can increase or decrease the `Risk` of not achieving the `Adoption goal`.

Context. is the current state of affairs or the interrelated conditions in which something exists or occurs [16]. It influences the method assessment because they change the `Benefits` perception, how the `Adoption goal` is defined, and the `Sacrifices` (e.g., a technically weak team increases effort and risk). The Context is constantly changing and can have a multitude of factors [10], whose relevance is dependent on the `Candidate method qualities` and `Adoption goal`. For instance, team size, a `Team's Context` factor, is relevant when adopting agile methodologies. In our model, Context is divided into four sub-types described in the following:

- **Environment's context** represents everything outside the boundaries of the `Team` and the `Candidate method` that influence the perception of value. For instance, methods compliant with regulations, preferences of stakeholders, requirements from interacting systems, or market competitors who are constantly raising the bar on what is necessary to fulfill the consumers' needs.
- **Team's context** is the team's intrinsic characteristics that influence the perception of value, including the methods the team employs before the method value assessment. For instance, larger teams might value processes and methods that develop a minimal amount of documents, whether smaller teams would praise agile more. Teams having many skillful members might perceive more advanced methods as more beneficial. If the employee turnover is high, documentation-oriented methods might be preferable.
- **Project characteristics** are elements srelated to the project's characteristics the `Team` is currently developing, which can influence the assessment of `Benefits` or be the `Adoption goal`'s reason. For instance, the availability of stakeholders belongs to this element and influences the value of agile methods. Instances of this element are time or budget constraints.
- **Product characteristics** describe the software developed by the team relevant to the method assessment. For instance, a product handling sensitive information would require methods to test its vulnerability. This element encompasses the code and artifacts, such as requirements documents and user manuals.

Benefits. are the perceived positive aspects of adopting the `Candidate` method. They stem from the `Candidate method qualities` within a `Context` that allows a `Team` to achieve an `Adoption goal`. It composes the `Assessment relationship` together with the `Sacrifices`.

Sacrifices. are the resources the Team must concede in order to adopt and exercise the Candidate method. Together with the Benefits, it composes the Assessment relationship. They can be influenced by the Context. Sacrifices can be of three different types (i.e., inheritance relationship):

- **Price.** is the monetary expenditure required to have the Candidate method implemented in a Team. Whatever is needed to have the method running and can be acquired through financial means is covered by this element. A few examples are tool acquisition, investments in training, setting up infrastructure, and licenses in general.
- **Effort.** is the time required to learn, put into use, or acquire the Candidate method. It has a qualitative dependency on the Candidate method qualities and can be of the following types [15] (not represented in the model diagram):
  - **Acquisition effort:** the sacrifice (e.g., time) needed to search for Candidate methods, evaluate and implement the method. For instance, some methods might require lengthy training sessions, thus increasing the associated efforts.
  - **Operations and maintenance efforts:** the maintenance and disposal costs, the time to learn how to use the Candidate method, the wait for it to perform, and monitoring. For instance, static analysis and code inspection aim to improve code quality, but the latter is much more effort-intensive.
  - **Complementary effort:** The time and cost needed to find and acquire complementary products or services associated with the Candidate methods.
- **Risk.** is related to the probability of the sacrifices to be more strenuous than predicted or even not fulfilling the goal at all with the Candidate method, which in both conditions incur on increased Sacrifices (e.g., money wasted). It has a qualitative dependency on the Candidate method qualities and can be classified in the following dimensions [15] (not represented in the model diagram):
  - **Safety:** physical risks related to the application of the Candidate method.
  - **Financial:** the risk that the financial expenditure is higher than usual. A possible kind is fluctuations in the exchange rate.
  - **Selection:** the risk of not choosing the best alternative for fulfilling the Adoption goal. This construct is relevant when informed decisions are not possible.
  - **Delay:** the risk that the Candidate method will take more time than expected to be implemented or not perform on time, thus, incurring opportunity costs. This element is very relevant for time-critical projects.
  - **Functional:** is the risk related to the possibility that the Candidate method will not perform as predicted, now or in the future.

Assessment Relationship. represents the significance attached to a Candidate method by the Team. It is influenced by two opposed elements: the Sacrifices and the Benefits. These two connect to the Assessment relationship through a composite relation, but the former has inverse qualitative dependency while the latter has a positive qualitative dependency.

4   Exemplification

This section provides a small example to illustrate the model elements. For this, let us consider a software development team that needs help with the quality of its code. Thus, they have defined the following Adoption goal: *Improve the code quality.* This team is considering between two Candidate methods, static program analysis, and code review.

Static program analysis consists of programs or algorithms designed to extract facts from another program's source code, which can be used to further understand, evaluate, and modify the associated code base [24]. The Candidate method qualities from this method are:

- Facts from different categories can be extracted from the source code.
- Less knowledge of developers is required to use the tools and find errors.
- Less time is required to perform de analysis.
- False positives can consume time to be investigated.
- Limited reach.

Code review (CRW) is a software quality assurance practice widely employed in open source and commercial software projects to detect defects, transfer knowledge and encourage adherence to coding standards [11]. The Candidate method qualities from this method are:

- Decreases the number of post-release defects.
- Improves the software quality.
- Promotes knowledge transfer.
- Promotes adherence to the project coding standards.
- Requires more experienced developers.

Market competitors of the development team are going for shorter release cycles, and there is a need to keep up, which is a Environment's context fact. Team's context characteristics relevant for assessing value are: personnel experience, since code review requires more experienced developers, team turnover rate, since the benefits of having knowledge transfer are lost once the employee leaves the team. Project characteristics that are relevant is the available time for project development. CRW is effort intensive, and if there is little availability, this can be a problem. Considering the Sacrifices, the Acquisition Effort for Static Program Analysis is slightly higher than the CRW. The Operation Effort is higher for CRW, which can sometimes be 15% of development time [11]. Two elements of Risk type can be elicited from the Candidate method qualities. The CRW has the risk of an over-optimistic evaluation of the time required, incurring a Delay risk. Static Program Analysis might miss the type of errors the team injects, incurring Functional risk.

5   Discussion

The CMSM conceptual description level allows it to be used for the interoperability of methods through semantic interpretation of the languages' constructs. This capability is possible because language integration is a semantic interoperability problem [21], and this can be applied to methods at different levels of granularity (i.e., vertically related, e.g., [12,14]), or at the same level (i.e., horizontally related, e.g., [2,6,17,18,21,22]). The CMSM is developed on level 2 of the Technical Readiness Level [13], which stands for *Technology concept formulated*.

The scope for method selection of the CMSM is the team. Other models consider bigger scope (e.g., organization, enterprise [17]). We understand an organization can have many teams, each requiring different methods. The CMSM considers a single adoption goal since the value assessment is related to how well the method can help achieve the goal. Thus, different goals provide different assessment outcomes. The modeling of goals (i.e., refinement into sub-goals and soft-goals) is not considered by this model. Additionally, the goal influences the relevance of more fine-grained characteristics.

Correctly categorizing the Context element in its sub-types allows the team to perceive what they can change (i.e., Team's context). The organization dictates some team characteristics, which are considered Environment's context since method adoption will not change these characteristics.

The proposed model describes the influencing factors for the method selection based on value. The model is useful for connecting goal models, process models, and value models. Some theories suggest the principle of separating strategy from implementation. Choosing the best method to achieve the strategy is not separate from the strategy itself. Additionally, the lack of traceability with associated rationale increases the risk of implementing the wrong solutions and failing to achieve the strategy. Thus the focus is on the interrelation of the elements that support the task of defining how the goal is to be achieved.

A limitation of our model is the need to use it together with other modeling approaches since it is described at the conceptual level. However, the state-of-the-art provides many modeling approaches that support the elements described in the CMSM. Some elements are more popular than others. Goal, Context, and Risk elements have many modeling approaches [10,14,21], while Price and Effort models are less popular.

Impact for the Industry. The proposed model can help decision-makers to assess the coverage of their process change roadmaps, i.e., whether some detail needs to be considered, thus, enabling more robust business plans.

Impact for Academia. Researchers can use our model to verify whether important aspects regarding adoption guidance based on value and context are considered when proposing new software engineering methods [7]. Additionally, the model stems further philosophical development of the elements and their relations. By providing direction for researchers on what to consider when suggesting new methods, the CMSM can impact method adoption research and stimulate discussion on the completeness of frameworks.

6   Conclusion

Selecting appropriate methods for software engineering process improvement is a complex and important task. By understanding the mechanics of the assessment process, better decisions can be made for effective method adoption. This paper has presented a conceptual model that can help decision-makers in this process by linking adoption goals and contextual characteristics with the benefits of method implementation. The discussion in this paper has highlighted the advantages of bridging the gap between process and decision modeling. Future work can refine the model by assigning attributes and redefining relationships. Another possibility is developing an operationalization method to perform the assessment as described. Finally, the model can be used to integrate different modeling approaches.

Acknowledgments. This work has been supported by the German Ministry of Research and Education (BMBF) within project SpesML (Sysml workbench für die SPES methodik) under grant 01IS20092C.

References

1. Project Management Institute. https://www.pmi.org/. Accessed: 07.05.2023
2. Ågerfalk, P.J., Wistrand, K.: Systems development method rationale: a conceptual framework for analysis. In: Proceedings of the 5th International Conference on Enterprise Information Systems (ICEIS'03) (2003)
3. Ali, R., Dalpiaz, F., Giorgini, P.: A goal-based framework for contextual requirements modeling and analysis. Requirements Eng. **15**(4), 439–458 (2010)
4. Amorim, T., Vogelsang, A., Dias Canedo, E.: Decision support for process maturity improvement in model-based systems engineering. In: Proceedings of the 16th International Conference on Software and System Processes (ICSSP'22) (2022)
5. Amorim, T., Vogelsang, A., Pudlitz, F., Gersing, P., Philipps, J.: Strategies and best practices for model-based systems engineering adoption in embedded systems industry. In: Proceedings of the 41st ACM/IEEE International Conference on Software Engineering: Software Engineering in Practice (ICSE-SEIP 2019) (2019)
6. Andersson, B., Guarino, N., Johannesson, P., Livieri, B.: Towards an ontology of value ascription. In: Proceedings of the 9th International Conference on Formal Ontology in Information Systems (FOIS 2016), vol. 283 (2016)
7. Arora, C., Sabetzadeh, M., Briand, L.C.: An empirical study on the potential usefulness of domain models for completeness checking of requirements. Empir. Softw. Eng. **24**(4), 2509–2539 (2019)
8. Booch, G., Rumbaugh, J., Jacobson, I.: Unified Modeling Language User Guide, The (2nd Edition) (Addison-Wesley Object Technology Series). Addison-Wesley Professional (2005)
9. Bourque, P., Fairley, R.E. (eds.): SWEBOK: Guide to the Software Engineering Body of Knowledge. IEEE Computer Society, Los Alamitos, CA, version 3.0 edn. (2014). https://www.swebok.org/, Accessed: 07.05.2023
10. Clarke, P., O'Connor, R.: The situational factors that affect the software development process: Towards a comprehensive reference framework. Inf. Softw. Technol. **54** (2012)

11. Ebert, F., Castor, F., Novielli, N., Serebrenik, A.: Confusion in code reviews: reasons, impacts, and coping strategies. In: 2019 IEEE 26th International Conference on Software Analysis, Evolution and Reengineering (SANER), pp. 49–60 (2019)
12. Gonzalez-Perez, C., Giorgini, P., Henderson-Sellers, B.: Method construction by goal analysis. In: Information Systems Development, pp. 79–91. Springer, US, Boston (2009)
13. Héder, M.: From nasa to eu: the evolution of the trl scale in public sector innovation. Innov. J. **22**, 1 (2017)
14. Horkoff, J., et al.: Goal-oriented requirements engineering: an extended systematic mapping study. Requirements Eng. **24**(2), 133–160 (2017). https://doi.org/10.1007/s00766-017-0280-z
15. Kambil, A., Ginsberg, A., Bloch, M.: Re-inventing value propositions. NYU Stern School of Business Research Paper Series
16. Merriam-Webster: Context. In: Merriam-Webster.com dictionary (2021). https://www.merriam-webster.com/dictionary/context. Accessed: 07.05.2023
17. Pankowska, M.: Business motivation model for information system architecture development support. J. Softw. Syst. Dev. (2021)
18. Papatheocharous, E., Wnuk, K., Petersen, K., Sentilles, S., Cicchetti, A., Gorschek, T., Shah, S.M.A.: The grade taxonomy for supporting decision-making of asset selection in software-intensive system development. Inf. Softw. Technol. **100**, 1–17 (2018)
19. PMI: PMI's Pulse of the Profession (2017)
20. Zúñiga y Postigo, G.: An ontology of economic objects. Mpra paper, University Library of Munich, Germany (1999)
21. Sales, T.P., Baião, F.A., Guizzardi, G., Almeida, J.P.A., Guarino, N., Mylopoulos, J.: The common ontology of value and risk. In: Proceedings of the 37th International Conference on Conceptual Modeling (ER'18) (2018)
22. Sales, T.P., Guarino, N., Guizzardi, G., Mylopoulos, J.: An ontological analysis of value propositions. In: 2017 IEEE 21st International Enterprise Distributed Object Computing Conference (EDOC), pp. 184–193 (2017)
23. Thalheim, B.: Towards a theory of conceptual modelling. In: Lecture Notes in Computer Science, pp. 45–54. Springer, Heidelberg (2009)
24. Thomson, P.: Static analysis. Commun. ACM **65**(1), 50–54 (2021)
25. Vogelsang, A., Amorim, T., Pudlitz, F., Gersing, P., Philipps, J.: Should I Stay or Should I Go? On Forces that Drive and Prevent MBSE Adoption in the Embedded Systems Industry (2017)

Towards Log-Driven Monitoring of Technical Degradation: An ERP Perspective

Pieter van de Griend[✉], Rob Kusters, and Jos Trienekens

Open University of the Netherlands, Heerlen, The Netherlands
`pieter.vandegriend@ou.nl`

Abstract. Change to business information systems, like enterprise resource planning (ERP) systems, is inevitable. The problem is that the processes degrading these highly complicated systems during their life cycle are poorly understood. To that end, we present an approach that operates as a degradation lens to view technical change data collected from ERP systems. We reconstruct a customization change stream from available log data and investigate structural degradation effects on one designated ERP system codebase in a system landscape. Our results indicate that, contrary to commonly held belief, changes do not maintain the customization in an initial architectural component but tend to evolve across several functionality clusters to evade degradation. Our data suggest that release-driven, complete redesigns of customized parts of ERP systems take place.

Keywords: degradation · structural degradation · ERP system · technical change · architectural evolution

1 Introduction

Enterprise resource planning (ERP) systems are an example of packaged information system software marketed as a commercial off-the-shelf product. ERP systems provide technical support along a considerable range of standard business processes. On the one hand, this explains their high adoption rate by businesses. On the other hand, it also demands that an ERP system changes at the speed of business. To meet that requirement, newly delivered ERP system codebases allow a standard configuration within a functionality bandwidth. Frequently, however, ERP system clients require additional customizations and augment their ERP system codebases accordingly. Proprietary codebase change is a client's responsibility as such technical change often falls outside license agreements with the vendor. As a stream of perpetual changes affects the codebase, it falls upon the clients to manage the consequences of their actions.

Subject to relentless change, the initial quality of an ERP system may degrade to levels where further change can expose the organization to considerable business disturbance risk. The problem is that the process of ERP system

B. Shishkov (Ed.): BMSD 2023, LNBIP 483, pp. 330–339, 2023.
https://doi.org/10.1007/978-3-031-36757-1_24

degradation on these highly complicated systems during operation is not well-understood [10]. This paper aims to demonstrate how, by viewing logged software change process (SWCP) data in a particular way, it becomes possible to obtain insight into degradation process aspects at the go-live phase.

The remainder of the current paper is structured as follows. In Sect. 2, we identify a gap in the business information system literature with respect to degradation. Section 3 develops a view to improve understanding of degrading systems. Section 4 presents the results we obtained by applying this view to 25 data sets. Section 5 discusses finds and concludes on the effectiveness of our approach.

2   Related Work

In general, software does not self-modify. It gets shaped under inevitable contextual influences that drive a business need to formulate functionality modifications. The customized part of the codebase, however, will remain relevant because client-owned processes are core to the respective businesses. Their mere existence is reported to be a major hindrance in ERP projects [14]. Migrating these customizations during the ERP system lifecycle requires sound understanding of their shared functionality [2].

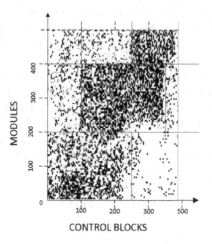

Fig. 1. Belady and Lehman (1985) - binary mapping example of control blocks against modules supporting the identification of functionality groupings [12, p366].

The idea of grouping associated functionality, reaching back to Alexander (1967), is a common approach in systems design [1]. Stegwee (1992) applied the principle when proposing a divide-and-conquer strategy to decide how to cluster functionality in an information system architecture [16]. Belady and Lehman (1985) introduced a practical way of representing software system change in a binary format [12]. By mapping the drift between 'modules' in a codebase against the 'control blocks' of functionality in used system resources under change, they provided diagrams similar to that reproduced in Fig. 1. Being able to recognize these design-theoretical clusters and determine how much drift they display over time suggests measures of system evolution or degradation.

Evolution provides a long-term view of how individual changes aggregate to keep the system relevant. Short-term information system changes, however, may have many causes. Such small-scale changes are classified as perfective, corrective, or adaptive maintenance when performed on individual components [17]. Although code is the primary artifact in the software process, numerous other controls are required to manage risk from degradational processes during the software change process. They may concern requirements, documentation, or test results [13]. A high-quality software development process supports evolution along all these dimensions. Zaidman et al. (2011) proposes to call this phenomenon co-evolution [18]. Two other important co-evolution drivers can be identified. A first driver is due to the collection of test systems instantiated to mitigate business disruption risk due to modification of the production system (PRD) [9]. A second driver is due to codebase synchronization challenges that emerge between the subsequently visited systems in the system landscape [4].

How any competence center, tasked with keeping an ERP system operational, deals with the factors driving degradation, is a question that has received little attention from researchers [3,7]. To reduce this gap in the literature, we developed a way to view structural degradation effects on ERP system architecture due to technical change. We expect this view to support insight into the degradation process. Therefore, we formulated two hypotheses to determine to what extent ERP system degradation can be assessed from change logs. First, we assumed that competence centers would have lost all control of the PRD architecture and maintainability would be badly affected. In this case random graph theory predicts that a so-called Giant Component will emerge in the codebase as ultimately all its objects will become path-connected [15]. Second, as an alternative hypothesis to the worst-case hypothesis, one would expect that codebases converge onto a stable architecture as businesses would endeavor to safeguard the functionality of their key business processes. In this case competence centers would have retained full control of the PRD architecture and its maintainability. To test our hypotheses we apply the developed view.

3   Approach

The view to be developed in this approach will be based on SWCP data. We first introduce relevant terminology, necessary to understand these data. Let the development system instance be the only codebase in the ERP system landscape that allows modification of its objects. Hence to get such modified object versions onto any other system instance will require two things. First, packaging of the modified versions into an entity we will call a container. Second, moving a single container between systems we will call a transport. By migrating container content, transports give rise to a change stream into the destination system. By chronologically ordering the m containers of the change stream, along a horizontal axis, one may map their payload, touching the n objects in the codebase, reflecting the modified part of codebase, along a vertical axis. This operation creates a two-dimensional binary matrix, of n rows and m columns, the so-called object version grid (OVG), consisting of unit and zero cells. We are interested in the changes collectively imported into the PRD system instance. The PRD-OVG provides a high-level expression of the codebase components that were touched by container imports.

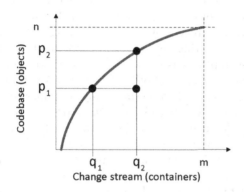

Fig. 2. A small example of an object version grid (OVG).

Figure 2 represents a generic PRD-OVG. Two containers, q_1 and q_2, are highlighted. Container q_1 only touches object p_1 whereas container q_2 touches a set consisting of objects p_1 and p_2, respectively. The red concave curve is the frontier due to the first touched object order and emerges naturally due to the chronological order of the change stream containers.

As outlined above, the data support a replay of recorded SWCP reality. Upon curtailing the changes to codebase customizations and identification of the production system, the PRD-OVG emerges as a tool to study the degradational nature of change into the system where business disruption is immediately felt. We now explain how we wish to interpret patterns concealed in the PRD-OVG by introducing a basic assumption that operates as an axiom in the following.

During development, the container creation phase determines how versions are collectively packaged. On the one hand, this has a practical purpose in that packing will ease release management and transportation across the various system landscape entities during testing before being promoted to production-level code. On the other hand, packaging suggests a functional dependency among the objects. Furthermore, developers and release managers often 'bucket' containers by collecting multiple developments in one transport. This action suggests that there exists a logical relationship between objects. For those reasons we formulate the following basic assumption:

versions packaged in one single container implies
that their objects' functionally belong together

The above statement has an interesting consequence. It can be shown that, as an equivalence relation, it induces a partition on that part of the PRD codebase that the change stream has modified. The resulting equivalence classes will be called domains here. These domains are architectural entities reflecting associated functionality that can be extracted directly from the PRD-OVG. By incrementally traversing the OVG change stream, domains can be used to reflect how object relations in the codebase have developed during change stream container import.

Consider the example of Fig. 2. Upon import of container q_1, a domain d_1 was created, which consists of one single object (p_1). Upon import of container q_2 the initial domain d_1 is extended with object p_2 because container q_2 associates two objects (p_1 and p_2). Other containers may create other domains, depending on how the basic assumptions associates their respective versions. If any of those versions relate to either p_1, p_2 or both, their domains will merge with d_1.

In an OVG it is not possible to permute any container columns in the change stream without risking different codebase status due to the swap. In any OVG, however, it is possible to permute object rows in the code base without any penalty. This OVG property turns out to be quite useful in that it allows us to arrange the vertical dimension into domains as they form under influence of the change stream. The resulting equivalence classes represent independent cores of associated functionality. Mapping the domains onto their containers produces a partition of the change stream. Due to this OVG property it is possible to diagonally decompose the OVG, as is illustrated in Fig. 3 for an example comprising three domains.

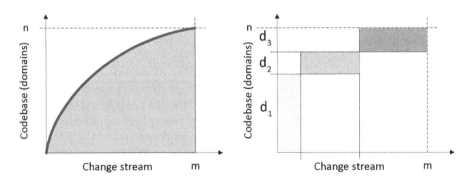

Fig. 3. Example of how the basic assumption induces a diagonal OVG decomposition (left). The three independent domains also partition the change stream (right).

If a domain consists of one single object, we will say it is of unitary type. If a domain consists of two or more objects, we will call it a compound domain. Under the basic assumption, domain types can express the software engineering concepts named coupling and cohesion [6]. Unitary domains reflect the highest degree of cohesion and zero coupling. Compound domains reflect a lower degree of cohesion and a higher degree of coupling than unitary domains. It follows that we must have a means to assess their respective levels.

As the change stream is imported into the PRD system instance, we can record the respective unitary and compound domain counts by means of the symbols K_u and K_c. Let these variables have a unit time-dependency denoted by q that is given by the change stream unit of measure, where $0 \leq q \leq m$. Hence these values can be graphed as curves $K_u(q)$ and $K_c(q)$ and will be named the unitary and compound kappa curve, respectively. As the change stream imports its containers into PRD, domains exhibit behavioral merging quite reminiscent to that encountered in a field called random graph theory and behavior described as 'attachment' [8,11]. The term 'random graph' is known to be misleading as such graphs are not truly random, in general [5]. Their development is conditioned to display preferential attachment, which leads to the emergence of a so-called giant component [15]. This will occur whenever edge selection is conducted from a uniformly distributed edge collection. If, alternatively, the edge selection is from a non-uniform distribution, it will take longer to develop such a giant component, but eventually it will occur provided edges are added faster than nodes to the 'random graph'.

Should graph theory of the uniform preferential type apply, it would predict that a giant component will emerge to dominate the domains [5,8,9,15]. In that case the giant component emergence can be detected by the necessary condition, $K_c(m) = 1$ and $K_u(m) = 0$. This situation is illustrated in the left image of Fig. 4 where $K_u(q)$ is given by the red curve and $K_c(q)$ is given by the blue curve. If the non-uniform preferential attachment type applies, we are not likely to witness the giant component emerging from the PRD-OVG when $q = m$. Direct observation of the PRD-OVG, often with thousands of containers and objects, does not readily yield giant component information although the laws of software evolution suggest that everything will ultimately connect to everything else [6]. Therefore, we formulated a testable null hypothesis for which we checked whether all available PRD-OVG contained a giant component [4]. Our alternative hypothesis tested whether the codebase would converge to a stable architecture.

4   Results

We collected SWCP-generated data sets from 25 SAP system landscapes. An individual data set is said to comprise a case. Per case the SWCP data allows the identification of three key global variable sets. The first variable identifies the system landscape magnitude and life span. Case size ranged from 8 to 154 system instances, whereas case ages ranged from 2 to 10 years. The second variable concerns containers packaging object versions, defining the topology of the system landscape, by delivering the arrows between systems. The third variable concerns transports moving containers between systems and provides the strength of the arrows between system pairs. The global construct provides a local view on change streams that feed into the PRD system.

As all technical change on ERP systems is logged, such data sets can grow quite large. Therefore, we only considered client-driven enhancements. Although customizations are fewer than vendor-driven enhancements, the former still provide a reasonably sized SWCP data subset. The PRD-OVG for a typical case would have more objects than containers, i.e. $m < n$.

Per case we identified the PRD-OVG and subjected it to the basic assumption. The implication of the assumption logically leads to a partition of the modified codebase. The equivalence classes of the partition support the identification of two mutually exclusive domain types. We can enumerate the so-called unitary and compound domain count as a function of the import of the change stream. This produces unitary and compound kappa curves that can be generated at any point in time along the change stream axis. The kappa curves were introduced to detect the emergence of a so-called Giant Component that random graph theory predicts. The typical patterns that our efforts produced over 25 cases, are shown by the right-hand side diagram in Fig. 4.

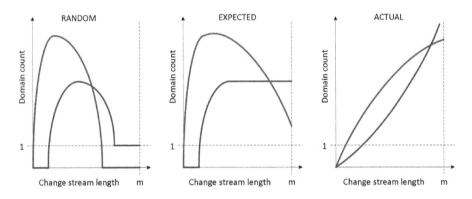

Fig. 4. Random Graph theory predicts the worst-case result, reflected by the leftmost image. The middle image reflects a more reasoned, expected result. The rightmost image shows the actual kappa curve sets extracted from the PRD-OVG. The unitary and compound kappa curves are red and blue, respectively. (Color figure online)

The results offer two immediate observations. First, this view does indeed enable us to obtain insight into the degradation process. Second, the actual curves take on a shape that is very different from the shapes our hypotheses predicted. Clearly, the obtained results demonstrate that the null hypothesis is untenable. The giant component, predicted by random graph theory, does not emerge. The rightmost image shows that its condition, $K_c(q) = 1$ and $K_u(q) = 0$, where $1 \leq q \leq m$, is not satisfied. Neither do the results indicate convergence of the number of compound domains $K_c(q)$. In fact, we see a continuous growth in the number of compound domains. This implies that the alternative hypothesis also cannot be accepted.

5   Discussion and Conclusion

The expected kappa curve shapes probably differ from the actual kappa curve shapes due to OVG dimensions. The OVG dimensions that are most likely to produce the giant component predicted by random graph theory, are those in which the change stream length (measured in containers and denoted by the symbol m) exceeds the cardinality of the touched codebase set (measured in object names and denoted by the symbol n). We say that such an OVG is wide $(m > n)$. If the number of containers in the change stream is less than the number of touched objects in the codebase, we say that such an OVG is narrow $(n > m)$. Evidently, narrow OVG will be more likely to produce compound domains as their average container size, measured in versions, will be higher than the average container size in a wide OVG. All our PRD-OVG were of the narrow type, which would explain the increasing and high K_c values but does not explain the increasing and high K_u values.

Even though the actual kappa curves are quite aligned, both with an increasing trend, the number of unitary domains initially exceeds the number of compound domains. This suggests that systems are first changed on individual objects before larger containers bring compound domains into play. If the changes would have been random, as our null hypothesis suggested, the narrow PRD-OVG should have resulted in considerably less unitary and more compound domains than we have observed. Not only is randomness ruled out, however. The container sizes in all PRD-OVG display a power law distribution. That means the number of containers carrying merely one single version would give rise to a relatively large number of unitary domains, which is exactly what is to be observed. This implies that cohesion remains strong for a considerable part of the system life cycle, but larger releases introduce coupling [6]. The actual kappa curves collective trends appear to be somewhat in line with the expected growth as illustrated for lower q-values of the random and expected kappa curves, at the early stages of the left diagram of Fig. 4. This suggests that the emergence of the giant component is actively avoided during releases.

The SWCP generates an abundance of information from which we have selected a well-defined and highly relevant subset. Although this subset is the most relevant from the client's perspective in terms of responsibility and business-criticality, focussing on one particular instance in the system landscape may not be fully representative for co-evolutionary developments across the entire landscape. Controls to manage architectural evolution risk and preventing PRD code base degradation may have been implemented elsewhere on the system landscape.

This paper presented a lens through which to view changes arriving at a production system in an ERP system landscape. The view was introduced to aid and increase understanding of structural degradation of ERP systems by interpreting technical change log data stemming from the software change process. After reconstructing the change stream targeting the production system from sources scattered across an ERP system landscape, we obtained an object version grid (OVG). Application of a self-evident basic assumption to the PRD-OVG change stream induced an equivalence relation on the touched part of the PRD codebase. The equivalence classes were split into two mutually exclusive types, called unitary domains and compound domains. By counting the respective domain types, so-called kappa curves were produced that displayed significant discrepancies between random, expected and actual behaviour, respectively. This supports the useability of the newly developed view to provide insight into the degradation process. By using the view, the formulated hypotheses were firmly rejected, suggesting that functional cores in the codebase are being rebuilt at every subsequent major release. Further research will address this suggestion.

References

1. Alexander, C.: Notes on the Synthesis of Form. Harvard University Press (1967)
2. Arbuckle, T.: Studying software evolution using artefacts' shared information content. Sci. Comput. Program. **76**, 1078–1097 (2011)
3. Bianchi, A., Caivano, D., Lanubile, F., Visaggio, G.: Evaluating software degradation through entropy. In: Proceedings Seventh International Software Metrics Symposium, pp. 210–219 (2000)
4. Brewer, E.: Towards robust distributed systems. In: Proceedings of the Nineteenth Annual ACM Symposium on Principles of Distributed Computing (2000)
5. Callaway, D., Hopcroft, J., Kleinberg, J., Newman, M., Strogatz, S.: Are randomly grown graphs really random? Physical Review E (2001)
6. Constantine, L., Yourdon, E.: Structured Design: Fundamentals of a Discipline of Computer Program and Systems Design. Pearson Technology Group (1979)
7. Eick, S., Graves, T., Karr, A., Marron, J., Mockus, A.: Does code decay - assessing the evidence from change management data. IEEE Trans. Software Eng. **27**(1), 1–12 (2001)
8. Erdös, P., Rényi, A.: On the evolution of random graphs. Publ. Math. Inst. Hungar. Acad. Sci (1961)
9. Fowler, M., Rice, D., Foemmel, M., Hieatt, E., Mee, R., Stafford, R.: Patterns of Enterprise Application Architecture. Addison Wesley (2002)
10. Herold, S.: An initial study on the association between architectural smells and degradation. In: Software Architecture, pp. 193–201 (2020)
11. Jeong, H., Neda, Z., Barabasi, A.: Measuring preferential attachment in evolving networks. Europhys. Lett. **61**(4), 1–19 (2003)
12. Lehman, M., Belady, L.: Program Evolution - process of software change. Academic Press (1985)
13. Mens, T., Wermelinger, M., Ducasse, S., Demeyer, S., Hirschfeld, R., Jazayeri, M.: Challenges in software evolution. In: Proceedings of the International Workshop on Principles of Software Evolution (IWPSE), pp. 13–22 (2005)
14. Parthasarathy, S., Sharma, S.: Determining erp customization choices using nominal group technique and analytical hierarchy process. Comput. Ind. **65**, 1009–1017 (2014)
15. Pittel, B., Wormald, N.: Counting connected graphs inside-out - series b. J. Combinatorial Theory **93**(2), 127–172 (2005)
16. Stegwee, R.: Division for conquest - decision support for information architecture specification. Groningen theses in economics, management and organization, Rijksuniversiteit Groningen (1992)

17. Swanson, E.: Dimensions of maintenance. In: ICSE'76 Proceedings of the 2nd International Conference on Software Engineering, pp. 492–497 (1976)
18. Zaidman, A., van Rompaey, B., van Deursen, A., Demeyer, S.: Studying the co-evolution of production and test code in open source and industrial developer test processes through repository mining. Empirical Software Engineering (2011)

A Development Example: From Conceptual Specification to OO Specification

Rein Smedinga and Bert de Brock[(✉)]

University of Groningen, Groningen, The Netherlands
{r.smedinga,e.o.de.brock}@rug.nl

Abstract. We illustrate, by using a practical example, how to map a Conceptual Specification (CS) systematically to an OO-implementation, using formal mapping rules or "semi-automatic" guidelines. Special attention will be paid to the "transfer" of constraints from the Conceptual Specification to the software, since programming languages usually lack constructs to express constraints.

We separate Model from View and Controller (MVC pattern) and create a default class diagram (statics/data) and default methods (dynamics/processes) from a CS. Our *enhanced* class diagrams inherit the constraints from the CS, which are subsequently worked out in the OO-specification in a systematic way. We generate pseudo-code such that a programmer in a specific (OO) language can easily translate this into real code.

Keywords: Conceptual Specification · Implementation-Independence · Object-Oriented Mapping · Implementation Design · MVC-Pattern · Guarding Constraints · Façade Pattern

1 Introduction

We illustrate how to develop an information system starting from a conceptual specification to an OO design in a systematic way using formal mapping rules or "semi-automatic" guidelines, as explained in general in [1].

Organization of the Paper. Section 2 illustrates by an example how to give the *statics* in the form of a *Conceptual Data Model* and the *dynamics* in the form of *textual* or *graphical SSDs* (*System Sequence Descriptions*). Together this forms the so-called Conceptual Specification (CS). Section 3 splits our (black box) system into a kernel and an interface, using the general MVC software design pattern. Finally, Sects. 4–7 show how to map a conceptual specification to an OO specification, via a so-called *Enhanced* Class Diagram, i.e., a class diagram that includes the constraints inherited from the CS (Sect. 4.1), and via grey box SSDs (Sect. 5) to white box SSDs (Sect. 6). Section 4.2 illustrates the handling of constraints, while Sect. 4.3 introduces so-called *managers*, in order to make the coupling between interface and model as small as possible.

B. Shishkov (Ed.): BMSD 2023, LNBIP 483, pp. 340–351, 2023.
https://doi.org/10.1007/978-3-031-36757-1_25

2 Conceptual Specification

A Conceptual Data Model can be partly depicted by a *graph* of which each *node* represents a <u>concept</u> and each *arrow* represents a <u>reference</u> relevant for the application at hand. Each node also enumerates the relevant <u>properties</u> of that concept.

2.1 Conceptual Data Model

Our running example concerns Courses with their Exams, Lecturers with their Teaching Activities, and Students with their Exam Enrolments and Exam Results (see Fig. 1). A lecturer can have several teaching activities for several courses and several lecturers can be involved in the same course. A student can enrol for several exams and an exam can have several enrolled students. There can be at most 1 result per exam enrolment. Furthermore, a phone number of a student *may be* known (but not necessarily) and a lecturer has a unique Employee ID and *maybe* a Social Security Number (SSN), which will be unique too in that case.

   In general, <u>optionality</u>, i.e. no value required for a property, is indicated by the brackets '[' and ']'. A <u>referencing property</u> is indicated by a '^' in front. A <u>uniqueness constraint</u> is indicated by a '!' in front of all properties involved. Another uniqueness constraint within the same concept is indicated by a '%' in front of the properties involved.

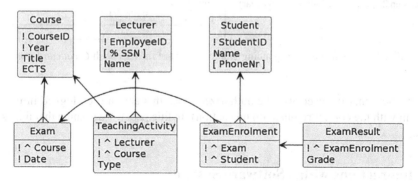

Fig. 1. Conceptual Data Model of our running example

2.2 System Sequence Descriptions

As an example of a *textual* and similar *graphical* SSD, we work out the elementary user wish *Create an Exam* in Fig. 2. Given our data model (Fig. 1), the *parameterized* user wish will be:

Create an Exam with a given date for a given course

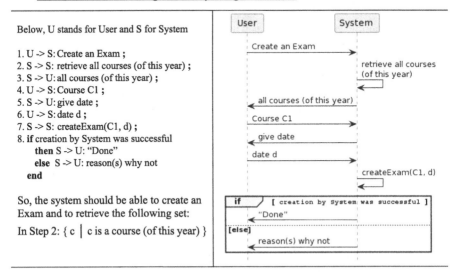

Below, U stands for User and S for System

1. U -> S: Create an Exam ;
2. S -> S: retrieve all courses (of this year) ;
3. S -> U: all courses (of this year) ;
4. U -> S: Course C1 ;
5. S -> U: give date ;
6. U -> S: date d ;
7. S -> S: createExam(C1, d) ;
8. **if** creation by System was successful
   then S -> U: "Done"
   else S -> U: reason(s) why not
   end

So, the system should be able to create an Exam and to retrieve the following set:

In Step 2: { c | c is a course (of this year) }

Fig. 2. Textual and corresponding graphical SSD of the user wish *Create an Exam*

We note that the user must be authorized to do this action (i.e., logged in into the system with the correct rights to do this action). In this paper, we assume that this is the case.

3   Interactions with a Software System

In the next sections, we go from conceptual specification to (software) system design. Following the MVC software design pattern, the *system* (as a 'black box') can be split into an *interface* and a *kernel*, becoming a 'grey box'.

In the next picture, we see the typical "analysis-SSD" transforming into the "design-SSD" with the system depicted as a grey box.

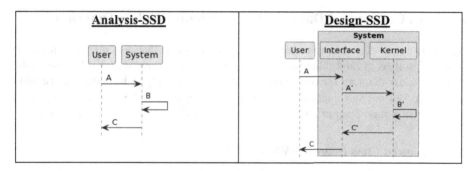

Explanation: In this general approach, B' expresses what the kernel must do to realize B. Preferably, B' is a method call or (stored) procedure call in the kernel's language. A' could simply be *do B'*, since the interface is supposed to address the kernel in the kernel's language. Finally, C' could be some machine-readable code, for instance, an (error) code with some parameters or a query-result expressed in some OO language. The interface must convert it into a user-readable message C and send it to the user. The user can be a human being or a system.

Sometimes the interface can handle things itself, e.g., checking whether a required property is indeed filled in. In that case, the arrows A', B', and C' above are replaced by an arrow B from Interface to Interface.

For our example *Create an Exam*, the split in an *interface* and *kernel* results in Fig. 3.

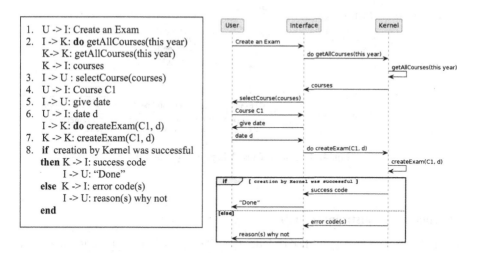

Fig. 3. Textual and graphical Design-SSD for the user wish *Create an Exam*

4 From Conceptual Data Model to Enhanced Class Diagram

By an *enhanced* class diagram, we mean a class diagram that also mentions the constraints specified in (and inherited from) the Conceptual Data Model. §4.1 shows the enhanced class diagram for our running example. §4.2 explains how these constraints can be worked out systematically into an OO-specification. §4.3 introduces so-called *managers* in a class diagram, meant to manage the different objects within a class.

4.1 Enhanced Class Diagram (V0.1)

This section describes how to get a 'Version 0.1' of a Class Diagram. Such a class diagram is actually an *enhanced* class diagram: It inherits the constraints from the CS.

Mapping a Conceptual Data Model to a 'Version 0.1' of a Class Diagram is simple:

- Each concept becomes a *class*
- Each property of a concept becomes an *attribute* in that class
- Each reference becomes a link to an instance of a class
- Each class has a third component, meant for its *methods* (or *operations*), which is initially 'empty'. Methods are used to implement the interactions with the system, e.g., those described earlier in SSDs.

Figure 4 shows the result for our running example.

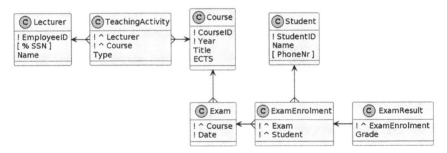

Fig. 4. Enhanced Class Diagram (Version 0.1)

4.2 Handling Constraints (V0.2)

When mapping a Conceptual Data Model to a Class Diagram, we have to incorporate constraints checking in our mappings. While 4th generation languages such as SQL have all kinds of language constructs to specify and check constraints, programming languages typically lack such constructs. Simple (datatype) constraints, such as Integer, String, and maybe enumeration types, can usually be expressed in the target programming language itself, using its datatypes. But, in general, this does not hold for all constraints. That implies that a straightforward modification statement must become a *conditional* modification statement. In particular, we will work out the important constraints *non-optionality, uniqueness,* and *referential* constraints.

For our running example, Table 1 gives the number of constraints per concept in case of *adding* or *deleting* an object (using the abbreviations Req: Required value, Uni: Uniqueness constraint, Ref out: Reference outgoing, Ref in: Reference incoming):

Table 1. Number of constraints per concept and type of modification

Modification → ↓ Concept	Adding				Deleting
	Req	Uni	Ref out	Total	Ref in
Student	2	1	0	3	1
Lecturer	2	2	0	4	1
Course	4	1	0	5	2
Teaching Activity	3	1	2	6	0
Exam	2	1	1	4	1
Exam Enrolment	2	1	2	5	1
Exam Result	2	1	1	4	0
Total	**17**	**8**	**6**	**31**	**6**

Applying [1], which explains in general how to construct conditional modifications, we define the following *conditionally Create* method for an Exam in our example (where ec stands for *error count* and c and d for the corresponding Course and date):

```
DEFINE conditionallyCreateExam(c, d) AS
  S -> S: ec := 0 ;
  if c = null then S -> S: ec := ec + 1;   S -> U: 'You should fill in the Course. ' end ;
  if d = null then S -> S: ec := ec + 1;   S -> U: 'You should fill in the Date. ' end ;
  if the combination of c and d already occurs in Exam
    then  S -> S: ec := ec + 1;
              S -> U: 'An Exam with that Course-Date combination already exists. ' end ;
  if course c is not known by the system
    then  S -> S: ec := ec + 1;
              S -> U: 'That Course is unknown to the system. ' end;
  if ec = 0
    then  S -> S: createExam(c, d) ;
              S -> U: 'The modification has been completed successfully. '
    else  S -> U: 'The modification could not be completed since there were errors. '
  end
END
```

The corresponding graphical SSD follows easily, see [2]. See Fig. 5 for the result.

We note that we start a class name and an attribute name with a capital, and an object name, a parameter, and a variable with a small letter.

The textual SSD for conditionally updating an *Exam e* with a new date d is similar to the textual SSD for conditionally *creating* an exam:

```
DEFINE conditionallyUpdateExam(e, d) AS
  S -> S: ec := 0 ;
  if d = null then S -> S: ec := ec + 1;  S -> U: 'You should fill in the Date. ' end ;
  if the combination of d and the course from e already occurs in Exam
    then  S -> S: ec := ec + 1;
          S -> U: 'An Exam with that Course-Date combination already exists. ' end ;
  if ec = 0
    then  S -> S: updateExam(e, d) ;  /* So, replace the old date in e by this new date d
          S -> U: 'The modification has been completed successfully. '
    else  S -> U: 'The modification could not be completed since there were errors. '
  end
END
```

The corresponding graphical SSD follows easily [2] and is similar to the graphical SSD for conditionally *creating* an exam.

The textual SSD for conditionally <u>deleting</u> an *Exam e* becomes as follows:

```
DEFINE conditionallyDeleteExam(e) AS
  S -> S: ec := 0 ;
  if there are exam enrolments referring to this exam
    then  S -> S: ec := ec + 1;
          S -> U: 'There are still Exam Enrolments belonging to this Exam. ' end ;
  if ec = 0
    then  S -> S: deleteExam(e) ;
          S -> U: 'The modification has been completed successfully. '
    else  S -> U: 'The modification could not be completed since there were errors. '
  end
END
```

We now have to add three extra methods per class in order to reach a 'Version 0.2'. E.g., for the class Exam, we have to add *conditionallyCreateExam(c, d), conditionallyUpdateExam(e, d),* and *conditionallyDeleteExam(e)*. However, in order to add these methods to the right class, we first need to introduce so-called *managers*.

4.3 Adding Managers (V0.3)

In this section, we use the general approach from [1] to create an extra set of managers. Since Lecture, Course, and Student do not have outgoing arrows, they should need a Manager. The other objects already have at least one suitable manager available. For example, an Exam has its Course as a potential corresponding manager and a TeachingActivity has both Lecturer and Course as possible managers. This leads to Version 0.3 of the class diagram, as given in Fig. 6.

Once we know all managers, we are able to put the conditional methods from the previous paragraph in the right class. Since there is no specific Exam-Manager, we need to choose the most likely manager for an Exam, which, in this case, will be the corresponding Course. Through this Course we are able to find each corresponding Exam. This leads to the additional methods as given in Fig. 7.

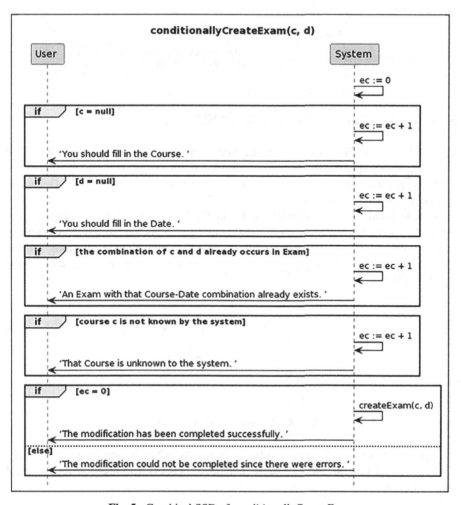

Fig. 5. Graphical SSD of *conditionallyCreateExam*

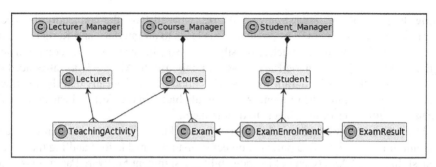

Fig. 6. Class diagram with a minimal set of managers added

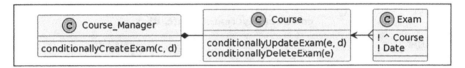

Fig. 7. Classes and methods in class diagram Version 0.3

5 From Textual SSD to Grey Box SSD

The condition in an **if**-, **while**-, or **repeat**-statement must also be checked, which is in fact a separate step (usually done by the system). For our three Exam-examples, we get five explicit checks for the Create, three for the Update, and two for the Delete, all because of their **if**-statements.

How to decide what the interface and what the kernel should check is explained in [1]. It also explains how to combine steps by using a combined request from Interface to Kernel (Fig. 8). This leads to a combined request in which the result of this request is also mentioned. In Fig. 8, R: = A means: send request A to the Kernel and return the result R to the Interface.

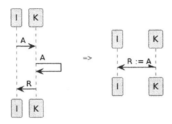

Fig. 8. Combined request to Kernel

Applying this to *conditionallyUpdateExam* results in 2 such combined steps (including 1 check) and 5 simple interface steps (including 2 checks). This results in the graphical SSD in Fig. 9.

6 From Grey Box SSD to White Box SSDs

Using the principle of *separation of concerns*, we will have the connection between Interface and Kernel as small as possible. This leads to an Interface and Kernel that are independent of each other as much as possible. Since the Interface needs to communicate with the object-structure in the Kernel, we will only use the Managers as introduced in Version 0.3 of the class diagram for this. This approach also means that the interface does not (need to) know the references to internal objects in the Kernel. Instead, we will use the key attributes of the objects to denote them.

In a white box, we use the objects as they are known from the Version 0.3 class diagram. Important is to find out what object is first responsible for handling the kernel request. In [3], GRASP (General Responsibility Assignment Software Patterns) is used to establish the object that is best suitable to be the first responsible object.

Let's now have a look at the kernel request.

so: = the combination of d and the course from e already occurs in Exam.

conditionallyUpdateExam(e, d)

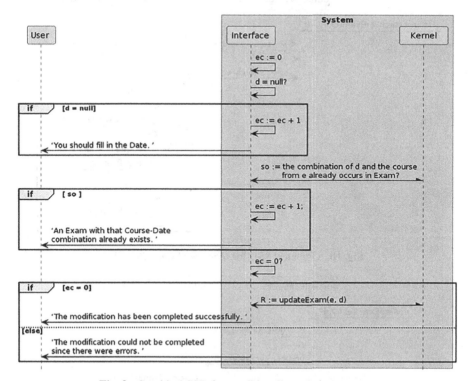

Fig. 9. Graphical SSD for conditionally updating an exam

First we reformulate this request so that it becomes a real method call:

so : = searchForExam(cKey, d)

where cKey is the unique reference to the course we are investigating (i.e., cKey contains the course code and the year since these uniquely identify a course) and d is the new date for the Exam. The method returns *True* if an Exam from the course already exists with the same d.

The responsible object for this request is the Course_Manager, which, in turn, knows the object c itself (from the given key values in cKey) and can pass through the request to this object. The complete white box SSD in graphical form will then be as in Fig. 10.

Note that, in contrast to [1], we now explicitly stated that we do not use a direct reference to object c, but instead use the key values of c to uniquely identify the object.

If the interface itself already has the correct reference to the Course object c, the first steps involving the Course_Manager can be skipped and the request can be sent directly to the Course c. But since MVC expects the interaction between model and view/controller to be as independent as possible, we prefer to involve the Course_Manager here as first responsible object. In this case, we are more independent of later changes in, e.g., the requests that can be handled by internal objects in the Kernel. In fact, we are using the Façade design pattern here, see [3, 4].

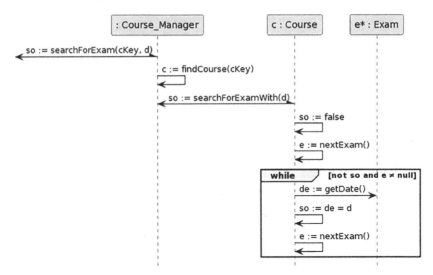

Fig. 10. Graphical SSD for *searchForExam(cKey, d)*

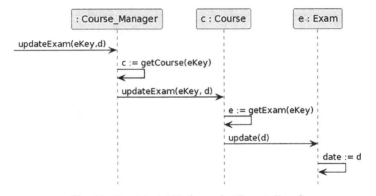

Fig. 11. Graphical SSD for *updateExam(eKey, d)*

For the updateExam-request we can create a similar white box SSD, assuming that the interface already knows the reference to the Exam under consideration; see Fig. 11.

Explaining Fig. 11: We start making the Course_Manager the responsible object. It finds the Course object c from eKey (since the key values of an Exam are date and Course) and then requests this c to change the date of the corresponding Exam. For this, we ask c to search for the corresponding Exam object e, given the key value eKey.

Both white box SSDs show that the designer will provide a more or less complete design to be used by the programmer to code this in the preferred OO language.

7 Updating the Class Diagram (V0.4)

When a white box SSD has been created, we have to extend the class diagram as well, since we then have more methods an object should react on. For the Exam-class, for instance, we have created two white box SSDs and introduced five methods that need to be added to the corresponding classes (Sect. 6). This results in a Version 0.4 class diagram, in Fig. 12. This should then be done for all classes. The red boxes denote a private method because we do not want other objects to call these directly.

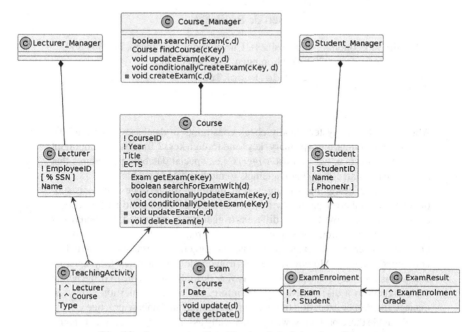

Fig. 12. A more complete Version 0.4 of the class diagram

8   Conclusion

We illustrated by example that the systematic approach of [1], how to go from a conceptual specification to an OO-implementation using formal mapping rules or "semi-automatic" guidelines, really works. The systematic approach leads to programme code in which all conditions are tested at the right times and all tests are complete. Using the grey and white box approach also leads to an Interface that is at much as possible independent of the Kernel and thus the most flexible when it comes to code refactoring and optimization. Working this way leads to software that is less vulnerable, since the systematic approach automatically deals with pitfalls like forgetting tests or have weird (in)dependences in the code.

References

1. de Brock, E.O., Smedinga, R.: From conceptual specification to OO-specification. In: Shishkov, B., (ed.): BMSD 2023. LNBIP 483, pp. 180–199. Springer, Cham (2023)
2. de Brock, E.O.: Developing Information Systems Accurately - A Wholistic Approach. Springer, Cham (2023). https://doi.org/10.1007/978-3-031-16862-8
3. Larman, C.: Applying UML and Patterns: An Introduction to Object-Oriented Analysis and Design and Iterative Development, 3rd edition, Addison Wesley Professional (2004)
4. Gamma, E., et al.: Design Patterns - Elements of Reusable Object-Oriented Software. Addison Wesley, Reading (1995)

Managing Database Trigger Design

Bert de Brock[✉]

Faculty of Economics and Business, University of Groningen, PO Box 800,
9700 AV Groningen, The Netherlands
E.O.de.Brock@rug.nl

Abstract. How to systematically check constraints in databases other than the
standard constraints, e.g., (primary) keys and foreign keys? To solve this important
problem in practice, one can use *triggers*, i.e., special database procedures that
automatically start ('fire') upon attempts to modify data in a table.

In practice, designing, writing, and maintaining triggers consistently is subtle, difficult, and error-prone, for many reasons: E.g., when multiple triggers are
activated 'at the same time' or different trigger-types are mixed, the behaviour
can become quite subtle or unpredictable, e.g., regarding their execution-order.
Or when triggers invoke external actions, the triggering transaction might not be
committed after all. Moreover, keeping triggers consistent when they must be
changed is also very error-prone. So, it is very desirable to be able to (re)generate
such triggers in a disciplined way. Therefore, our research question is how to
manage the proper execution of checking constraints in database practice.

To tackle these problems, we systematically assemble the triggers that should
be activated 'at the same time' into one trigger. In that way, we keep control over
what happens, and when. It keeps the trigger-order platform-independent as well.
Using standard templates, we describe a generic way for generating triggers from
a *declarative* specification. We intensively used and evaluated this approach in
practice. Constraints *between* and *within* tables can be treated in this way. Using
triggers, we also propose a straightforward implementation of SQL's *assertions*.

To develop triggers consistently, several design-decisions must be made. E.g.,
should the trigger stop checking after detecting the first violation or find and
mention all violations? And what to do when there is a violation? E.g., a rollback or
some 'repair', e.g., a cascading delete? We discuss and answer all these questions.

Keywords: Constraints Checking · Database Triggers · Trigger Design · Design
Decisions · Generators · Rollback · Assertions in SQL

1 Introduction

We can use *triggers* to systematically check constraints in databases other than the standard constraints, such as (primary) keys and foreign keys, for which there already exist
language constructs. This is possible because *triggers* are special database procedures
that automatically start ('fire') upon modification attempts of data in a table.

B. Shishkov (Ed.): BMSD 2023, LNBIP 483, pp. 352–364, 2023.
https://doi.org/10.1007/978-3-031-36757-1_26

A modification attempt can be one of 3 types: Insert, Delete, or Update. A DBMS usually already has several 'mechanisms' for constraints checking, e.g., 'domains', check-constraints, (primary) keys, and foreign keys. But triggers can be used for checking other constraints as well, i.e., constraints for which there is no standard mechanism.

However, designing and writing triggers and keeping them consistent is subtle, difficult, and error-prone for several reasons [1]. E.g., in order to safeguard one constraint, four to six (mutually consistent) triggers might be needed. Furthermore, a small change in one constraint (e.g., because of changing circumstances) might lead to changes in several triggers. Moreover, triggers might become quite complex, e.g., in case of cascading deletes. Therefore, it would be very beneficial to be able to (re)generate triggers in a systematic manner. So, developing triggers is very 'triggy'.

Ref. [1] clearly describes the important and broad benefits of triggers: *'The main recognized advantages of trigger-based applications are still the ability to move shared application logic and business rules into the database (rather than hard-coding the behavior into all applications), and the ability to specify integrity constraints that go beyond the specific types of built-in constraints supported by SQL'*.

1.1 Our Work Versus Related Work

A very thorough and complete overview of the issues involved in using triggers is given by Ceri, Cochrane, and Widom in *Practical Applications of Triggers and Constraints: Successes and Lingering Issues* [1]. It is a successor of their influential and price-winning paper [2]. It identifies many problems with database triggers and mentions the relevant literature. Also other papers point out the problems with triggers [3–5]. Some of the stubborn issues are still lingering. We will cite the most subtle and lingering issues mentioned in [1], and react to them.

Since *'the execution of a row-level trigger effectively enumerates through the modified rows in an undefined order'* (p.260), we prefer *statement-level* triggers. Moreover, *'many systems still lack a means of prioritizing when multiple triggers are activated at the same time'* (p.260). Triggers on the same table to be fired at the same event should be fired in the order in which they were created, according to the standard SQL specification [6]. In that case, you might create those triggers in the order they should be fired... However, when your software will change, this might not be maintainable anymore.

An RDBMS might implement this standard SQL behaviour, or specify in which other way they decide for the order (e.g., name order), or don't specify or guarantee any order. Anyway, it is better to control the trigger-order yourself, keeping it platform-independent. Therefore, we assemble the triggers that should be activated 'at the same time' into one trigger! In that way, we can arrange their execution order ourselves.

This also softens the problem of *'Subtle behavior, particularly when mixing different types of triggers'* (p.260), because you yourself can control the mixing of different types of triggers that should be activated 'at the same time'. For instance, the problem that *'if triggers invoke external actions, there is no way for the external actions to know if the triggering transaction committed'* (p. 260) can be avoided by invoking external actions only if it is sure that the triggering transaction commits; see Sect. 2.3.

In the same sentence, [1] also mentions *'Subtle behavior, particularly when ... mixing triggers and built-in constraints'*. Indeed, we noticed that already in the late eighties when using Sybase. For instance, you didn't control their execution order nor (the order of) the messages to the user. In order to control that, we also used our general trigger generation mechanism to replace built-in constraints. This is illustrated in Sect. 5.2.

Although '*a generic system for generating triggers from a declarative specification does not seem feasible*' (p.258), we (try to) do just that in our current paper.

According to [3], using active rules or triggers to verify integrity constraints is a serious and complex problem because these mechanisms have behaviour that could be difficult to predict in a complex database. Ref. [3] states that automatic support for trigger development and verification would help database developers to adopt triggers in the database design process. Well, that is just what we built as database developers. Ref. [3] itself only suggests a visualization tool that represents and verifies triggers execution by using UML's sequence diagrams. It simulates the execution sequence of a set of triggers when a DML operation is produced. However, it actually is symptom control.

Ref. [4] gives a technique to improve efficiency of existing methods by defining the order in which maintenance of integrity constraints should be performed. However, we propose a method to control that order and the (error) messages completely ourselves.

Ref. [5] introduces a debugging tool to identify and understand problems that a composite set of triggers may cause, but only after the triggers have been programmed and simulated. In our approach, we simply try to avoid those problems. The many proposals for end-user development ('Empowering End Users') work well for simple cases only.

1.2 Contribution

To tackle these problems, triggers must be designed - or even *generated* - in a controlled and systematic manner. We systematically assemble the triggers that should be activated 'at the same time' into one trigger. In that way, we can keep control over what should happen, and when. Using templates, this paper describes a generic system for generating triggers from a declarative specification.

We did develop and apply this in an industrial setting in the late eighties (using Transact-SQL in Sybase). Because we urgently needed something like this in our industrial environment, we intensively tested, validated, used, evaluated, and improved our approach and our software until it worked properly *and* efficiently. It resulted in the approach described in this paper.

We can treat the constraints between tables as well as within tables with this approach. One could even include the classical (primary) key constraints, foreign key constraints, domain constraints, and check constraints, as will be discussed in Sect. 5.

To develop triggers consistently, several design decisions must be considered as well. E.g., should the trigger stop checking after detecting the first violation or should it find and mention all violations? And what to do if there is a violation? E.g., a rollback or some kind of repair (e.g., a cascading delete)? We decided to let a trigger find and mention all violations, in principle, and to roll back the transaction if there is a violation.

1.3 Paper Outline

The paper is organized as follows. Sect. 2 presents a basic trigger design. Sect. 3 explains why (and how) constraints might need to be rewritten/reformulated first. Sect. 5 presents a more refined trigger design but before doing so, Sect. 4 explains the auxiliary *trigger test tables*, only existing during the execution of the modification. Sect. 6 proposes a straightforward implementation of SQL's *assertions* using triggers (for the moment ignoring concurrency). Finally, Sect. 7 contains a summary and Sect. 8 our conclusions.

2 A Basic Trigger Design

Central in our approach is that (and how) we combine various trigger-clauses into one trigger. Each table gets at most three triggers: an insert-, a delete-, and/or an update-trigger. Therefore, we can identify a trigger by its table and its modification type: Insert, Delete, or Update. In SQL, it is possible to restrict an update trigger to only some specified attributes of that table. In that case, the trigger only 'fires' upon an update of those attributes. Example 1 illustrates this.

We will usually follow the trigger syntax as described in [7]. That site also gives further background on triggers. We start with a straightforward trigger design.

Each of our triggers consists of three parts, simply called:

(1) *begin part*   (2) *middle part*   (3) *final part*

For readability, some SQL keywords are written in **bold**.

2.1 Begin Part

The *begin part* of our trigger on a table T for modification type M (Insert, Delete, or Update) names the trigger and declares it as an 'after trigger', meaning that the trigger 'fires' after the transaction has been done (but not yet committed). The transaction can still be undone in the trigger. The begin part also declares and initializes a counter called @*errcount* for the number of errors found until then.

Begin part
```
create trigger T_M after M on T
BEGIN atomic
    declare @errcount integer;
    select  @errcount = 0;
```

2.2 Middle Part

The *middle part* of the trigger on a table T contains *for each modification type* M the following check clause/statement *for each constraint* C in which table T is mentioned:

<u>Ingredients of the middle part</u>

if not (C)
begin select @errcount = @errcount + 1;
    execute mess N, T, M
end;

where *mess* is a stored procedure meant to inform the user about the 'error', essentially saying that this modification M on T would violate the constraint. C is the constraint expressed as a Boolean expression in SQL (as in Example 1), and N is an identification (a unique name) of the constraint C. The message *mess N, T, M* could be something like **'This M on T would violate the *N*.'**

In principle, for each modification type M, the middle part of a trigger on a table T should contain such a clause for each constraint C in which T is mentioned. But it can be left out if the type of modification on the table cannot violate the constraint at hand, as Example 1 concretely shows. As another, generic and important example, we mention foreign key constraints; see Fig. 1 in Sect. 3. As a consequence, trigger T_M is not needed if there are no constraints that mention T and can be violated by M.

If checking a certain constraint C is very 'expensive' in time or space (or money), then you might consider to put it at the end of the middle part and only check it if there were no errors found until then. The code then becomes:

if @errcount = 0

if not (C) **begin select** @errcount = @errcount + 1; **execute** mess N, T, M **end;**

In that case, the counter @*errcount* represents the number of errors found until then in the *checked* constraints only. Moreover, if there are violations, the trigger might not find and mention *all* violations anymore.

2.3   Final Part

The *final part* of each trigger first checks whether there were any errors. If so, the transaction is rolled back and the user is informed about it. If there were no errors, then the transaction commits and the system executes the actions that should apply only if the transaction commits. Typical examples are: invoking external actions, performing replication, updating materialized views, et cetera.

The final part also contains the '**END**' belonging to the initial '**BEGIN atomic**':

Final part

    if @errcount > 0
    begin rollback transaction;
        execute rlbkm T, M, @errcount
    end
    [**else** execute actions that should apply only if the transaction commits]
    END

where *rlbkm* is a stored procedure meant to further inform the user, essentially saying that the proposed modification could not take place because of the potential constraint violation(s), and maybe also mentioning the number of errors found. The message *rlbkm T, M, @errcount* could, for instance, be something like '**The M on T cannot take place due to the** @errcount **mentioned potential constraint violation(s).**'

This is related to the so-called ECA-rules [8], where ECA stands for *Event-Condition-Action*, meaning: When the *event* happens and the *condition* is satisfied, then the (follow-up) *action* executes. In our case, the original transaction constitutes the *event*, the conjunction of the applicable constraints (see Sect. 2.2) constitute the *condition*, and the actions mentioned in the **else**-part in the Final part constitute the *action*.

Example 1 illustrates how an 'arbitrary' constraint C can be treated; rewrite it as a Boolean expression in SQL, say C_{SQL}, and use that SQL-expression:

    if not (C_{SQL}) **begin ... end;**   /* see Sect. 2.2

Example 1: A basic trigger design
Consider the constraint that there should always be less than 100 open orders.
Formally, this constraint could be expressed as something like

$$| \{ x \mid x \in \text{ORDERS and } x.\text{STATUS} = \text{``Open''} \} | < 100$$

In SQL, this Boolean expression can be expressed as

(**select** count(*) **from** ORDERS **where** STATUS = "Open") < 100

The only table mentioned in this constraint is ORDERS, so ORDERS is the only table potentially influenced by this constraint. Clearly, this constraint should be checked upon an insert into ORDERS (of an open order), not upon a delete from ORDERS, and upon an update of a STATUS attribute.

Suppose that this constraint is known under the name *Open order limit*. Then the insert-trigger on ORDERS according to our rules would become:

```
create trigger ORDERS_INSERT after INSERT on ORDERS
BEGIN atomic
    declare    @errcount integer;
    select     @errcount = 0;
    if not ( (select count(*) from ORDERS where STATUS = "Open") < 100 )
    begin select @errcount = @errcount + 1;
          execute mess Open order limit, ORDERS, INSERT
    end;
    if @errcount > 0
    begin rollback transaction;
          execute rlbkm ORDERS, INSERT, @errcount
    end
END
```

As suggested earlier, message *mess Open order limit, ORDERS, INSERT* could be something like '**This INSERT on ORDERS would violate the *Open order limit*.**' Similarly, message *rlbkm* ORDERS, INSERT @*errcount* could be '**The INSERT on ORDERS cannot take place due to the** @errcount **mentioned potential constraint violation(s).** ', although in this case there can be only one violation.

The *update*-trigger on ORDERS is almost the same: The word 'INSERT' must be replaced by 'UPDATE' and the expression '**if not** (… < 100) **begin** … **end**' must be preceded by '**if update**(STATUS)'.

3 Rewriting Constraints Where Needed

The constraints to be checked might have a form which needs some formal rewriting before it can be directly translated to SQL. This might lead to SQL-expressions which are not immediately obvious. Therefore, we will rewrite such constraints step by step, using formal rewriting rules from predicate logic.

Often, an 'inter-table' constraint on instances x of a particular concept has the form:

For each <concept> x, <constraint on x>

An example could be that for each employee x, there is a department where x belongs to. This cannot be directly translated to SQL, since SQL is a 'set oriented' language. We will rewrite the constraint, in two alternative ways. It is logically equivalent to:

(a) *'There does not exist a <concept> x for which <constraint on x> does not hold'* and
(b) *'The number of <concepts> x for which <constraint on x> does not hold, is zero'.*

This is based on the following logical equivalences:

$$\forall x \in A: \varphi(x) \;\;\Leftrightarrow\;\; \neg\, \exists x \in A: \neg\, \varphi(x) \;\;\Leftrightarrow\;\; \big|\, \{x \in A \mid \neg\, \varphi(x)\,\}\,\big| = 0$$

Now we can use the following general SQL-patterns to express such a constraint:

(a) NOT EXIST S (SELECT * FROM A x WHERE NOT <constraint on x>) or
(b) (SELECT COUNT(*) FROM A x WHERE NOT <constraint on x>) = 0.

where x can be considered as a 'row variable' over the table A.
We recall that the fragment in Sect. 2.2 is *'if not (C)'*, which would then lead to:

(a) IF EXIST S (SELECT * FROM A x WHERE NOT <constraint on x>) or
(b) IF (SELECT COUNT(*) FROM A x WHERE NOT <constraint on x>) ≠ 0.

An important special subclass of this form are ***foreign keys***, which occur multiple times in any practical application. Essentially, they are of the following form:

For each x in table A, there is a y in table B such that 'x refers to y'

A bit more formally: $\forall x \in A: \exists y \in B:$ 'x refers to y'.
Applying the previous translation rules here, leads to:

(a) *There does not exist an x in A for which there is no y in B such that x refers to y.*
(b) *The number of x in A for which there is no y in B such that x refers to y, is 0.*

With our translation rules, the *foreign key* constraint translates to the SQL-forms:

```
(a) NOT EXISTS (SELECT * FROM A x
                WHERE NOT EXISTS (SELECT * FROM B y
                                  WHERE 'x refers to y'))
(b) (SELECT COUNT(*) FROM A x
    WHERE (SELECT COUNT(*) FROM B y WHERE 'x refers to y') = 0 ) = 0
```

(a) in words: There is no occurrence in A without a corresponding occurrence in B.
(b) in words: The number of occurrences in A for which the number of corresponding occurrences in B is zero, is zero.

If table B has attribute b1 as its key and table A has a foreign key attribute a1 that is referring to b1 of B, then the condition *'x refers to y'* concretely becomes 'x.a1 = y.b1'.

Similarly for *composite* keys: if table B has the attribute combination b1, b2 as its key and table A has the combination a1, a2 as the corresponding foreign key referring to B, then the condition '*x refers to y*' becomes 'x.a1 = y.b1 **and** x.a2 = y.b2'. Et cetera.

For a foreign key constraint '*A referring to B*' it is clear that an Insert into B or a Delete from A cannot violate this constraint. But an Insert into A, an Update on A on its relevant foreign key attributes, a Delete from B, or an Update on B on its relevant key attributes can violate this constraint. See Fig. 1. (By the way, an Update on a key attribute is usually considered 'harmful' anyway.)

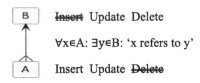

Fig. 1. A foreign key constraint and its potential constraint violations

4   Trigger Test Tables

How are triggers implemented, essentially? Well, during the execution of a modification in a DBMS, the DBMS has two so-called *trigger test tables*. Trigger test tables are temporary tables, only existing during the execution of that modification. Depending on the DBMS, there is a pair called *OLD TABLE* and *NEW TABLE* or a pair called *Deleted* and *Inserted*, for instance. We will use *Deleted* and *Inserted*.

The old and new sets of rows of a table T during the execution of a modification expressed in a simple formula per modification type (with Deleted $\subseteq$ T) are:

Create:	new T-value = old T-value $\cup$ Inserted	(Deleted = $\emptyset$)
Update:	new T-value = (old T-value − Deleted) $\cup$ Inserted	
Delete:	new T-value = old T-value − Deleted	(Inserted = $\emptyset$)

In summary, in all cases we have: new T-value = (old T-value − Deleted) $\cup$ Inserted.

5   Refined Trigger Design

5.1   Standard and Stricter Foreign Keys

A standard foreign key constraint is of the form.

For each row x in table A, there is a row y in table B such that 'x refers to y'

Sometimes we have a 'stronger foreign key', namely such that the reference is restricted to certain rows in table B only. This leads to the following form:

For each x in table A, there is a y in table B such that $\varphi(y)$ and 'x refers to y'

where $\varphi(y)$ expresses the limiting condition involved.

But this already holds for all the rows in the old A-value. So, for an Insert into the referencing table A, the check can be limited to *Inserted* only:

For each x in table Inserted, there is a y in table B such that $\underline{\varphi(y)}$ and 'x refers to y'

Following Sect. 3, this leads to the following two alternative SQL-forms:

```
(a) NOT EXISTS (SELECT * FROM Inserted x
                  WHERE NOT EXISTS (SELECT * FROM B y
                                      WHERE φ'(y) AND 'x refers to y'))
(b) (SELECT COUNT(*) FROM Inserted x
        WHERE (SELECT COUNT(*) FROM B y
                  WHERE φ'(y) AND 'x refers to y') = 0 ) = 0
```

where $\varphi'(y)$ is the limiting condition expressed in SQL.

An existing table might already have grown (very) large, while the number of rows in *Inserted* might be small, so this will then be a considerable efficiency improvement.

For a Delete from referenced table B, something similar holds: If each x in A refers to at most one y in B, as usual, no x in A should refer to a y in *Deleted*. In a formula:

$\neg\ \exists x \in A: \exists y \in Deleted: \varphi(y)$ and 'x refers to y'

which leads to the following two alternative SQL-forms:

```
(a) NOT EXISTS (SELECT * FROM A x
                  WHERE EXISTS (SELECT * FROM Deleted y
                                  WHERE φ'(y) AND 'x refers to y'))
(b) (SELECT COUNT(*) FROM A x
        WHERE (SELECT COUNT(*) FROM Deleted y
                  WHERE φ'(y) AND 'x refers to y') ≠ 0 ) = 0
```

If each x in A refers to at most one y in B, as usual, the condition $\varphi'(y)$ can be left out.

5.2 Constraints Within a Row

Constraints within a row in a table, on one of its columns or between its columns, can be expressed using built-in constraints such as *domain* constraints or *check* constraints.

But, as explained in Sect. 1.1, in order to control the behaviour when mixing triggers and built-in constraints, e.g., controlling their execution order or (the order of) the messages to the user, our general trigger generation mechanism can be used to replace built-in constraints. We can incorporate them in our trigger mechanism, similar to the foreign key constraints, for instance. Constraints within a row in a table A are of the form: $\forall x \in A: \varphi(x)$. As explained in Sect. 3, we have the next formal and SQL-equivalences:

$$\forall x \in A: \varphi(x) \iff \neg \exists x \in A: \neg \varphi(x \iff \big| \{x \in A \mid \neg \varphi(x)\} \big| = 0$$
$$\iff \texttt{NOT EXISTS (SELECT * FROM A x WHERE NOT } \varphi'(x)\texttt{)}$$
$$\iff \texttt{(SELECT COUNT(*) FROM A x WHERE NOT } \varphi'(x)\texttt{)} = 0$$

where $\varphi'(x)$ is the condition expressed in SQL. This already holds for all 'old' rows in A, so upon an Insert into A, the check can be limited to the trigger test table *Inserted*:

```
NOT EXISTS (SELECT * FROM Inserted x WHERE NOT φ'(x)) or
(SELECT COUNT(*) FROM Inserted x WHERE NOT φ'(x)) = 0
```

We mention a few examples of such constraints. For each row of table A, the value for:

- attribute a in A should be divisible by 10: $\varphi'(x)$ then becomes 'x.a mod 10 = 0'.
- attribute MIN should be less than its value for MAX: $\varphi'(x)$ becomes 'x.MIN < x.MAX'.

Clearly, a delete from table A cannot violate any constraint on an individual row in A and an update on A can only violate a constraint on an individual row in A if the update concerns at least one of the columns involved.

6 Implementing SQL'S Assertions Using Triggers

Official SQL has so-called *assertions*, which are suitable to express and check constraints between tables or between rows within a table, among others. (For further background on assertions, see, e.g., [9].) However, hardly any commercial DBMS has an implementation of SQL assertions yet! But with our approach, practitioners in the field can simulate the functionality of SQL's assertions. The SQL syntax for assertions is:

CREATE ASSERTION <constraint name> CHECK (<constraint>)

where <constraint> is a Boolean expression in SQL. For instance, the constraint in Example 1 expressed as an assertion, would become:

CREATE ASSERTION Open_order_limit

CHECK ((**select** count(*) **from** ORDERS **where** STATUS = "Open") < 100)

Well, it might be clear now how we can simulate the functionality of SQL's assertions: An assertion with constraint name N and constraint C, so of the form.

CREATE ASSERTION N CHECK (C)

can be treated just as the constraint C with name N in Sect. 2. Therefore, it leads to the following ingredient for the middle part for each constraint C that mentions T and can be violated by M:

if not (C)
begin select @errcount = @errcount + 1;
      execute mess N, T, M
end

7 Summary

The central procedure in our approach can be summarized as follows:

1. Given a constraint C, each table T mentioned in C gets for each modification type (Insert, Delete, Update) a clause in its middle part, in principle (Sect. 2.2)
2. A clause can be left out if the type of modification on T cannot violate C (Sect. 2.2)
3. Sometimes, a constraint needs some rewriting before it can be translated to SQL because SQL is a 'set oriented' language (Sect. 3)
4. In several cases, the check of the constraint can be limited to the trigger test table *Inserted* or *Deleted* only (Sect. 4 and Sect. 5)
5. Also *domain* constraints and *check* constraints could be treated in this way (Sect. 5.2)

The structure of a Trigger T_M is: <u>1 begin part</u>; <u>n check clauses</u>; <u>1 final part</u>.
where n is the number of constraints that mention table T and can be violated by M.
If $n = 0$ for Trigger T_M, then that trigger can be left out.

8 Conclusions

Using templates, we sketched a generic way to design triggers starting from declarative specifications, such that we can avoid the stubborn problems and drawbacks sketched in Sect. 1.1. The crucial idea is to assemble the triggers that should be activated 'at the same time' into one trigger.

In that way, we can arrange their execution order ourselves and we can control the mixing of different types of triggers. Moreover, we are able to invoke external actions only if it is sure that the triggering transaction committed. Furthermore, in order to control the subtle interactions between triggers and built-in constraints, we can extend our general trigger generation mechanism to replace built-in constraints. In that way, we have complete control over the content and the order of messages to the user. Any Boolean expression that is also expressible in SQL, can be treated in this way. We intensively used, evaluated, and successfully improved this approach in an industrial setting.

As a bonus, we also proposed a direct implementation of SQL's *assertions* by means of triggers, which is also useful for practitioners in the field. All in all, we proposed a fruitful general approach for generating triggers from a declarative specification.

References

1. Ceri, S., Cochrane, R., Widom, J.: Practical applications of triggers and constraints: successes and lingering issues. In: Proceedings of the 26th VLDB, pp. 254–262 (2000). https://www.vldb.org/conf/2000/P254.pdf. Accessed 24 Apr 2023
2. Ceri, S., Widom, J.: Deriving production rules for constraint maintenance. In: Proceedings of the 16th VLDB, pp. 566–577 (1990). https://www.vldb.org/conf/1990/P566.PDF. Accessed 24 Apr 2023
3. Al-Jumaily, H.T., de Pablo, C., Cuadra, D., Martínez, P.: Using UML's sequence diagrams for representing execution models associated to triggers. In: Bell, D.A., Hong, J. (eds.) BNCOD 2006. LNCS, vol. 4042, pp. 36–46. Springer, Heidelberg (2006). https://doi.org/10.1007/11788911_3
4. Mayol, E., Teniente, E.: Structuring the process of integrity maintenance. In: Database and Expert Systems Applications, pp. 262–275 (2006). https://doi.org/10.1007/BFb0022037
5. Corno, F., et al.: Empowering end users in debugging trigger-action rules, pp. 1–13 (2019). https://doi.org/10.1145/3290605.3300618
6. SQL standard: https://www.itl.nist.gov/div897/ctg/dm/sql_info.html. Accessed 24 Apr 2023
7. Triggers in SQL: https://crate.io/docs/sql-99/en/latest/chapters/24.html. Accessed 24 Apr 2023
8. Berndtsson, M., Mellin, J.: ECA Rules (2009). https://doi.org/10.1007/978-0-387-39940-9_504
9. Assertions: https://crate.io/docs/sql-99/en/latest/chapters/20.html#create-assertion-statement. Accessed 24 Apr 2023
10. Bell, D.A., Hong, J. (eds.): BNCOD 2006. LNCS, vol. 4042. Springer, Heidelberg (2006). https://doi.org/10.1007/11788911
11. Proceedings of the 2019 CHI Conference on Human Factors in Computing Systems, (2019)
12. Liu, L., Özsu, M.T. (eds.): Encyclopedia of Database Systems. Springer, New York (2018). https://doi.org/10.1007/978-1-4614-8265-9

A View on Vulnerabilities Within IoT Devices in the Smart Home Environment

Annika Nykänen and Andrei Costin[(✉)]

Faculty of Information Technology, University of Jyväskylä,
P.O. Box 35, Jyväskylä 40014, Finland
{TODO,ancostin}@jyu.fi
https://jyu.fi/it/

Abstract. The number of different devices connected to the Internet is constantly increasing. There is a high demand for these devices, and their benefits are clear for certain groups of users. Some of these devices, the Internet of Things (IoT), are part of smart homes, making the residents' everyday lives easier and safer. In general, the security of IoT devices is constantly improving, but overall, they are still full of vulnerabilities. The purpose of this paper is to explain the most significant threats to IoT devices in the smart home environment and propose a number of different ways to eliminate these threats and vulnerabilities in smart home IoT devices. It is important to acknowledge that both the manufacturers of IoT devices and their users are responsible for taking care of the vulnerabilities.

Keywords: Internet of Things · smart homes · cybersecurity · vulnerability

1 Introduction

Cybersecurity has gained a lot of visibility in recent years compared to before, as the number of information security and cyberattacks is increasing. For example, the number of malware detected annually increased from 100 million to more than 700 million during the years 2012–2017. This means an average of 400,000 new malware every day [17].

The objects to be protected can be anything within cyberspace, for example, the Internet of Things devices of a smart home. The Internet of Things (IoT) refers to devices whose purpose is to connect virtual environments to the physical environment and maintain communication with people [6]. IoT devices are an integral part of a smart home, which consists of various devices connected to the same home network, so-called smart devices, such as smart appliances, smart watches, and smart TVs, and their goal is to make everyday life easier and, for example, make an apartment safer. Because these IoT devices are connected to the Internet, they at risk of becoming or already are vulnerable [11,12], which leads to them being prime targets for IoT specific malware attacks [10] further leading to Internet-wide botnets and attacks [3].

B. Shishkov (Ed.): BMSD 2023, LNBIP 483, pp. 365–374, 2023.
https://doi.org/10.1007/978-3-031-36757-1_27

1.1 Motivation and Contribution

According to Wirth [36], Symantec revealed in their study that an average of 5,200 IoT devices per month were under attack. Of these, almost 15 percent were surveillance cameras connected to the network. Thus, security and privacy should be of primary importance in the design of IoT technologies and services. Unfortunately, many commercial IoT products are provided with inadequate, incomplete, or poorly designed security mechanisms [22]. Currently, there is still relatively little research on the cybersecurity vulnerabilities of IoT devices in smart homes, even though the number of these devices has been growing significantly for several years, which means a growing threat to cybersecurity. Therefore, it is vital to increase awareness about the ways to make these devices safer to use.

In this paper, we concentrate on the vulnerabilities of these kinds of IoT devices and suggest several means to increase the safety of these devices. In Sect. 2, we define the central concepts regarding the vulnerabilities in IoT devices. In Sect. 3, we present the most common vulnerabilities. In Sect. 4, we explain possible ways to protect these devices. In Sect. 5, we summarize the paper.

2 Literature Review

2.1 Information Security

The Vocabulary of Comprehensive Security [34], published by The Security Committee and The Terminology Center TSK, defines information security as follows: "Information security means arrangements that aim to ensure the availability, integrity, and confidentiality of information. These arrangements include, for example, access control, data encryption and backup, and the use of a firewall, anti-virus program and certificates."

2.2 Cybersecurity

The Security Committee and The Terminology Center TSK defines [34] cybersecurity as follows: "Cybersecurity is a state in which the threats and risks arising from the cyber operating environment to society's vital functions or other functions dependent on the cyber operating environment are under control. Disruption of the operation of the cyber operating environment is often caused by a realized information security threat, so information security is a key factor when striving for cybersecurity."

2.3 Cybersecurity Vulnerabilities

According to a couple of different definitions, a vulnerability is an error or weakness in a program that an attacker can exploit to gain access to the system [35] or that can cause damage to the system [30].

According to the last definition to be considered, a vulnerability is an opening or weakness in an application that allows an attacker to cause harm to the application's users, the owner, or other parties dependent on the application. The vulnerability described above can be the result of an error during either the design or implementation of the application [27].

For this paper, it is meaningful to look at the last definition presented. Thus, a vulnerability can be thought of as a technical feature that is the result of an application's faulty design.

2.4 Internet of Things

The IoT can be described as devices whose purpose is to shape people's daily lives and completely change the way some tasks work [33].

There is no defined standard for the IoT architecture so far. Previously, the architecture was considered to be three-layered, with a perception, network, and application layer. Following this, researchers also proposed architecture of four and five layers. Each of these layers has its own vulnerabilities and risks [24]. The five-layer architecture is the most common nowadays, so this report examines the structure according to the five-layer model [24].

The first layer, the perception layer, includes all physically identifiable devices. The function of the sensors is to bring into an electronic form information about things that usually are not electronic, such as temperature or air humidity. By combining the data from the sensors, large-scale information can be collected [8].

The second layer is the network layer, which connects the devices of the perception layer to the network. Typical examples of the network layer are the wireless local area network (WLAN), i.e., Wi-Fi and wireless data transfer, such as Bluetooth Low Energy [14]. The advantage of Wi-Fi is its speed, the strength of its range, and the possibility for a large number of devices to be connected to the same network. The strengths of Bluetooth technology are its affordability and its integration into new systems [8].

The third layer in the IoT architecture is the processing layer, which uses many technologies, such as databases and cloud services. On this layer, for example, the TCP/IP protocol that uses packet-based communication is located [5]. IoT-aware process models are used in various execution environments. The requirements of the IoT service must be defined before a suitable IoT process model can be used correctly [5].

The application layer is the fourth layer, and it is responsible for implementing application-specific services for the user. The application layer contains new types of applications for which the IoT is used [32]. This means smart environments, such as traffic, construction, cities, retail stores, factories, and smart homes. The task of the application layer is to structure the received information in such a way that the production of applications for users is concrete and thoughtful [29].

The last layer of the IoT architecture model is the business layer. It ensures that the services structured on the other layers are brought to market.

This includes the entire IT business, such as applications, business revenues, and user privacy protection. Examples of the business layer are big businesses such as Google, Oracle, and Cisco [32]. Each layer must work in line with other layers so that the IoT architecture remains as intact as possible throughout the entire process.

2.5 Smart Homes

A smart home is a technology that enables the control and monitoring of various home devices automatically using advanced technologies [13]. The most common smart home systems include, for example, various lighting systems connected to the network.

As a rule, different beneficiaries can be divided into three different groups according to different needs. The first group is older people or families who have challenges performing everyday tasks such as cleaning. Another group is people with certain incurable diseases. A smart home can, for example, remind a person to take their medication on time and thus reduce the likelihood of medication abuse. The third group is people living alone. Smart home systems can identify situations when a resident is in danger and call for help [7].

However, no technology is perfect, so like any other technical thing, smart homes also have some drawbacks, such as the problem of managing and controlling several different applications and devices [13]. Also, smart home systems are complex systems because they consist of many different devices and different subsystems, which are all connected to each other [21]. Another drawback is that every time the user's needs change, the configuration of the smart home system must be changed [15].

Despite the disadvantages of smart home technology, it is inevitably coming to people's homes to make everyday life easier. It is estimated that in the near future, approximately 90 million people will live in smart homes and use technology to improve home safety, increase comfort, and reduce energy consumption [26].

3 System Vulnerabilities in IoT Devices

Because a modern smart home environment with IoT technology is connected to the Internet, its attack surface increases considerably. In addition to physical vulnerabilities, devices can be attacked remotely, either through interfaces or by downloading malicious programs to the hardware [18].

Although the smart home as an environment is unique compared to other IoT environments, its vulnerabilities are theoretically very similar. However, a smart home differs from other IoT environments because smart homes are often managed by a private individual. Compared to companies and other legal entities, they do not have the same resources to maintain the data security of the IoT system [18].

This paper, however, presents vulnerabilities that are not caused by the end user of IoT devices.

IoT Security Vulnerabilities

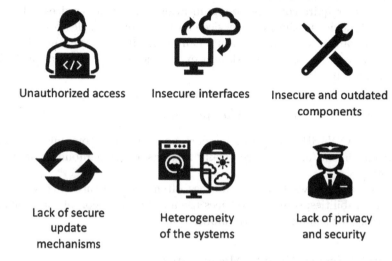

Unauthorized access   Insecure interfaces   Insecure and outdated
                                                              components

Lack of secure   Heterogeneity   Lack of privacy
   update   of the systems   and security
mechanisms

Fig. 1. Summary of the main types of IoT security vulnerabilities.

3.1 Unauthorized Access

In 2018, the Open Worldwide Application Security Project (OWASP) listed weak, guessable, hardcoded passwords, and insufficient authentication as the biggest IoT technology vulnerabilities [28]. In this paper, we will call these unauthorized access.

Unauthorized access can lead to an attacker gaining access to sensitive information [18]. Unauthorized access is aimed at the application level and, in the worst case, can lead to life-threatening situations, such as if an outsider manages to adjust the settings of medical devices or turn on electronic devices when the residents of the smart home are not present.

In addition to the above, the voice command feature increases the risk of unauthorized access. Attackers have been able to create voice commands that are not even audible or comprehensible to the human ear and thus gained unauthorized access to devices [23]. Other vulnerabilities can also indirectly expose the user to unauthorized access.

The risks of unauthorized access would be significantly lower if manufacturers of IoT devices set stricter identification requirements, which would prevent the use of excessively weak passwords [18].

3.2 Insecure Interfaces

IoT communication protocols are not based on cryptographic mechanisms [19], and often, IoT devices use different technical interfaces [20]. Unnecessary or insecure interface services exposed to the Internet may run in the background of the system. Insecure web, backend API, cloud, or mobile interfaces may also exist in the ecosystem outside the device [28].

IoT devices require constant communication with cloud services. The route from the IoT device to the cloud service can be distorted or destroyed, and the flow of data transferred along the route can be blocked. Insecure interfaces and interface services increase that risk and expose devices to information leakage and eavesdropping [19].

3.3 Insecure and Outdated Components

According to OWASP, the use of insecure and outdated components, lack of device management, and insecure default settings are vulnerabilities of the IoT technology [28].

Research also shows that IoT devices often use software with commonly known vulnerabilities; some IoT devices use a reduced version of the Linux OS, which is risky for leaking sensitive information [9].

3.4 Lack of Secure Update Mechanisms

OWASP lists the lack of a secure update mechanism as one of the IoT vulnerabilities [28]. Firmware is vulnerable, as regular software updates are available for only a few devices designed for smart home use. Manufacturers have very little motivation to provide continuous updates to maintain the systems of inexpensive devices. Cybercriminals are constantly finding new vulnerabilities and developing new attack methods, so non-updated devices are more vulnerable to attacks [18].

Because fixed software contains a lot of incomplete data security settings, there is a fair amount of insecure software and incomplete data security settings in IoT smart homes. Naturally, these vulnerabilities increase the risk of a cyberattack and data leakage, which can expose the system to unauthorized access and use.

3.5 Heterogeneous System Within a Smart Home

A smart home is a heterogeneous system and characteristic to it are many types of devices, different connection technologies, applications, and service models [1].

Even though IoT devices are becoming increasingly general, smart home IoT devices are rarely installed in a smart home during the construction phase. Often, the devices also have very little or no documentation about the security mechanisms installed in the internal software [18].

This exposes the smart home to network-level information security vulnerabilities, such as the presence of insecure interfaces, which can lead to equipment and system operation being compromised and information leaking [16].

3.6   Privacy and Security

OWASP lists insufficient privacy protection and insecure data transfer and storage as security vulnerabilities of IoT devices [28].

Many smart homes have sensors that are always on that collect and transport data about users and their movements. Often, the network traffic of a smart home is susceptible to eavesdropping by other parties. Because a large portion of smart home devices do not work without a network connection, data protection and privacy problems cannot be avoided [4].

4   Safe Use of IoT Devices

As previously stated, IoT devices are usually connected to the Internet. Data security does not depend only on the IoT device itself. It is also affected by other devices and connections. In particular, other devices on the same network can compromise the security of the IoT device. Next, we will review a few examples of how IoT devices can be secured.

4.1   Encryption

It is said that encryption is the most important operation to ensure confidentiality during communication [22]. Even with IoT devices, it is wise to prepare for the possibility that a possible attacker gets the data from the device. With IoT devices, encryption comprehensively secures confidentiality and data privacy, regardless of whether the data is located in cloud or local storage.

4.2   Intrusion Detection Systems

It is vital to be able to detect ongoing attacks in addition to prevent them. For example, anomalies in system parameters may refer to an ongoing attack [22]. An intrusion detection system provides a solution by which it could be possible to detect anomalies and other malicious events. By preventing ongoing attacks, it could keep all the IoT devices in the same network safe.

4.3   Software Updates

The manufacturers of IoT devices have the main responsibility for the safe operation of the devices. That is because software updates for IoT devices in particular are problematic: Some devices have no update options at all, whereas other devices are too old for new updates. Updates are usually not up to date in cases where the equipment was purchased many years ago, such as a smart refrigerator, whose updates may only be up to date for the first few years. Even if updates for older devices are still available, applying them is challenging. Some devices require users to update the devices themselves, whereas others are automatically installed to download new software updates [4]. One solution could be to create a standard for secure software updates for IoT devices to improve the secure usage of the devices.

4.4   Physical Security

With good physical security of the devices, attacks on the perception layer in particular can be prevented. To improve physical security, equipment components, such as radio frequency, must have a high level of protection [31]. The technical challenges are largely related to information security problems when designing and manufacturing IoT devices. Security should be considered at every architectural layer of the device application. Heterogeneity of IoT devices should be avoided in order to mitigate security threats. To guarantee the safety of the devices, they must be manufactured in compliance with appropriate safety measures [25].

5   Discussion and Conclusion

The security of IoT technology is still in the development phase, and although there are already methods to improve it, there are currently not enough resources to implement them in practice.

For this paper, the aim was to find out the most important cybersecurity vulnerabilities of IoT devices in a smart home environment and suggest proper measurements to improve the safe use of IoT devices.

The best way to protect IoT devices from security threats is to only use devices that are sufficiently well protected. Manufacturers should offer better opportunities to maintain IoT devices safely, for example, with automatic software updates. In addition, manufacturers should clearly present what cybersecurity measures have been taken and what updates have been made to the devices. Users, on the other hand, should try to keep their smart homes safe through their own actions, for example, by using strong passwords and two-step authentication. It would also be worthwhile for users to familiarize themselves with the manufacturers of different IoT devices before making purchase decisions.

Using information security products as an aid to protection is probably becoming more common because IoT device users do not always necessarily want or have time to take the necessary protection measures themselves.

Both manufacturers and users are responsible for taking care of the vulnerabilities of smart home IoT devices. However, the low motivation of manufacturers to provide continuous software updates for inexpensive devices is a problem that makes it difficult to implement solutions in practice. Providing updates is inherently expensive, so adding them would also mean an increase in the prices of IoT devices. As long as users prioritize convenience and trust IoT device manufacturers, and stricter data security standards are not mandated by law, few will find it economically viable to manufacture devices with better data security [37]. In future, there should be international frameworks mandating the use of minimum-security standards in heterogeneous IoT devices and applications [2].

5.1   Future Research

Currently, there is still relatively little research on the cybersecurity vulnerabilities of IoT devices in smart homes. Although, as technologies, IoT and smart home are no longer very new, their combination is a subject area that is still in the development stage. In further research, it would therefore be meaningful to investigate methods by which the cybersecurity of IoT smart homes could be improved. Other possible research topics could be how the security of a cheap IoT device differs from that of a device from a trusted manufacturer or the security differences between heterogeneous and homogeneous smart home systems.

References

1. Amadeo, M., Campolo, C., Iera, A., Molinaro, A.: Information centric networking in IoT scenarios: the case of a smart home. In: 2015 IEEE International Conference on Communications (ICC), pp. 648–653 (2015)
2. Anand, P., Singh, Y., Selwal, A., Alazab, M., Tanwar, S., Kumar, N.: IoT vulnerability assessment for sustainable computing: threats, current solutions, and open challenges. IEEE Access **8**, 168825–168853 (2020)
3. Antonakakis, M., et al.: Understanding the mirai botnet. In: 26th {USENIX} security symposium ({USENIX} Security 17), pp. 1093–1110 (2017)
4. Apthorpe, N., Reisman, D., Feamster, N.: A smart home is no castle: privacy vulnerabilities of encrypted IoT traffic (2017)
5. Bassi, A., et al.: Enabling Things to Talk: Designing IoT solutions with the IoT Architectural Reference Model. Springer, Berlin Heidelberg (2013)
6. Borgohain, T., Kumar, U., Sanyal, S.: Survey of security and privacy issues of Internet of Things (2015)
7. Chan, M., Campo, E., Estève, D., Fourniols, J.Y.: Smart homes - current features and future perspectives. Maturitas **64**(2), 90–97 (2009)
8. Collin, J., Saarelainen, A.: Teollinen internet. Talentum (2016)
9. da Costa, L.T., Barros, J.P., Tavares, M.: Vulnerabilities in IoT devices for smart home environment. In: International Conference on Information Systems Security and Privacy, vol. 1, pp. 615–622 (2019)
10. Costin, A., Zaddach, J.: IoT malware: comprehensive survey, analysis framework and case studies. BlackHat USA **1**(1) 1–9 (2018)
11. Costin, A., Zaddach, J., Francillon, A., Balzarotti, D.: A large-scale analysis of the security of embedded firmwares. In: 23rd {USENIX} Security Symposium ({USENIX} Security 14), pp. 95–110 (2014)
12. Costin, A., Zarras, A., Francillon, A.: Automated dynamic firmware analysis at scale: a case study on embedded web interfaces. In: 11th ACM on Asia Conference on Computer and Communications Security, pp. 437–448 (2016)
13. Gaikwad, P.P., Gabhane, J.P., Golait, S.S.: A survey based on smart homes system using internet-of-things. 2015 International Conference on Computation of Power, Energy, Information and Communication (ICCPEIC), pp. 0330–0335 (2015)
14. Giri, A., Dutta, S., Neogy, S., Dahal, K., Pervez, Z.: Internet of things (IoT): a survey on architecture, enabling technologies, applications and challenges. In: 1st International Conference on Internet of Things and Machine Learning. IML 2017, Association for Computing Machinery, New York, pp. 1–12 (2017)
15. Kadam, M., Mahamuni, P., Parikh, Y.: Smart home system. Int. J. Innov. Res. Adv. Eng. **2**(1), 81–86 (2015)
16. Lee, C., Zappaterra, L., Choi, K., Choi, H.A.: Securing smart home: technologies, security challenges, and security requirements. In: 2014 IEEE Conference on Communications and Network Security, pp. 67–72 (2014)

17. Lehto, M.: Muuttunut turvallisuustilanne ja uhkakuvat. Jyväskylän yliopisto (2018)
18. Lin, H., Bergmann, N.: IoT privacy and security challenges for smart home environments. Inf. **7**, 44 (2016)
19. Ling, Z., Luo, J., Xu, Y., Gao, C., Wu, K., Fu, X.: Security vulnerabilities of internet of things: a case study of the smart plug system. IEEE Internet Things J. **4**(6), 1899–1909 (2017)
20. Mahmoud, R., Yousuf, T., Aloul, F., Zualkernan, I.: Internet of things (IoT) security: current status, challenges and prospective measures. In: 10th International Conference for Internet Technology and Secured Transactions (ICITST), pp. 336–341 (2015)
21. Majumder, S., et al.: Smart homes for elderly healthcare-recent advances and research challenges. Sensors **17**(11), 2496 (2017)
22. Meneghello, F., Calore, M., Zucchetto, D., Polese, M., Zanella, A.: Iot: Internet of threats? a survey of practical security vulnerabilities in real IoT devices. IEEE Internet of Things J. **6**(5), 8182–8201 (2019)
23. Meng, Y., Zhang, W., Zhu, H., Shen, X.S.: Securing consumer IoT in the smart home: architecture, challenges, and countermeasures. IEEE Wirel. Commun. **25**(6), 53–59 (2018)
24. Mrabet, H., Belguith, S., Alhomoud, A., Jemai, A.: A survey of IoT security based on a layered architecture of sensing and data analysis. Sensors **20**(13), 3625 (2020)
25. Nguyen Duc, A., Jabangwe, R., Paul, P., Abrahamsson, P.: Security challenges in IoT development: a software engineering perspective. In: Proceedings of the XP2017 Scientific Workshops, pp. 1–5 (2017)
26. Oracle: The internet of things: Manage the complexity, seize the opportunity (2014)
27. OWASP: Owasp category: Vulnerability (2016)
28. OWASP: Internet of things (IoT) top 10 (2020)
29. Patel, K., Patel, S., Scholar, P., Salazar, C.: Internet of things-IoT: definition, characteristics, architecture, enabling technologies, application & future challenges. Int. J. Eng. Sci. Comput. **6**(5) (2016)
30. Pfleeger, C.P., Pfleeger, S.L., Margulies, J.: Security in Computing (5th Edition), 5th edn. Prentice Hall Press, USA (2015)
31. Rao, T., Haq, E.: Security challenges facing IoT layers and its protective measures. Int. J. Comput. Appl. **179**, 31–35 (2018)
32. Sethi, P., Sarangi, S.R.: Internet of Things: architectures, protocols, and applications. J. Electr. Comput. Eng. (2017)
33. Tewari, A., Gupta, B.: Security, privacy and trust of different layers in Internet-of-Things (IoTs) framework. Future Gen. Comput. Syst. **108** 909–920 (2020)
34. TSK, S.: Kokonaisturvallisuuden sanasto (2017)
35. Wang, J.A., Guo, M., Wang, H., Xia, M., Zhou, L.: Environmental metrics for software security based on a vulnerability ontology. In: 2009 Third IEEE International Conference on Secure Software Integration and Reliability Improvement, pp. 159–168 (2009)
36. Wirth, A.: Cyberinsights: reviewing today's cyberthreat landscape. Biomed. Instrum. Technol. **53**(3), 227–231 (2019)
37. Zheng, S., Apthorpe, N., Chetty, M., Feamster, N.: User perceptions of smart home IoT privacy. Proc. ACM Hum.-Comput. Interact. 2(CSCW), 1–20 (2018)

On Tools for Practical and Effective Security Policy Management and Vulnerability Scanning

Ilkka Urtamo and Andrei Costin[(✉)]

Faculty of Information Technology, University of Jyväskylä,
P.O. Box 35, Jyväskylä 40014, Finland
ilkka@urtamo.com, {ilkurt,ancostin}@jyu.fi
https://jyu.fi/it/

Abstract. An organization's ability to protect itself against risks originating from system vulnerabilities is determined by its ability to apply and maintain an operating system security policy and detect, prioritize, and timely apply patches to known system vulnerabilities. This paper discusses the usability of openly available Security Content Automation Protocol (SCAP) tools and source data for system security policy management and vulnerability scanning. Usability evaluation was conducted with use a case where installation of the tools in the target environment was coupled with election, setup, and execution of the security policy and vulnerability scanning. The use case revealed variation in tool usability depending on implemented features and availability of published source data. Implementing security compliance automation with SCAP tools was found to be feasible in operating systems that provide adequate source feed and supported by OpenSCAP.

Keywords: Security · Vulnerability · SCAP

1 Introduction

Organizational risk management and compliance with authority regulations require effective system security policy and vulnerability management. Effective system security policy requires defining, applying, and auditing of the rules. Continuous protection against system vulnerabilities requires periodical investigation of the system for vendor updates. Security Content Automation Protocol (SCAP) framework provides technical specifications for these tasks, but are the tools and required vendor publications feasible for the task?

The aim of this study was to examine usability of openly available SCAP tools to develop, apply, and verify a security policy and conduct system vulnerability scanning. The usability of the selected tools was evaluated via use cases in Linux and MacOS environments. The security policy use case consisted of the selection of a suitable security baseline, tailoring of the policy, and execution of

B. Shishkov (Ed.): BMSD 2023, LNBIP 483, pp. 375–382, 2023.
https://doi.org/10.1007/978-3-031-36757-1_28

an automatic policy audit. Vulnerability scanning consisted of selecting a proper vendor-published source and conducting the scan. Consideration was given to source data availability in the proper format, tool ease of use, and the quality and usability of tool reporting capabilities. Adaptation was evaluated based on the availability of SCAP tools and vendor-released source data for the scanning.

The remainder of this paper is organized as follows. Section 2 discusses the technological background related to SCAP, security policy, vulnerability scanning, and the tools evaluated. The use case is discussed in Sect. 3, followed by the tool results in Sect. 4. Section 5 concludes the findings.

2   Technological Background

2.1   Security Content Automation Protocol

SCAP is a framework of specifications developed by the National Institute of Standards and Technology (NIST) since 2009 [15]. SCAP defines human- and machine-readable technical specifications for system security compliance and vulnerability management tasks. Among others, it defines a machine-readable security policy (XCCDF) and automated evaluation test format (OVAL) for security policy automatizing and system configuration scans against known vulnerabilities. SCAP defines system component identification schemes such as Common Platform Enumeration (CPE), which is used in both automatic security policy auditing and in vulnerability protection tasks to identify software components. SCAP also defines scoring systems for system vulnerability reporting, via Common Vulnerability Scoring System (CVSS), which can be used for risk assessment and subsequent prioritizing [10,18].

These specifications create common communication interfaces between publisher and consumer organizations and make it possible for tools to be developed. With SCAP tools, organizations can identify software and hardware in various systems, verify security policy, and provide evidence of security policy compliance as well as continuously monitor system status against known vulnerabilities and apply actions accordingly [16].

2.2   System Security Policy

System security policy consists of rules and guidelines to strengthen the target system's effective security. Policy comprises parameters of proper configuration, such as password strength rules, system monitoring, and disabling of services that are not used or contain unacceptable risks. Rules dictate what options and services are available for the user. Security policy rules crafted by government or security organizations are called security baselines. Baselines can be required by an authority or elected based on organizational risk assessment. In the most common case, organizations elect a predefined security policy baseline and tailor it to fit the requirements of their risk assessment [13,17]

2.3   Vulnerability Scanning

Vulnerability scanning is a technique for discovering security issues by scanning the target system against a known vulnerability database. Vulnerability scanning methods can be credentialed and non-credentialed [11]. This paper focuses on credentialed scanning by software component version comparison against known vulnerabilities, called vulnerability scanning [9] or auditing [1]. Vulnerability scanning is done by comparing target system software component versions to it's vendor-released list of the known vulnerabilities of those component versions. SCAP-compatible tools use vendor-published source data streams. Source freed files include a combination of system configurations and tests defined with OVAL and based on relevant CVEs coupled with associated CPE information.

2.4   OpenSCAP

OpenSCAP is an open source project to develop SCAP-validated [12] tools to automate continuous security compliance and vulnerability assessment. Open-SCAP also develops guidelines and configuration baselines to be used as part of an organization's security policy, such as *SCAP Security Guide*. OpenSCAP tools include *OpenSCAP base*, which is a command line utility to parse and evaluate SCAP compliant artifacts. This tool is used to scan a system against XCCDF and OVAL definitions and produce reports. For supported systems, this tool can be used to evaluate the system security policy, as well as for vulnerability scanning. *SCAP Workbench* is graphical interface tool designed to ease tailoring security-related configuration policy and provides a user interface to execute configuration and vulnerability scans. [5]

2.5   macOS Security Compliance Project (mSCP)

The macOS Security Compliance Project (mSCP) is an open-source project that provides a programmatic approach to generating and using macOS security configuration baselines. It is used to generate security policy baselines and automatic tests for compliance scanning. mSCP tools are the result of collaboration between NIST and other US government agencies, such as NASA. mSCP is not SCAP validated. [10,17]

3   Tools Analysis

Analysis of the tools was conducted through the following steps. Security policy compliance verification was done by tailoring the selected source and analyzing the results of the scan. Scanning against known vulnerabilities was done by selecting a source and analyzing results of the scan. Similar steps were followed for the reference environment.

3.1   Security Policy Rules and Compliance Verification

The target environment was installed as a VirtualBox virtual machine using a standard Ubuntu 22.04 server installation image. OS was brought up to date using Ubuntu distribution package management tools.

Security policy checklists using XCCDF format are published by different entities. These are OS vendors such as Ubuntu [2], security organizations such as CIS [3], and government entities such as NIST [7]. Table 1 lists the sources considered for the security policy baseline.

Table 1. Security policy checklist providers

Policy	Publisher	Comments
National Checklist Program	NIST	No baseline for Ubuntu 22.04
SCAP Security Guide	OpenSCAP	PCI DSS,STIG, and USGCB compatible. No Ubuntu support
CIS Benchmark List	CIS	Wide range of systems supported. Free in PDF format only
Ubuntu Security Certifications	Canonical	20.04 onward Ubuntu Security Guide tool. No 22.04 support

None of the publishers provided XCCDF format baselines that could be directly used in the experiment. The baseline was either nonexistent for the target system version, required a subscription, or had a format other than SCAP format.

The solution to get a proper XCCDF format security policy baseline was to build appropriate files from the SCAP Security Guide (SSG) published by the OpenSCAP project [14]. As a result of the build, several different SCAP source data streams were available. `ssg-ubuntu2204-ds-1.2.xml` was used for the experiment. This file contained several profiles that could be viewed with the `oscap info` command, from which the *CIS Ubuntu 22.04 Level 1 Server Benchmark* profile was selected. Tailoring of the profile rules was conducted using the *SCAP Benchmark* graphical tool to experiment with the usability of the files for conducting modifications for organizational needs. Tailoring results were saved as a separate tailoring file to avoid altering the original file, which would make it harder to maintain tailoring during baseline profile changes.

The security policy was then scanned against the selected profile combined with the tailoring file using te `oscap xccdf eval` command combined with `--profile`, `--tailoring-file`, `--results`, and `--report` command-line option switches. This command executed the scan and produced a results file, the content of which is discussed in Chap. 4. Vulnerability scanning was conducted against and within the same system.

Apple macOS Ventura 13.2.1 was used as the reference target environment. No SCAP-validated tools were available for direct comparison. Security policy rules and associated scanning were done using tools provided by mSCP [6]. The required tools were installed in target environment by using the `git clone --branch ventura` command. Following provided online help, a moderate-level security policy baseline was created by `./generate_baseline.py -k 800 -53r5 _moderate`, and a compliance test script was created by `generate_guidance.py -s 800-53r5_moderate .yaml`, which created the actual scanning script. This script was then executed with the `800-53r5_moderate_compliance.sh --check` command, yielding the results discussed in Chap. 4.

3.2 Scanning Against Known Vulnerabilities

A system vulnerability scan was conducted after the security policy scan. For the vulnerability scan, an up-to-date OVAL-compatible feed file was acquired from an official Ubuntu source [8]. The scan was executed using the `oscap oval eval` command with `--report` switch, which produced the results discussed in Chap. 4.

For macOS, there was no tool available to make an operating system distribution package comparison to known CVEs like, OpenSCAP OVAL scanning discussed above. OVAL-compatible file for macOS Ventura 13.2.1 was also not found. The CVE Binary Tool [4] is available to conduct similar scanning against the NVD database, but this tool was not experimented with at this time.

4 Scan Results

The OpenSCAP scanner produced an informative report detailing the results of the security policy scan. The verification scan against the non-hardened vanilla target system resulted in an expected large amount of fails (138 fails out of 275 rules). In addition, one rule was suppressed by tailoring and therefore not required to be compliant. A summary of the scan is illustrated in Fig. 1. Scan results created by the OpenSCAP tool can be sorted using a web browser in such a way that high-ranking discrepancies are seen on top. The ranking view illustrated in Fig. 2 can be used to prioritize any configuration changes most urgently requiring corrective actions.

The results from the mSCP compliance scan were considerably more limited as only a summary with a number of passed and failed rules was indicated, as illustrated in Fig. 3. A report in which details such as which rules passed and which failed could not be found. The lack of such a report could make efforts to fix compliance discrepancies harder than necessary.

A summary from the OpenSCAP vulnerability scan is illustrated in Fig. 4. The executed OVAL scan resulted in one patch suggestion out of 680 objects considered. The issue found had a low CVSS score and was related to known vulnerabilities in the OpenEXR package used and installed on the system.

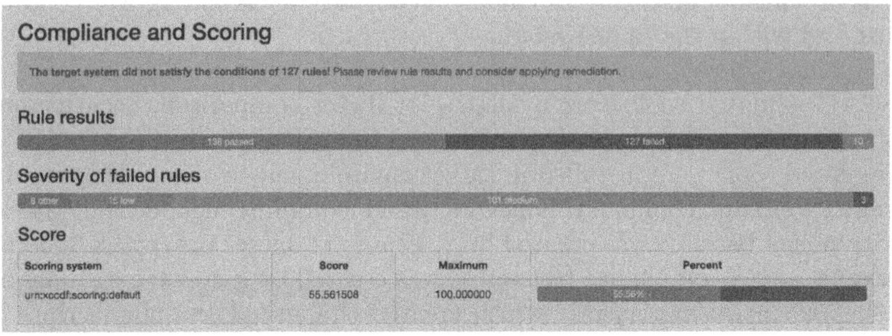

Fig. 1. OpenSCAP compliance report - summary

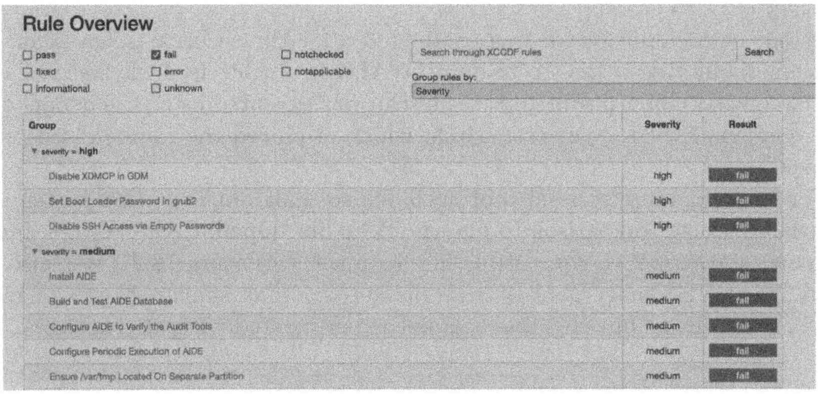

Fig. 2. OpenSCAP compliance report - priority rules

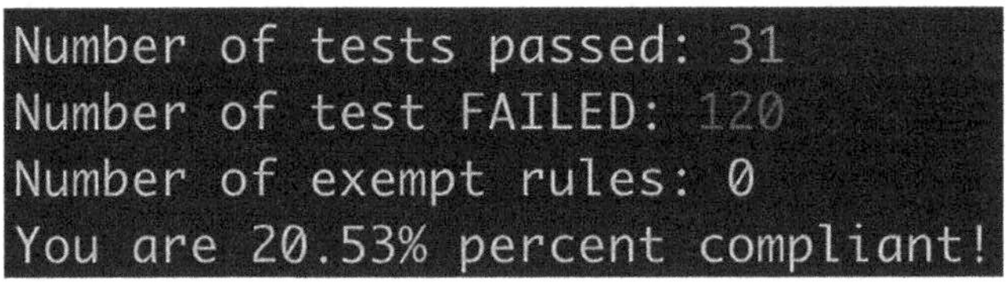

Fig. 3. mSCP compliance results - summary

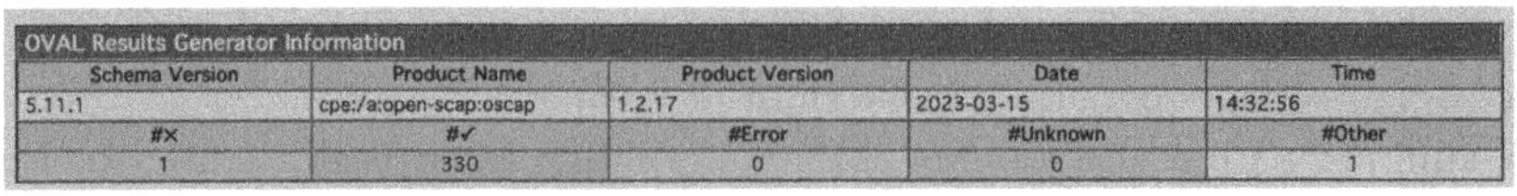

Fig. 4. OpenSCAP vulnerability results - summary

5 Conclusions

The aim of this study was to explore the adaptation and usability of openly available SCAP tools to develop, apply, and verify a security policy and conduct system vulnerability scanning.

Implementing security policy compliance with SCAP tools was found to be possible as authorities and security organizations release carefully thought-out rules using SCAP-defined formats. Diverse tools and source data formats are used depending on the operating system vendor and flavor. Not all operating system vendors release patch information using XCCDF and OVAL formats.

A security policy can be defined and compliance audited without extensive knowledge of SCAP formats or deep technological know-how. Vulnerability scanning meets the objectives of detecting software components with known vulnerabilities. The effectiveness of the scan relies on the quality of the publisher's OVAL source and its suitability for the system being scanned.

There were notable differences in scan results reporting. The OpenSCAP tool had adequate reporting capabilities. mSCP lacked detailed reports which, was found to be a downside. For compliance purposes, the summary report provided by mSCP can be sufficient, but the lack of detailed reporting affects the feasibility of the tool's usability in developing and tailoring security policy rules.

There is variation in tool usability depending on what and how features are implemented within a tool. The availability of published source data affects usability as well. Implementing security compliance automation was found to be effective in operating systems providing an OVAL source feed and being supported by the OpenSCAP project.

This study was done with a limited amount of target systems. Only one Linux distribution was used, and Windows, as one of the popular operating system, was not considered. The tested tools had automatic remediation possibilities for security policy compliance. There is an opportunity to study the feasibility of these features.

References

1. Auditing for Vulnerabilities By Using OVAL Definitions. https://docs.oracle.com/en/operating-systems/oracle-linux/8/oscap/auditing_for_vulnerabilities_by_using_oval_definitions.html#topic_q4t_znf_m5b
2. Canonical security certifications—Security. https://ubuntu.com/security/certifications
3. CIS Benchmarks™. https://www.cisecurity.org/cis-benchmarks/
4. CVE Binary Tool. https://github.com/intel/cve-bin-tool
5. Home—OpenSCAP portal. https://www.open-scap.org/
6. macOS Security Compliance Project. https://github.com/usnistgov/macos_security
7. NCP - National Checklist Program Checklist Repository. https://ncp.nist.gov/repository
8. Ubuntu Oval — Security. https://ubuntu.com/security/oval

9. Vulnerability Scanning Red Hat Enterprise Linux 7—Red Hat Customer Portal. https://access.redhat.com/documentation/en-us/red_hat_enterprise_linux/7/html /security_guide/vulnerability-scanning_scanning-the-system-for-configuration-com pliance-and-vulnerabilities

10. Aksu, M.U., et al.: A quantitative CVSS-based cyber security risk assessment methodology for it systems. In: 2017 International Carnahan Conference on Security Technology (ICCST), pp. 1–8. IEEE (2017)

11. Chen, A., Zhang, Z.: A comparative study of credentialed vulnerability scanning and non-credentialed vulnerability scanning. In: 2021 IEEE International Conference on Parallel & Distributed Processing with Applications, Big Data & Cloud Computing, Sustainable Computing & Communications, Social Computing & Networking (ISPA/BDCloud/SocialCom/SustainCom), pp. 1613–1616. IEEE (2021)

12. Computer Security Division, I.T.L.: SCAP Validated Products and Modules - Security Content Automation Protocol Validation Program — CSRC — CSRC. https://csrc.nist.gov/Projects/scap-validation-program/Validated-Products-and- Modules

13. Hamdani, S.W.A., et al.: Cybersecurity standards in the context of operating system: practical aspects, analysis, and comparisons. ACM Comput. Surv. (CSUR) **54**(3), 1–36 (2021)

14. Project, O.S.G.: OpenSCAP Security Guide. https://github.com/ComplianceAs Code/content/wiki/Home

15. Quinn, S.D., Waltermire, D.A., Johnson, C.S., Scarfone, K.A., Banghart, J.F.: The technical specification for the security content automation protocol (scap): Scap version 1.0 (2009)

16. Torchio, M.: Security assessment and threat response through SCAP. Ph.D. thesis, Politecnico di Torino (2022)

17. Trapnell, M., Trapnell, E., Souppaya, M., Gendler, B., Scarfone, K.: Automated secure configuration guidance from the macos security compliance project (mscp). Tech. rep, National Institute of Standards and Technology (2022)

18. Waltermire, D., Quinn, S., Booth, H., Scarfone, K., Prisaca, D.: The technical specification for the security content automation protocol (scap): Scap version 1.3. Tech. rep., National Institute of Standards and Technology (2016)

Linking Computers to the Brain: Overview of Cybersecurity Threats and Possible Solutions

Tuomo Lahtinen and Andrei Costin[✉]

Faculty of Information Technology, University of Jyväskylä,
P.O. Box 35, Jyväskylä 40014, Finland
tutalaht@jyu.fi, ancostin@jyu.fi
https://jyu.fi/it/

Abstract. The brain-computer interface (BCI) is a growing field of technology, and it has become clear that BCI systems' cybersecurity needs amelioration. When BCI devices are developed with wireless connection capabilities, more often than not, this creates more surface area for attackers to concentrate their attacks. The more invasive BCI technology is used, the greater the threat to the users' physical health. In this paper, we summarize and outline the main cybersecurity threats and challenges that BCI systems may face now and in the future. Furthermore, we present avenues for the future BCI systems including cybersecurity solutions and requirements. We emphasize the importance of the health layer to be considered as important as technical layers in BCI systems as people cannot endure life-threatening situations where attackers could cause permanent brain damage to the BCI user.

Keywords: Brain-Computer Interface · Deep Brain Stimulation · Cybersecurity · Vulnerability · Privacy

1 Introduction

The brain-computer interface (BCI) is a growing field of technology among researchers [29] that can make people's lives easier. Initially, BCIs were mainly made for medical purposes, but in the last ten years research direction has been shifting into non-medical research [42]. BCI applications are influential in the fields of healthcare and well-being, gaming, smart homes and cities, military, and more. BCIs are not a new research topic; BCI research was established in the early '70s at the University of California [43]. In this early BCI research, researchers tried to prove that direct brain-computer communication was plausible through multiple experiments. At first, BCI systems were used only for brain activity recording, but nowadays BCI systems are also capable of stimulating brain activity, which makes BCI systems bidirectional.

Cybersecurity development of the BCI is at the early stages as cybersecurity has not been considered a consequential part of the BCI. The lack of cybersecurity requirements is real in BCI systems [5,11,28]. BCI systems' cybersecurity

B. Shishkov (Ed.): BMSD 2023, LNBIP 483, pp. 383–392, 2023.
https://doi.org/10.1007/978-3-031-36757-1_29

can be evaluated with security the triangle "CIA," where "C" stands for **confidentiality**, "I" for **integrity** and "A" for **availability**. Bernal et al. [11] added one more "security and safety" component to the CIA triad. The CIAS is a new approach to security in BCI systems, where "S" stands for **safety**. CIA focuses on the technical side of a BCI system, but safety refers to the user's physical integrity. In other words, is the use of a BCI device safe for the user, and can the device cause harm to the physical integrity of the user?

In this paper, we state some of the challenges that BCI systems may encounter in the future (Sect. 3). One of the challenges is that attacks and breaches against the medical healthcare industry are rising [31, 38, 45] and BCIs can be used for medical purposes as well. Sensitive medical data is attracting malicious attackers and could be worth hundreds of dollars on the dark web [38].

In Sect. 3 we address more specifically the rising technologies such as transcranial direct current stimulation (tDCS) 3.1 and deep brain stimulation (DBS) 3.2. DBS devices nowadays have wireless connection possibilities that are creating a threat to the integrity of the BCI user's health.

Finally, we present possible future layers to secure the BCI system in Sect. 4. The layer-based cybersecurity model (Fig. 1) includes eight layers that all need to be considered when a BCI system is designed and developed.

2 Brain-Computer Interface: Applications

BCI systems have many different use purposes, and there are also multiple technologies that are separated into two categories, which are brain wave acquisition techniques and brain stimulation techniques. The most common techniques in brain wave acquisition are electroencephalography (EEG), electrocorticography (ECoG), functional magnetic resonance imaging (fMRI), and magnetoencephalography (MEG). The most common stimulation techniques are transcranial magnetic stimulation (TMS), transcranial electrical stimulation (tES), transcranial focused ultrasound (tFUS), tDCS and DBS. Neural dust is technology that is used for both purposes [10].

Kapitonova et al. [28] listed a range of domains, from working and employment, productivity, cognitive enhancement, education, art, gaming, entertainment and virtual reality (VR), neuromarketing, smart homes and smart cities, to security and military-related BCI applications. Using BCIs for medical purposes can be seen as a primary purpose. There are two types in the medical domain. BCIs can be used for diagnosing or supportive purposes [29]. Supporting could mean, for example, treating Parkinson's symptoms or controlling a wheelchair, and diagnosing could mean diagnosing Alzheimer's disease. Of course, some BCI use can be partly seen as being for medical purposes if a patient with restriction in moving/lifting/completing normal daily routines gets help by using a BCI, for example, to control smart home devices. Teles et al. [40] used the union of Internet of Things (IoT) and BCI systems to achieve control, which was called the Brain-to-Thing Communication (BTC) system. The Michael J. Fox Foundation [24] listed three different manufacturers that offer DBS-based BCIs that

are approved by the U.S Food and Drug Administration (FDA). All three manufacturers' devices are used to treat Parkinson's symptoms. Devasia et al. [20]
introduced a BCI system that assisted quadriplegic people (the state of paralysis
where the body is paralyzed from the shoulders down) in performing some of
their daily activities by themselves.

Although BCIs have been used mostly for medical purposes in the past, we
have seen the direction shift in the last 10 years from medical to non-medical
as non-medical domains have more potential users around the world [42]. Usage
such as aerial device control has been presented in a few studies. Rosca et al. [36]
introduced a quadcopter controlled via a BCI, and Prasath et al. [34] conducted
research in a similar field where an unmanned aerial vehicle (UAV) was controlled
using a BCI. One of the richest research field using BCIs is smart home control
or BTC, as Teles et al. [40] called their solution. Often, integrating BCI and
IoT together is driven by the urge to make life more convenient and to help
impaired patients. A few different IoT-related studies are those of Saboor et al.
[37], where BCI-controlled smart glasses were used to control devices; Chicaiza
et al. [16], who used a P300 speller to command IoT devices; and Parui et al.
[33], who used Muse headband sensor, which captured EEG signals with an
eye blink. In research conducted by Saboor et al. [37], participants controlled
a smart home system with an accuracy of over 80%. Elshenaway et al. [23]
demonstrated a new method for authenticating IoT devices using EEG signals
and hand gestures. The accuracy was 92%, which could be acceptable for using
some smart home IoT devices, but what if your door refuses to unlock every tenth
time? Moreover, researchers demonstrated that a large population of IoT devices
are vulnerable [18,19], which leads to them being prime targets for IoT specific
malware attacks [17] further leading to Internet-wide botnets and attacks [6].

Another venue for BCI usage is gaming, but there is a problem with satisfactory user experience. Better user experience often requires more invasive BCI
techniques, such as ECoG [11]. Marshall et al. [30] conducted a survey about
using BCIs in gaming. Their conclusion was that using BCI technology is limited, and BCIs in gaming can be used for training or testing purposes of BCI
technology. Simple games can be developed to use BCIs, such as Tetris [44], or
"Neuro Wander" – a game based on the fairy tale Hansel and Gretel [46].

3   Brain-Computer Interface: Challenges

There are privacy concerns about the future of BCIs, and privacy seems to be the
most noted challenge in BCI systems. Takabi et al. [39] wondered the question,
Is it possible that in the future, we will be able to get more results from the
raw brain data analyzed, and can this later reveal critical data? This was noted
especially when the brain data is handled publicly because of open research.
The critical data is always anonymized in research but is that enough? If data
is exposed to a malicious attacker, it could put the user's life at risk [39].

Kapitonova et al. [28] stated that security and privacy should be handled as
defaults and part of the design of BCI systems. The problem in this vision of

Table 1. Attacks organized under CIA

Confidentiality	Integrity	Availability
Noise adding [29]	Noise adding [29]	Neuronal jamming [8,9]
- Goal: Disrupt data sending	- Goal: Disrupt data sending	- Goal: Denial of service
- Complexity: High	- Complexity: High	- Complexity: Low
Stimuli altering [29]	Stimuli altering [29]	Neuronal flooding [8,9]
- Goal: Misdiagnosis or misuse	- Goal: Misdiagnosis or misuse	- Goal: Collapse of network
- Complexity: Medium	- Complexity: Medium	- Complexity: Low
Artificial input [29]	Artificial input [29]	Drain the battery [14,35]
- Goal: Misdiagnosis or misuse	- Goal: Misdiagnosis or misuse	- Goal: Denial of service
- Complexity: High	- Complexity: High	- Complexity: Low
Modified input (MitM) [29]	Modified Input (MitM) [29]	Interfere BCI connections [14]
- Goal: Misdiagnosis or misuse	- Goal: Misdiagnosis or misuse	- Goal: Denial of service
- Complexity: High	- Complexity: High	- Complexity: Low
Data leakage [29,35]	Data leakage [29,35]	Switch off IPG [35]
- Goal: Misuse of obtained brain data	- Goal: Misuse of obtained brain data	- Goal: Denial of service
- Complexity: Medium	- Complexity: Medium	- Complexity: Medium
Neuronal spoofing [9]	Neuronal selective forwarding [9]	
- Goal: Steel data	- Goal: Selectively drop packets	
- Complexity: Very high	- Complexity: High	
Neuronal sybil [9]	Neuronal sinkhole [9]	
- Goal: Computer hijack	- Goal: Manipulate routing	
- Complexity: Very high	- Complexity: High	
Neuronal nonce [9]	Tampering data [14,35]	
- Goal: Replay attack	- Goal: Modify data	
- Complexity: Low	- Complexity: High	
Neuronal scanning [9]		
- Goal: Identify vulnerable services		
- Complexity: Medium		

security and privacy as defaults is that it is not clear how that would be achieved in effective practical terms. To mitigate security and privacy problems, we need to address issues by recognizing possible cybersecurity challenges and threats that BCI systems are facing or may face in the future.

Bernal et al. [11] created an informative list of attacks, impacts, and counter-measures for BCI systems. Attacks have various effects in corresponding CIAS (confidentiality, integrity, availability and security) domains. Safety can be considered the most important aspect for the BCI user. If use of the BCI system puts a user's life at risk, it is not worth using the system. Safety can be threatened in two ways: technology- or attack- created threat. Section 3.1 explains more about the threat created by technology in tDCS.

The concern is that causing harm to the BCI user is easier than manipulating data. Bernal et al. [7] and Pycroft et al. [35] stated that if an attacker is only trying to cause harm to the user or patient, the attacker hardly needs any knowledge about brain stimulation or specific information about the patient. This kind of attack can be described as a blind attack [35]. In Table 1, attacks are listed under CIA according to the attack surface. Some attacks affect multiple fields and in that case, the attack is mentioned in more than one or in the most suitable field of the CIA.

3.1   Challenges in tDCS

In recent years transcranial direct current stimulation (tDCS) has gained popularity because of its potential to improve mood and cognitive function [2]. tDSC is a non invasive brain stimulation technique that directs a low electric current to the scalp, but it is not approved by the FDA [4]. tDSC has shown that it can enhance brain functioning, such as learning, attention, creativity and memory. Although there is still research to do with tDSC, it could be used as an effective tool to boost mental performance and well-being without being invasive [2].

As a BCI technology, tDCS seems quite harmless, as side effects (e.g., minor burns) tend to be rare, with mild or disappearing symptoms after the experiment; still there are some issues with this technology. Moioli et al. [32] envisioned that in the future, there will possibly be a need to consider undesired signals that affect the brain stimulus through wireless networks in BCI systems. BCIs could receive unwanted read and write signals, which could affect human behavior, thus having individual and social influence [32]. Boccard-Bine and Sen [12] suspected that tDCS had caused seizures, and the same suspicion was raised by Ekici [21]. When buying a tDCS device, buyers should always make sure that the device is safe to use. This can be elevated when choosing a known brand [2].

Besides the upper neural change or damage cases, if tDCS devices are connected to the Internet, they are vulnerable to all the most common attacks against networks and devices. Also, data sent, handled, and stored on a network is vulnerable to attacks such as sniffing, MitM, phishing, and DoS.

3.2   Challenges in DBS

DBS is a technique used mainly for health care, for example, treating neurological disorders. In DBS, electrodes are implanted in the deep regions of the brain by stereotactic neurosurgical techniques [26], and DBS can be included in the most invasive BCI technology. According to the Michael J. Fox Foundation [24], there are currently a few different DBS devices approved by the U.S FDA. The devices are from the manufacturers Abbott, Medtronic and Boston Scientific and are designed to help reduce symptoms of Parkinson's disease. Parkinson's disease is a neurodegenerative disorder of aging that is affecting both motor and cognitive function. Parkinson's disease is progressive and cannot be cured, but there are effective medications to treat it, and DBS can also be used for reducing symptoms, especially in medication-resistant cases [25]. These DBS devices are invasive and use directional stimulation where pulses are sent directly to the target areas of the brain.

The Michael J. Fox Foundation [24] stated that Abbott developed the first device offering remote programming, and this capability is likely to become more widely available in the future. This trend is inevitably increasing threats that BCI systems will face as BCIs are becoming remote controllable and more attack surface is exposed [41]. In terms of DBS-based BCIs where the stimulus is invasive and pulses are sent straight to the brain, there is a serious threat against the physical integrity of the patient. In Table 1, there are eight different neural attacks presented that could be used against DBS.

In the research by Bernal et al. [8], it was highlighted that using wireless communications, such as Bluetooth, can expose sensitive knowledge about the instant of attack, the voltage used in a device, or the list of targeted neurons in the BCI. The need for remote control must be well motivated in the sense that remote control should create more value to the user than it creates health-related threats. For example, CVE-2022-25837 [1] permits an unauthenticated MitM to acquire credentials.

4 Discussion

BCI systems are becoming more advanced, and as they are developed, more threats will emerge. We need a general design guide or framework for BCI systems. Kapitonova et al. [28] presented a good framework for preserving privacy and cybersecurity in BCIs, but this does not cover every aspect of the BCI system (e.g., physical threats caused by the BCI). The world is full of different standards and guides trying to explain, clarify and enhance security in IT systems. For example, OSI 7 created by the International Organization for Standardization (ISO) 1984 is an architecture where seven layers are linked together to transmit data from one layer to another. OSI 7 defines layers and functions at layers in order to secure data transfer between layers [3,13]. There are many other layer-based guides similar to OSI 7 that can be used to evaluate data security. For example, Elijah et al. [22] presented seven cybersecurity layers for Industry 4.0.

Normally, IT systems do not cause harm to the users, but there is a growing amount of health care devices that have a risk of malicious attackers cause harm to the user. As mentioned in Subsect. 3.2, DBS devices pose life-threatening risks, and Jackson et al. [27] explored the Medical Internet of Things (MIoT) and found several mentions of life-threatening risks. The risk comes when the MIoT device is wirelessly connected and there is a possibility to monitor and control the device remotely [27].

To understand BCI system requirements, we provide BCI system layering in Fig. 1. These layers can be used to describe the cybersecurity of the BCI system and enhance cybersecurity awareness. The layers follow the seven cybersecurity layers of Elijah et al. [22], but we added an eighth layer, the **Health Layer**, to provide a better understanding about the BCI system as a whole.

In Fig. 1, the layers are as follows: 1) Human Layer, 2) Perimeter Security, 3) Network Security, 4) Application Security, 5) Endpoint Security, 6) Data Security, 7) Critical Assets, and 8) Health Layer. Layers from 1 to 7 are related to data inside the BCI system. Layer 8 contains health-related issues, such as the physical integrity of the user and surgery for BCI implants. As the health layer holds the biggest threat against users, it is important to research actions to reduce risks in this layer. For example, Chiaramello et al. [15] studied how DBS could be improved to be less invasive. They discovered that minimal invasiveness and proven biocompatibility, makes magneto-electric nanoparticles (MENP)

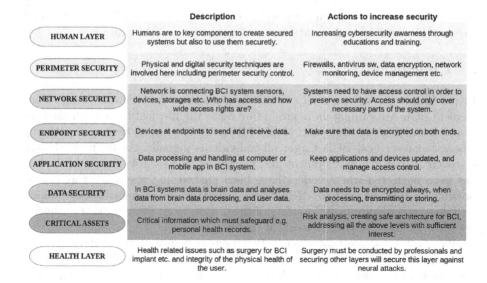

	Description	Actions to increase security
HUMAN LAYER	Humans are to key component to create secured systems but also to use them securely.	Increasing cybersecurity awarness through educations and training.
PERIMETER SECURITY	Physical and digital security techniques are involved here including perimeter security control.	Firewalls, antivirus sw, data encryption, network monitoring, device management etc.
NETWORK SECURITY	Network is connecting BCI system sensors, devices, storages etc. Who has access and how wide access rights are?	Systems need to have access control in order to preserve security. Access should only cover necessary parts of the system.
ENDPOINT SECURITY	Devices at endpoints to send and receive data.	Make sure that data is encrypted on both ends.
APPLICATION SECURITY	Data processing and handling at computer or mobile app in BCI system.	Keep applications and devices updated, and manage access control.
DATA SECURITY	In BCI systems data is brain data and analyses data from brain data processing, and user data.	Data needs to be encrypted always, when processing, transmitting or storing.
CRITICAL ASSETS	Critical information which must safeguard e.g. personal health records.	Risk analysis, creating safe architecture for BCI, addressing all the above levels with sufficient interest.
HEALTH LAYER	Health related issues such as surgery for BCI implant etc. and integrity of the physical health of the user.	Surgery must be conducted by professionals and securing other layers will secure this layer against neural attacks.

Fig. 1. Layers to secure BCI systems.

mediated DBS, representing a big improvement towards less invasive and more secured stimulation of the deep neural tissues. This kind of research is welcome, as less invasive techniques lower not only physical threats caused by surgery but also neural attacks as the invasiveness level decreases.

The second important layer is the Human Layer, as humans make errors. It cannot be precisely stated how many successful data breaches are caused by human error, but it is the most effective layer to make improvements in the cybersecurity field. BCI system users need education and knowledge to avoid misuse of BCI devices or being affected by phishing attacks, malware, viruses, and so on. Education and training are mentioned in many studies to reduce data breaches [10,31,38,45].

Other layers require technical security. For privacy attack prevention, the commonly suggested techniques are access control, efficient encryption, and adding noise into brain data passed back and forth between various hardware and software components of the BCI system. Takabi et al. [39] mentioned that a BCI application should never have access to the raw brain data, as it is more easily accessible by an attacker. All the devices that are part of the BCI system should be protected by keeping them up to date with the latest software/firmware updates and fixes [18]. Firewalls, antivirus, data traffic monitoring should be used if possible to detect malicious data and unauthorized access.

When conducting future and further research among BCI systems, there is a need to carry out hands-on testing to see how secure BCI systems really are. Testing should involve as many layers as possible in the BCI system. Related to the testing, it poses some ethical issues and it is not possible to use human volunteers in research when conducting tests for neural attacks, as this could cause at least a skin burn or at most serious damage to the brain.

5   Conclusion

In the future, the cybersecurity of BCI systems must be followed closely. Non-medical BCIs are gaining more ground by replacing medical BCIs from the lead research and development post. Medical BCIs focus on small targets of patients, whereas non-medical BCIs target all individuals globally. As we have already discovered from IoT development and marketing, the security aspect of devices has been neglected when devices have been pushed into the market as fast as possible to maximize profit. Regulation, validation or standardization among BCI devices could improve the safety of the devices (e.g., FDA or other authority approval for using devices in medical treatment).

We must be aware that when a BCI system is designed and developed, it is needed to address all the layers from Fig. 1 to ensure that the BCI system's security is at an adequate level. A BCI system is as strong as the weakest link in the system, which means the weakest layer defines the rigorousness of BCI systems.

References

1. Cve-2022-25837 detail (2022). https://nvd.nist.gov/vuln/detail/CVE-2022-25837. Accessed 24 Apr 2023
2. Best TDCS devices of 2023 (2023). https://tdcs.com/best-tdcs-devices/. Accessed 18 Apr 2023
3. Layers of osi model (2023). https://www.geeksforgeeks.org/layers-of-osi-model/. Accessed 18 Apr 2023
4. What is transcranial direct current stimulation? (2023). https://neuromodec.org/what-is-transcranial-direct-current-stimulation-tdcs/. Accessed 24 Apr 2023
5. Ajrawi, S., Rao, R., Sarkar, M.: Cybersecurity in brain-computer interfaces: RFID-based design-theoretical framework. Inform. Med. Unlocked **22**, 100489 (2021)
6. Antonakakis, M., et al.: Understanding the mirai botnet. In: 26th {USENIX} security symposium ({USENIX} Security 17), pp. 1093–1110 (2017)
7. Bernal, S.L., Celdran, A.H., Maimo, L.F., Barros, M.T., Balasubramaniam, S., Perez, G.M.: Cyberattacks on miniature brain implants to disrupt spontaneous neural signaling. IEEE Access **8**, 152204–152222 (2020)
8. Bernal, S.L., Celdrán, A.H., Pérez, G.M.: Neuronal jamming cyberattack over invasive BCIS affecting the resolution of tasks requiring visual capabilities. Comput. Secur. **112**, 102534 (2022)
9. Bernal, S.L., Celdrán, A.H., Pérez, G.M.: Eight reasons to prioritize brain-computer interface cybersecurity. Commun. ACM **66**(4), 68–78 (2023)
10. Bernal, S.L., Celdrán, A.H., Pérez, G.M., Barros, M.T., Balasubramaniam, S.: Cybersecurity in brain-computer interfaces: State-of-the-art, opportunities, and future challenges. arXiv preprint arXiv:1908.03536 (2019)
11. Bernal, S.L., Pérez, M.Q., Beltrán, E.T.M., Pérez, G.M., Celdrán, A.H.: When brain-computer interfaces meet the metaverse: Landscape, demonstrator, trends, challenges, and concerns. arXiv preprint arXiv:2212.03169 (2022)

12. Boccard-Binet, S., Sen, A.: Safety of transcranial direct current stimulation in healthy participants. Epilepsy Behav. Rep. **15** (2021)
13. Briscoe, N.: Understanding the OSI 7-layer model. PC Netw. Advisor **120**(2), 13–15 (2000)
14. Camara, C., Peris-Lopez, P., Tapiador, J.E.: Security and privacy issues in implantable medical devices: a comprehensive survey. J. Biomed. Inform. **55**, 272–289 (2015)
15. Chiaramello, E., et al.: Magnetoelectric nanoparticles: evaluating stimulation feasibility of the possible next generation approach for deep brain stimulation. IEEE Access **10**, 124884–124893 (2022)
16. Chicaiza, K.O., Benalcázar, M.E.: A brain-computer interface for controlling IoT devices using EEG signals. In: 2021 IEEE Fifth Ecuador Technical Chapters Meeting (ETCM), pp. 1–6. IEEE (2021)
17. Costin, A., Zaddach, J.: IoT malware: comprehensive survey, analysis framework and case studies. BlackHat USA **1**(1), 1–9 (2018)
18. Costin, A., Zaddach, J., Francillon, A., Balzarotti, D.: A large-scale analysis of the security of embedded firmwares. In: 23rd {USENIX} Security Symposium ({USENIX} Security 14), pp. 95–110 (2014)
19. Costin, A., Zarras, A., Francillon, A.: Automated dynamic firmware analysis at scale: a case study on embedded web interfaces. In: 11th ACM on Asia Conference on Computer and Communications Security, pp. 437–448 (2016)
20. Devasia, D., Roshini, T., Jacob, N.S., Jose, S.M., Joseph, S.: Assistance for quadriplegic with BCI enabled wheelchair and IoT. In: 2020 3rd International Conference on Intelligent Sustainable Systems (ICISS), pp. 1220–1226. IEEE (2020)
21. Ekici, B.: Transcranial direct current stimulation-induced seizure: analysis of a case. Clin. EEG Neurosci. **46**(2), 169 (2015)
22. Elijah, O., et al.: A survey on industry 4.0 for the oil and gas industry: upstream sector. IEEE Access **9**, vol. 144438–144468 (2021)
23. Elshenaway, A.R., Guirguis, S.K.: Adaptive thresholds of EEG brain signals for IoT devices authentication. IEEE Access **9**, 100294–100307 (2021)
24. Foundation, M.J.F.: Currently available deep brain stimulation devices. https://www.michaeljfox.org/news/currently-available-deep-brain-stimulation-devices. Accessed 18 Apr 2023
25. Fröhlich, F.: Chapter 23 - parkinson's disease. In: Fröhlich, F. (ed.) Network Neuroscience, pp. 291–296. Academic Press, San Diego (2016)
26. Hemm, S., Wårdell, K.: Stereotactic implantation of deep brain stimulation electrodes: a review of technical systems, methods and emerging tools. Med. Biolog. Eng. Comput. **48**, 611–624 (2010)
27. Jackson Jr, G.W., Rahman, S.: Exploring challenges and opportunities in cybersecurity risk and threat communications related to the medical Internet of Things (miot). arXiv preprint arXiv:1908.00666 (2019)
28. Kapitonova, M., Kellmeyer, P., Vogt, S., Ball, T.: A framework for preserving privacy and cybersecurity in brain-computer interfacing applications. arXiv preprint arXiv:2209.09653 (2022)
29. Landau, O., Puzis, R., Nissim, N.: Mind your mind: EEG-based brain-computer interfaces and their security in cyber space. ACM Comput. Surv. (CSUR) **53**(1), 1–38 (2020)
30. Marshall, D., Coyle, D., Wilson, S., Callaghan, M.: Games, gameplay, and BCI: the state of the art. IEEE Trans. Comput. Intell. AI Games **5**(2), 82–99 (2013)
31. McLeod, A., Dolezel, D.: Cyber-analytics: modeling factors associated with healthcare data breaches. Decis. Supp. Syst. **108**, 57–68 (2018)

32. Moioli, R.C., et al.: Neurosciences and wireless networks: the potential of brain-type communications and their applications. IEEE Commun. Surv. Tutorials 1599–1621 (2021)

33. Parui, S., Samanta, D., Chakravorty, N.: An advanced healthcare system where internet of things meets brain-computer interface using event-related potential. In: 24th International Conference on Distributed Computing and Networking, pp. 438–443 (2023)

34. Prasath, M., Naveen, R., Sivaraj, G.: Mind-controlled unmanned aerial vehicle (UAV) using brain-computer interface (BCI). Unmanned Aerial Veh. Internet Things (IoT) Concepts Tech. Appl. 231–246 (2021)

35. Pycroft, L., et al.: Brainjacking: implant security issues in invasive neuromodulation. World Neurosurg. **92**, 454–462 (2016)

36. Rosca, S., Leba, M., Ionica, A., Gamulescu, O.: Quadcopter control using a BCI. In: IOP Conference Series: Materials Science and Engineering, vol. 294, p. 012048. IOP Publishing (2018)

37. Saboor, A., et al.: SSVEP-based BCI in a smart home scenario. In: Rojas, I., Joya, G., Catala, A. (eds.) IWANN 2017. LNCS, vol. 10306, pp. 474–485. Springer, Cham (2017). https://doi.org/10.1007/978-3-319-59147-6_41

38. Seh, A.H., et al.: Healthcare data breaches: insights and implications. In: Healthcare, vol. 8, p. 133. MDPI (2020)

39. Takabi, H., Bhalotiya, A., Alohaly, M.: Brain computer interface (BCI) applications: privacy threats and countermeasures. In: 2016 IEEE 2nd International Conference on Collaboration and Internet Computing (CIC), pp. 102–111. IEEE (2016)

40. Teles, A., Cagy, M., Silva, F., Endler, M., Bastos, V., Teixeira, S.: Using brain-computer interface and internet of things to improve healthcare for wheelchair users. In: 11th International Conference on Mobile Ubiquitous Computing, Systems, Services and Technologies (UBICOMM), vol. 1, pp. 92–94 (2017)

41. Uppal, R.: Brain-computer interfaces (BCI) are vulnerable to cyber attacks and need security and safety measures (2023), https://idstch.com/cyber/brain-computer-interfaces-BCI-vulnerable-cyber-attacks-need-security-safety-measures/. Accessed 24 Apr 2023

42. Värbu, K., Muhammad, N., Muhammad, Y.: Past, present, and future of EEG-based BCI applications. Sensors **22**(9), 3331 (2022)

43. Vidal, J.J.: Toward direct brain-computer communication. Ann. Rev. Biophys. Bioeng. **2**(1), 157–180 (1973)

44. Wang, Z., Yu, Y., Xu, M., Liu, Y., Yin, E., Zhou, Z.: Towards a hybrid BCI gaming paradigm based on motor imagery and SSVEP. Int. J. Hum.-Comput. Inter. **35**(3), 197–205 (2019)

45. Wikina, S.B.: What caused the breach? an examination of use of information technology and health data breaches. Perspect. Health Inf. Manag. **11**(Fall) (2014)

46. Yoh, M.S., Kwon, J., Kim, S.: Neurowander: a BCI game in the form of interactive fairy tale. In: 12th ACM International Conference Adjunct Papers on Ubiquitous computing-Adjunct, pp. 389–390 (2010)

Author Index

Printed in the United States
by Baker & Taylor Publisher Services